THE MUSIC OF MY TIME

JOAN PEYSER

The Music of My Time

WITH A FOREWORD BY MILTON BABBITT

AND ROSALYN TURECK

PRO/AM MUSIC RESOURCES, INC.
White Plains, New York

KAHN & AVERILL
London

FIRST EDITION

Published in the United States of America 1995 by
PRO/AM MUSIC RESOURCES, INC.
63 Prospect Street, White Plains, New York 10606
Tel/Fax (914) 448-9327
ISBN 0-912483-99-7

U.S. School & Library Distribution by
PRO/AM MUSIC RESOURCES, INC.

U.S. Trade & Retail Distribution by
THE BOLD STRUMMER, LTD.
20 Turkey Hill Circle, Box 2037, Westport, Connecticut 06880
Tel (800) 375-3786 ● Fax (203) 259-7369

Published in Great Britain 1995 by
KAHN & AVERILL
9 Harrington Road, London SW7 3ES
ISBN 1-871082-57-9

To Frank Driggs
for the unanticipated happiness
of these years

SERIES TITLE:
SOMETHING ABOUT THE MUSIC
Guide to Contemporary Repertory

AVAILABLE IN THIS SERIES:

THE MUSIC OF MY TIME
(Something About the Music 1)
by Joan Peyser. 1994.
ISBN 0-912483-99-7

SOMETHING ABOUT THE MUSIC 2
Anthology of Critical Opinions
edited by Thomas P. Lewis. 1990.
ISBN 0-912483-66-0 (cloth)
ISBN 0-912483-54-7 (paper)

ACKNOWLEDGEMENTS

I extend my profound appreciation to Jacques Barzun who, for more than ten years, encouraged me to create a new book comprised of my interviews, essays and lectures. It was Barzun who suggested these pieces be organized into the particular sections you will find in this volume.

In each of my books I have acknowledged the help of Stanley H. Brown, writer and editor and my friend for 30 years. Brown not only helped with the books but with most of the articles printed here. When we met I had just emerged from the world of academia and was guilty of many of the sins common to scholarly writing. Brown taught me how to say what I mean in a simple and direct way.

Five years ago I met Frank Driggs, the photo archivist, and my attitude towards pictures changed. Instead of using them to support my text, as an accompanist supports a soloist, writing and photographs began to share center stage. I thank Driggs not only for those pictures here that come from his remarkable collection but also for his skill and expertise in selecting and reproducing the ones that do not.

Paul Wittke was senior editor at G. Schirmer for decades and gave his help unstintingly to me during those seven years when I was the editor of *The Musical Quarterly*. Our friendship continues to this day. For the purposes of this book outdated references had to be removed and the overlap between articles eliminated. For Wittke's help in these matters I am in his debt.

For more than forty years Paul Bacon has been one of our preeminent book jacket designers and illustrators. For this book Bacon presented me with a gift I hold very dear: its cover's plan and its realization.

Thomas P. Lewis, publisher of Pro/Am Music Resources Inc., believed in the importance of *The Music of My Time* and attacked its production with devotion, care and energy. For all of that I express my gratitude.

JP

ACKNOWLEDGEMENTS

*

The author and publisher extend their gratitude to the following newspaper, journal and other publishers for permission to include in this volume material originally published in their pages.

The American Scholar: Igor Stravinsky, Autumn 1983 (winner of Deems Taylor/ASCAP Award for 1984)

Aperiodical: Mel Powell, Spring 1988

The Columbia University Forum: Marc Blitzstein, Winter 1966 (winner of Deems Taylor/ASCAP Award for 1968); The Beatles, Fall 1967

Commentary: Lincoln Center, 05/61

The New Grove Dictionary of American Music, 1986: Leonard Bernstein

The New York Times and *The New York Times Book Review:* José Quintero, 01/01/67; Luciano Berio, 01/03/67, 02/15/70; Evelyn Lear and Marie Collier, 04/09/67; Symphony of the New World, 11/26/67; Vladimir Ussachevsky at Bell Labs, 03/03/68; John Crosby and the Santa Fe Opera, 06/02/68; Hopkins Center at Dartmouth, 08/25/68 (winner of Deems Taylor/ASCAP Award for 1970); Anton Webern, 09/08/68; The Beatles, 09/29/68; Milton Babbitt, 01/12/69, 10/17/82, 05/04/86; Elliott Carter, 03/02/69; Pierre Boulez, 03/09/69, 06/20/71, 12/07/80; Benjamin Britten, 11/06/69; Columbia-Princeton Electronic Music Center, 05/03/70; Seiji Ozawa, 08/23/70; Stefan Wolpe, 02/06/72; Edgard Varèse, 04/23/72; Hans Werner Henze, 07/16/72; René Leibowitz, 09/10/72; Betsy Jolas and Barbara Kolb, 06/17/73; New York Philharmonic, 01/26/75; Harvey Sollberger, 03/28/76; Robert Mann, 07/06/80; Arnold Schoenberg, 09/21/80; Maria Callas, 03/15/81; John Harbison, 08/16/81; Karlheinz Stockhausen and Hans Werner Henze, 09/06/81; Henry Cowell, 12/06/81 (winner of Deems Taylor/ASCAP Award for 1982); Roger Sessions, 02/14/82; Leonard Rosenman, 08/29/82; Charles Wuorinen, 04/10/83, 06/05/88; Minna Lederman and *Modern Music,* 12/25/83; Leon Kirchner, 01/01/84; Richard Tucker, 03/25/84; Tod Machover at IRCAM, 05/06/84; Nina Beilina, 12/09/84; David Diamond, 07/01/85; Morton Gould, 05/25/86; Ned Rorem, 05/03/87

Newsday: New York Philharmonic, 08/20/89

TV Guide: George Gershwin, 11/21/87

The following pieces are published in this volume for the first time:

Jerome Lowenthal (for *The New York Times*), 02/81; Béla Bartók (for Indiana University, 03/81); Parents and Genius Children (for the Phi Betta Kappa Society, 05/22/84); Virgil Thomson (for *People* Magazine, 11/86).

CONTENTS

CONTENTS

CONTENTS

xi

PHOTOGRAPHS & ILLUSTRATIONS

FOREWORD

IN RESPONSE TO the foreseeable charge that I am engaging in a
self-serving act by offering these words in appreciation of Joan
Peyser's writings about music and musicians, I need but cite
how well, how valuably these writings have served so many of
us of the contemporary music community, so many of us whose
works and lives taken together span, chronologically and dis-
positionally, virtually the whole of the fast passing century, and
who heard music change before our very ears from that more
than symbolic moment between the final two movements of
Schoenberg's *Second String Quartet.*

Along the tangled pathways of our pluralistic musical world
Joan Peyser's writings lead the plain as well as the fancier listener, those listeners ranging from those unaware that there is a
contemporary cultivated music (or "classical" music as they, like
Presidents, might term it) with living composers who create it,
to those self-alleged "music lovers" who appear to believe that
because they think they know what they like, therefore they
think and know about music, while the music they affect to love
is only the familiarly old and restful, performed by the mana-
gerially and journalistically created and manipulated stars of
show business performance.

Joan Peyser never trivializes the fundamental and deeply
motivated fragmentation of contemporary composition by
presenting composers as a parade of passing fashions, as a succession of compositional flavors of the month, nor does she
regard the works themselves primarily as vehicles of contention
and competition, for all that many of the composers seem to. She
avoids the customary journalistic traps of the biographical "in-
tentional fallacy" by not presuming to invoke the composer's life
to "explain" his music, but—rather—by invoking his music to
"explain" his musical and extra-musical life. For, as music has

been transformed, so—therefore—has the composer's position been altered, as has the position of music as it has descended in prestige among the disciplines of creative intellection, as musical education has disappeared, as categories have been confused, as compositions have been as misrepresented verbally out of malice and ignorance as by inadequate performance.

I recall, perhaps first recall, Joan Peyser when she, as a graduate student in music history at Columbia University, visited our just a-building Columbia-Princeton Electronic Music Center. She came not in awe of technology, for she was not one to be impressed musically by artefacts for artefacts' sake, but she also did not come as a musical Luddite, asking "but where is the human element?" She understood that a total machine, such as the RCA Synthesizer, was conceived of and constructed by humans to meet the crucial needs of human composers, and that the communication channel from human composer to human receptor never before had been so little obstructed. She also understood that this new fusion of the roles of composer and performer, of the acts of creation and recreation into a single act of realization was not concerned to eliminate the "human" performer and conductor, for our new musical medium was to be employed not to displace or replace any of the traditional musical functions, but to expand and extend music's resources.

But the reality of musical performance without "performers" as such did inter or, at least, alter the thrust of that absurd slogan that "music is a performing art", with its strong suggestion that it matters not what is performed, but only who performs it, a tenet to which our "music lover" obviously subscribes. And Joan Peyser's articles, if not explicitly, then surely effectively redress if not the balance of power, the balance of ultimate importance between the composer and the performer. Of course, she recognizes the necessity and even celebrates the contribution of the performer, but not the sufficiency, just as she understands that divergence in ambition and disposition between the composer and performer from the first stages of their training, and — therefore — the need for the special care and training of those rare performers and conductors of not only extraordinary musical ability, but the curiosity, conviction, and courage to become true colleagues of, collaborators of the admittedly demanding contemporary composer, since into the mix goes the administrator, the manager, the entrepreneur, and if the fate of informed, mature contemporary music is to be placed in the hands of the likes of (to cite just one of Ms. Peyser's subjects and objects) the eponymous Mr. Peter Gelb (and I am assuming he knows more of the German language than of the language of music), then Joan Peyser may look forward to a future as writer in which she will be able to do little more than write the obituaries for those composers, performers, conductors, and thinkers about music who all are to be hung together.

MILTON BABBITT
Princeton University
January 1995

JOAN PEYSER has been interviewing composers over a substantial period of years, and her writings represent a wide range of diverse channels of creative thought in the 20th century, a century remarkable for its variegated approaches to form, structure, style, performance and their resultant multiple productions. Her writings form a significant contribution to the perception of a composer, supplementing the direct study of actual music in a way that fleshes out the image and the aesthetic position of the composer.

I have been greatly enriched by knowing virtually all the composers interviewed by Peyser and having lifelong friendships with them entailing both professional collaborations and personal relationships. Having performed works by composers interviewed by Peyser, such as David Diamond and Roger Sessions, and having rehearsed their works with them individually, I cherish a direct tie with their compositional foci and their performance intentions all of which are brilliantly illuminated in these dialogues. In creating the organization, Composers of Today, one devoted to performance of contemporary music, both American and international, I came in close contact with many composers as varied in style as Henry Cowell, Leon Kirchner and Milton Babbitt, as well as with the products of electronic music. In reading Peyser's articles, I relish the accurate representation of all that I know, as well as her insights and assessments.

If we possessed such portraits of composers of the 14th, 15th, 16th, 17th, and 18th centuries, some crucial gaps in our knowledge and perceptions of older music would be bridged, providing us with invaluable connections to the past.

Posterity will benefit from the interviews and contemporaneous impressions of 20th century creative minds presented here. These narratives and descriptions illuminate, for both the professional musician and the lay reader, divergent paths of artistic interest in this century. Peyser's newly written passages, placed between the individual portraits, fill out the picture by clearly and succinctly charting the crucial aesthetic constructs of our time.

ROSALYN TURECK
Oxford University
November 1994

PREFACE

When I wrote these pieces I had no plan to present them in a collected edition. It is only now, after a lifetime in the field, that I have decided to bring them together in one volume. In rereading this material, I find they illuminate much that lay behind the various paths that music took during the present century. So that they be seen to be based not on whim but rather on years of study and reflection, I shall give a brief account of my life in music.

From the age of five, I spent many hours at the piano each week. By the time I was 13 I played well enough to perform in a recital at New York's Town Hall. When I entered the High School of Music and Art, I was told to select a second instrument so I could play in one of the school's orchestras. I chose the viola. That meant that in addition to courses in theory and orchestration, I was practicing two instruments every day. Despite this concentration on music, when I completed high school I still did not know that serious composers were writing music in my own time. That is because my repertory had never extended further into the 20th century than Debussy and early Stravinsky.

At Barnard, where I majored in music, I learned even more about harmony and counterpoint, but remained almost as oblivious as ever to the music created after World War I. Then I enrolled in the music department of Columbia University's Graduate School. One of two routes was open to me: composition or musicology. Although I chose musicology, all the courses were held in the same building and I came to know well those composers who were teaching and studying there.

I had not been alone in being generally unaware of current activity in my field. It was only after World War II that American culture began to emerge from a provincialism that extended to all of the arts. In an article on Meyer Schapiro, the eminent art historian, which appeared in the August 14, 1994 issue of *The New York Times Magazine*, the art critic Deborah Solomon wrote: "During the '50s, when Abstract Expressionism reigned, Schapiro dragged Barnett Newman and Adolph Gottlieb up to Columbia to speak to a roomful of awed art-history students: they had never seen a real live artist before."

While working for a Ph.D. I began to send articles to music magazines such as *Opera News, Hi-Fi Stereo* and *The American Record Guide.* Everything I submitted was published. Still I did not feel I had embarked on a real career until the winter of 1966 when the *Columbia University Forum,* an intellectual journal published by and for the university's graduates, presented an essay I wrote on the composer, Marc Blitzstein, who had recently been murdered on Martinique. What I set out to do was describe how American politics, musical aesthetics and Blitzstein's personal life combined.

On the basis of this article, Delacorte Press gave me a contract for a book on 20th century music. Titled *The New Music: The Sense Behind the Sound,* it was written with the same approach as the Blitzstein essay: it charted the outer circumstances and inner lives of Arnold Schoenberg, Anton Webern, Igor Stravinsky and Edgard Varèse, those pioneering musical figures who were the models for the Columbia composers. The Blitzstein article also attracted the attention of Seymour Peck, then the editor of the Drama section of the Sunday *New York Times.* While I continued to contribute to the Columbia *Forum* and to journals such as *The American Scholar,* I started to write for the Sunday *Times.* In all I contributed almost 60 articles to the *Times,* most of them during Peck's tenure.

In 1969 Pierre Boulez came to the United States as a guest conductor for four major orchestras. I interviewed him for the *Times* and the piece appeared before his first performance in New York. Soon after he was given the post of music director of the New York Philharmonic beginning in the fall of 1971.

When *The New Music* appeared in 1970, I sent a copy to Boulez and asked if he would cooperate with me on a new book which would concentrate on him. He said yes. My biography treated not only Boulez

2

but his European colleagues as well as the American composer John Cage whom Karlheinz Stockhausen and other Europeans had followed down a relentlessly anti-art path. But Boulez remained obsessed with a particular compositional idea, one that had originated with Schoenberg in the early 1920s and had been reinforced by Stravinsky several decades later. Boulez not only believed in it; he longed for audiences to want only that kind of music and not the music of past centuries.

To help him realize his goal, Boulez had at his disposal the New York Philharmonic as well as the support of a powerful press. During his guest appearances in 1969 and 1970, Boulez presented large doses of the music he loved. But the audience cancelled subscriptions and wrote angry letters. After Boulez's first season here in which he conducted much Alban Berg, he moved steadily backwards — under public pressure — to a second season of Haydn and Stravinsky, a third of "Early and Late Romanticism", and a fourth of "Nineteenth Century Nationalism".

The denouement was clear: the new style and syntax that had crystallized in the early part of the century never succeeded in being accepted into the ears, heads or hearts of most listeners. I wrote exactly that in the Preface to *Boulez: Composer, Conductor, Engima* which was published in 1976.

Early in 1977 I became the editor of *The Musical Quarterly*, a learned journal with an international distribution. I remained in the post until 1984 when I agreed to create a reference book for Scribner that came to be called *The Orchestra: Origins and Transformations*. A one volume collection of original essays, it documents the history of the orchestra from the 15th century to the present time. It was also in 1984 that I found myself eager to write about music in the United States as I had written about music in Europe: through biographies of seminal figures. Because I believe the American vernacular — jazz and popular song — lies at the heart of virtually all American music, I selected as my subjects for two books George Gershwin and Leonard Bernstein, men whose gifts lay in that arena and who, because of the use of popular material in their concert works, have been called "cross-over" composers.

It is dangerous to predict what will happen in any art. Perhaps the cross-over phenomenon will become the major trend. Perhaps composing styles built on Schoenberg's 12-tone technique will gradually infiltrate the consciousness of the majority of the concert-going public. Or perhaps it is all over. Cultural historian Jacques Barzun and composer-conductor Giuseppe Sinopoli are among those who believe that the tradition of art music in Western civilization — the writing of new music meant for performance in the traditional settings of the concert hall and opera house — has come to an end.

Whatever is true, the music of the 20th century has been characterized not by a single highway but by diverging roads. It is the nature of many of these roads that I hope to illuminate in *The Music of My Time*.

Joan Peyser
January 1995

I

THE PIONEERS

ARNOLD SCHOENBERG

ANTON WEBERN

IGOR STRAVINSKY

EDGARD VARÈSE

HENRY COWELL

BÉLA BARTÓK

Portrait of Arnold Schoenberg painted by George Gershwin.
Gershwin studied with Schoenberg in 1933, when the great
Viennese composer first arrived in New York. This painting is
Gershwin's last, completed just before he died at 38.
Reproduced from the collections of the Library of Congress

Introduction

In 1993 Giuseppe Sinopoli, the conductor and composer, told *The New York Times:* "One problem for composers today is that all the good materials seem to have been used. And there is the feeling that new works are often paraphrases of earlier music. You know, I am very interested in archaeology, and one thing I have seen is that there have been some fantastic periods in which cultures flourished for two, three or four centuries and then came to an end. I don't know if the period of Western musical composition is finished. It is possible: it has been three hundred years.

"I still compose. But what I think led me to conducting is that I preferred to conduct the music that I would be paraphrasing if I were composing."

What is most striking about Sinopoli's remark is its tone of inevitability. He does not attack living composers for eschewing the musical language of Bach, Mozart, Brahms or Wagner. He knows, as Heraclitus wrote, that one cannot step into the same place in a river twice.

Tonality, the system of seven-note scales in which one note is the focal point or tonic key, has been the foundation of Western musical culture certainly since the end of the Renaissance. From the moment it crystallized, it has changed continually. By the beginning of the twentieth century, certain composers concluded that it had yielded all it could give.

In tonality, the function of each of the other notes in the scale is determined by its relationship to the tonic key. The listener hears fundamental attractions of one tone to another as though they were part of a natural order of things. Gradually, over three hundred years, the half tones between the whole tones of the scale contributed more than the color for which these chromatic notes were named. The elevation of the significance of these tones led to the breakdown of tonality.

By the late 19th century, Debussy turned his back on the seven note scale in favor of a five note scale of whole tones. Wagner went further; his perpectual shifting of key centers undermined the tonal structure. By 1911, when Arnold Schoenberg published his *Theory of Harmony*, the tonal system appeared to have been spent. After that, any futher use of it could only fall into the paraphrases of ealier music to which Giuseppe Sinopoli referred.

What were composers to do? The most striking solution was dodecaphony, the 12-tone method, articulated by Schoenberg in 1923, on the eve of his 50th birthday. Fifteen years earlier he began his journey with a move into atonality, where there is no key signature. In an atonal work, the unity previously achieved through tonality was often provided by a literary text.

Schoenberg's first step into the atonal world occurred in the 13th song of a cycle of poems, *The Book of Hanging Gardens*, by Stefan George. Born September 13, 1874, Schoenberg grew up superstitious about the number 13. He numbered his measures 12, 12A and 14 believing that any measure numbered 13 would cause a creative block for him. He even believed he would die at an age that was a multiple of 13. After he survived his 65th year, he told friends he felt safe until he turned 78. But on his 76th birthday, an astrologer and numerologist warned him: seven plus six equals 13. Never having considered *adding* the digits of his age, Schoenberg became deeply disturbed. On Friday, the 13th, of his 76th year, the composer stayed in bed, anxious and depressed. Shortly before midnight his wife whispered: "You see, the day is almost over. All that worry was for nothing." Schoenberg look at her and died.

To reveal the power that Schoenberg's beliefs exerted on his life, his death and his work is not to suggest the 12-tone method was nothing more than the arbitrary notion of one obsessed man who invested the technique with profound significance because 12 was the number that came just before 13. It was, in fact, a logical development that grew from the aesthetic requirements of the time. Josef Matthias Hauer, Anton Webern and Igor Stravinsky all were working in similar ways. Still, the power that this technique exerted on the music of the century was at least in part due to the strength of Schoenberg's personality and the symbolism with which he invested numbers.

In 1933 the rise of Hitler forced Schoenberg from his teaching position in Berlin, and he went to Paris, New York, Boston and finally settled in Los Angeles. There, in addition to teaching at the University of Southern California and the University of California at Los Angeles, he accepted private students. In 1939 Dika Newlin, then a 14-year-old prodigy, now a Schoenberg specialist, began to study with Schoenberg and to keep a diary. The diary was published in 1980 and I reviewed it for *The New York Times Book Review*.

The portrait Newlin paints is reinforced in the second article published here. While reporting on the music program at the Hopkins Center at Dartmouth College, I met Amalie Webern Waller, Anton Webern's daughter. Webern was one of Schoenberg's early pupils. I believe it is because he and Alban Berg worked with Schoenberg during his earlier years that they were able to survive the oppression and harsh criticism that Schoenberg unleashed on his pupils at a later period. After 50, Schoenberg's paranoia and grandiosity went out of control. At the least he inhibited, at the most destroyed, the army of students who came to study with him. Here in my article, which originally appeared in the Arts and Leisure section of the *Times*, Amalie Weber Waller reveals how Webern and his family suffered from the blows Schoenberg dealt them throughout his life.

In the first half of the 20th century, no composer appeared to be more at cross purposes with Schoenberg than Igor Stravinsky. Initially Stravinsky attacked the problem of what composers at the beginning of the second decade could do by creating a radical concept of rhythm in his 1913 *The Rite of Spring*. But, in the early 1920s, when Schoenberg emerged from an extended silence with the 12-tone idea, a technique in which each of the half tones between, for example, one C and the next assumes equal importance, Stravinsky appeared with something else that has come to be known as neoclassicism, a reserved musical style removed from the anguished, post-Romantic Schoenberg sound. It also brought forth music quite separate from the classical works of Mozart and Haydn for, although Stravinsky used the seven-note scale, he turned his back on sonata form, that organic outgrowth of tonality endemic to the 18th and 19th centuries.

For 30 more years Stravinsky was the model for a large school of composers on both sides of the Atlantic. In the United States they were led by Aaron Copland, the most important of the many American composers who traveled to Paris to study with the renowned teacher Nadia Boulanger. Thirty years later, in the mid-1950s, when Stravinsky took the then unimaginable step of discarding neoclassicism for a variety of dodecaphony, Copland and many others followed.

In the third essay, first published in *The American Scholar*, Robert Craft, Stravinsky's amanuensis, takes much of the credit for steering the then artistically paralyzed composer into the 12-tone world of Schoenberg. Still, I believe even Craft would agree that Stravinsky would never have made this move had Schoenberg been living; his pride was too great. After 1951, when Schoenberg died, Stravinsky began to make the change that kept him working prodigiously for the rest of his life. Yet Stravinsky never acknowledged a debt to Schoenberg; he said Webern was at the center of his new aesthetic.

I first met Vera Stravinsky after her husband died. By then her emotional world was focused entirely on Craft. Her conversation always returned to how young and slender Craft had been when he entered the Stravinsky household in 1948. At the time of our conversations, she was distraught because Craft had decided to marry Rita McCaffrey, the Stravinsky nurse who bore his child. She need not have worried. The marriage was exceptionally brief and Craft returned to the Stravinsky apartment on Fifth Avenue in Manhattan and lived with her until she died.

Louise Norton Varèse, Edgard Varèse's second wife, was a sophisticated woman who symbolized for me the spirit of the 1920s. The

Varèses had been frequent guests on Leopold Stokowski's houseboat and Stokowski's milieu was Hollywood and the very rich.

One of the significant facts of Varèse's life was a catastrophic one that haunted Louise; it had a profound effect on her own life. In the 1930s, when socialist realism had all but annihilated advanced music in Europe, that philosophy took hold in the United States too. The composers who joined the Federal Works Progress Administration program in the arts, with the booming new media of radio and records, promoted a more accessible music, putting the avant-garde virtually out of business. In a conversation in May, 1994, 81-year-old composer Henry Brant said that after 1932, composers had to write conservative music, similar to radio and film scores: "The boom was lowered on everyone. Music for symphonies was like commercial music; there was no way out."

According to Louise Varèse, her husband became so depressed he spoke of suicide. Even after World War II, when advanced music came back into vogue, Varèse and misfortune seemed inseparable. In 1958 he was invited to mount a major electronic work at the Brussels World's Fair. But stories circulated of his mistreatment there by U.S engineers. After he died, the eulogies included one by Stravinsky who had never said a word about Varèse while he was alive.

Varèse and Cowell were far more eager to escape the shackles of the European tradition than Schoenberg, Webern or Stravinsky. Varèse left Europe not in the 1930s, when Schoenberg and Stravinsky were forced to flee because of the rise of Nazism, but in 1915. He longed for something more radical than a different method of organizing old sounds.

Varèse did not interest himself in Schoenberg's dodecaphony and expressed contempt for the retrogression of Stravinsky's neoclassicism. Creating increasingly dense scores, he produced a non-melodic fabric that depended on rhythm and sonority. Until World War II, Varèse had neither the technology nor the audience he needed. But his work led directly to the recording of unpitched sounds on tape that helped bring forth electronic music both in Europe and the United States.

Cowell was less solitary than Varèse. He took lessons with Schoenberg in Berlin and later visited him in his California home. Nevertheless, he was not indebted to the Viennese.

In 1933, Cowell identified himself as part of a group of composers that included Charles Ives, Carl Ruggles, and Roy Harris, writing that they worked with "indigenous materials" and reflected an "independent spirit". Wallingford Riegger and Henry Brant could have been included in this group. But Cowell's most famous pupil was John Cage, who has publicly acknowledged his profound debt to him.

In his anti-art stance, which sprang not only from Erik Satie, the French dadaist composer, but also from Cowell's irreverence, Cage, probably more than anyone else, pulled the rug from under Schoenberg, the modern Viennese school and Stravinsky and his followers.

Bartók, the last of my group of "pioneers", also remained independent of the Schoenberg-Stravinsky dichotomy. In assimilating his scholarly studies of folk music, Bartók created a compositional idiom that held little relevance to the Austro-German or the Franco-Russian domains. *Mikrokosmos,* a collection of piano pieces designed for beginners, was intended to initiate children into a world of unfamiliar tonal and rhythmic complications.

The essay included here—published for the first time—was presented as a lecture for the Bartók Centenary in 1981 at Indiana University. When invited to speak, I decided to concentrate my remarks on Bartók's last years not only because little attention had been paid to them but also because I had been close to that particular time and place. I began my graduate studies in the music department at Columbia less than ten years after Bartók worked there. The major participants in the Bartók drama were still at the university when I was there.

1

ARNOLD SCHOENBERG

In 1935, Dika Newlin was eleven years old and living with her parents in Cincinnati. She had been studying composition for three years with Arthur Farwell, founder of the music publishing house, the Wa-Wan Press. She was also a piano prodigy. At a party, she met Vladimir Bakaleinikoff, the associate conductor of the Cincinnati Symphony. He looked at one of her piano pieces and admired it so much that he orchestrated and conducted it. He also did one other thing for her: he insisted she study with Arnold Schoenberg, who had fled Europe for the United States two years before.

Dika waited until she was 14 and had graduated from high school. Then she and her mother settled in Los Angeles so that she could begin working with Schoenberg. At Christmas of that year, Mrs. Newlin gave her daughter a diary, instructing her that these would be important years.

Schoenberg Remembered consists primarily of the diary entries from 1939 through 1941; it also briefly describes Miss Newlin's career since then, which has been devoted to teaching and to writing about Schoenberg. Prodigies are often emotionally immature, and Dika's perceptions at the time she made the entries may suffer from some lack of wisdom. But whatever is lacking is more than compensated for by the author's absolute ingenuousness: she does not seem to have censored anything.

There are teachers who try to bring out the very best in their students. There are others who appear to say with every breath: "You want to become better than me? Not on your life!" Schoenberg was among the latter, particularly by the time he reached his mid-40s and founded The Society for Private Musical Performances in Vienna,

Review of SCHOENBERG REMEMBERED: DIARIES AND RECOLLECTIONS (1938-76) by Dika Newlin in *The New York Times Book Review*, September 21, 1980.

Walter Goehr, Arnold Schoenberg, Edward Steuerman
Berlin, c. 1930
CREDIT: Frank Driggs Collection

with statutes giving him total control and the requirement that each member come to every concert armed with an identification card and photograph. At 50, after crystallizing the 12-tone technique, Schoenberg's superstition, mysticism, paranoia and tyranny knew virtually no bounds. Because he composed such remarkable music, and because he was so perverse, he, more than any other single figure, was responsible for moving music along a course that can only be described as antagonistic to the average listener. Those who knew Schoenberg have remained as secretive as he. That is why Miss Newlin's book is both revelatory and important.

There were those composers who sensed the risks in becoming a disciple of Schoenberg. Marc Blitzstein, the American composer who had studied with him in Berlin in the 1920s, wrote of Schoenberg's anticipated arrival here: "A danger for his pupils lies in his insistence on genius, on perfection, in his ruthlessness with the near-perfect; the danger of paralysis and despair."

Most of Schoenberg's European pupils gave up composing altogether after studying with him. Many of the Americans also did, while those who persisted cannot be said to have made any special or original marks. Small wonder. Here are two of Miss Newlin's entries, chosen virtually at random:

February 21, 1939
    S.: Now, Miss Newlin, you will make the best use of your counterpoint—namely, erase it. [She does that, adding two eighth notes, she explains, for variety.]
    S.: All right, Miss Newlin (with a stubborn toss of his head), take away those eighth notes.
    I: Can't I possibly use them here?
    S.: Well, I suppose no one will kill you. (To class) Do you know why I do not let her use eighth notes? (No answer. He starts to shake all over laughing.) Why, because she *wants* to use them!

March 24, 1939
    He still thinks my string quartet style a little too pianistic. I

15

said, 'Of course, I realize it isn't the best string quartet writing.' He... replied, 'No, it is not the best — nor even the second best — perhaps the fiftieth best, yes?' But at least I had the advantage of having done some work, whereas the others are so afraid of criticism that they never write anything.

Repeatedly Miss Newlin notes the "hilarity" which greets Schoenberg's remarks.

In his book, *On Wit and Humor*, Freud claimed there is a kernel of truth in every joke, one which the teller could not articulate if it were not camouflaged with irony because he is intent on concealing his true feelings. Those close to Schoenberg, who imitated the composer in so many of his ways, picked up this particular facility too. Here is another diary entry:

October 7, 1939
It seems that, instead of taking money by the week, he wants 'sixty dollars month' in advance! (Funereal note: what guarantee do I have that he will not die within said month? Very little, I should say.)

Schoenberg's second and much younger wife apparently learned as well as Miss Newlin. One day when Schoenberg asked Dika and her mother to help him fill out citizenship papers, Mrs. Schoenberg was present. Here is the diary account:

One of the questions is, 'Have you ever been committed to an insane asylum? If so, why?' (Mrs. S. was heard to utter under her breath, 'If not, why not?')

Through the diary we learn that Schoenberg kept his piano badly out of tune, boasted that his treatise on harmony, *Harmonielehre*, caused him to be treated "as Hitler is now treated in Germany," believed that nothing done for a purpose could be art, said the only way to appreciate a building is by studying the blueprint, and was convinced he suffered from a fever and "warm breath" 24 hours before each rainfall because the air is then "full of little microbes or deathrays" which got right into his bronchial tubes. Once, on entering a classroom, he saw this equation on the blackboard: $16 + 53 = 69$. Puzzling over it obsessively, he determined to find the teacher of the previous class to question him "because the numbers must mean something."[*] Miss Newlin quotes Schoenberg as saying: "This composing is a serious business. It does not matter if what you write is not good — what matters is the *pain* you had in writing it."

The German musicologist, Hugo Leichtentritt, wrote, "How poor our descendants will be if they take this joyless, careworn Schoenberg as the sensibility of our age." The formidable power of Schoenberg's art was such that his descendants did exactly that. A man makes art in the same way that he breathes, eats, teaches and loves; his art reflects the deepest aspects of his personality. Miss Newlin's diary entries reveal not only Schoenberg's awesome intellect but the hostility and rage that infused everything he did. We should, therefore, not be surprised that many of the composers for whom Schoenberg set the example have pursued an approach that often carries messages of derision and rebuke and is generally uninterested in enhancing peoples' lives.

---

[*] As he grew older, Schoenberg invested not only numbers but the arrangement of letters with symbolic significance. When, with his second wife he had two children, he named the first Ronald and the second Roland, both anagrams of his own name. On discovering adverse numerological implications in Roland, he changed it to Lawrence Adam, which contains all the letters of Arnold except the O. A generation later, when Ronald had his own son, he named him Randol, yet another scramble of Arnold.

17

Anton Webern

2

ANTON WEBERN

Hanover, New Hampshire
At the end of the symposia conducted during the fourth International Webern Festival held at Dartmouth, a Yale professor played a tape by Mel Powell appropriately titled *No Song, No Dance.* He played it, he said, to illustrate the "aphysical, atemporal music — without beginning, middle or end" that characterizes much current work. He added that the piece reveals a deeper understanding of Webern's art than the "start-stop-pause music" of many of Webern's earlier followers.

The professor's point was clear. "New" musicians participated in the latest Webern festival not because they still adhere to the totally organized approach to music that the composer inspired ten and 15 years ago, but because they wanted to do homage to Webern for opening new doors. By starting to organize the duration of notes as composers had been organizing the pitch of notes, Webern removed melody from its position at the head of the musical hierarchy and promoted other attributes of musical sound. The de-emphasis of pitch and the consequent emphasis on the very matter of sound itself lies at the core of much new composition.

The public knows Webern as Schoenberg's pupil, but composers have assessed him in quite another light. Since his music emerged after World War II, Webern has caught up with his teacher and actually outdistanced him. His tight, quiet, extremely short works (one of the *Five Pieces for Orchestra* lasts 19 seconds) first attracted such figures as Stockhausen in Germany and Boulez in France. Rejecting Schoenberg for his old-fashioned Expressionism, his rhetorical manner, and his exploration of the serial technique in only the direction of pitch, these men eagerly embraced the Webern esthetic. If Schoenberg was the grandfather of new music, Webern was surely its posthumous father.

Originally published in *The New York Times* as "Two Masters Who Were in Conflict: Music at Dartmouth", September 8, 1968.

But during his life he received few accolades. Infrequent performances of his work occurred under the aegis of the International Society for Contemporary Music and even these enlightened audiences preferred other composers' noisy works to Webern's very quiet ones. In 1945, when Webern was accidentally shot and killed in Austria by an American soldier, not many musicians either understood or appreciated his art.

What could have caused this long-standing neglect? At least part of the answer is clear: Schoenberg stole the show. While Webern characteristically remained silent, Schoenberg proclaimed to the world his own singular destiny.

The central figures at the recent Dartmouth festival were Amalie Webern Waller, the composer's daughter, Hans Moldenhauer, President of the International Webern Society, and Ernst Krenek, composer and close friend of Webern. In private conversations with me, each revealed that the relationship between Schoenberg and Webern was far more complex than has generally been known.

Amalie Waller characterizes Schoenberg as "an autocrat, a tyrant," who continually shouted at the Webern children. Mrs. Waller said that he dominated the Webern household in a very harsh manner, despite the fact that Webern supported him with monthly checks until the end of World War I. (Webern was a member of the minor nobility; his father was an engineer and administrator in the Austrian imperial regime and left him an inheritance.) Much later, Mrs. Waller added, when her family needed help and her mother wrote Schoenberg asking for it, the composer refused, accusing Webern and the family of being Nazis because they remained in Austria.

Moldenhauer mentioned that the dissension between the two composers was longstanding and that he possessed letters which reveal that Webern wanted to break away from Schoenberg as early as 1914, but that the older composer "would not allow the separation."

Krenek indicated that these bits of information supported his own observations:

"Schoenberg believed in authority above all else. He had fantastically high standards, and was unbelievably opinionated. He used to make the most outrageous statements just to see how far he could go unchallenged, and he could go very far. One composer I know thinks Schoenberg tried to prevent people from writing music; he may be right. Of Schoenberg's hundreds of pupils, only Berg and Webern succeeded. The only approach he appreciated was one of total worship and he gathered around him a group of thoroughly devoted disciples who remain as devoted to him today. During the 1950s, I published an article in *The Musical Quarterly;* it dealt with the general evolution of the 12-tone technique, in which Webern also played a role. A member of the Schoenberg circle called and reprimanded me: 'Schoenberg discovered the 12-tone technique suddenly and all by himself.' Thus one is pledged to maintain the official position."

Webern triumphed over this attempt to rewrite history. In an impassioned article written in the early 1950s, Boulez asked his readers to admit that "Schoenberg is dead" and that "a certain Webern has been too easily forgotten." Stockhausen also announced: "All music must begin with Webern; there is no other choice." And in 1966, Stravinsky summed up the ideology of the age: "All of us owe something to him, if not in rhythmic vocabulary, then in our sensibility to musical time, for I think Webern has raised everyone's sense of refinement in this regard (well, nearly everyone's)." Webern's lonely lyricism, his crescendos and diminuendos on a single tone, his unwasted notes and uncomfortable intervals, opened a formidable world of sound to a new generation of musicians.

But a pianist and scholar brought Webern to the attention of the general public. In 1959, Hans Moldenhauer passed through Mittersill, the town in Austria in which Webern was killed, and called on Mrs. Waller. Discouraged by her own country's neglect of her father, Mrs. Waller transferred to Moldenhauer Webern's musical manuscripts, sketches, diaries, letters, notes, photographs, and a stage play that had been in the family's hands ever since Webern's death.

In the introduction to a book he wrote about the circumstances of Webern's death, Moldenhauer cites a number of musicians who have been influenced by the composer. These include Berio, Nono, Roch-berg, Henze, Dallapiccola, Schuller, Ginastera, Petrassi, de la Vega, Foss and Penderecki. This is an impressive legacy and Mel Powell, who produced *No Song, No Dance,* is a significant addition to the list. During the 1940s, Powell played piano with Benny Goodman and ar-ranged many of the swing hits of the Goodman era. How far removed from swing is Powell's cerebral tape played before the Festival's as-semblage of scholars!

Webern is reported to have suffered from a physical fear of noise. His personal silence is reflected in his scores: characteristic instruc-tions are "like a whisper", "scarcely audible", and "dying away". Col-leagues report that he actually hesitated before conducting the works of others, knowing in advance that the largeness and coarseness of the approaching orchestral sound would torture him.

3

IGOR STRAVINSKY

In a centenary article, entitled "My Life with Stravinsky", published in the June 10, 1982 issue of *The New York Review of Books*, Robert Craft wrote: "I dread to contemplate the prurient hypotheses and tendentious projections of music historians concerning the nature of the glue that held us together."

Craft's concern is understandable in light of the hostility he provoked from those who knew the circumstances of his arrival in the Stravinsky household in 1949. The situation was this: Stravinsky's first wife, Catherine, the mother of his four children, had been dead for ten years. Soon after her death, the composer married Vera de Bosset, with whom he had been having an open liaison for almost 20 years. In 1940, at the time of the marriage, the Stravinskys settled in Los Angeles and, after the end of World War II, invited the composer's second son, Soulima, to join them in the United States.

Soulima Stravinsky, then living in Paris with his wife and young son, was the only one of Stravinsky's children to have pursued a career in music. In the 1930s, along with his father, he played the Stravinsky *Concerto for Two Solo Pianos* on tours in Europe and South America. They even made a recording of that particular work. Soulima also performed the solo piano part in performances of his father's *Concerto for Piano and Wind Instruments* and the *Capriccio for Piano and Orchestra* under the direction of Stravinsky and several other conductors as well. In June 1948, Soulima and his family accepted the invitation to make a new life in California and took up residence in a small cottage rented and furnished by the Stravinskys about two miles from the composer's own house.

Originally published as "Stravinsky-Craft, Inc." in *The American Scholar*, Autumn, 1983.

In little more than a year, Craft, who first met the composer and his wife in March 1948, began spending time in the Soulima Stravinsky house. He was there in the summer of 1949 and, again, in October and November of that year when the young family was in Santa Barbara. Then, in 1950, when according to Vera, she herself helped procure a teaching position for Soulima at the University of Illinois, the Soulima Stravinskys moved out and Robert Craft moved in.

From that moment on, Craft's displacement of Soulima in Stravinsky's life has led many writers to impugn the motives behind most of Craft's actions. Here is one such example: In a review of the 31-record set issued by CBS under the title of *Igor Stravinsky: The Recorded Legacy*, which appeared in the October 1982 issue of the *New Criterion*, Samuel Lipman, a concert pianist and critic of the contemporary repertoire, suggests that the reason the early recording of the *Concerto for Two Pianos* by Stravinsky and Soulima was omitted from the CBS set can be traced to Craft's influence. But Lipman is almost certainly wrong about this. Craft insists he had nothing to do with this project, which was produced by Vera Zorina Lieberson. In fact, soon after the records appeared on the market, Craft sent me a copy of a letter he wrote to CBS attacking that omission, among others.

So Craft is correct in fearing that mistakes will be made. Still, many conclusions based on the presumed involvement will be correct. My own view is that, however eccentric and even repugnant many of the details of this Stravinsky-Craft relationship were, Craft's effect on Stravinsky was positive and that future historians will be generous to him.

At the outset I think it important for me to state my own relationship with the principal figures. I never knew Stravinsky. I did know the late Vera Stravinsky and conversed privately with her a number of times. I know Soulima and his wife, Françoise. I also know Robert Craft, and *The Musical Quarterly* [of which I was then editor] has published several of his essays.

I view Craft not merely as companion and chronicler, but rather as an influential force, as important to Stravinsky in the 19 years from

Milton Babbitt, Igor Stravinsky, Claudio Spies
Rehearsal for *Threni*
CREDIT: Don Hunstein

George Balanchine, Igor Stravinsky
Cabin in the Sky —Backstage, 1940
CREDIT: Frank Driggs Collection

1948 to 1967, the year of his last sketches, as Diaghilev had been in the composer's career during the 19 years from 1909 to 1928. Those who prefer the earlier works to the serial pieces of the late years are probably reacting as much to the evolution of music in general as they are to Stravinsky in particular. For, as this century moved on, being "interesting" displaced other attributes, such as beauty, expressivity, and profundity, as the ultimate musical criterion. And who can deny that Stravinsky's late works are among the most interesting not only of his career but also of the musical literature of the 20th century?

It has been argued that everyone is replaceable. In his essay in *The New York Review of Books* Craft wrote: "From the first, Mrs. Stravinsky believed that I, or someone like me, was essential to her husband if he were to remain in the midstream of new music. She sensed, as she had done in the early twenties, when she introduced Arthur Lourié to Stravinsky, that he needed a musical confidante and sounding board."

Lourié, ten years younger than Stravinsky and a fellow alumnus from the St. Petersburg Conservatoire, first met Stravinsky in Paris in 1925 and served him as "musical confidante and sounding board" for roughly a decade. In 1935, he was replaced by Alexis Kall, an old friend of Stravinsky from St. Petersburg who assisted Stravinsky both during the frequent trips he made to the United States and after he moved here in 1939. When making arrangements to deliver the Norton Lectures at Harvard, *Poetics of Music in the Form of Six Lessons*, Stravinsky wrote to ask that Kall be put up with him at Eliot House. When the request was denied, Stravinsky wrote again, this time noting that Kall's presence "was important to me for psychological and moral reasons," that Kall had already given up his own work "to share my solitude and look after me throughout my stay in America."

Stravinsky accepted with ease the idea and the fact of others making sacrifices for him. Lourié and Kall were only two soliders in a veritable army of devoted acolytes. In the January 1983 issue of the *London Review of Books*, the musicologist and psychoanalyst Hans Keller wrote that "Stravinsky treated human beings as mere, sheer material." Two Californians, Sol Babitz and Ingolf Dahl, were among that "mere, sheer material."

But it is also important to note that Stravinsky did not use others only to perform musical chores. He often used them as ghostwriters for his prose. Vera Stravinsky told me that her husband did not publicly acknowledge the work of these others because he did not want to share the glory with them and, more important, because he wanted to keep all the royalties for himself. Walter Nouvel wrote *The Autobiography*; Roland-Manuel and Pierre Souvchinsky *Poetics of Music*. Robert Craft recently submitted to *The Musical Quarterly* 1500 words that he claims are the only words that Stravinsky contributed to those six hours of Norton Lectures. Craft's own involvement with Stravinsky was more encompassing than that of anyone else, for he worked on both musical and literary projects and, in addition, immediately became the necessary "musical confidante and sounding board."

Just as Stravinsky had predecessors for Robert Craft, so Craft had at least one for the role Stravinsky played in his life: the bandmaster at the military academy he attended as a boy. Growing up in Kingston, New York, with an older and a younger sister, Craft's early life seems to have been unremarkable. His father inherited a supermarket business, then went into real estate with a partner. He was a Republican, a Methodist, and liked to dance. Craft's mother, the dominant figure in the family, was literary, Episcopalian and, along with her husband, supported her son in his ambitions. One neighbor remembers the boy as "thinking and complicated", another as "unnecessarily verbose". By his adolescence Robert was fanatic about music. He played the trumpet and spent hours each day conducting to records as he read the scores. He was unaffected by the social distinctions or political conservatism of small-town life. Craft was early drawn to Jewish women. He was an impassioned liberal. His open-mindedness was to have resonance with Stravinsky in later years.

In 1937, Craft entered the New York Military Academy at Cornwall on a music scholarship. A former classmate, now on the school's board of trustees, remembers Craft as somewhat less than an average student, excelling only in music. He also remembers him as a follower, not a leader. "What I remember most," the man recalled recently, "was his wholehearted dedication to the bandmaster. He tried to learn everything he could from him. In return he helped him enormously. He checked the scores, copied the parts, made the arrangements, even carried the music. He spent virtually all his free time with him."

Of the New York Military Academy, the same man remarked: "There was a particularly high-class clientele at the school. The sons of the heads of Paramount and MGM went there. The son of Bill Tilden, the tennis player, went there. Celebrities were always hanging around. Fifteen or twenty planes came in every weekend for the tennis matches. Rolls-Royces were everywhere. The music scholarship Bob received must have been viewed by his parents as the opportunity of his life."

The scholarship also provided Craft with four years of glamorous living that he — not expecting to inherit money, not being endowed with leadership qualities, not excelling in traditional academic pursuits — must have feared he could never acquire on his own. He seems to have decided, on some level, that the good life once removed was better than none at all; for, in 1941, when he entered Juilliard at 17, he told at least two classmates that his goal was to become an amanuensis to a great composer. Over the years, Craft wrote to several European composers including Schoenberg, but it was only when he wrote to Stravinsky that the complex chemistry of the two correspondents meshed in practical, psychological, even philosophical ways.

Craft was probably one of the first Americans Stravinsky met after moving to the United States who viewed art in much the same manner as he did. For his early American years were radically different from those he had known in Europe. Living in Los Angeles, Stravinsky was at first surrounded by Russians — friends, gardeners, cooks, and so on. Russian was the principal language in the Stravinsky household. Professionally, Stravinsky became involved with a kind of West Coast Tin Pan Alley. Possibly unaware that music in America could be anything *but* pop, he produced a cabaret piece, the 1940

Tango; reharmonized *The Star-Spangled Banner*; fulfilled commissions for Paul Whiteman and Benny Goodman; wrote *The Ebony Concerto* for Woody Herman; conducted a rehearsal of the Army Air Force Band; provided a polka for elephants in the Barnum and Bailey Circus; and composed music for Hollywood films, which was turned down. During this time, Stravinsky's music was performed infrequently.

The day on which Stravinsky met Craft was also the day the composer was handed his first libretto in English. Aldous Huxley, Stravinsky's Los Angeles neighbor, had introduced the composer to W. H. Auden. Stravinsky's having to deal with an English libretto — even if there had been nothing else at stake — made Craft immediately useful to him. Auden was to deliver the libretto to Stravinsky in a Washington, D. C., hotel room on March 31, 1948. In a conversation three years ago, Vera Stravinsky recalled some of the events that had led to that first meeting between her husband and Robert Craft:

"I remember when the first letter from Bob arrived. Stravinsky came into the room and said, 'I received a letter. It is from a young man. It is marvelously written. And so true. He is young, but he knows everything.'

"They continued to write," Mrs. Stravinsky went on, "for a number of years. Then, when Stravinsky was going to be in Washington, he wrote to Bob asking him to meet him there. In the hotel room, Auden said: 'There is a young man who wants to see Stravinsky.' Well, of course, there were always young men who wanted to see Stravinsky. Who was it this time? Robert Craft.

"When Auden and Stravinsky talked, Bob mostly listened. Then he moved to the side and asked me what I read. Then he told me what I *should* read."

And so did Craft begin to select and to order for the Stravinsky library.

Craft went even further. Although Mrs. Stravinsky had painted a little in her native Russia, after 1920 she had been using her very real talent to design items that could be found in boutiques. Handpainted scarves were her specialty. But, in 1952, Craft persuaded her to set up a studio for herself in a small house in which he himself had taken an apartment only one block from the Stravinsky ménage. Thus Mrs. Stravinsky found an outlet that not only gave her a sense of her own identity—not easy to come by when one is the wife of Stravinsky—but she also occupied herself during those hours everyday when Stravinsky needed to be alone to compose.

Igor, Vera, Robert—each of the three had everything to gain, nothing to lose in this new arrangement. Stravinsky, who in those days surely determined his own arrangements, profited more than the other two. From the beginning, Craft proved useful in finding the errors in Stravinsky's scores. Then, as conductor of the Chamber Art Society, from 1947 to 1950, Craft conducted Stravinsky's music when New Yorkers had no other access to it.

How did Craft influence Stravinsky, the man?

When he first learned of my explorations of these matters, Craft sent me two letters. The first, handwritten, included these observations:

1) Stravinsky and Politics: Can anyone imagine that he would ever have returned to Russia in 1962 if I had not been there?
2) Would Stravinsky have written *Abraham and Isaac* without my presence for fifteen years? What became of the "traditional Russian anti-Semitism" found in the family and other correspondence in the 1920s and '30s (and found, too, surprisingly in Prokofiev)?
3) Why did Stravinsky *stop* attending the Russian Orthodox Church after 1951 and for the rest of his life? Did my "freethinking" have any connection, any influence on his reading?

As to the depth of Stravinsky's receptivity, Craft has commented frequently over the years on that particular element of the master's temperament. Soulima's wife, Françoise, not generally in accord with Craft's views, has emphasized that same personal characteristic to me. "Father was extremely impressionable," she said. "Sometimes he would come home and say 'Renoir is finished' or some such thing if he had heard it from one of Vera's friends."

30

As for the crucial subject of Craft's influence on the music itself, here I quote from several typewritten letters Craft sent to me in August 1982:

What requires immediate and categorical refutation... is the notion that when I met Stravinsky he was already acquainted with the works and methods of the New Viennese School. In fact he did not know a single measure of the music of any member of this group, and the last time that he had heard a piece by Schoenberg – the *Septet-Suite* – in Venice, in 1937, he admitted in print to having understood nothing in it. He had *never* heard music by Berg and scarcely knew Webern's name....

My guilt is not in having directed or controlled the 'spiritual interests of a composer of genius' – this is in reference to an attack on Craft by Mikhail Druskin in a book on Stravinsky published by Oxford University Press in 1980 – but rather in trying to bury my tracks for having done so. I destroyed several pages of notes (verbal) that I had prepared for Stravinsky when he was composing *The Flood* – one of them mentions the film music in *Lulu* as a model (in construction) for the storm scene – and which he pasted at the center of his sketch-score.

To borrow Harold Bloom's phrase, 'the anxiety of influence' (but not in his sense of the Oedipal child's 'resented dependence on the progenitor'), I did not want the responsibility of influencing Stravinsky. Having assumed since my twelfth year that he *had* to know more about every aspect of music than I could ever *learn*, I was dumbfounded during our first sessions at the piano together, when he asked for my opinion about doubling a note in a chord, choosing between two alternatives in a modulation, the advisability of repeating a certain figure, and so forth. Here was the man whom I had believed to be completely sure of himself seeking confirmation in the very crucible of his creation. Naturally I tried to give the answers I felt he wanted, and not react instinctively. But what I wanted most was simply to disappear....

In 1949, with the ascendancy of the Webern cult... Stravinsky, for the first time in his life, suffered from a fear

31

that his music was being superseded. Most of *The Rake's Progress* was yet to be written and the crisis was slow in coming. One afternoon in March 1952, during a drive to Palmdale in the Mojave Desert, he sat silently, then choked up, suddenly said he was afraid that he could no longer compose. And for a moment or two he wept. I tried to encourage him by proposing that he orchestrate his *Concertino* using, in addition to the obligato violin and cello, wind instruments employed in the *Octet* and *Mass....* He started work on the *Concertino* arrangement immediately, but did not compose new music until after a concert tour in Europe. There he watched the Parisian public rave over *Wozzeck* and hiss and boo Cocteau in *Oedipus Rex*, though the real target was not Cocteau but the piece itself and its aesthetics as I think Stravinsky understood. Three weeks later, in Brussels, he heard Paul Collaer discuss Berg and Webern with me after which Collaer sent him a tape of *Das Augenlicht*. In October and November, in Hollywood, I conducted four Schoenberg memorial concerts. Stravinsky, scores in hand, did not miss a rehearsal, some of which even took place in his own home. The remainder of the story, part of it, at least, goes from private to public record.

Stravinsky confirms Craft's influence on his late music. On page 1 of the *Monumentum* manuscript he wrote: "To Bob, who forced me to do it, and I did it." Craft quotes this in his *New York Review* essay and adds that the "statement might have been inscribed on *The Flood* and the *Canticles* as well and that could serve as an *apologia pro vita mea*."

If Stravinsky's serial period can be traced directly to the influence of Craft — as Craft claims in these passages — so can Stravinsky's neoclassic period be traced directly to Diaghilev. In fact, the composer might well have inscribed on page 1 of the *Pulcinella* manuscript: "To Serge, who forced me to do it, and I did it." For in 1920 Diaghilev handed the composer several 18th century manuscripts, then thought to be by Pergolesi, and told him to string them together, adding, of course, his own harmonies. In making this recommendation, Diaghilev pointed to a rich and varied source of material — the art of the past as opposed to the folk material from Russia — with which

Stravinsky was to work for the next 30 years. His last neoclassic work, the Mozart-influenced *Rake's Progress*, was conceived just before he met Craft.

Craft's influence on history's perception of Stravinsky is probably the most difficult arena to assess in any account of the Craft-Stravinsky connection. But here again, Craft has performed remarkable services. He has illuminated the details of Stravinsky's past, particularly his relations with men and women who, in some instances, were unknown and, in others, were distorted in such outright diplomatic tracts as the *Autobiography*. Stravinsky appears to have held onto everything, and Craft has been tireless in sorting out and organizing the material.

The greatest difficulty comes when we approach the writings presented to us as "by" Stravinsky in his last decades. How can Craft tell us that, in the late 1930s, Stravinsky wrote only 1500 words of the 30,000-word *Poetics of Music* without ever acknowledging his collaborators publicly, and then expect his readers to believe that Stravinsky's post-1954 prose was written entirely by the composer himself? This is particularly hard to accept in light of the style of these writings. Those who had firsthand knowledge of Stravinsky knew the composer to be fiercely intelligent, capable of identifying a problem right away, witty and pungent in his expression, and always free of pretension. They also knew he was no intellectual in the sense in which he has been presented to us in these late writings. Although the ideas that relate to music and aesthetics are most probably Stravinsky's own, the articles and books published under his name in the late 1950s and 1960s use the jargon of modern psychology, physics, mathematics, and musicology in a way that is as alien to Stravinsky's own character and temperament as it is congenial to the interests and personal style of Craft himself.

The portraits Craft has offered of Stravinsky have become increasingly harsh. In the *New York Review* article, Craft writes that Stravinsky was "extremely anal, exhibitionistic, narcissistic, hypochondriacal, compulsive and deeply superstitious. He was also quarrelsome and vindictive, which is stated not as moral judgment but merely as description of behavior." Such words, in fact, represent a quantitative rather than a qualitative difference in Craft's treatment of Stravinsky when the composer was alive. In the same article, Craft writes:

"Stravinsky discovered that I was more independent than he had initially supposed, and markedly unlike his children and the numerous acolytes schooled by Nadia Boulanger. Yet I think that after the initial shock, he welcomed this difference in me. No one before seems ever to have contradicted him, or questioned a patently foolish statement (of which he was as capable as anyone else.) No doubt my bad manners were to blame when I talked back, as much as the feeling that disagreements should not always be swallowed. But we did adjust to each other."

They did more than adjust. Craft appears to have sensed that an irreverent, abrasive attitude was the only attitude that would nourish Stravinsky, for even in his strongest years, the composer was never influenced by anyone who was *not* in a combative relationship with him. Like an oyster, he needed an irritant to produce a pearl. That was his history. His mother was the prototype of those who insulted him. She did not hear *Le Sacre du Printemps* until its 25th anniversary performance and then told friends she did not expect to like it, that it was not her kind of music. Rimsky-Korsakov, Diaghilev, and Arnold Schoenberg all treated Stravinsky with very real abuse.

And Stravinsky's feelings toward each were infused with intense ambivalence. Not only did he take from these people their most seminal ideas, but then, resenting their power over him, he retaliated in the most striking way. According to Craft, Stravinsky repeatedly said he wrote *Le Sacre du Printemps* to send everyone connected to his past to hell. Making great art *is* the final triumph, and Stravinsky, again, in his late years, continued to send everyone in his recent past to hell. Craft was certainly high on that list, not only because of the composer's genuine dependence on him, but also because of Craft's persistent humiliation of Stravinsky in front of servants and musicians as well. And the music kept flowing from Stravinsky like wine.

34

It is reasonable to suppose that if we were to look closely at the lives of many artists, we would find hidden collaborators lurking everywhere. While few have been as willful or as aberrant as Craft, few have been as skillful with words or as intellectually lively as he is. Early in life, Craft knew precisely what he wanted to do. He chose the right man who also chose him. And the right woman, Vera Stravinsky, made the connection work.

From 1920 to 1939, Stravinsky had lived in a triangle with his first wife, Catherine, and Vera. Catherine's death left Stravinsky and Vera alone, and it is just possible that this simple twosome seemed empty and inadequate to them both. With Craft's entrance into the household, turmoil returned, jealousies abounded, life became exciting, and Stravinsky turned his back on pop art to create the exalted works of his late years.

Over that period, Robert Craft's personality changed. In Stravinsky's life, he went from amanuensis to alter ego. He remained a figure always powerfully in the shadows, yet never permitting himself to be quite invisible. The "thinking and complicated" adolescent remained, but in addition, there were mixed with him bits of Machiavelli, Svengali, and John Alden. Craft conducted Stravinsky's life from his own carefully constructed score.

As Stravinsky became weaker with advancing age, Craft became stronger, more manipulative. As Stravinsky's will to create lessened, Craft, through sheer determination and single-mindedness of purpose, revived him with regular and powerful transfusions of empathetic energy. Few men could set out to walk a high wire without a net and do it so brilliantly and for so long as Craft. Whatever fault we may find in his ways, whatever extraordinary behavior took place, here is one set of circumstances in which the end clearly seems to have justified the means.

For, none of us would wish Stravinsky's career had stopped with the *Rake's Progress*. Nor would we want a last picture of the composer to be that of a man in despair, weeping in the Mojave Desert, fearing years of creative paralysis. Craft was only 25 years old when he joined

Stravinsky in Los Angeles. Intuitively, he did what had to be done so that the composer could make art throughout the rest of his life, and he succeeded, brilliantly.

For much memorable music, we are in debt to Robert Craft.

4

EDGARD VARÈSE

In 1923 Lawrence Gilman, music critic for *The Herald-Tribune*, reviewed Edgard Varèse's *Hyperprism:* "Hearing Schoenberg's notorious *Five Pieces for Orchestra*... you will remember that Wagner once lived; hearing Alfredo Casella's *Alta Nottee,* you will remember that Schoenberg still lives. Hearing Varèse's *Hyperprism,* you will remember only Varèse. It is lonely, incomparable, unique."

Edgard Varèse is the composer who, in 1916, hungered for sounds that would eventually be provided by electronic instruments. He rejected traditional form, and as a conductor he played advanced music. Now, seven years after his death, his widow has completed the first of two biographical volumes. Not a musician, psychologist or historian, but a woman who loved her husband very much, she tells the story without attempting to explain it. Still, she has given plenty of clues.

Varèse began to study music at 17, knew Debussy and Romain Rolland in Paris, Busoni and Richard Strauss in Berlin, and the Whitneys and Vanderbilts when he first arrived in New York. Varèse hated Mozart, refused to read Proust, thought "Pierrot Lunaire" a "trashy" poem. Here is Varèse on Arnold Schoenberg: "Schoenberg liberated music from tonality, but it was as though, frightened by so much freedom, he retreated to the refuge of a system. Beware the codification of systems and, in spite of all revolutionary slogans, their latent academicism."

Varèse was a handsome and charming man who liked to cook and eat and drink with friends. But underneath it all, one dark theme prevails: Edgard hated his father, Henri. Mrs. Varèse suggests that his

---

Review of *Varèse: A Looking-Glass Diary* by Louise Varèse in *The New York Times Book Review,* April 23, 1972.

Igor Stravinsky, Edgard Varèse
CREDIT: Don Hunstein

Milton Babbitt, Edgard Varèse
CREDIT: Clemens Kalischer

rebellious attitude towards such men as Clemenceau, from whom he got an exemption from the military service, and Vincent d'Indy, then his teacher and head of the Schola Cantorum, stemmed from his bitterness towards his father. She presents a convincing case history: Henri repeatedly beat Edgard who would engage in street fights to "release his pent-up resentment." When Edgard's mother lay dying, she told him to protect his younger brothers from their "assassin" father. In a violent scene, Edgard attacked Henri and left home; he refused to see him in later years.

Louise Varèse agrees with Dr. William Flies, Freud's former friend and Varèse's physician in Berlin, that her husband was *"un grand nerveux"*. She documents his severe depressions (he destroyed his early score *Bourgogne* during one sleepless night) and characterizes them as "not sullen and brooding. They were fierce and furiously resentful." She quotes Varèse's "I can't breathe" and comments that she heard it repeatedly. She writes that her husband suffered a "sense of suffocation" whenever he walked under the arches of the Rue de Rivoli, could not bear an enclosed elevator, and regarded with apprehension "forests cluttered up with trees, high mountains closing one in like a 'prison,' and lakes that lay unmoving, 'dead,' among them."

One cannot escape the possibility from this account that Varèse's hatred for his father served him in his attack on the music of the past, and that his fear of enclosure played a large role in his quest for "liberating sound," for "instruments freed from the tempered system," and for the seemingly boundless space that his sounds occupy. To say this is not to deny Varèse's genius; it is rather to chart—in a small way—that mysterious passage from self to symbol.

The first half of the book deals with Varèse up to 1917, before he met the author, Louise Norton. She was then separated from her first husband. At this point, the narrative really springs to life, for the author now relies on memory rather than on information which, even though it came from Varèse himself, is nevertheless, secondhand. He was 34 when they met. (He, too, had been married once before.)

Varèse was pursuing a conducting career in New York, determined to bring newly composed music to people "eager to listen and learn." In 1919, he founded the New Symphony Orchestra. Three pairs of concerts were scheduled, but Varèse conducted only the first. After the initial performance, the Board notified him that he'd have to compromise on the programming; Roussel, Busoni, Casella, Debussy, Satie, Ravel and Bartók would not do. Varèse refused, and lost the post to Artur Bodanzky who took over with the traditional repertoire. Shocked and angry, Varèse now condemned this new orchestra on the ground that it was following the "same pattern as the two which already only aped each other."

In 1922, Varèse formed the International Composers Guild that was to provide a showcase for his *Hyperprism, Octandre, Offrandes* and *Integrales,* as well as for works by the greatest contemporary composers. Shortly after its inception, Louise Varèse recalls, the I.C.G. named Mrs. Arthur Reis Executive Secretary. Mrs. Reis's connections were "many and moneyed... she was indefatigable... she was a treasure—or so we thought."

Soon after Claire Reis entered the I.C.G., the Varèses left New York for Berlin to visit Busoni who was ill. During their absence, Mrs. Reis and her clique "assumed that theirs was the power and glory to come. They began, not yet frankly but with determination of pique, working *democratically* to dethrone him."

The clash of personalities intensified. "Activities that season tended to center around Mrs. Reis's house: the folding, stuffing, licking, stamping and the meetings... and the afterconcert receptions, which Varèse ungratefully called 'those delicatessen parties,' ostensibly on account of the mounds of mayonnaise which covered chicken salad that he happened not to like, but really because of what he felt as an alien atmosphere.... For us, something had gone out of the Guild—something which, lacking an English word, I fall back on that precious overworked *Gemütlichkeit.* I stress 'for us,' as probably for Mrs. Reis and her followers, everything was as cozy as possible." Claire Reis

40

broke from the parent group and formed the League of Composers, which promoted neoclassicism — new works that drew on the tonality of the past — at the expense of advanced composition. Music critic Paul Rosenfeld sided with Varèse; he characterized the League as a "social function" in which performance of music served the "ambitions of mediocres... and music a prelude to... chicken salad at close quarters." In a B.B.C. interview, Varèse commented on patronage; music, he said, would be saved only by the instinctive listener and the aristocratic intelligentsia, "but there is little to be hoped from the bourgeoisie."

In 1927, as the author observes at the close of Volume I, the I.C.G. died of lack of funds. With it went Varèse's principal access to an audience. In her consistently open, unpretentious way, Louise Varèse confesses to prejudice: "Observing indelibly only what I observe emotionally, I am a bad reporter and it is my hope that some impersonal music historian will... write an account of Varèse's pioneer I.C.G. more complete and unbiased than mine."

In the March 19, 1972, Sunday *Times,* a listener attacked Pierre Boulez, another French composer-conductor, for his attention to the 20th-century repertoire and threatened to withdraw financial support. What Varèse confronted 50 years ago, makers of "the new music" still face.

5

HENRY COWELL

The late Henry Cowell was best known for his tone clusters, great fist and forearm smashes on the keyboard. He is also fondly remembered virtually climbing into the gut of the piano, with fingers plucking, strumming and scratching the strings in previously unimagined ways. Cowell wrote a work in which the performer decided in what order the movements were to be played. That anticipated the chance music pioneered by John Cage by at least 20 years.

"Pulse", to be performed by the New Music Consort, is oriental, percussive, brief and to the point. It is also characteristic Cowell. The composer thought in short, quick terms and expected the same of everyone else. Once he asked his wife how quickly she typed to determine how long she would take to write a book.

Cowell's scores were never elaborately worked out. If he wanted to change a note, he preferred to start again with a brand new piece. By the age of 17, with no traditional schooling or musical education, the composer had reached Opus 100. By 1965, when he died at the age of 68, he had completed 20 symphonies, 30 other large orchestral works, 18 Hymn and Fuguing Tunes, eight string quartets and countless smaller pieces.

*

Cowell was born in 1897 in a tiny cottage in Menlo Park, California. This short, energetic man, with a fringe of white hair ringing his head and eyes peering brightly through spectacles, not only anticipated many of the techniques of the post-World War II avant-

Originally published in *The New York Times* as "Henry Cowell: An Influential American Original", December 6, 1981.

Henry Cowell
CREDIT: Clemens Kalischer

garde; he also anticipated its tone. In Cowell, there is neither sentiment nor tragedy. Often he seems calculatedly shallow; he is quoted
as having said he never composed "while in an emotional or intellectual fever." Still, Cowell belongs firmly to the Western tradition of
high art.

To say Cowell symbolized the irreverence, brashness, high spirits
and playfulness that lie at the heart of the American character is not
to suggest his countrymen loved him for it. After his first Carnegie
Hall recital in 1924, the New York *World* critic warned that the next
time he aired his tone clusters in public, the paper would send a
sportswriter to cover the event. After the second concert, the headline
read: "Kid Cowell and Battling Knabe".

But artists and intellectuals outside the United States were quick
to recognize Cowell's innovative genius. Béla Bartók and Artur
Schnabel helped arrange his concerts in Europe between 1923 and
1933 and, after a meeting in London, Bartók asked Cowell for permission to use tone clusters; apparently Bartók thought Cowell had a
patent on them.

In 1922, Breitkopf & Härtel published 15 piano pieces and a few
years later issued six more. In the mid-1920s, Vasily Kandinsky invited
Cowell to perform at the Bauhaus and, in 1929, Cowell concertized in
Moscow and Leningrad after which the Soviet State Music Edition
printed two of his pieces, tone clusters and all. In 1932, Schoenberg
asked Cowell to demonstrate his techniques to his own master class
in Berlin, and Webern, the same year, conducted two performances of
the Scherzo movement of Cowell's *Sinfonietta* in Vienna.

Although Cowell grew up very poor, by his early 30s he was able
to sponsor a variety of ambitious publishing, recording and concert
management projects designed to disseminate far-out music.

In 1928 Cowell began to lecture at the progressive New School for
Social Research in New York; in 1929, on a Guggenheim Fellowship,
he studied the Hornbostel collection of cylinders of folk and primitive

music at the University of Berlin; in 1933 he edited a book *American Composers on American Music,* to which he contributed several articles.

That same year, Germany refused Cowell a visa and he was unable to return to Berlin. His widow says that because the composer did not provide the place of his paternal grandmother's birth — he did not know the particular city in Ireland — the authorities assumed that he was Jewish. During the next few years, Cowell helped European friends emigrate to the United States.

The harsh political climate of the 30s inhibited radical art. The Marxist philosophy of socialist realism attracted large numbers of artists and intellectuals, and accessible, popular music became the fashion. Those committed to breaking barriers had nowhere to go. In 1936, Edgard Varèse, another pioneer, sank into a deep depression and began throwing away all the music he wrote.

That same year Cowell was arrested on a morals charge and was sentenced to San Quentin prison. In 1940, pressure from distinguished musicians brought about Cowell's release and, a year later, the Governor of California pardoned him.

When he got out, he began to work as secretary to Percy Grainger and renewed his acquaintance with a California friend, Sidney Hawkins Robertson, whom he had known, on and off, since she was 13 and he was 20. Mrs. Robertson came from a wealthy, cultivated family. She was bilingual, a pianist and a folk music collector. As Cowell was small, unassuming, laconic, Mrs. Robertson was large, expansive, wordy. They were married in September 1941.

Today she characterizes the relationship as "More a long friendship than a romance." She says that one of her responsibilities was to take three sentences by Cowell and expand them into a two- to three-thousand word article. But she adds that "Henry used words in a direct, forceful way, and I could never make mine sound like his." Since Cowell's death in 1965, Mrs. Cowell has devoted considerable energy to disseminating information about his life and ideas. "There is no Henry Cowell biography," she explains, "and I am the only reference work around."

Here is some generally unfamiliar information gleaned from Mrs. Cowell:

Cowell's mother, Clarissa Dickson, was 46 when Henry was born. She was a philosophical anarchist and believed in no laws or regulations. Cowell's father, Harry Cowell, was only 26 at the time of his child's birth. He came from a distinguished Irish family. Harry Cowell wanted to be a poet but rarely published nor could he hold a job. Very soon he left Clarissa but continued to move in and out of his son's life.

Henry did not attend school. Twice he went for a matter of weeks, but he wore long curls and a Lord Fauntleroy suit, and the children humiliated him. The elder Cowell pressed Henry to study the violin and become a prodigy. Henry worked on the traditional repertory with an aged teacher and at 7 gave his first recital. At 8, he developed a nervous disease which a physician attributed to the pressure to perform. Henry stopped playing the violin, and his father never forgave him for it. Decades later, at Cowell's concerts, Harry Cowell would rise in the audience and take lengthy, repeated bows. Henry Cowell confided to his wife the rage he still felt toward a father who had rejected him for so much of his life.

Henry searched for a father-figure all of his life. The first of these was John Varian, an Irish poet. At 15, the young composer arrived at Varian's house with a piece dedicated to the poet's son. Varian liked it and asked him to write a prelude that could open a dramatic reading of one of his own poems. Cowell wanted rolling effects to suggest the Irish sea. He played chords, but they were too neat. He played octaves, but they were not right. Impatiently, he hit the keyboard and — right out of a Hollywood scenario — he knew he found what he wanted. *The Tides of Manaunaum* was Cowell's first tone-cluster piece.

Cowell's last father-figure, and the most important one, was the awesome composer Charles Ives, whom Cowell first brought to public attention. Here is how Cowell met Ives:

In 1929, Cowell started New Music Editions; his purpose was to publish radical scores. He sent out 8,000 circulars, one of which went to Ives. In response, Ives sent money for two subscriptions. When New Music Editions' first publication, Carl Ruggles' *Men and Mountains* came out, Ives sent money for additional subscriptions. Grateful, Cowell visited Ives at his insurance company office in New York City. Ives showed Cowell other pieces, among them *The Fourth of July*, which Cowell accepted right away. Ives insisted on paying enough to publish his own work and that of one other composer. Then Ives began sending New Music Editions $100 each month.

But when Cowell was arrested, Ives broke with him. The friendship was repaired later, and the Cowells wrote the first biography of Ives. Mrs. Cowell reports that one could only ask Ives specific questions, that he would never talk on or discuss issues. "Ives had a heart condition, and he could get excited easily. Mrs. Ives forbid us to question relatives, so we had to kind of crawl up on him. This is a book written by two friends. It has been attacked as too sentimental, but there was no way to get more information than we did."

Although Cowell's wild experiments were over by the 1940s, he never did anything afterward that was inconsistent with the way he viewed art and life. That view may be characterized as one of a child playing with a great, beautiful toy. In the post-Webern period, when discipline was the *sine qua non* of musical thought, Cowell continued to disregard all scholarly techniques. Instead, he concentrated his efforts on another lifelong interest, non-Western music, and he and his wife spent time in the East. Cowell also drew on a collection of Southern rural hymns arranged by William Walker in the 1830s and, for the rest of his life, sporadically drew on them for his *Eighteen Hymn and Fuguing Tunes*, which remain among his most engaging pieces.

Henry Cowell was a great American original. He almost singlehandedly initiated the focus on percussion that became a significant characteristic of much modern music. He turned the piano into an idiosyncratic percussion instrument and alerted Western culture to the values of Eastern music. John Cage, who copied by hand a book by Cowell on rhythm and then hitch-hiked from California to New York to study with him, acknowledges a great debt. Karlheinz Stockhausen, Mauricio Kagel, Philip Glass, Steve Reich and dozens of composers in Europe and the United States all owe much of their tone and musical ways to Cowell indirectly through his influence on Cage.

In 1923, Schoenberg wrote that he had developed a technique — dodecaphony — which would assure the supremacy of German music for the next hundred years. The supremacy did not last that long. Exuberant Americans — Henry Cowell and Charles Ives — came along with their eccentric, freewheeling ways and created yet other possibilities for new music.

6

BÉLA BARTÓK

In covering a seminar held in New York in November 1994 entitled "Mahler in America, 1907-1911", Edward Rothstein wrote in The New York Times: *"In recent years there have been scholarly examinations of Dvorák in America, Tchaikovsky in America, Wagner in America: encounters of European composers, their music and the United States. As American culture becomes more self-consciously brooding about its past and future, these encounters are taking on mythic status."*

The present paper is being published here to stimulate comparable work on Bartók in America.

Many musicians and scholars believe the United States, particularly Columbia University, treated Béla Bartók, the great Hungarian composer and scholar of folk and ethnic music, badly during the last years of his life. I do not wish to refute entirely that charge but to shed light on it. I was a musicology student at Columbia several years after Bartók's death. During these years, I was in almost daily contact with those figures who, in large measure, determined Bartók's fate immediately after he arrived in the United States.

In the fifth edition of *Grove's Dictionary of Music and Musicians*, Eric Blom, the editor, used the word "shameful" to characterize Bartók's treatment here. Blom added, however, that "how he lived during his last years we still have no clear picture."

Vera Lampert and Laslo Shomfai, authors of the Bartók entry in the sixth edition of Grove, generally known as *The New Grove*, give the reader a more complete picture of the composer's late years. In this essay, published in November 1980, they at least indicate where much

---

Paper delivered at Indiana University's centennial celebration of the composer's birth, March, 1981, as "Bartók in the United States".

49

of Bartók's problem lay: "Bartók," they write, "was employed at Columbia from March 1941 to the end of 1942 at a salary of $3,000 a year though since the post was renewable each term, he could never feel secure."

The problem, then, was the insecurity of the post, not the work itself. Bartók refused to teach composition because he believed it would interfere with his creativity. Instead, he studied and transcribed into musical notation the material from 2600 discs of Yugoslav folk music at Harvard University collected by Milman Parry in 1933 and 1934. The arrangement he made with Columbia also provided him with a house at 117th Street and Broadway in which he kept his equipment and papers. Bartók often called his research his "life work" suggesting he considered it more central to him than composing. Even then, $3,000 a year was not a lot of money; it was equal to about $15,000 today. What is hard to understand is the demand that Bartók behave like a young student applicant and request a renewal of the grant at the beginning of every term. Why was he obliged to do this?

To illuminate a dark period of any person's life, it is useful to recreate the activities of those years just prior to the ones under investigation. This should help us understand what led Bartók to leave Hungary and choose the United States.

In Budapest, the composer had enjoyed a secure income as a professor at the Conservatory of Music, a house, a pension for his later years, an impressive library, a beautiful garden, and his own vast collection of folk music. He had longstanding, loyal friends with whom he conversed in Hungarian, avoiding the German language that had become the vogue. It was the rise of Nazism that made life there unbearable for him.

Although the Nazis had not yet entered Hungary when Bartók left for the United States, problems had been growing for almost a decade. As early as 1930, when Toscanini was under attack by the Fascists, Bartók wrote on behalf of the Hungarian section of the International Society for Contemporary Music a letter that said he hoped to "protect

Joseph Szigeti, Béla Bartók, Benny Goodman record
Bartók's *Contrasts* for Violin, Clarinet & Piano
Columbia Records / Los Angeles / May 13, 1940
CREDIT: Frank Driggs Collection

Benny Goodman and Béla Bartók in conversation
CREDIT: Frank Driggs Collection

the integrity and autonomy of art." After the first performance of his *Second Piano Concerto* conducted by Hans Robaud in Frankfurt on January 23, 1933, Bartók forbade broadcasts of his music in Germany and Italy and renounced his membership in the Austrian Performing Rights Society on the grounds that it was Nazi-inclined. He joined the London branch. Probably for the same set of reasons, he left Universal Edition, his Austrian publisher, for the London office of Boosey and Hawkes. This was in 1937.

Bartók was constantly being attacked in the Hungarian and Romanian papers of the time and began to look towards some Swiss friends for help. In a letter in 1938, he wrote to one Müller-Widmann: "The political situation in Hungary becomes more and more crooked. At least my manscripts should be somewhere safe." The next year, he directed his papers be sent to London, making it clear he would have preferred they find a proper place in the United States. It was then he considered emigration, but love for his mother apparently tied him to Hungary. When she died, in 1939, Bartók inquired about the possibility of settling elsewhere. When he decided on the United States, it was his Swiss friends who paid for the trip.

During the five-week period between April 11 and May 18, Bartók gave a concert at the Library of Congress with Joseph Szigeti, recording *Contrasts*, his own composition which he and Szigeti played with Benny Goodman. He also lectured on his folk music research. It was during this five-week visit that Nicholas Murray Butler, then President of Columbia University, informed him that the university wanted to confer upon him the honorary degree of Doctor of Music for "distinguished service to the art of music". In a handwritten letter, Bartók replied he would not be able to attend the ceremony because he was returning to Hungary: "This is to save my life work: the collection of many records of Hungarian folk music." Bartók added he planned to return to New York in the fall and remain for a few months. Butler answered he would hold the honor in reserve: "I quite understand why you should feel it necessary at such a time as this to return to Hungary promptly."

Bartók's visit to the United States during that spring of 1940 was not the first time he had experienced American appreciation and American generosity. On his first American tour, in 1927, Blanche Walton, a wealthy Quaker woman, gave parties in his honor and invited distinguished guests. Walton also befriended Arnold Schoenberg. Ignoring those composers most of us now think of as prototypical Americans — Aaron Copland, Virgil Thomson and Roy Harris — she supported Schoenberg and Bartók as well as those idiosyncratic, eccentric Americans such as Charles Seeger, Ruth Crawford and Henry Cowell who were experiencing even more difficulties in their professional lives than Copland, Thomson and Harris, who were at least being played by the League of Composers and being written about in *Modern Music*, the major outlets for serious music in the United States before World War II.

Considering Bartók's experiences in these early visits, it would seem he would have had every reason to expect decent treatment in the United States. The difficulties he encountered came from two sources. One was his own personality: icy, remote, uncompromising. He never performed from memory, and that was interpreted as a lack of preparation or lack of courtesy by audiences. The other difficulty came from the outside. But it was not Columbia, the university, putting obstacles in his way. Rather it was the music department itself, which was guided in its actions by Paul Henry Lang, who believed composers had no place in an institution devoted to learning, ridiculed scholarship that dealt with anything outside the main traditions of Western Europe, and identified with Germanic rather than Hungarian culture.

The correspondence between Bartók and the highest officials of Columbia University rests in a special collection of rare manuscripts in Butler Library, the library named for the president of the university who conferred the doctor of music degree on Bartók.

In May 1940, just after Bartók received that degree, Douglas S. Gibbs, assistant treasurer of the university, received this letter from Frank D. Fackenthal, then provost at Columbia:

"Is it likely that any of the Ditson bequest money will be available for 1940-41. There is an opportunity to do a distinguished piece of work through Béla Bartók if we can provide a Research Associateship or some such position for him. It is assumed that if the appointment is made, it should carry a stipend of about $4,000."

Gibbs replied on June 10, saying that "it is unlikely that it will be available for 1940-41." The Ditson fund had just been set up in memory of Mrs. Charles Ditson, widow of the publisher, and there had been no recipients thus far.

In October 1940, Fackenthal sent Bartók a letter asking if he would be able to attend a special convocation for those who had been honored but could not attend the Commencement the previous spring. Bartók was unable to be at the ceremony on December 2 because he was scheduled to perform at Oberlin Conservatory. The event was moved to November 25. Bartók was honored by Columbia University along with Paul Hazard, the French historian, Karl T. Compton, the American physicist, and Sir Cecil Thomas Carr, the British jurist.

The citation was a perfectly correct assessment of Bartók's contribution to world culture. It signified that Columbia University knew precisely who Bartók was and chose to honor him for his achievements. The citation read: "Master performer and distinguished teacher of the piano. Internationally known authority on Hungarian, Slovakian, Rumanian and Arabic folk music. As composer, creator of a musical style universally recognized as one of the greatest contributions of the twentieth century literature of music. An artist of humility, originality, and unswerving idealism, he has brought great distinction to the spiritual and artistic life of his country."

What went wrong, then?

Two months later, on February 3, 1941, Fackenthal wrote to Bartók:

"My dear Sir: I have the honor to advise you that you have been appointed to be Visiting Associate in Music at Columbia University at a salary of $1,500 payable monthly." That appointment was for one term. University documents show that the go-between, the man who had arranged for this post, was George Herzog, then a specialist in American Indian music and linguistics in Columbia's department of anthropology and a fellow Hungarian admiring of and sympathetic to Bartók.

Immediately Fackenthal sent the following note to the publicity director of the university:

"This appointment was sponsored by the Alice M. Ditson Foundation in music, on the recommendation of the Advisory Committee provided for by Mrs. Ditson's will of which Carl Engel is chairman. This is the first assignment of income from the Alice M. Ditson Fund."

A few weeks later, Fackenthal wrote to Bartók enclosing a guest card for the Columbia University Club "because of its convenient midtown location, you may find the facilities of the club helpful during your stay in New York." Such a blanket invitation may not seem very important today, but it was certainly a considerate gesture, once again indicating the university authorities concerned themselves about Bartók's comfort in New York.

What follows is what I find to be the most interesting of the exchanges.

On April 19, 1941, Fackenthal wrote to composer Douglas Moore, then chairman of the music department and head of the Ditson Fund, asking if "Bartók is to be reappointed from the Ditson Advisory Group?" Such a question suggests that all Fackenthal required of Moore was a one-word answer: yes. But the day before, Bartók had sent Moore a letter justifying his need for a reappointment. Someone in the music department must have told him to do this. Bartók wrote "there are over 2600 records... the only collection of Yugoslav folk music on accoustical recordings" and so on. Certainly a degrading act for a man of his stature.

Bartók then received confirmation that his assignment would continue from September 1941 to June 1942. Yet in January 1942, there is another letter from Bartók to Moore:

"The situation is this: the material of the Parry Collection proves to be richer and the transcription of the single pieces more wearisome and harder than it seemed at first glance. On the other hand, the musical and scientific value of this material is far higher than I first thought. In fact, it is unique in its kind and reached nowhere in the world.... I will be through with little more than half of the material next June, at best."

Why was Bartók put in a position of being a continual supplicant when on June 4, 1941, the end of his first term there and seven months before this letter, Columbia University wrote to the American Consul General:

"In connection with the application of Béla Bartók of 3242 Cambridge Avenue, Bronx, New York, for a visa, I desire to state that he has been, during the academic year 1940-41, a Visiting Associate in Music at Columbia University and that he has been appointed Associate in Music for the academic year 1941-42 at a salary of $4,000.

"The appointment is technically for one year, but it may be assumed that the relationship is likely to continue and that Dr. Bartók may reasonably expect there be no dimunition of income from this source."

Jacques Barzun, at the time professor at Columbia and later provost of the university, recently told me that "the feeling was that Bartók was being treated like a young man making a beginning. I know that the administration would have done anything at all for him if they had had the support of the music department."

That support was not forthcoming. In June 1942, Bartók's association with Columbia came to an end. He was ill at the time. The word went out that Columbia had behaved in an evil way to him, so different from the way Yale supported Hindemith or some of the other universities gave sustenance to the other great European composers who had fled Hitler's Europe.

BÉLA BARTÓK

In March 1981, the centennial of Bartók's birth, Lang, by then
retired from Columbia, wrote an article about the Bartók-Columbia
situation. Lang, a musicologist, had studied at the Budapest Conservatory when Bartók was on the faculty there. As committed as Bartók
was to his native culture, Lang was committed to international
scholarship. In 1924, he left Hungary and never went back. First he
studied at the University of Heidelberg, then the Sorbonne in Paris
and finally at Cornell where he obtained a Ph.D. in 1934 with the dis-
sertation, *A Literary History of French Opera*. In 1933, he became associate professor of musicology at Columbia and, in 1939, was appointed full professor. The composer Douglas Moore was chairman of
the department. Lang soon took command. In his article, Lang wrote:
"By 1942, the funds gave out. And what with wartime conditions,
the university felt unable to budget a non-teaching position." Jack
Beeson, the present chairman of the department and head of the Ditson Fund, told me that Ditson money never ran out. When Beeson
was informed that Lang said the money Bartók had received never
came from Ditson funds at all but from an appropriation of the anthrol-
ogy department, Beeson expressed shock at this "misinformation". He
said Lang had always been "jealous of the Ditson Fund because it
served projects outside of musicology."

Lang expended, throughout his teaching career, considerable energy making certain no composer would ever receive a Ph.D. at Columbia. He believed the university to be a place of learning, designed for
the accumulation of knowledge and not for anything that involved
creativity. Today a composer receives a doctor of musical arts degree
in a separate department under a separate dean. Lang was also
profoundly opposed to the inclusion of ethnomusicology in the music
department. He had no respect either for the art of primitive cultures
or for what he considered to be the "pseudoscientific" research used
in this domain. Benjamin Suchoff, director of the Bartók Archives, says
Lang called that material "grunt and groan music." Lang also persistently fought the other great composers of his time, railing against Ar-

57

nold Schoenberg and Igor Stravinsky not only in class but in his columns for *The New York Herald Tribune*. Bartók received even more pernicious treatment than Schoenberg and Stravinsky in Lang's major work, *Music in Western Civilization:* he is not mentioned.

The cutting off of funds from Columbia was bad for Bartók but turned out to be good for the world for it shifted the focus of his energies from research to creative work. The American Society of Composers, Authors and Publishers — and Bartók was not even a member — paid for two summers rest at a clinic at Saranac Lake and an autumn in Asheville, North Carolina. It also paid all of his hospital bills. Between June 1942 and September 1945, when he died, Bartók composed the *Concerto for Orchestra*, the *Viola Concerto*, the *Sonata for Solo Violin*, the *Third Piano Concerto* as well as a theme for a seventh quartet.

In December 1944, Serge Koussevitzky led the Boston Symphony Orchestra in Bartók's *Concerto for Orchestra* at Carnegie Hall. The composer attended not only the rehearsals but also the performances. Koussevitzky, who had commissioned the work, reportedly told him: "This is the best orchestral work of the last fifty years."

Many would agree with Koussevitzky's assessment. And Bartók composed this remarkable work in his adopted land during a burst of creative energy that seems to have been released just as soon as he was freed from 18 months of oppression. The United States need not accept Eric Blom's word that it has behaved in a "shameful" way regarding Bartók. For it finally gave him an environment in which he produced some of his, and the century's, greatest music.

II

AMERICANS AT THE BOULANGERIE

VIRGIL THOMSON

ELLIOTT CARTER

DAVID DIAMOND

NED ROREM

MINNA LEDERMAN OF
MODERN MUSIC

Introduction

In 1984 *Copland: 1900 through 1942,* co-authored by Aaron Copland and Vivian Perlis, appeared in which the composer said, "Perhaps my three student years in France are so vivid in my memory because they had such an enormous influence on my future career.... It was in France that I reached my majority, that my ideas came of age, and it was there I came to know those who were to be the major and contributing influences on my life... Nadia Boulanger, my teacher, and Serge Koussevitzky, the great Russian conductor. I cannot imagine what my career would have been without them."

Copland began studying with Boulanger in 1921. In 1924 Boulanger introduced him to Koussevitzky, who was then conducting modern music concerts in Paris. Koussevitzky promised him that the very next year, when he began his tenure with the Boston Symphony Orchestra, he would introduce a Copland work there. Not only did Koussevitzky keep that promise with the *Symphony for Organ and Orchestra;* very soon he presented Copland as soloist in his own composition, and also presented works by other Americans, most of whom had studied with Boulanger. These composers were following the neoclassical Stravinsky. Koussevitzky also conducted Russian composers and occasionally the Viennese Alban Berg. The ones in disfavor with him were Schoenberg, Webern, and the idiosyncratic American artists such as Varèse, Cowell, Ruggles, Riegger, Brant and Ives.

In my review of *Varèse: A Looking-Glass Diary,* I quoted Varèse saying that the League of Composers, devoted to new music and headed by Copland, was dominated by delicatessen parties and that "little was to be hoped from the bourgeoisie."

A few weeks later, a letter from Copland was published in the *Times Book Review.* It challenged Varèse's remark and indicated irritation that I had given it credence. I understand why Copland wrote this. For although he adhered to the Stravinsky-Boulanger idiom, his programming at the League was far broader than that. I mention this here so the reader can know why I never interviewed Copland, surely one of the most seminal figures in American music: I anticipated he would reject such a request.

My categories in this book are not rigid. Ned Rorem, for example, is included here yet he never studied with Boulanger. But he worked long and closely with Virgil Thomson who did, virtually ingesting Boulanger through Thomson. Marc Blitzstein, on the other hand, who *did* study with Boulanger is not here, because his ties to the American vernacular transcended anything he brought back to the United States from France.

David Diamond and Elliott Carter, both Boulanger pupils, have enjoyed long and rich careers that have taken them far afield from their student days in Paris. After the decline of serialism in the 1970s, Diamond enjoyed a renaissance with commissions, performances and recordings. Carter is widely celebrated both here and abroad. The May 9, 1994 *New Yorker* devotes a lengthy review by Paul Griffiths around the time of Carter's 85th birthday, celebrating his "majestic achievement".

Virgil Thomson, whose Boulanger days go back to 1921, the year Copland began working with her, remained a Francophile all his life. Commissioned by *People* magazine for his 90th birthday, the article I wrote did not appear in that magazine. This is its first publication.

My article on *Modern Music,* the magazine that covered the contemporary scene for about twenty years, gives an overview of what was going on in the field during that period. The composers were not only tied to France, but to Nadia Boulanger, their teacher. Boulanger's major effect was to get the United States out of the tradition of Griffes, MacDowell, Gregory Mason and Henry Hadley, Americans who had emulated 19th century German music. The Guggenheim Foundation had a hand in promoting this exodus by giving fellowships to those who went to Paris, starting with Copland. The Boulangerie deserves a place in the history of American music, because it shifted its center of gravity away from 19th century Germany to 20th century France.

Virgil Thomson
CREDIT: Naomi Savage

1

VIRGIL THOMSON

No living composer has exerted a stronger influence on American music than Virgil Thomson. Aaron Copland insists it was Thomson, with his invented folk songs, who moved him away from the complex writing he was doing in the 1920s to his accessible ballets of the 1930s. Another important composer, Philip Glass, says Thomson "is definitely a source for me. With Virgil you have a completely American spirit. He can be abstract, whimsical, and serious at the same time."

On November 25, Thomson will be 90. Orchestras around the country are playing his symphonies, the Opera Ensemble of New York is presenting *Four Saints in Three Acts,* one of the two operas he wrote with Gertrude Stein, and The Museum of Modern Art is screening the films to which Thomson provided scores. On the birthday itself, The American Composers Orchestra will host a dinner at Manhattan's Plaza Hotel which will include performances of his music and Summit Books is publishing 1,000 of Thomson's 25,000 letters, edited by music critic Tim Page. Described as looking like a combination Roman senator and kewpie doll, Thomson also calls to mind Truman Capote, with his high-pitched voice and bulging eyes, and the stage character Sheridan Whiteside, The Man Who Came to Dinner and stayed, torturing everyone around with his rapier-like wit.

Thomson was born in 1896 in Kansas City, Missouri, to what he describes as a "Confederate family of slaveowners." His father lost his money in the Depression of 1893, went to work as a grip man on a cable car, then spent the rest of his working life in the postal service. Neither parent was musical.

Written in November 1986 for *People* Magazine, to commemorate Thomson's 90th birthday, but never published. Virgil Thomson died on September 30, 1989.

Before he was five, Virgil improvised on the piano. He says he played very loud, always keeping the pedal down, and that he would name his pieces after the Chicago Fire or similar events. He was precocious in many ways, and by the time he graduated from high school, he had memorized just about all of Mark Twain. Samuel Clemens knew how to puncture the pompous with humor and provided a lesson in writing not lost on the young Missourian.

After serving in the Army during World War I, Thomson, with borrowed money, entered Harvard. There he won scholarships and earned enough playing the organ in a church to get him through. It was at Harvard that he met Maurice Grosser, a painter who writes on art and who remains his closest friend today.

After his junior year, Thomson went to Europe with the Harvard Glee Club but did not return for his senior year. Instead he remained in Paris to study with Nadia Boulanger, that remarkable teacher of composition who went on to teach literally dozens of Americans. Thomson was one of the very first to study with her. Nor was it out of character for him to do this. He was always drawn to strong women. He says his sister lived "until 92 or 93," and the first musical piece he composed was to a poem by Amy Lowell, the cigar-smoking New England poet.

From Paris Thomson sent back reviews to the Boston *Transcript* that led to Koussevitzky's appointment as conductor of the Boston Symphony Orchestra. After a year, Thomson returned to Harvard to get his degree.

But he told friends that when he went "home" to Paris, he would brook no obstacle in his efforts to meet Gertrude Stein. Stein, a wealthy American who ran a salon in Paris for years, wore men's clothes and wrote high-brow nonsense poetry like "a rose is a rose is a rose." One evening, a friend brought Thomson to her living room. Today Thomson recalls that he and she "got along like two Harvard men." Thomson set some of her verse; *Capital, Capitals* is probably the most famous of these early pieces. Stein found the sound of words more captivating than their meaning. Stein and Thomson got on so well that he asked her to write a libretto for him. She did that, then Thomson composed the score, then Grosser transformed the combination into a workable scenario, indicating the action and the characters. When the piece was completed, Thomson was 32 and Stein, 54.

Because words mean nothing to Stein, *Four Saints in Three Acts* had dozens of saints in four acts. In a recent interview Thomson said, "The text is so obscure. The words have to go besides—not integrated with—the music. That is so the two can go on without being simultaneous. It has to be a very loose arrangement."

Not even Stein's elevated position among the intellectual elite could maneuver a performance of this work with its representation of the Holy Ghost in the line, "Pigeons on the grass alas." Thomson's music, as always, was plainspoken and pleasingly direct, with evocations of hymns and ballads that seem familiar but were, in fact, his own. Stein was vocal in her support: "It's not at all banal," she said. "He frosts his music with a thin layer of banal sounds to put people off, but what's underneath is pure and special."

Projected productions in Paris and Darmstadt, Germany, failed to materialize. But any time Thomson found himself with a piano and any audience at all, he would promote the work by sitting down and playing through the entire score, singing all of the parts himself. Six years after he had completed the work, those efforts paid off. In 1934, the first Picasso retrospective in the United States was being mounted in Hartford, Connecticut. As part of that event, the opera received its world premiere. Stein was far better known than Thomson, and the work was known as hers. It was, in fact, Thomson's first opera, Stein's first libretto, Frederick Ashton's first ballet, and director John Houseman's first work in the theater. It was also the first theatrical effort of Florent Stettheimer who wrapped her figures and sets in white cellophane creating a shimmering transparent texture not altogether unlike Thomson's music.

Although Grosser had done the invaluable work of transfering the incoherent text to the stage, his name was omitted from that first program. As Thomson began by working in Stein's shadow, Grosser was willing to live in the shadow of his lively, forthright and multi-talented friend.

It was Thomson's own idea, however, to cast the work entirely with blacks. He says he did it because he sensed they would be less self-conscious with Stein's incoherent passages and because of the grace with which they moved and even stood. This stereotype is appropriate for a man who claims descent from a Confederate slaveowning family. Thomson says that Gershwin attended a performance in New York that followed those in Hartford and took many of the same blacks Thomson had recruited for *Four Saints* for his own *Porgy and Bess* which opened on Broadway the following year. However, before *Porgy, Four Saints* achieved a reputation through its sixty performances and its celebration by people in the arts that made 1934, Thomson says, the best year of his life.

But its success did not translate into profitable work and, on his return to Paris, Thomson spent his time composing film scores. Those most frequently played on their own are *The Plow that Broke the Plains* and *The River*, two Pare Lorentz documentary films. (Later he wrote the music to Robert Flaherty's *Louisiana Story*, which won a Pulitzer Prize.) Thomson also composed incidental music to plays and wrote his first book, *The State of Music* which was published by William Morrow in 1939.

After his early articles for the Boston *Transcript*, Thomas wrote for national magazines such as *The American Mercury* and *Vanity Fair*. In *Vanity Fair*, he published one of the first serious essays on jazz. But when he tried to compose jazz, he was never successful. Composer Ned Rorem, whose first job in music was as Thomson's copyist more than forty years ago, says that "while his contribution to American music is incalculable, Virgil's jazz comes out square and hickish."

World War II forced Thomson to leave Paris, but he was so reluctant that he waited until only two days before the Germans occupied the city in 1940. Even then he could not bring himself to leave France and moved south. Stein, with Alice B. Toklas, her lover, moved south, too, and although she waited out the war over there, hidden and generally cared for by neighboring villagers, Thomson returned to the United States that fall. He was broke. But even then, he wore his Lanvin suits and appeared to eat nothing but haute cuisine.

About the time he arrived in New York, the music critic for the New York *Herald Tribune* died. Geoffrey Parsons, the chief editorial writer for the paper, was told to find a replacement. He picked Thomson both because of the stir that had been created by *Four Saints* and because *The State of Music,* Parsons has said, showed that he "could write like an angel."

Angelic in style, not temperament. From the beginning, Thomson was on the attack, savaging everything from the New York Philharmonic, Toscanini, Beethoven and Sibelius. Once he likened Heifetz's playing of a minor piece to taking the Queen Mary to get to Brooklyn.

In the mid-1940s, Columbia University commissioned another opera from Thomson and Stein which turned out to be *The Mother of Us All,* with its central figure Susan B. Anthony, the suffragette. Thomson says Stein chose Anthony because she identified with her. Far less obscure than *Four Saints,* this second Stein-Thomson collaboration has had several thousand performances. Both operas assume a very large position in the history of American opera, yet neither has been presented by the major New York opera companies.

But Thomson has never said much about his feelings about that slight or about any other personal matter. Not even in his autobiography, published in 1966, where he devoted more than 400 pages to a picture of the contemporary music scene interwoven with a variety of listings: early piano teachers, itineraries, menus and furnishings. Never did he touch on intimate reminiscences or explore his relationship with Grosser.

His refusal to reveal himself continues even now. In a recent conversation, Thomson attacked those against whom he bears grudges.

They included Charles Wuorinen, "one of the 12-tone boys"; William Schuman, the composer who became president of Lincoln Center, and "got into heavy power swinging"; Koussevitzky, who never programmed Thomson, for "conducting the Americans as though they were Europeans; Roy Harris came out sounding like Bruckner;" and Gershwin for working in a "playwriting tradition in which white men tell stories about negroes, which is not very admirable." To specific questions, he replied without missing a beat but all the while managing to avoid applying his remarks to himself. Here, then, is Thomson on the matter of sexuality and music:

> Sir Thomas Beecham was fond of pointing out that many composers were bachelors — Beethoven, Brahms, and Bruckner were all bachelors. But that doesn't mean they were queer. I can't find any pattern among those I have read about. Bach had twenty children and two wives. Handel had no wife and no children but ate like a hog. He always ordered for three ....
>
> Some composers are oversexed, some undersexed, some are married to one wife, some sleep around with anyone they can lay their hands on. Conductors are not supposed to sleep around. That can lose them a job. Opera singers serve as a whorehouse for the trustees. Toscanini passed for being sexually quite active. Mahler did not amount to much in that direction. His wife was more active than he. Boulez has kept very quiet.

Since the late 1920s, Thomson has composed about 150 pieces, most of them for piano, which he calls musical portraits. The subject sits for him as he would for a painter while Thomson, usually within 90 minutes, puts his impressions into music. Thomson's sitters include casual acquaintances, friends, New York Mayor Fiorello LaGuardia and Picasso.

POSTSCRIPT: Thomson was reported to be composing portraits until shortly before he died.

2

ELLIOTT CARTER

The concert honoring Elliott Carter on his 60th birthday drew such disparate composers as Aaron Copland, Milton Babbitt, Mario Davidovsky, Jack Beeson, Eric Salzman, Hugo Weisgall and Benjamin Boretz. The audience included representatives of virtually every composing style from traditional tonality through serialism and electronics to multi-media happenings. Carter himself is essentially a musical loner, not readily identified with any specific musical current. However stylistically independent he may be, he does not disdain the acclaim of his peers: Carter flew in from Rome only to attend the event.

Several days before his birthday concert, the composer spoke about his current project, a work commissioned for the New York Philharmonic's 125th anniversary. The piece is scheduled for performance on May 1, but it may not make it. Carter says that he rarely finishes pieces on time:

"My experience is that it is far better to produce a good composition than to concentrate on getting one out on time. I don't know whether I like this piece enough to let it out for the scheduled performance. My Piano Concerto, over two years late, has had as many as six or eight performances and Erich Leinsdorf has recorded it. The most important thing is to write a decent work."

Gentle and rumpled in a gray business suit, Carter expressed a concern for the performer that is unusual among composers these days:

"A composer's first interest must be the performer, so that the performer will want to use his work as a vehicle. I never write passages too difficult to handle, nothing like some you find in Debussy and Richard Strauss. One must remember than an orchestra is a group of

Published as "Elliott Carter: Acclaim for a Musical Loner" in *The New York Times*, March 2, 1969.

men, and the members of the New York Philharmonic are men of good will. I always try to make interesting parts, so that each musician has at least one moment in which he has something special to give."

Carter's expansive and generous nature extends not only to performing musicians but to American composers as well. Active throughout his life in the League of Composers and the American Branch of the International Society for Contemporary Music, he has pushed for performances of his colleagues' work. When asked to cite the best Americans composing today, he started by naming Babbitt and Gunther Schuller. Then he stopped, saying he couldn't do it because he was afraid he might leave someone out.

*

From time to time, the composer lit harshly into some aspects of the American musical scene:

"There is a great problem in New York. The city has only one newspaper in which music is extensively reviewed. Thus the coverage is subject to one point of view. In Berlin, there are six daily papers and two more fed in from the outside; all of them contain intelligent music criticism. A few lines written about a performer are more important than a dozen Lincoln Centers. But in New York the performer cannot be certain of even getting a review. So the city will inevitably become the center for the tried and true, while others stay away in droves, playing in cities where there is greater coverage. It will kill the musical life of New York."

Carter also complained about the many orchestras that give commissions to composers for new works when they have never played their old ones: "If these orchestras are not interested in playing compositions by that composer, why do they commission him to write another piece? The orchestra reveals it's not interested in that man's music but only in his reputation. I frequently reject commissions made under these circumstances."

Igor Stravinsky, Elliott Carter
CREDIT: Frank Driggs Collection

Then why is he doing one for the New York Philharmonic which has played only one short Carter piece before? "I admire the orchestra, and I've lived in New York all of my life."

The son of a wealthy lace importer, Carter was educated at the Horace Mann School and traveled to Europe often from the time he was 12. During his prep school years, he began listening to advanced composers such as Varèse and Charles Ives. While he was still in his teens, he wrote a letter to Ives expressing his admiration and they became friends. After entering Harvard, where he majored in English, Carter frequently shared Ives's box at Koussevitzky's Boston Symphony concerts. Probably no other composer knew Ives as well as Carter did.

Carter turned his attention entirely to music and did graduate work under Walter Piston at Harvard. Then he joined other Americans such as Copland, Marc Blitzstein, Virgil Thomson and Roy Harris in Paris to study with Nadia Boulanger. It was during these years that he says his style changed:

"Between 1933 and 1935, during the turbulence of the social unrest, we questioned whether avant-garde stuff wasn't just a little trivial. I decided it was and tried to write differently. I tried to reach a larger audience rather than just a special elite. Most of us wrote in a more accessible way. It simply was the thing to do in those days."

During that period, Carter wrote such pieces as the incidental music to a production of *The Merchant of Venice*, some settings of poems by Whitman and Frost, and several ballet scores. Although he refers to this music as being "accessible," it was light years away from Blitzstein and Thomson. But his lack of success in what he considered to be a more popular style caused him to change again:

"It turned out that the public was no more interested in my 'accessible' music than it had been in my advanced work. So I decided I might as well go back to the music in which I believed."

After settling on his own private path, Carter produced such intense, expressive works as the First String Quartet, the elegant Sonata

74

for flute, oboe, cello and harpsichord, the *Variations for Orchestra* and the Second String Quartet, which won the 1960 Pulitzer Prize and the New York Music Critics Circle Award.

Today Carter and Babbitt are the leading candidates for the office of father-figure in serious American music. Reflecting on the most current composition, he said:

"Apart from Boulez and some of the new Polish composers— Penderecki, Lutoslawski and Serocki—I find music to be in a most perplexing state. The desire to be advanced at all costs leads only to a dead end. It is like guerilla warfare, with all kinds of activity branching out in all directions."

*

Carter noted that long ago European composers had stopped taking American composers seriously: "The only one who interests them is John Cage. And it's not Cage's music but what he writes in his books. The aleatory principle has gained such momentum.

"Stockhausen's latest work is just a philosophical game. He has not written down any notes; thus the performer bears full responsibility. I don't like this aspect of contemporary music. The purpose of a musical score is to prevent the performer from lapsing into his old routines. When there is no instruction from the composer, the performer falls back on familiar tricks. Most improvised music is far less free than music that a composer has scored. A composer is in command of time; he lives above time, controlling all of his material at will. He can correct the beginning of a work while the performer is literally caught in the flow of time."

Carter compared today's advanced trends with those of the late 1920s and early '30s:

"I am afraid that the present path toward what some composers think of as freedom will inevitably lead to a violent reaction. This is what happened in the 1930s. The same patterns prevail now as prevailed then. The same turbulence exists, the same racial troubles grow. Once again, all this can make advanced art seem foolish."

Carter hopes it will not.

3

DAVID DIAMOND

On a Sunday afternoon last May, Gerard Schwarz conducted the Waterloo Festival Orchestra in the first New York performance of David Diamond's *Suite No. 1*. The work was culled from a two-and-a-half-hour score for a ballet, *Tom*, with a scenario by E. E. Cummings which Diamond composed almost 50 years ago. After acknowledging the warm response from the audience, Diamond leaned toward a friend and whispered, "Not bad for a 20-year-old."

Not bad at all. In some ways, Diamond is a fortunate man. He was born early enough in the century to have composed a piece seen by George Gershwin, who asked him: "Where'd ya learn to orchestrate that way, kid?" And he has survived long enough to see a pluralism emerge that allows his traditional kind of composition to achieve recognition alongside serialism, aleatoric work and all the rest. In fact, at his 70th birthday concert in April Milton Babbitt, the leading advocate of serialism in the United States, was seated on the stage. About that evening, Diamond remarks: "To see Babbitt on the stage made everything seem worthwhile."

Diamond, whose natty appearance matches his courtly manner, defies categorization on virtually every level. Unlike many of his colleagues, he never earned his living through a long-time appointment at a university. To do that requires some inhibition and control. Diamond's explosions are legendary. Recently he reported one that took place more than 40 years ago. According to his own recollection, he was at the bar in the Russian Tea Room when Artur Rodzinski walked in. He had sent the conductor of the New York Philharmonic a score, so he asked him what he thought about it. "Too much like

Published as "David Diamond: A Composer Who Defies Categorization" in *The New York Times*, July 7, 1985.

David Diamond
CREDIT: Louis Ouzer

Shostakovich," Rodzinski replied. Whereupon the short, delicately boned Diamond called the big, bear-like Rodzinski a pig and proceeded to punch him in the face. According to Rodzinski's widow, her husband responded to whatever attack had been made by saying that although Diamond was a troubled soul, he was a talented man, and then served as a go-between in arranging for a commission for a large orchestral work.

*

David Diamond was born in Rochester, New York, to Eastern European parents; his father was a cabinetmaker, and his mother a dressmaker for the Yiddish theater. At the age of five, he discovered a three-quarter size violin at the house of a friend on the next block.

Rochester was a rich, cultivated city — Bernhardt and Duse played there — but Diamond says: "We lived in a kind of ghetto. I was exposed to different languages and different sounds. Our neighbors were Italian, and I loved to hear them speak. On one side was the Negro neighborhood with its Baptist singing; on the other was the Russian church."

When Diamond was nine, Howard Hanson, director of the Eastman School of the University of Rochester, invited Martha Graham to head a dance division there. "I remember," Diamond says, "peeking through the curtains and seeing three beautiful girls and a woman — a remarkable looking woman with her mouth open — and hearing music I had never heard. It was Scriabin, and I fell in love with it. I began to take theory then."

Economic troubles later forced the Diamonds to move in with relatives in Cleveland where David studied at the Cleveland Institute of Music. But within a few years they were back in Rochester, and Diamond enrolled at Eastman. He met Rouben Mamoulian, a stage director at Eastman who later became a Hollywood film director, and Goddard Lieberson, Alec Wilder and Mitch Miller, all of whom went

79

on to big careers in music. In 1933-34, Diamond's sophomore year, Hanson's criticism of his work as being "too modernistic" moved him to look for a more congenial atmosphere. At the New Music School and Dalcroze Institute in New York, he entered an analysis class taught by Roger Sessions that included the composers Hugo Weisgall, Miriam Gideon and Vivian Fine. He also studied privately with Sessions, as did Babbitt, and the two met there. When he first got to New York, he lived with an aunt in Brooklyn. But soon his parents began sending $5 a week for a room in the YMHA. For food, he mopped floors at Dalcroze and worked behind the food counter at Walgreen's drugstore.

Despite having met Gershwin and Graham, and having known Sessions and Babbitt — all extraordinary Americans — Diamond was drawn to Europe. In 1936, he angered Sessions by using his first prize money to go to Paris and study under Nadia Boulanger. He went again the following summer and, in 1938, a Guggenheim Fellowship — he was the youngest person ever to receive one — permitted him to go back to France. But World War II intervened, and in the spring of 1939 the American Embassy insisted all Americans go home.

By the end of the war, Diamond had made enough of an impression to have had performances of his music under conductors Hanson, Monteux, Koussevitzky and Mitropoulos. Mitropoulos even commissioned a work, *Rounds for Orchestra,* that won the New York Music Critics' Circle Award in 1944. All this meant prestige but no money. In the mid-1940s, he joined the Hit Parade Orchestra. "I loved being with the Hit Parade crowd," he says, "Sinatra, Mildred Bailey and Bea Wain." But his association with the group upset Koussevitzky, who believed a composer of art music should project only the classiest of classical, European-type images. In fact, in a *Life* magazine article, Koussevitzky asked how it was possible for a musician of Diamond's stature to be reduced to work like this. The story was accompanied by a photograph of Diamond holding up his viola.

*

Diamond was in trouble, both financial and psychological trouble. Many composers needed money but few mopped floors or worked as soda jerks. In addition, he says he was "making scandalous scenes" and notes that his friends Aaron Copland and Leonard Bernstein "got together a kitty so I could begin psychoanalysis."

In 1951, Diamond received an appointment as a Fulbright Professor at the University of Rome. In 1952, the Fulbright was renewed. In 1953, the political climate, he says, was "so dominated by the McCarthy hearings that I decided to remain in Europe."

Diamond visited the United States in the mid-1950s to work while waiting for the Fulbright to be renewed. One day while he was rehearsing in the pit of a Broadway show, a woman walked down the aisle and handed him a subpoena to appear before the House Un-American Activities Committee. Diamond suffered no serious problems; he had never been a card-carrying Communist. But that experience moved him to return to Europe right away, and he settled in Florence. There he supported himself on royalties and advances on royalties from ASCAP.

Europe, never hospitable to American music and then in the throes of the serial avant-garde, paid virtually no attention to him. But premieres continued in the United States: Charles Munch and the Boston Symphony presented his Symphony No. 6; Eugene Ormandy and the Philadelphia Orchestra, the Symphony No. 7; Leonard Bernstein and the New York Philharmonic played *The World of Paul Klee* during the orchestra's tour of the Soviet Union in 1959.

In 1965, at a time when serialism in the United States was pushing out more conventional modes, Diamond came home with, he says, his "psychological wrinkles ironed out."

He makes his home in Rochester now and commutes each week to Juilliard. Soft-spoken, highly intelligent, with a formidable memory for literature, music and movies, he says: "There is nothing in me any more that pushes this fighting thing." Still he remains an outspoken man. Here he is on some musical matters:

"Today grants and awards are given to composers who have no craft at all. Many do a mix of music theater and aleatoric combinations. We have this even in university-based composers, and their works are atrociously conceived. Their counterpoint is nil. Their knowledge of theory is deadly. They are bad orchestrators. When I speak of this to them they say: 'But we were told we didn't have to have traditional technique.'

"The teaching everywhere seems a delicatessen department of tastes of the past and a delicatessen department of the avant-garde. There is a mishmash of foods. When I returned from Europe I had students asking me, 'Mr. Diamond, in what style shall I compose?'

*

"I had performances by Koussevitzky, Szell, Mitropoulos and Bernstein. We were treated royally. Today I can't get an answer from a conductor's secretary."

Though major orchestras may not be playing his works now, he has many compensations. First, he is a remarkably prolific artist, and there is the fulfillment found in the work itself. Second, he has a number of commissions. Finally, he can look back on a life in which he crossed paths with the likes of Ravel, Massine, Gide, George Antheil, Carson McCullers, Tennessee Williams, and Truman Capote. He says Capote can be heard on a privately-owned tape advising him to have a facelift. After reporting this suggestion, Diamond, a serious, even dour looking man, placed his hands on his cheeks, lifted them to his ears and asked, "Can you imagine me looking like this?"

4

NED ROREM

"I am as insecure as I ever was," says Ned Rorem, the 63-year-old Pulitzer Prize-winning composer. "If I don't have tangible proof every day of the week that I am appreciated—a commission, a letter from a stranger, a performance by someone somewhere—I suffer."

This spring Rorem should feel gratified. Performances of his work abound, as usual, including his *Picnic on the Marne: Seven Waltzes for Saxophone and Piano,* which will be played by the saxophonist Gary Louis, and an Australian premiere for his *Winter Pages* quintet. In June *The Nantucket Diary,* covering the last 13 years of his life, will be published by North Point Press. Rorem describes it as "a self-portrait of the artist as a middle-aged man; shocking, gossipy, dull, unique in its picture of music backstage, and spectacularly accurate about critics, stars and colleagues."

Rorem says he knew all of Stravinsky backward by the time he was 14 and that, as a child, he not only composed but wrote stories and poems and kept a diary he has continued to the present day. "It was always a toss-up whether I would be a composer or a writer, so I became a little bit of both."

*

Born in 1923 in Richmond, Indiana, Rorem was brought to Chicago while still an infant. As a child, he took piano lessons with Margaret Bonds, a teacher who was well enough known to be listed in *The New Grove Dictionary of American Music.* He then attended, in this order, Chicago's American Conservatory of Music and Philadelphia's Curtis Institute, where he now teaches composition.

Published as "Ned Rorem Delivers a Solo on the State of Music" in *The New York Times,* May 3, 1987.

In 1944, Rorem came to New York to go to Juilliard. It was then he took his first paying job, working four hours a day as musical copyist to Virgil Thomson. Thomson paid him $20 a week and gave him lessons in orchestration. Rorem says he "learned more from Virgil in six months" than he had from all the schools he attended. That seems unarguable. Rorem also says — he tends to speak in pronouncements — that "one imitates what one loves. You steal what you admire, then feel so guilty about it you try to disguise it." It would seem that at the time he came of age, Rorem loved and admired Thomson, because he appropriated a great deal from him. Both use a diatonic language that resists the abrasiveness as well as the adventure of much 20th-century music. Both are composers who also write: each of them had composed for years, receiving little recognition, and finally broke through to the public with beautifully written prose. What Thomson's book, *The State of Music*, did for him in 1939, Rorem's *Paris Diary* did for him in 1966. It was their writing that put them on the musical map.

Thomson and Rorem are not alone in being composers who are skillful with words. In this century, the capacity to be articulate seems to be required for the composer who succeeds. Consider Schoenberg, Stravinsky and Boulez in Europe; Bernstein, Babbitt and Wuorinen here. Like these composers, Thomson and Rorem stir up controversy. But unlike these composers, Thomson and Rorem invariably name names. Rorem claims — though it stretches the listener's credulity — that "it never occurred to me anything you say about someone can be the wrong thing to say. But there are people who have stopped talking to me."

These days Rorem moves between a house on Nantucket and an apartment off Central Park West. He shares them with Jim Holmes, a church organist who has been his close friend for almost 20 years. Rorem says his interest in the organ derives in part from the harmony lessons he had at 15 with Leo Sowerby, one of the country's prominent organ composers, and in part from his connection with Holmes.

The walls of Rorem's Manhattan living room are covered with

84

Ned Rorem, 1992
CREDIT: Jack Mitchell

paintings by friends: Jane Wilson, Rosemarie Beck, Jean Cocteau, Balthus, Larry Rivers and Nell Blaine, who paints flowers. In the dining room, there is a still life of flowers by Rorem himself. He did it while he was at Yaddo, a retreat for artists, during a period when Nell Blaine was there. "She told me," he says, "to have more fun, to think bigger. She said I was too concerned with detail in the flower and not enough with the canvas I was going to cover."

A similar criticism of his music was voiced by Francis Poulenc, the French composer who, with several others, including Darius Milhaud and Erik Satie, was a member of the famous composers' group, *Les Six*. "When Poulenc heard my music," Rorem says, "he asked, 'Why do you have to be so Protestant, so inhibited?'"

Composers generally use words the way they use notes. Not so Rorem. The inhibition Ms. Blaine finds in his painting and Poulenc in his music is nowhere apparent in his prose or conversation. Here Rorem pulls out all the stops. If he senses an interviewer may be timid and fail to report what he says, Rorem admonishes the journalist to "print it all. This finally must be heard."

The kind of attack Thomson used to make on Heifetz, Toscanini and Beethoven, Rorem makes on our current icons. After saying, "I can't really look at myself, and I don't believe that anybody can," Rorem takes off on virtually everyone in the contemporary music scene.

"I can't table-hop the way Lukas can," Rorem starts, referring to Lukas Foss' shifts in musical styles. "I never had to come back from 12-tone music, like George Rochberg and David Del Tredici did," he says, emphasizing the tonal language he uses today is one from which he never veered. I can't be classified as one of the 'New Romantics' because 'The New Romanticism' comes from the Austro-German sound, particularly Mahler." Like Thomson, Rorem sees himself descending from the French: the scores are lucid, thinly textured.

Rorem's hostility to dense, modern music is relentless. "The great composers of the 20th century," he says, "do not include Schoenberg.

One good thing is that we are out of the 12-tone mess. The music was so complicated you couldn't know what was going on. Elliott Carter has been a pernicious influence for too long. Some of his early music has flavor but no charm. His last piece, the fourth quartet, is actually hostile. It is so filled with information that nothing is able to come through." Rorem does not restrict his anger only to the "intellectual" composers. He also lashes out at Philip Glass: "While Carter presents what is a maze, Glass gives too little unless you are zonked out on drugs. I am not against Glass' premise, that we need an antidote to what has gone on. But a C major chord played hundreds of times does not seem to me to be the right solution."

People often attack when they are sad. Rorem's sadness may come from his belief that "the art song died in 1955" and that this was the genre in which he excelled. Long recognized as one of America's foremost composers of the art song, Rorem has produced more than 250 of them. Although it is true he never hit the spectacular peak that Carter and Glass did, Rorem has enjoyed a career that extended well past the mid-50s. He received his Pulitzer in 1976 for an orchestral work, has commissions now that stretch three years into the future and, perhaps most important, has always been blessed with performers of extraordinary caliber who are thoroughly devoted to him. Leonard Raver plays all of Rorem's organ works. Gregg Smith conducts the choral pieces. Years ago Donald Gramm and Phyllis Curtin and, more recently, Phyllis Bryn-Julson have disseminated the songs with understanding and skill.

*

Rorem speaks warmly of his parents. He also looks back with gratitude on Margaret Bonds, his teacher. He says that living in France, which he did from 1948 to 1957, "showed me what it meant to be an American as far as an artist is concerned. I learned how different the American 'language' is from the French, which has no rhythm, no tonic accent, no syllabic stress. We are what we speak, like we are what we eat. And I feel deeply American."

Rorem says he deplores those American composers who use European poems as the words to their songs: "George Perle sets German," he notes, "George Crumb, Spanish; John Harbison, Italian; and Lou Harrison, Esperanto. If they composed an equal amount on American texts I would say O.K. But they do not." Such a remark seems surprising coming from a man who, at 25, used his George Gershwin Memorial prize money of $1,000 to go to Paris and then stayed for years. While there, he lived in an 18th-century mansion of a vicomtesse and learned to speak perfect French. He also set French texts with success. *Poèmes pour la paix,* a cycle based on medieval French poetry, was selected for performance at a prestigious Paris festival in 1954.

But that was more than 30 years ago. Today Rorem says he is "chauvinistic." In his music, he works only with English-language texts. And in his polemics, he attacks only American colleagues, treating the Europeans as though they didn't even exist.

5

MINNA LEDERMAN OF *MODERN MUSIC*

For the last 50 or 60 years, negotiation, hustling and internecine warfare have been common practice among American composers struggling to get their works performed. *Modern Music*, a magazine published in the 20s, 30s and early 40s, made it possible for composers to do an important part of their work: publicize themselves and pick the right fights. But *Modern Music* did even more than that. A vehicle for reportage, it conveyed information, ideas and standards to an intelligent, non-specialized audience. And those composers whom it celebrated most—Aaron Copland, Roger Sessions and Virgil Thomson—are the grand old men of music today.[*]

The Institute for Studies in American Music at Brooklyn College has published a book, *The Life and Death of a Small Magazine* (Modern Music, 1924-1946) that consists of excerpts from some of the original articles with an introduction and commentary by Minna Lederman, the editor who presided over the magazine through its entire life.

Modern Music was conceived in 1923, the year a group of musicians and new-music enthusiasts launched the League of Composers in New York. The chair of the board of the League was Claire Reis, another dynamic, autocratic woman. Minna Lederman and Claire Reis legislated much of the course of music in the second quarter of the 20th century in New York.

Lederman, who says of her age only that she is a "turn-of-the-century" person, graduated from Barnard College, did some reporting on *The Evening Mail,* and took piano lessons with a Juilliard teacher who

---

[*] All three composers have died since this piece was published.

Published as "A Power Broker Who Helped Shape American Music" in *The New York Times,* December 25, 1983.

Minna Lederman

"Herewith one of the half dozen shots taken by an ASCAP
photographer at my home, then on 9th Street, in 1937.
ASCAP had been impressed by a piece I wrote at the
time about how the Carnegie Hall charwomen received a
higher compensation for their work than did Stravinsky
on the night he conducted there—quite their style."
—from a letter to the author.

avoided 20th-century repertory. The daughter of well-to-do New Yorkers who donated a small room in their apartment as an office for the magazine, Lederman writes that "the household maids — German and enthusiastically musical — took messages; elevator boys ran errands to and from the printer," and "an old armoire held current material, a single shelf for reference books, dictionaries and a telephone extension."

In a recent conversation, Lederman explained that she joined the League's board to "help with the performances in the most casual way. Everyone was terribly upset that the first concerts given by the League had been so badly reviewed. The critics had absolutely no knowledge: at the time we were receiving those splendid little magazines from abroad — like *La Revue musicale* — and someone said: 'Let's have a magazine.' So I undertook to do it."

The first issue appeared in February 1924. "No one was paid for the work," Lederman recalled. "We sent most of the copies to the press. The press was our real target and the press fell in love with the magazine."

Although *Modern Music* is intimately tied to the League of Composers in most musicians' minds, Lederman says there was conflict from the start. First called *The League of Composers' Review*, the name seemed too restrictive to its editor. "I didn't want it viewed as a house organ," she said. "In 1925 we changed it to *Modern Music*, but I certainly had trouble with the League over that. Composers with the League felt they should receive the bulk of the attention, more than their fair share of the space. I never felt the magazine was as career making as the composers did."

*

Modeled on European journals, *Modern Music*'s first issues were filled with short essays by such European scholars as Henri Prunières, Alfred Einstein and André Coeuroy, the associate editor of *La Revue musicale.* But soon the magazine took on an idiosyncratic American tone: fresh, brash, brusk, contentious. That tone started with an article by Aaron Copland on George Antheil, the American composer then living abroad. Copland wrote it in 1925, just after he returned from Paris where he had studied with Nadia Boulanger. Here is some of what he said:

"Although Antheil has a considerable list of works to his credit, few of them withstand close examination. The Symphony for Five Wind Instruments has no backbone, no structural significance, the Sonata for Violin and Piano lacks a sense of climax, the Jazz Sonata is simply a poor re-statement of Stravinsky's *Piano-Rag Music.* And if Antheil's music did not make us suspect his lack of natural feeling for form, the articles he has written on musical subjects would."

Antheil responded with predictable rage, misspelling Cop(e)land's name. Lederman printed the letter with the error intact.

According to Lederman: "It was just after Aaron's article that he visited me and asked: 'Why make this magazine an echo of *La Revue musicale?*' That was the start of composers dominating the pages. It began with Copland and Copland introduced me to other composers. I lunched with Bartók and, as though in exchange for the lunch, he sent in a piece on purity in music. It was short and elegant, just like the man. We often invited Stravinsky to write but he always refused, saying he was too busy composing." (At that time it was not known that Stravinsky rarely – if ever – wrote his own prose.)

Modern Music published some genuinely informative essays not infused with bitterness. "To Revitalize Opera", by Roger Sessions, was just such an article. But often composers used the magazine to promote their own works and punish their enemies. Take, for example, the following:

After the publication of *The Musical Scene,* a collection of articles selected from Virgil Thomson's columns in the New York *Herald Tribune,* Thomson, Lederman writes, "suggested it be reviewed by Walter Piston, professor of music at Harvard, of which both composers

George Antheil, 1930
CREDIT: Frank Driggs Collection

were alumni, and, an admirer of Piston himself, I gladly agreed. The tone of irascibility which marked the first version of Piston's review both surprised and alarmed me."

Lederman never did publish that version. Instead, in *The Life and Death of a Small Magazine*, she prints the letter she sent to Piston, asking him to rewrite it and make it "less personal, less edgy." She tells him she cannot understand why he told the reader that "Thomson has not to my knowledge reviewed any of my work." Piston replied he did it "because I anticipated many evil-minded persons thinking I was getting back at V.T." This is a *non sequitur,* for every composer, painter

93

and writer knows that to be ignored is far more damaging to a reputation than receiving a harsh review. Piston sent in a toned-down article which is reprinted in the book.

*

There is no doubt that Lederman feels betrayed by members of the League who allowed the magazine to die. But the bitterness is tempered by some rewards. Although she concedes "there is a reaction again today," she believes the magazine succeeded in "eroding" the critics' hostility to contemporary music. And she enjoys warm memories of the composers with whom she worked, most of whom were taught by still another powerful woman, Boulanger.

It may be, as Lederman suggests here, that irritation felt by some contributors generated by what they viewed as autocratic editing played a role in bringing the magazine down. It may be, as she also suggests, that rising costs and absence of sufficient funding played a role in bringing the magazine down. But there was something else afoot: just after the end of World War II 12-tone music burst on the American scene with such force that any astute observer could have predicted it would soon replace the hegemony of the more accessible neotonal French style. In fact Lederman was just such an observer: after the 1944 "crisis" and before her last issue in 1946, Schoenberg's writings appeared in *Modern Music* not once but twice. Clearly she was shifting gears in an attempt to survive.

Half a century later the angry words, the demonstrable untruths, the bitter animus, even the pointed truths may seem interesting but beside the point. But as an opinionated and articulate power-broker, Lederman probably shaped pre-world War II American music more than any single composer did.

94

III

U.S. & ENGLISH VERNACULAR

GEORGE GERSHWIN

MARC BLITZSTEIN

LEONARD BERNSTEIN

MORTON GOULD

MEL POWELL

THE BEATLES

Introduction

There were probably more than one reason for Copland to return from Paris to New York in the spring of 1924. One was Koussevitzky's move and his promise to program Copland with the Boston Symphony Orchestra. Another may well have been the stunning impact on the classical music world made by George Gershwin's *Rhapsody in Blue* in February of that year. The classical music domain was one Copland had staked out as his own.

Copland and Gershwin had similar backgrounds. Born in Brooklyn two years apart — Gershwin was the older — they were Jews who rose to great heights without the benefit of college education. Gershwin took a few lessons with Rubin Goldmark, one of Copland's composition teachers. But there the similarities end. Copland's family wished him well as he set sail for Paris while Gershwin's never let him forget that it depended on him for financial support.

Gershwin left high school at 15 to become a song plugger on Tin Pan Alley. His rise was as meteoric as Copland's but it took place in the commercial music world of Broadway, from which Copland distanced himself. In fact, towards the end of his life, when a composition student at Juilliard asked Copland what he though of the man who composed not only *Rhapsody in Blue*, but *Concerto in F, An American in Paris, Cuban Overture, Second Rhapsody, I Got Rhythm Variations* and *Porgy and Bess,* Copland said, "He was a good Broadway composer."

Most of the academic and critical community has taken the same view of Gershwin. Even Gershwin himself often agreed. To rectify what he saw as deficiencies in his technique, he studied with one teacher after another until, in 1933, when Schoenberg first arrived from Europe, he took a few lessons from him.

However much Gershwin borrowed from art music, he never turned his back on the American vernacular — popular song and jazz —

as his primary source material. Nor was he the only composer to combine these elements with a European approach to art. The line is clear: Gershwin, Blitzstein, Bernstein and Sondheim. Stephen Sondheim studied for years with Milton Babbitt, as abstruse a composer as there is, and a disciple of Schoenberg.

The short piece on Gershwin is reprinted from *TV Guide*, which commissioned it to accompany a four-hour PBS Special: *Gershwin Remembered*. I wrote it just before I began *The Memory of All That*, my biography of Gershwin. The only line I would alter today is the reference to the "intimate connection" between George and his lyricist brother Ira. The connection, of course, was intimate, but now I know it to be far darker than I realized; the complexity of the relationship between these remarkable artists has never been fully and adequately deciphered.

Complexity is also the word to characterize Marc Blitzstein. The essay reprinted here, first published in the *Columbia University Forum*, emphasizes Blitzstein's struggle with the shifting musical language and the politics of his time. It inevitably deemphasizes the wide range of his musical endeavors beginning with ballet pieces, through the radio plays, a cantata, cabaret songs and his opera *Regina*. Blitzstein is important not only for his work, but because he was an important link between Gershwin and Bernstein.

During our first interview in 1983, Bernstein said that in 1935, when he was 17, he attended a performance of *Porgy and Bess* and was overwhelmed by it. A few years later Gershwin was dead and he met Blitzstein, who became his mentor and friend. It has always seemed to me that Blitzstein was more crucial to Bernstein's development than Copland, whom Bernstein identified as his "father figure in composition." Bernstein's Broadway musicals, which I think the best of his work, owe a large debt to Blitzstein.

The essay on Bernstein is one I wrote for *The New Grove Dictionary of American Music*. Nothing in *Bernstein : A Biography*, which I began soon after completing this essay, and which was published in

98

1987,[*] contradicts anything I wrote in the Grove entry. What is added in the biography is a portrait of Bernstein's character and temperament as well as my interpretation of why he did not concentrate more on Broadway.

Bernstein enjoyed both composing and conducting but gave up composing for Broadway because Koussevitzky told him in 1944, after seing *On the Town*, that if he were ever to write anything like this again, Koussevitzky would stop helping him in his conducting career. Bernstein did not return to Broadway for almost ten years, until after Koussevitzky died in 1951. When, two years after *On the Town*, his collaborators—Jerome Robbins, Betty Comden and Adolph Green—had conceived *Billion Dollar Baby*, the score was by Morton Gould.

Like Bernstein, Gould is a composer and conductor. Like Bernstein he juggled jazz, art and commerce. One of the finest musical craftsman living, Morton Gould, after a life of continuous musical activity, says he covets the advantages of those who had gone to Europe to study.

Mel Powell is also a man with roots in jazz but he has no connection to Broadway musicals. In his teens he played piano at Nick's, a jazz club in Greenwich Village, then he joined the Benny Goodman band. Powell wrote many memorable arrangements, the most famous probably his "String of Pearls". After World War II he became a student of Paul Hindemith and entered the academic music community, teaching at Yale and serving as dean at the California Institute of the Arts. Powell has been composing now for many decades with the same aesthetic underpinnings as the post-Schoenberg, post-Webern artists.[**]

---

[*]   This book is also reprinted by Pro/Am Music Resources, in a format uniform with the present volume.

[**]   Not only did some Americans whose roots were in jazz appropriate European forms. By 1918 jazz had invaded Europe and many of the continent's most prominent composers appropriated its rhythms for their concert works. Debussy, Stravinsky, Darius Milhaud, Maurice

*

Jazz and the Broadway musical are among the United States' greatest contributions to world culture, and popular music of one sort or another is present in every country of the globe. Often the most serious composers dabbled in it. Even Schoenberg, in 1901, just after he married, left Vienna for Berlin to score and conduct light music in a cabaret. This was not his first choice of a post; he took it because he needed a paying job.

Pragmatism had little to do with the Beatles' beginnings. They started without the benefit of much education. Yet in time they were seduced, as Gershwin was, by serious music. Here is what led me to write the Beatles pieces:

Peter Spackman, then the editor of the now defunct *Columbia University Forum*, a journal distributed to all Columbia graduates, admired my Blitzstein piece and asked me to write an essay about the Beatles. At first I said no; pop music was not my field. But I had two adolescent children who had bought all 13 of the Beatles records then available. So I listened, became captivated and finally said yes. As I was working on it, *Sergeant Pepper's Lonely Hearts Club Band* was released. My article appears to have been the first attempt to analyze it. Translated into many languages, the article was published in half a dozen pop culture anthologies and prompted the editor of the *Times Book Review* to assign me reviews of two Beatles biographies.

Ravel, Ernst Krenek and Kurt Weill were among those who transmuted what they considered to be jazz into their formal compositions. Copland, who generally took his cues from France and Stravinsky, also moved in this direction, most strikingly in his *Music for Theater* (1925) and *Piano Concerto* (1926). In August 1994 a work by the Dutch composer Louis Andriessen was the centerpiece of a long program at Tanglewood. *The New York Times* described it as an "uncommon syntheis of 20th century sounds from Stravinsky to Minimalism to boogie-woogie and hints of disco."

1

GEORGE GERSHWIN

The picture most of us have of George Gershwin (1898-1937) is that of
a vigorous young man, jutting jaw, impressive nose, black hair com-
bed back, cigar sticking straight up from his mouth — in profile at a
piano. Always nattily dressed, sporting a yellow cane with an ivory
handle, this American musical genius projected an air of being completely at one with the post-World War I New York environment. His
picture appeared on the cover of *Time* and his music was performed
by such world-renowned artists as Fritz Reiner and Jascha Heifetz.

Yet he grappled with the problem of failure. Throughout his career,
music critics' reactions ranged from condescension to attack. Vain and
insecure, Gershwin often asked people if they thought his tunes
would live. The most frequently quoted answer was, "Yes, if you are
there to play them." However, more than 50 years after Gershwin
stopped monopolizing the piano at New York parties, such songs as
"Embraceable You", "How Long Has This Been Going On?", "Someone
to Watch Over Me", and "I'll Build a Stairway to Paradise" show no
sign of lessening their hold.

What the Italian Renaissance was to painters, the 1920s and 1930s
were to American songwriters. In those days, about 40 musicals were
staged on Broadway each year and the newly invented radio distributed the songs everywhere. Irving Berlin, Jerome Kern, Richard
Rodgers and Cole Porter were, along with Gershwin, the best of the
melodists of the time. Neither Gershwin's nor anybody else's genius
is explainable, but the humanity in the music, a joy mixed with vul-
nerability, helped separate him from his gifted colleagues.

In an article published in May 1930, Gershwin complained that the
situation may have become too much of a good thing. He wrote that

First published in *TV Guide*, November 21, 1987.

Above: George Gershwin, *c.* 1933
Below: "Music by Gershwin",
CBS Radio Network, September 1934
CREDIT: Frank Driggs Collection

the competition was so fierce that a song could not survive more than a few weeks. Five years later, in *The New York Times,* he claimed he had composed the longer classical-type works — *Rhapsody in Blue, Concerto in F, An American in Paris* and *Porgy and Bess* — because it was only through the serious forms that his melodies had a chance of staying alive.

The melodies in those big works are still very much alive. But Gershwin was wrong about the songs. Just listen to those that Johnny Green, a songwriter and bandleader, presents in the *Great Performances* Gershwin tribute. "They Can't Take That Away From Me", "Let's Call the Whole Thing Off", "They All Laughed", "A Foggy Day", "Love Walked In", "Love is Sweeping the Country" and "Love Is Here to Stay" have had staying power that was unimaginable to Gershwin.

Growing up on the Lower East Side, George was an unruly kid with wild black hair who was a good wrestler and an even better roller skater. He jeered at the boys who took piano lessons. Yet at 14, he selected as his teacher a sophisticated musician who, he later said, made him conscious of harmony and had him playing Chopin and Liszt. At 15 he left high school for a job in Tin Pan Alley. Gershwin worked as a song plugger for a music publisher, playing new tunes for possible use by entertainers.

But echoes of Chopin and Liszt remained in his head along with the more jazz-like strains and they merged in his large-scale works. After Gershwin's death, Irving Berlin said of him: "He was the only songwriter I know who became a composer." Being a "composer" gave Gershwin a kind of status that was denied the other great tunesmiths. But that does not account for the Gershwin legend.

What does?

Part of the credit goes to Ira, his older brother, a shy man who began to write words for George's tunes regularly in 1924. That was the year they wrote their first Broadway musical, *Lady, Be Good!,* and the songs "Fascinating Rhythm" and "The Man I Love." 1924 was also the year of *Rhapsody in Blue* which Gerswhin composed for a famous concert by

Paul Whiteman and his orchestra in New York's Aeolian Hall. That concert made jazz respectable to highbrow audiences. Even in this work, which had no words, Ira played a crucial role. He suggested taking a blues melody from one of the notebooks George kept of his tunes, putting it into the then entitled "Rhapsody" and creating a new name: *Rhapsody in Blue.*

Ira's work as George's lyricist, of course, was invaluable to the success of the songs. He used slang cleverly and came to the point of a song quickly. Most important, Ira's lyrics told a lot about the brothers and their lives. "(They're Writing Songs of Love,) But Not for Me" seems to have been about George's inability to fall in love, a problem that one biographer claims brought him to a psychoanalyst. George never married. And, to the last song George wrote before he died of a brain tumor at 38, Ira later wrote the lyric: "(Our) Love Is Here to Stay." It speaks volumes about the intimate connection between these two remarkable artists.

As for the music itself, George once told an interviewer: "The tunes are simple. The trick is in the rhythms." Sometimes the tunes *are* simple. " 'S Wonderful" is made up essentially of two notes, "The Man I Love" of three. But more often the tunes are far more complex, and they apparently just kept bubbling up in George's head. One time he lost a notebook containing melodies, but it didn't bother him. He knew there would be more.

2

MARC BLITZSTEIN

Art for Art's sake,
It's smart, for Art's sake,
To part, for Art's sake,
With your heart, for Art's sake,
Be blind, for Art's sake,
And deaf, for Art's sake,
And dumb, for Art's sake,
Until, for Art's sake,
They kill, for Art's sake,
All the art, for art's sake.
   —Marc Blitzstein, *The Cradle Will Rock*

In holding such a point of view, a man takes a stand, identifies himself with it, and hopes that time will not pull the rug out from beneath him. Marc Blitzstein was unfortunate; time did exactly that. On Tuesday evening, January 21, 1964, the American composer had dinner with a friend on Martinique. After they finished, he went on alone joining the crowds in a carnival. At 3:00 a.m., he was found lying on the street, robbed and badly beaten. Of the generation of composers that gave America its first musical identity, Blitzstein was the first to die.

During the last four years of his life, he had been working on an opera based on the Sacco and Vanzetti case that presented him with a number of especially agonizing problems. Tired, depressed, anxious for a change, the composer decided to spend the winter swimming and working on Martinique.

Shortly before leaving the country, he ran into John Gutman, the administrator of the Metropolitan Opera Company. The Met had an option on the Sacco and Vanzetti work but as yet had seen nothing of

Originally published as "The Troubled Time of Marc Blitzstein" in *The Columbia University Forum*, Winter 1966.

the score. Gutman asked Blitzstein why he had been "so stubborn." It was four years since the work had been commissioned and he and Rudolph Bing, director of the Met, wanted to hear a little of it. Blitzstein agreed to come in and sing and play a few pieces, but on the day of the appointment, he wired his apologies and canceled it. Instead, he put the score into the trunk of his Peugeot and drove to a garage in Westchester where friends said he could leave his car while he was in the Caribbean. Blitzstein told no one the location of the manuscript that represented more than four years of work—an uncharacteristic act, for he was a meticulous man. His abandonment of the score must have reflected his attitude toward it.

Throughout the 50s and early 60s, Blitzstein had been a witness to one of the most dramatic changes in the history of music. He and his contemporaries were all but crushed in the shift. Although the new composers have not acquired the affection of the large concert-going public, they do have a hard core of devoted disciples all over the world, which Blitzstein's contemporaries no longer have. Indeed, Blitzstein's own commitment to melody, harmony, and the musical setting of words was in direct conflict with the new sound and techniques.

Born in Philadelphia on March 2, 1905, an only son, Blitzstein was raised in affluent surroundings among people committed to the eastern European Jewish tradition of social democracy. He showed early musical talent, was a piano prodigy, and developed into a young man of great charm, with a gallant manner and a wry sense of humor. After excelling in academic work at the University of Pennsylvania, he went on to study at the Curtis Institute. The high point of his musical training came in the late 20s—in Berlin with Arnold Schoenberg and in Paris with Nadia Boulanger. Although Blitzstein became technically adept at Schoenberg's 12-tone technique, he and most of his colleagues who were studying with Boulanger grew to love Stravinsky and adopted his style, discarding the Schoenberg idea. Blitzstein had described his early pieces as "wild, dissonant, percussive." Few of them were performed, and in later years, he disowned them all. Significantly, the last dramatic work of this early period was a one-act choral opera, *The Condemned,* based on the lives of the two men who occupied his thoughts for so much of his life: Sacco and Vanzetti. The critics were hard on the piece, judging the central characters to be "remote and inhuman."

The conflict between Blitzstein's social conscience and his position in a sophisticated, intellectual circle may have provided the primary source of difficulty he had with this opera; he did not write another dramatic work for three years. A man of enormous personal integrity, he was unable to reconcile his attraction to the elegant with his concern for the oppressed (a dichotomy that affected both his life and his work). He lectured frequently and wrote regularly for the journal published by the League of Composers, *Modern Music,* to which Aaron Copland, Virgil Thomson, and other articulate composers contributed. On its pages, he often criticized serious musicians who debased their standards to reach a large audience. In January 1933, he called Kurt Weill's songs "bourgeois ditties," implying that although social justice was for everyone, art was still for an aristocracy.

Suddenly he changed. One afternoon in Times Square, shortly after his marriage to Eva Goldbeck, a writer of the radical left, Blitzstein met his friend and colleague, Douglas Moore, well groomed and conservatively dressed. His comment, "You look like a banker," was not meant as a compliment. The political ideology he had always been attracted to was now crystallized and was reflected in his behavior, his literary pieces, and his music. An article, *Coming, the Mass Audience!* was followed by a piece for piano and speaker, *Send for the Militia,* which was written in 1934 after the Spanish government had suppressed a revolt in Asturias with bloody retribution. Blitzstein was now 29 years old; "wild, dissonant, percussive" music was a style of the past. His expressed view was that "music must teach as well as entertain—must have a social as well as an artistic base; it should broaden its scope and reach not only the select few but the masses."

Writing in *Modern Music*, he repudiated his earlier criticism of Kurt Weill.

Many of his colleagues did not share his political convictions nor did they all reject esoteric techniques, but the image of the lonely figure composing in a solitary and often very advanced fashion — as earlier figures such as Charles Ives had done — was no longer part of the American scene. Instead, the men returning from study in Europe became actively involved in the musical life of New York. They worked as critics for the major papers and held teaching jobs in the universities. Their works were performed in concert halls, experimental theaters, on the radio and in Hollywood films. The generation of which Blitzstein was a member may not have made much money through the performance of its music, but there was room enough for each of its members to operate with dignity and friendliness toward one another.

During the winter of 1935-36, Blitzstein's wife became very ill. He remained with her constantly, allowing no one to relieve him. After her death, he plunged into work on *The Cradle Will Rock*, and within months it was finished. A bitter satirical piece, *The Cradle* is a plea for unionism made through the conventions of popular music and ordinary speech. The style was new, although Weill's *Johnny Johnston* and Aaron Copland's *Second Hurricane*, both similar in concept, were written about the same time. This was the year Robert Sherwood was preparing *Abe Lincoln in Illinois*, John Steinbeck *Tortilla Flat*, and Ben Shahn a mural for a garment workers' resettlement project in Roosevelt, New Jersey.

The initial performance of *The Cradle Will Rock* was the most spectacular moment of Marc Blitzstein's life. Not long after he had completed the work, arrangements were made for John Houseman to produce it, with Orson Welles as director, for the WPA Theater Project. Houseman got in touch with Howard DaSilva, then earning $33.18 a week as director of the Federal Theater of the Air. Blitzstein sang and played through the score and DaSilva immediately resigned from his permanent directing job and accepted the role of Larry Foreman at a $10 a week cut in salary. Virgil Thomson, after seeing a preview, wrote that "an important revelation" would soon be made. There was a lavish dress rehearsal with sets, costumes, and costly lighting equipment. It was a composer's dream. In the final scene, the whole stage rocked, blinding lights shot up from below, and the steelworkers' trumpets, fifes, and drums blared from loudspeakers throughout the house.

The play was set in a fictitious city, Steeltown, U.S.A., but just before it was to open, steelworkers actually went on strike. The libretto, which made heroes of steelworkers and blackguards of capitalists, would have appeared to be the Federal government's point of view if presented with W.P.A. support. Moreover, the Act of Congress that had set up the Federal Theater Project was due to expire within weeks of the opening and drastic cuts in production were anticipated. Three days before the premiere, the play was canceled.

Houseman and Welles appealed the ruling but President Roosevelt himself called the director of the Federal Theater Project to say the show could not open. However, the enthusiasm of those committed to *The Cradle Will Rock* was not to be stayed. The audience arrived on opening night to find the doors of the Maxine Elliot Theater sealed. A new theater, The Venice, twenty blocks north, was found. Welles and Houseman called the musicians' union and were told that its members could not appear in the pit of any house; they could be on stage, however—that would be a "recital." The actors' union said that their performers could not appear on stage but could buy tickets and sit in the audience. Jean Rosenthal, the lighting specialist, found an upright piano and a pick-up truck to haul it. She, Welles, and Houseman boarded the truck while the actors, led by DaSilva and Will Geer, started the march up Sixth Avenue to the Venice Theater. The audience followed them, picking up a band of stragglers as they paraded through Times Square.

When the lights at the Venice Theater went down and the curtain went up, Marc Blitzstein was sitting in his shirtsleeves, alone at the piano. He planned to take all of the roles himself, but as he began the Moll's song, the original cast member seated in the balcony began to sing it too. When Blitzstein started the Gent's song, the same thing happened. One by one, the cues were picked up by actors and actresses who had joined the the mile-long walk and were sitting all over the house. Blitzstein remarked later that the audience resembled spectators at a tennis match, looking from left to right as each member of the cast rose to sing. It was, Archibald MacLeish wrote, "the most exciting evening of theater this New York generation has seen."

For Marc Blitzstein, it was the perfect moment, everything converged brilliantly: moral conviction, natural talent, psychic energy, and public taste.

*

An ancient dialogue pervades all of art. Art either exists to serve a purpose or it exists for its own sake. Plato held that "poets should be compelled to impress upon their poems only the image of good or they should not make poetry in our city." Aristotle took the other stand, that the object of poetry is pleasure which can be derived solely from the absorption of the hearer in the poet's words.

Whether or not a piece of music exists purely for pleasure or serves an extra-musical function can be seen very clearly: either there *is* a relation between the word and the tone that accompanies it, or there is *not*. Both philosophies have strong traditions. All absolute music — that is, music without words, titles, a story or other conceptual implications — belongs to one. Gregorian chant, the Renaissance chanson and madrigal, the 19th-century program symphony and the music produced by the current school of socialist realism belong to the other.

Marc Blitzstein expressed his own attachment to the latter philosophy in his personal, political, and professional life. In 1938, he joined the Communist Party. His ideological commitment was firm, and the formal aspects of composition were of secondary importance. It was a prolific time. After finishing *The Cradle*, he wrote the incidental music to Orson Welles' production of *Julius Caesar*, composed a radio song-play, *I've Got the Tune*, collaborated with Virgil Thomson on music for a film, *Spanish Earth*, and wrote another satirical opera, *No for an Answer*. In 1942, he was assigned the post of Musical Director of the American Broadcasting Station in London. While there he composed an orchestral work, *Freedom Morning*, dedicated to the U.S. Army Negro troops, and *The Airborne*, a 55-minute symphony for speaker, soloists, men's chorus, and full orchestra, which dealt, in the composer's words, with the "history of human flight, flight viewed as an agent of man's destruction of tyranny, as a device for building the better world." *Regina*, an opera based on Lillian Hellman's play, *The Little Foxes*, was finished in 1949, when Blitzstein was 45 years old, and represents the culmination of his efforts to narrow the gap between the learned and the vernacular. He used the popular language of both words and music, yet, through his craftsmanship, created a thoroughly valid opera.

While he was at work on this traditional project, something important and radically new began to happen in New York, although the roots of the development extend back to the beginning of the 17th century when tonality began to replace the church modes as the organizing principle of music. By the 20th century, with tonality virtually spent, the time was ripe for dodecaphony, a method of composing with twelve tones, each of them equal in importance to any other. The composer who uses this technique arranges the 12 notes in a particular order, the tone "row", and it is then this row — whether in its original state, inverted, played backwards or with its inversion played backwards — that determines the structural organization of the work. It is a horizontal, melodic concept rather than a vertical, harmonic one.

Schoenberg had a devoted following in Berlin early in the century, but here in the U.S., the Depression, the WPA, and the new radio audience interfered with the acceptance of dodecaphony. Instead, a

111

tuneful, accessible, uniquely American style was wrought by composers such as Aaron Copland, Virgil Thomson, Douglas Moore, William Schuman, and Marc Blitzstein. Another group of American composers, however, most of whom grew up during World War II, behaved as though Blitzstein, Thomson, and Copland never lived; they became engrossed with Schoenberg and his disciple, Anton Webern. And then, at just about the time *Regina* appeared, Igor Stravinsky, the force behind Boulanger and a man opposed to Schoenberg throughout his life, became attracted to 12-tone composition, later declaring that it was supported by a great tradition and that his own, such as *Le Sacre du printemps*, was not. When Stravinsky, in his late sixties, embraced dodecaphony, it was apparent that form had become the overriding principle and content was secondary. "Art for art's sake" was no longer a subject for parody.

The current extension of dodecaphony, "serialism," goes beyond a technique governing pitch relations. The same principles organizing the treatment of the pitch "row" are used to organize rhythm, tone qualities, and dynamics; the aim is total control of all the elements of musical composition. Today this music is international. It is complex and difficult to perform. Composers either serve as their own interpreters or else work tirelessly with a select group of able musicians devoted to the new style. Electronic music, also a postwar development in the U.S., avoids the problem of performance altogether; composers put their sounds directly on tape and manipulate them in a countless variety of ways.

Along with the total organization of sound, the opposite approach developed, the aleatory or chance method of composition, which depends on a throw of the dice or a turn of the dial. The performer actively participates in this kind of work, improvising according to guidelines set by the composer.

The breeding ground of much of the new music (particularly the non-aleatory work) is the university. Avant-garde composers are rarely found on Broadway, off-Broadway, or anywhere near the ordinary

112

concert world. Princeton, UCLA, Michigan, Illinois, Iowa, Yale, and Columbia are all active centers of the new music. Many of these institutions have the IBM 7094 computer available for their composers. A champion of the new style, Antoine Golea, has described this new activity as the "total dismantling of music and its total reconstruction under new laws."

The Music Department at Columbia University encapsulates the current somewhat schizophrenic situation. The University endorses concerts of new music by the Group for Contemporary Music, acknowledged to be among the best anywhere in the world. Columbia also supports, with Princeton, a tape center which has produced large numbers of electronic scores, and houses the giant RCA synthesizer, a unique machine that generates sound electronically. Yet in this same department, the powerful influence of MacDowell Professor Emeritus of Music Douglas Moore continues to be felt in such operas as Jack Beeson's *Lizzie Borden*. This work, presented last spring by the New York City Opera Company and televised this winter by National Eductional Television, is an aesthetic world apart from the pieces performed by the Group for Contemporary Music.

Although broadcasting networks, foundations, symphony and opera boards give primary support to the more accessible, harmonically based music, it is the new music — heady, tight, unsentimental pieces — that, for the past decade and a half, has been in favor among most vigorous, young, articulate composers. These were the works talked about in European ministries of culture and placed high on the lists of festival committees while Blitzstein was writing an opera, the very genre an anachronism in this abstract, formal milieu.

Most of the American composers born at the turn of the century have had little to communicate to the men using the new language, and many of them are bitter about it. Blitzstein was not. He enjoyed attending contemporary concerts and always expressed his delight at the anti-Establishment nature of the material. In fact, as early as 1951, when Orson Welles asked him to write incidental music for *King Lear*, the composer agreed and suggested that Welles get in touch with Columbia University's Vladimir Ussachevsky and Otto Luening to see whether some electronic sequences could be worked out for particular passages in the play. Having made the suggestion, Blitzstein withdrew from the electronic scene in his characteristic gentlemanly manner and wrote the remainder of the score in a stylish but more conventional fashion.

He wanted to move on, wanted to, as Leonard Bernstein put it, "enlarge his vision." His problem was that he didn't know how to do it. Some of his colleagues have coped with the crisis in style simply by avoiding confrontation with the new sound. They are presidents of culture centers, administrators of conservatories, and advisors to foundations. Some have attempted a kind of ping-pong, writing a work that is comfortable for themselves and the public, and following it with a work for the avant-garde. Several have never questioned the correctness of their vision of music as serving a social function. They remain inactive except, for example, to teach in private schools where students perform their old works, or new ones written in the old tradition.

Blitzstein stayed with the crisis until the end. His increasing anxiety was poetically conveyed by the protagonist of his next major work, *Reuben, Reuben*. This musical play, produced by Cheryl Crawford in 1955, was semi-autobiographical; its hero was unable to find his way, even to the local subway station. The work was inspired by the Faust legend, an *idee fixe* throughout Blitzstein's life and one that preoccupied him in much the same manner as the story of Sacco and Vanzetti. The heroic fight against the Established Order of Things — whether it was Faust's or an Italian cobbler's — was, in some sense, related to his own personal struggle in the world.

Leonard Bernstein, in a tribute to Blitzstein for the National Institute of Arts and Letters, wrote that he always thought of his close friend as the "chief survivor of the welts of passion, the agony of commitment, of a long chain of beautiful work-failures." *Reuben, Reuben* was the classic beautiful work-failure. Although it contained much lovely music, the libretto was so vague that the audience didn't know what was going on. The show closed after one week in Boston and never reached New York. Blitzstein followed it with a musical version of Sean O'Casey's *Juno and the Paycock*, a few scores of incidental music, and a cantata for interracial chorus, but his major contribution between *Regina* and *Sacco and Vanzetti* was the translation and adaptation of Kurt Weill's *Three Penny Opera*, appropriately enough a bitter social satire. With a libretto by Bertolt Brecht, it was first performed at Brandeis College in 1952 and later became one of the most successful of all off-Broadway productions. From 1960 to 1964, Marc Blitzstein worked on the *bête noire* that had defeated him in 1933: Sacco and Vanzetti.

His circumstances at that time had little in common with the embattled conditions of *The Cradle Will Rock*. Arrangements were made for the Ford Foundation to pay him $15,000 for what he anticipated would be two years of work. (This is an unprecedented grant for a musical work, yet how little compared with the time, energy, and work involved in such a project.) There was no written plan presented to any board of directors or administrators. There were no pressures of an external nature on the composer. When the work was half-completed, the Met was to hear it and decide, then, whether to produce it. So Marc Blitzstein, a man dedicated to anti-Establishment principles all of his life, approached his final test under the gentle aegis of the most established of Establishments: the Ford Foundation and the Metropolitan Opera Company.

He maintained his integrity by persisting in his choice of subject, but the opera was doomed from the start. The 600,000-member Federation of Music Clubs issued a formal protest because of the composer's political past (he left the Communist Party in 1949) and nobody expected the audience at the Met to empathize with a fishmonger and a cobbler. (The story is that when the Viennese-born director of the Met,

Marc Blitzstein and Leonard Bernstein reading through
Three Penny Opera at Brandeis University, June 1952
CREDIT: Morris Beck / Frank Driggs Collection

Jam session: Marc Blitzstein and Sam Bernstein (composer's
father) flanking Leonard Bernstein, with Rose Gershwin (the
composer's mother) over Bernstein's shoulder
CREDIT: Whitestone Photo / Heinz H. Weissenstein

Rudolph Bing, was told the name of the opera, he thought Sacco and Vanzetti were a pair of lovers.)

Plagued by efforts to reconcile his affection for tonality with the current style of composition, and unable to handle the balance of his social concerns with the aesthetic demands of a good libretto, Blitzstein turned to two stories written by National Book Award winner, Bernard Malamud. He left the score of *Sacco and Vanzetti* in the trunk of his unwatched car and took *Idiots First* and *The Magic Barrel* with him to Martinique.

Blitzstein's conscience was a severe one. Obligated to the Met, he sent Bing and Gutman a note saying that "guilt assailed" him for not playing anything for them before he left. Enclosed was some music identified as "Sacco's aria: *With a Woman to Be.*" This song, the only one the Met has ever seen, was not newly composed but a borrowing from *Reuben, Reuben* where it had been part of the *Hills of Amalfi*. The rest of the score was found, half completed, by a used car dealer months after the composer's death. *Sacco and Vanzetti* remains a creative impasse.

Had Blitzstein been one of the great composers of his era, he would have transcended the abrupt change in aesthetic philosophy that occurred here after World War II. He was not, and the works written after that period have neither the vitality of *The Cradle* nor the artistry of *Regina*. Had he been an insular person, he would have continued to write in the style of the thirties. He was not this either: unable to ignore the contemporary idiom, he experimented with serial technique in *Idiots First*, his last work. Blitzstein was a gifted musician, an able craftsman, a warm human being and a very smart man, caught, with his eyes wide open, in an era not his own. Precisely because he was neither parochial nor a genius, Marc Blitzstein exemplified the predicament of the composer in our time.

3

LEONARD BERNSTEIN

LEONARD BERNSTEIN (*b.* Lawrence, Massachusetts, 25 August 1918. Composer, conductor, teacher, and pianist.[*]

As a composer Leonard Bernstein has straddled the worlds of serious and popular music, playing a major role in lifting the Broadway musical theater towards the realm of opera. Through his appearances on television, Bernstein has probably done more than any educator for the general understanding of music. He was the first American to be appointed musical director of the New York Philharmonic; also a gifted pianist, he often performed simultaneously as soloist and conductor.

1. Childhood and Student Years, 1918-43. Bernstein was a first-generation American whose artistic temperament derived as much from his Russian-Jewish roots as from his American experience. His father, Samuel, the oldest child of a scholar-rabbi, was 16 when he left the Ukraine for New York, where he took a job in the Fulton fish market; his mother, Jennie Resnick, was seven when she arrived in Lawrence, where she worked in the mills from the age of 12. The eldest of three children, Leonard attended the highly competitive Boston Latin School. His introduction to music came late for one who was to become a professional musician; he was ten when the family acquired an upright piano. Immediately he was drawn to it, but his father bitterly opposed this interest, expecting him to join his beauty supply

---

[*]   Leonard Bernstein died on October 14, 1990.

Reprinted by permission from *The New Grove Dictionary of American Music* ed. by H. Wiley Hitchcock & Stanley Sadie (London: Macmillan & New York: Grove Dictionaries, 1986).

business. Bernstein began lessons, however, with a neighbor, Frieda Karp, and went on to study with Susan Williams, a faculty member of the New England Conservatory; Helen Coates, an assistant to Heinrich Gebhard, Boston's foremost piano teacher; and finally with Gebhard himself.

In 1935 Bernstein entered Harvard University, where he studied with Edward Ballantine, Edward Burlingame Hill, A. Tillman Merritt, and Walter Piston. While an undergraduate he wrote incidental music for a production of *The Birds* (Aristophanes), directed and played the piano for Blitzstein's left-wing musical *The Cradle Will Rock*, and met Dimitri Mitropoulos, who exerted a profound influence on his musical life. After graduating in 1939 (BA), Bernstein studied at the Curtis Institute: piano with Isabella Vengerova, score reading with Renée Longy, orchestration with Randall Thompson, and conducting with Fritz Reiner (winters of 1939-40 and 1940-41). He also studied conducting with Serge Koussevitzky at the Berkshire Music Center (summers of 1940 and 1941), where in 1942 Koussevitzky appointed him his assistant. Meanwhile, he had become involved with the Revuers (a group of popular entertainers that included Adolph Green and Betty Comden), who composed and sang sophisticated songs at the Village Vanguard, New York, where Bernstein often spent the evening and occasionally played the piano (without pay). In the autumn of 1942 he began working at Harms-Remick, arranging popular songs for piano, transcribing band pieces, and notating improvisations by such jazz artists as Coleman Hawkins and Earl Hines; these were published under the pseudonym Lenny Amber (Amber being an English translation of the German "Bernstein").

In August 1943 Artur Rodzinski, the newly appointed music director of the New York Philharmonic, named Bernstein his assistant conductor. On 14 November 1943 Bruno Walter, who was scheduled to conduct the orchestra, fell ill, and Bernstein substituted for him in a concert that was broadcast throughout the US. His performance was reviewed on the front page of *The New York Times* and in other newspapers across the country; the widespread publicity not only launched his conducting career, it make him instantly recognizable to millions.

2. Early Career: 1944-50. After serving in 1944-45 as guest conductor of seven major orchestras, including the Pittsburgh Symphony Orchestra and the Boston Symphony Orchetra, Bernstein was appointed music director of the New York City Symphony Orchestra, replacing Leopold Stokowski. During his tenure with the orchestra (1945-48), he conducted mostly 20th-century compositions, concentrating on works by Stravinsky, Bartók, Chávez, Hindemith, Prokofiev, and Shostakovich; although he did present exerpts from Berg's *Wozzeck* (with Rose Bampton), he felt little affinity for the music of the Second Viennese School. In the summer of 1946 he conducted the American première of Britten's *Peter Grimes* at the Berkshire Music Center. That year he also led the Czech Philharmonic Orchestra in two programs devoted to American music including pieces by Copland, Barber, Roy Harris, Schuman, Gershwin, and himself. He proved to be an effective ambassador of American music; not only did he look the role, with his wide smile and informal manner, but he captured American music, with its special inflections and particular rhythms, more successfully than anyone else. In Tel Aviv in 1947 he conducted the first of a series of concerts with the Palestine Philharmonic Orchestra (later Israel Philharmonic Orchestra), of which he was music adviser during 1948-49. Also in 1948 he conducted a concert given by concentration camp survivors in a refugee camp near Munich, appeared with orchestras in Milan, Vienna, Budapest, Paris, Munich, and Scheveningen (the Netherlands), and in the USA was appointed to the faculty at the Berkshire Music Center. He was not yet 30.

The Clarinet Sonata (1941-42) was Bernstein's first published composition. His works of this period possess both the vitality of popular genres and the restraint normally associated with art music. The first such work for orchestra was the Symphony Nr. 1, *Jeremiah*, which he conducted with the Pittsburgh Symphony Orchestra in January 1944; it won the New York Music Critics' Circle Award as the best American work of the year. In April, at the Metropolitan Opera, Hurok presented *Fancy Free,* a ballet choreographed by Jerome Robbins; this became the basis for the musical *On the Town* (with book and lyrics by Comden and Green), which opened on Broadway in December of that year and enjoyed great popularity as well as considerable critical acclaim. During these years Bernstein also continued his activities as a pianist and in 1948 appeared as soloist under Koussevitzky in his own Symphony Nr. 2, *The Age of Anxiety.*

3. **Years of Path-Breaking Activity: 1951-63.** After Koussevitzky died in June 1951, Bernstein became head of the orchestra and conducting departments at the Berkshire Music Center. He also married Felicia Montealegre Cohn, a Chilean actress, and was appointed professor of music at Brandeis University, where he served until 1955. He continued to compose works for the stage: *Trouble in Tahiti,* his first opera (one act), was produced at Brandeis in 1952; *Wonderful Town* opened on Broadway in 1953; and *Candide,* a musical based on Voltaire's novel, was completed in 1956. The musical theater work *West Side Story,* conceived and choreographed by Robbins, was finished in 1957. The last, widely acclaimed as a musical of unprecedented dramatic, choreographic, and musical integrity, was to become extraordinarily successful in the USA and abroad in both stage and film versions. Other works of this period include the *Serenade,* commissioned by the Koussevitzky Foundation, and music for the film *On the Waterfront* (starring Marlon Brando), which was released in 1954.

In 1953 Bernstein became the first American to conduct at La Scala when he directed Callas in Cherubini's *Medea.* And, after serving in 1957 as co-director (with Mitropoulos) of the New York Philharmonic, he became in 1958 the first American-born musical director of the orchestra, organizing its seasons around themes such as "Keys to the 20th Century", "The Middle European Tradition", "Spring Festival of

Theater Music", and "The Gallic Approach". In 1960 he conducted the orchestra in a Mahler festival (Bernstein came to be identified with the anguished composer-conductor—claiming that, while Copland was his musical father, Beethoven and Mahler were his forefathers). At the inaugural gala for John F. Kennedy, he presented his *Fanfare I* written specially for the occasion, and, in September 1962, he led the orchestra in the opening concert of Philharmonic Hall at Lincoln Center.

During the 1950s and early 1960s Bernstein's international reputation flourished. He was the first to take the New York Philharmonic to South America, Israel, Japan, New Zealand, the USSR, Turkey, and several European countries; his first book, *The Joy of Music*, was published in 1959; *West Side Story* was performed widely in the US and abroad; and he made his debut at the Metropolitan Opera conducting Verdi's *Falstaff* (1963). Especially important to Bernstein's career at this time was his recognition of the potential of television for reaching a large audience. After his remarkable success as a lecturer on the television series *Omnibus* in 1954, he began other series in 1958: the *Young People's Concerts* which ran for 15 years, and two programs for adults, *Lincoln Presents* and *Ford Presents,* all with the New York Philharmonic. These televised lectures were both musically literate and accessible to people with no knowledge of music, and in them Bernstein set the standard for those who would follow him. He said that his efforts to teach music to his own children (born in 1952, 1955, and 1962) lay behind his success with his television programs.

From the beginning of his career, Bernstein had profited from exposure in the mass media. It was fortunate for him that the concert in which he substituted for Walter was broadcast nationally; others were not. Radio brought him initial recognition, and then print, recordings, and television increased his popularity. He played a central role in the burgeoning of performing arts and the building of cultural centers in the US, and he transformed the image of the American musician from a somewhat forlorn figure to a remarkable and exciting one.

4. Later Years: From 1963. Partly because he was welcome at the White House and partly because the youthful President appeared to share many of his liberal political views, Bernstein exulted in the brief period of Kennedy's tenure. On 22 November 1963 the President was assassinated. In many public statements made since, Bernstein returned obsessively to that event, and it marked a turning point in his career. Although negative criticism of his conducting style had begun as early as 1947, it escalated in the early 1960s; in *The New York Times*, the music critic Harold Schoenberg consistently ridiculed his gestures, once saying "Bernstein rose vertically, à la Nijinsky, and hovered there a good 15 seconds by the clock." This was also a difficult period for Bernstein as a composer. The widespread use of 12-tone techniques among his contemporaries, including his friend and mentor Aaron Copland, as well as criticisms leveled against him for adhering to tonality undoubtedly undermined his confidence.

In December 1963 Bernstein completed his Symphony Nr. 3, *Kaddish;* in it he uses serial techniques in the first part and tonal writings in the second, a lullaby. Bernstein explained this alernation of language thus: "the agony expressed with 12-tone music has to give way... to tonality and diatonicism." In order to confront 12-tone music, Bernstein arranged for a sabbatical from the orchestra in 1964. He claimed that during this period he threw away more 12-tone pieces and bits of pieces than he had written otherwise. At the end of the sabbatical he confirmed his commitment to tonality with the *Chichester Psalms.*

It was not as a composer, however, that Bernstein enjoyed international renown throughout the 1960s and 1970s but as a conductor, and he was invited to conduct on many notable occasions. The Viennese in particular held him in high regard. In 1966 he conducted *Falstaff* at the Staatsoper; in 1969, to celebrate the Staatsoper's centennial, he conducted Beethoven's *Missa solemnis;* and in 1970 (in honor of Beethoven's 200th anniversary) he conducted *Fidelio.* In Berlin Bernstein began filming a series of concerts of Mahler's music with the

Vienna Philharmonic (1971), and he also led the Vienna Staatsoper and the Vienna Philharmonic in performances at La Scala to celebrate the latter's 200th anniversary (1978).

Bernstein remained as musical director of the New York Philharmonic until 1969, when he retired as conductor laureate. His concerts had attracted capacity audiences, and during his tenure the orchestra made more recordings than ever before. Additional income from television programs brought about unprecedented financial stability. On 15 December 1971 Bernstein returned to conduct his 1000th concert with the New York Philharmonic, and he continued to tour with the orchestra. Despite his reputation as a musical conservative, Bernstein always did conduct numerous nontonal works including more than 40 world premieres, among them Carter's Concerto for Orchestra, Babbitts' *Relata II*, Schuller's *Triplum*, and Cage's *Atlas eclipicalis*. In the late 1970s, however, he began to devote himself primarily to the standard repertory, emerging as America's most overtly Romantic conductor. He refined his approach to Brahms and Schumann, continued to explore Mahler, and in 1983 recorded Wagner's *Tristan und Isolde*.

Bernstein was also in demand as a public speaker, and as Charles Eliot Norton Professor of Poetry at Harvard University (1973), he gave a series of lectures in which he discussed music ranging from Hindu ragas through Mozart to Copland; these were later published as *The Unanswered Question* (1976). All music, Bernstein believed, is rooted in a universal language comparable to Noam Chomsky's universal grammar of speech, and this conviction underlies these lectures (as well as his earlier television series and even his undergraduate thesis); it also illuminates his belief that good music can be found in jazz and popular song as well as in the symphony. His own compositions are an eloquent testimony to this belief. Bernstein's works from the early 1970s included *Mass*, composed for the opening of the Kennedy Center (8 September 1971); he wrote relatively little during the remainder of the decade, perhaps due to his wife's long illness and her death (1978), but

Top: Leonard Bernstein during rehearsal of the Los Angeles
Philharmonic Institute Orchestra, California State University
at Northridge, 1983. Bottom: with Michael Tilson Thomas
CREDIT: Robert P. Millard

in 1980 he began the opera *A Quiet Place* (commissioned by the Houston Opera, La Scala, and the Kennedy Center), which he considered his most important work. Conceived as a sequel to *Trouble in Tahiti*, it was first performed on a program with that opera; later *Trouble in Tahiti* was incorporated into *A Quiet Place*, as a flashback. Despite problems of structure and text, the work is bold and ambitious, and contains some of Bernstein's most complex and beautiful music. In 1984 *A Quiet Place* became the first American opera ever to be performed at La Scala. Bernstein was elected to the Academy of the American Academy and Institute of Arts and Letters in 1981, and in 1985 he received the Academy's Gold Medal for Music, in recognition of his achievement as a composer.

Bernstein did not, in his music, expand the boundaries of musical thought; nor did he crystallize a style associated with a past era. What he has done above all was proclaim that an American can be a remarkable and exciting musician. No musician of the 20th century has ranged so wide. As a composer, Bernstein wrote symphonies, chamber music, and opera as well as music for dance, film, voice, and Broadway. As a public personalty, he conducted, wrote books, appeared on television, lectured at universities, and remained a thoroughly professional pianist. As a conductor, he not only showed himself a searching interpreter but he also introduced American works around the world. In consequence he achieved an unparalleled renown.

4

MORTON GOULD

In January, Morton Gould—at 72—was elected to the American Academy and Institute of Arts and Letters, filling the vacancy left by Roger Sessions' death. In April, he was elected president of ASCAP, the American Society of Composers, Authors and Publishers, the oldest performing rights organization in the world. Elected unanimously by its 24-member board of directors, Gould succeeds Hal David, the lyricist for "Raindrops Keep Falling on My Head", who had six years before succeeded Stanley Adams, the lyricist for "What a Difference a Day Makes".

The last few years have been a microcosm of Gould's productive life as a composer; his output is enormous and ranges from symphonic work to scores for Broadway, Hollywood and television, and even as the new pieces receive their first performances, older ones are revived. Currently, the New York City Ballet is dancing *Interplay*, choreography by Jerome Robbins; the Dance Theater of Harlem and the Boston Ballet are performing his *Fall River Legend,* choreography by Agnes de Mille; and the New York Philharmonic is playing his *Tap-Dance Concerto* as part of its Horizons '86 series.

Gould is the first composer to be president of ASCAP since Deems Taylor (1942 to 1948). An active administrative post, it brings with it a salary comparable to that of a chief executive officer of a large corporation. ASCAP can afford it; last year its income, from the collection of licensing fees, was $240 million. These fees, paid for the non-dramatic performance in public of copyrighted works by the thousands of ASCAP members, are distributed to the members. (Staged performances of operas, musicals and the like, being dramatic, are not covered.)

Originally published as "Morton Gould: Composer, Conductor and—Now—Executive" in *The New York Times*, May 25, 1986.

*

In terms of both art and commerce, Gould is the right man for the job. A piano prodigy at five, a scholarship student at the Institute of Musical Arts (later the Juilliard School) at eight, he went on to become a kind of crossover artist, a serious composer of popular serious music before that became acceptable to the trendsetters among the intellectual elite.

ASCAP itself never suffered from snobbism. From its beginnings under Victor Herbert in 1914, it has served composers on both sides of the aesthetic fence.

Igor Stravinsky and Irving Berlin were members of ASCAP. In fact, when serious composers suffer financial hardship, ASCAP dips into its pocket, full of money from pop musicians, and bails them out. Béla Bartók, at the end of his life, after Columbia University withdrew support of his ethnomusicological research, received ASCAP support.

Probably the single most important question about Gould is why the recognition he is getting now came so late. Just look at some of the conductors who have performed his work: Toscanini, Stokowski, Rodzinski, Reiner, Mitropoulos, Ormandy, Solti, Fiedler, Dorati, Mester, Ehrling, Maazel, Comissiona, Previn, Slatkin and Michael Tilson Thomas. Nor is Gould only a composer. As a conductor, he has made more than 100 recordings; 12 received Grammy nominations. One, his conducting of Ives' First Symphony with the Chicago Symphony Orchestra in 1966, won the Grammy Award for the best classical recording of the year.

A listing of a few of the early Gould composition titles suggests the nature of those scores: *Pavane, Latin-American Symphonette, Spirituals for Orchestra, Lincoln Legend, Chorale and Fugue in Jazz.* Many of the melodies are so familiar that on hearing them one first thinks past Gould to perhaps Sousa or Stephen Foster. Any explanation of why Gould has not been taken seriously enough must take into account

128

Morton Gould, a Kennedy Center honoree in 1995
CREDIT: Frank Driggs Collection

not only the fact that he writes accessible work. It must also acknowledge his genuine modesty, for he is a man who does not reveal a trace of the arrogance, aggression, or competitiveness that characterizes the personalities of so many who have succeeded as serious composers. He regrets most in life, he says, "that I don't have more talent." Then he adds that he also regrets not having had an adolescence that permitted him to "go to school, attend a conservatory and study abroad. I was off and running at an early age."

When he was only six, he played piano in a concert at the Brooklyn Academy of Music; and during his first year in public school, a piece he composed at the piano was notated by a teacher and published. When asked recently about its length, Gould said with his self-deprecating wit, "As short as it was, it was too long."

*

Morton was the oldest of four boys of a non-musical New York couple who lived in Richmond Hill, Queens. A player piano in the living room, Gould says, taught him all the chestnuts. At eight, he auditioned for Frank Damrosch at the Institute of Musical Arts [later the Juilliard School]. "He was very impressed," Gould says, "because I arrived with a briefcase with music in it. He turned pages and assumed I could read and count. But I was playing what I had in my ears and could neither read nor count.

"The Institute was very rigid," Gould recalls. "I was just a little kid, and there were no other kids in the school. Everyone there was supposed to read and count music, and the authorities told my father to teach me to count. I remember him cutting apples in half and then in half again and my saying each time that what remained was a half. It is peculiar because I have never had the slightest difficulty with the most complicated rhythmic configurations."

At the Institute, Gould would wait outside the piano room to which he was assigned, and when the bell rang, whoever was playing would

130

stop – even if in the middle of a musical phrase – and he would enter and play. Once, when his teacher walked in and discovered him improvising, she shouted, "How dare you?"

Because he was far too young to be in this environment, one ill-equipped to deal with a child who could play the piano well by ear, but had not yet been taught to read or count, the teacher began to send harsh letters home using the boy as messenger. Not surprisingly, Morton failed to deliver them. When this was discovered, the school insisted that the nine-year-old be examined at Columbia's Neurological Institute.

At the Neurological Institute, the examining physician put him in a chair, wheeled him around the room, and observed him as he played with blocks. Then he summoned the teacher. When she refused to appear, the doctor advised Morton's parents to take him out of the school right away. "I was enormously relieved," Gould says, "because I had not enjoyed what I now call my marine boot camp training of musical life." He went on to study with a piano teacher in New York and learned everything he was expected to know.

At 14, Morton came home one day from school to find the piano gone. His family could not meet the payments, and the instrument had been repossessed. Then, when his father became ill, Morton had to leave high school to earn a living by playing for vaudeville acts. "It was the very last thing I ever thought I'd be doing," he says, "when I was a child playing concerts and seeking to have my pieces published. I had thought it would be all serious study, that I'd be doing only important things."

During his teens, with one foot in vaudeville, the young Gould kept the other in serious music. Along the way, he auditioned for Fritz Reiner. "He put a full score on the piano," Gould says. "it turned out to be Strauss' *Elektra*.

"Reiner went about his business – washing, shaving, eating breakfast, reading his mail – and every time I stopped playing he told me to keep right on. I was a fairly good sight reader and a pretty good pianist, and I had been spending whatever free time I had at the old 58th Street music library reading scores. Afterward, Reiner sent me a letter saying he had arranged for a scholarship for me at the Curtis Institute, where he was teaching conducting. Just before he died, I visited him in his Connecticut home. His wife Carlotta showed me my reply; I had thanked him but turned it down, saying I had to keep playing vaudeville to support my family."

In 1931 and 1932, Radio City Music Hall opened with the 18-year-old musician as its staff pianist. "We did two shows a day in the old European tradition," Gould says. "There was a 100-piece symphony orchestra in the pit, and the pit [on an elevator] would start at audience level and then go down six levels. I would jump off, rush into a Hungarian Hussar uniform and jump onto a revolving stage playing the Liszt *Hungarian Rhapsody* as it was on the way up. I was a busy bee. On Washington's birthday, I wore a Colonial outfit and played Haydn on the harpsichord."

From 1934 to 1942, Gould ran the *Music for Today* series on the Mutual Radio Network and throughout much of the 1940s headed the Cresta Blanca program on CBS Radio, which was a tremendous commercial success. He says he was aware that while Stokowski or Rodzinski might conduct his work in a concert hall before an audience of 2,000, he was reaching millions on the radio. His work in radio probably strengthened his natural instinct to use the American vernacular in his art.

*

Since 1982, years during which he was hospitalized with rheumatoid arthritis and had to cope with a legal separation in a long marriage, Gould has completed ten commissions of major works. These include the *Cello Suite,* commissioned by the Chamber Society of Lincoln Center and given its premiere in 1982; *I'm Old Fashioned (Astaire Variations),* based on the song by Jerome Kern, commissioned by

132

Morton Gould

the New York City Ballet and premiered in 1983; *American Sing,* commissioned by the Los Angeles Philharmonic, Michael Tilson Thomas conducting, which had its premiere in 1984, and the Flute Concerto, commissioned for the Chicago Symphony, conducted by Georg Solti in 1985. In the fall of 1986, Lorin Maazel will conduct the Pittsburgh Symphony in a work commissioned by the Pittsburgh *Post Gazette* to celebrate the paper's 200th anniversary.

A parallel can be found in the careers of Gould, Robert Frost and Edward Hopper. During their youth and middle years, they were dismissed by contemporary critics as naive, accessible craftsmen, and it was only in the later years that the genuine merit of the work was seen.

Gould is, above everything else, a creative artist. "Composing is my life blood," he says. "That is basically me, and although I have done many things in my life — conducting, arranging, playing piano and so on — what is fundamental is my being a composer, which has shaped everything else rather than the other way around. Any piece I'm working on becomes that particular wrestling match. Once I'm through with it, the performances are nice and all that but almost beside the point."

POSTSCRIPT: *In 1995 Morton Gould won the Pulitzer Prize in Music.*

5

MEL POWELL

Powell is in a class with Benny Goodman, Duke Ellington,
Count Basie, and Dizzy Gillespie. I don't use the word
"genius" lightly but I've always considered Mel a genius. Mel
was trying to raise money for a repertory playhouse that had
been founded by his wife, actress Martha Scott. He asked me
to round up a few of the old musicians for a benefit. I can still
hear him saying as we played, 'Man, I gotta keep doing this.'
And I can still see Benny Carter shaking his head as he listened to Mel for the first time in so many years: 'Once you got
it, you always got it.' Mel was like a little kid. We talked about
Louis Armstrong, Charlie Parker, all the jazz greats. I know his
heart still is in jazz. His going on the S. S. Norway, the jazz
cruise ship, last year and the year before and now thinking of
doing it a third time, proves he has come back to his roots.
            —Louis Bellson, December 1987

Mel left popular music for the same reason I did: as much as
we liked it, after half an hour we got tired of it and wanted
something more. Mel doesn't miss it at all. He is attached to
jazz historically, not emotionally.
            —Milton Babbitt, December 1987

Bellson is a renowned big-band drummer, in the same league as Gene
Krupa and Buddy Rich. Babbitt is probably the leading composer of
post-Schoenberg serial music in the United States. Few higher compliments could be paid any musician than to have Bellson and Babbitt
each claim him for his own camp.

    Powell was born Melvin Epstein on February 12, 1923. He began to
take piano lessons at six and soon was working on Beethoven and

Originally published as "Mel Powell: The Artist at 65" in
Aperiodical, Vol. 2 Nr. 1 (Spring 1988).

Mel Powell (left) and Milton Babbitt, 1962
CREDIT: Popsie Randolph / Frank Driggs Collection

Brahms with a German woman he says was very strict. During his teens, Powell won third prize in a city-wide competition for young pianists. In a *New Yorker* profile, Whitney Balliett quotes him on this event: "It was bruited about in the family that the judges must have been anti-Semitic because I had not won the first prize."

The Bronx apartment where Powell grew up overlooked Yankee Stadium, a fact that colored his life: his dreams of glory shifted between music and baseball. A Talmudic grandfather set the tone of the home. The only fighting Powell says he recalls was with his older sister over who would scrape the chocolate pudding pot. Lloyd, his younger brother, introduced the 13-year-old boy to remote broadcasts of the big bands. He remembers his first trip to the Paramount Theater to hear the Benny Goodman band. He and Lloyd sat through five shows. Powell was so taken with the improvisations of Teddy Wilson that, at his next lesson, he embroidered Beethoven in the same ways. His teacher slapped his hands with a ruler.

Soon he was moving around the city with a local musician who introduced him to the downtown clubs. At Nick's on Tenth Street and Seventh Avenue, he heard Sidney Bechet, Bobby Hackett, and Zutty Singleton. At 15 Powell began to sit in and play. In between sets, Nick used to hide him in the men's room because he was too young to be in the union. Once Art Tatum paid him a great compliment: "You're going to be a real one," he said.

At 18 Powell entered City College, then a highly competitive school. About the same time, he was accepted by Goodman. It was before entering the band that he changed his name to Powell, borrowed from a Polish uncle who changed his name from Poljanowsky. The band took precedence over school and soon Mel dropped out. In place of an academic life, this thin, six-foot-two, blond, handsome musician sat alongside Sid Catlett, Cootie Williams, and Billy Butterfield as the great stage of the Paramount Theater rose into the view of a screaming, adoring, packed house.

When Powell was drafted for World War II, Glenn Miller called on him to play with the Army Air Force's band. It was during these years that Powell composed his first serious works. He wrote string trios and brass quintets, and the Miller musicians tried them out for him. After the war, he returned to Goodman, and it was then he and Louis Bellson met. Bellson remembers Powell spotting him carrying scores of Ravel and Stravinsky. Like Powell, Bellson had had a traditional music education stressing the European masters. He says Powell asked him to go along to visit Bela Bartók, the Hungarian composer living in near poverty in a midtown hotel. Powell brought Bartók money from time to time, according to Bellson.

After a year with Goodman, Powell was seduced to Hollywood. He says he had gotten tired of playing the same arrangements of the same pieces day after day. But Hollywood proved to be no better. Powell sums up his experiences there: he composed music to a mouse running up a clock.

From Hollywood Powell went to Yale to study with Paul Hindemith. Hindemith was a neoclassic composer, at the other end of the spectrum from Arnold Schoenberg, the initiator of the 12-tone idea. Few placed jazz in any relation to either one: neoclassicism or dodecaphony.

During the 50s, Powell still played some jazz. He sat in occasionally on a recording for John Hammond or did a gig for Goodman. Recently he explained that when he was young, jazz connected in his own mind "to the bordello, sex, fallen women, and drugs. How was I, who had grown up with a Talmudic grandfather in the house, supposed to relate to that?" Powell says he always thought of jazz as the "son" and European art music as the "father".

To feel grown up, Powell needed a respectable job, and what was more respectable than teaching old European-style music in an Ivy League university? But no such post was available to him then. A friend, composer Norman Dello Joio, introduced him to Joseph Machlis, then chairman of the music department at Queens. Machlis

Paul Hindemith
CREDIT: C. T. Alburtus / Hindemith Archive, Yale University

says he told Powell that "ivy doesn't grow in Jamaica" and hired him to teach theory and composition.

In the late 50s, Powell moved on to Yale. He says his first course was late Renaissance polyphony and that he sometimes spent five days preparing a single lecture. Eventually he replaced Hindemith as head of the composition department.

Babbitt dates Powell's reinvolvement in jazz to a party in New Canaan in the late 60s when he was still at Yale. Benny Goodman was one of the guests. Powell and Babbitt, a jazz pianist himself and an expert in the field of American pop, sat down at the piano and played four-hands. Goodman was impressed and after that, Powell played with some frequency. He even has performed the pop songs that Babbitt had written for a Broadway musical in 1946.

A few years after the New Canaan party, Powell was invited to start a music school at Cal Arts. The pieces he has composed the fifteen years he has been there display total control of his craft. Recently Bellson attended a performance of Powell's *Modules* given by the Los Angeles Philharmonic. Here is what he says:

"It was so beautiful, the way Mel had laid it all out. It is a truly great work. Of course, the reaction of the audience there was very different from the reaction to a recent performance we gave that included *Mission to Moscow*, a piece Mel composed and arranged for the old Goodman band. At the jazz concert, the people were screaming. The response to *Modules* was cooler, but while the composition may not be recognized today by more than a small group, future audiences will understand it for what it is."

Bellson loving *Modules*, Babbitt a composer of pop songs, Glenn Miller's musicians playing string trios and brass quintets — where are the neat categories so beloved by our music historians?

In conversation Powell stresses the nonexistence of categories in art. In an essay on Brahms, he notes that Brahms' contemporaries viewed him as a relic, an old-fashioned plodder, and states that in his own view Brahms was "entirely attuned to just those cabalistic 'difficulties', the same ingenuities and modes of complexity that eventually come to inform our century's strongest and most advanced musical thought."

Then, in an interview with the composer Frans van Rossum, Powell expands on this idea and shows his contempt for those who insist on imprisoning artistic expression in one camp or another. "What I'm doing now," he says, "is inventing. I'm making things up. Please don't talk to me about processes. Please no more about system. Please don't be childish. I am really making things up.... When Babbitt was visiting Cal Arts, we talked about a piece of his which was going to be played. And I said, 'You know Milton, I think it is all an improvisation,' and he said, 'You are right'... We were agreeing about this."

The critical fact here is that these two composers, whom the outside world labels cerebral and addicted to complex methodology, agree that "improvisation", a word intimately tied to jazz, best characterizes the way they put notes together today.

In *Bernstein: A Biography* I used Powell to help illustrate my primary theme: that Americans moved away from jazz and Broadway, their most valuable and idiosyncratic birthrights, because they had been intimidated by the European model.

Then something ironic happened. Alfred H. Kingon, the American Ambassador to the European Community, used my thesis in an address he delivered in London to point up the strength of Europe's hold on American intellectual and artistic life before, during, and after World War II. Then he chastised his European listeners for no longer providing Americans with the models they once did.

But it wouldn't matter what the Europeans did now. Jazz itself has become a standard, and American composers draw from it what they wish. They also draw on what they wish from Europe. They are even able to sit down at the piano and swing with *Mission to Moscow* without guilt.

That is what has happened to music in the United States during the last 50 years. It has grown up. It has lost some of its freshness, vitality,

and joyousness, but what hasn't? The late 80s is a time for sophisticated people equipped with enormous information and the technique
to deal with it. No person I know has charted the path from innocence
to what we have in its place today in a more clear-cut and humane
way than Mel Powell, for whom I wish the most gratifying of
birthdays.

6

THE BEATLES

Many people ask what are Beatles? Why Beatles? Ugh, Beatles? How did the name arrive? So we will tell you. It came in a vision — a man appeared on a flaming pie and said unto them, 'From this day on you are Beatles with an "A".' Thank you, Mister Man, they said, thanking him.
And so they were Beatles.

— John Lennon, 1960

A thousand years ago small groups of uncultivated, bizarrely dressed, oddly named musicians traveled from town to town, singing and accompanying themselves on the vielle. The most famous of these — Jumping Hare, Little String, Ladies Praiser and Rainbow — were rewarded with such fame and luxury that they were imitated by hordes of less gifted, envious men. During the late Middle Ages chronicles refer to "large armies of minstrels", the better ones playing for nobility while lesser troupes entertained at peasant celebrations. Despite the demand for their performances at all levels of society, these itinerant poet-musicians were held in contempt throughout the era. The animus stemmed principally from the Church, which held that their obvious secular *joie de vivre* posed a threat to the spiritual welfare of its people.

Once again, to a degree unparalled since the 14th century, Western society loves and rewards its itinerant minstrels. The Beatles, royalty of rock and roll, were received by the Queen of England ("she was like a mum to us"), have appeared on satellite television with Alexander Calder, Van Cliburn, and Joan Miro ("we would rather be rich than famous — that is — more rich and slightly less famous"), and live in a

Originally published as "The Music of Sound, or, The Beatles and the Beatless" in *The Columbia University Forum*, Fall 1967.

state of growing luxury ("we're not rich by rich standards. I could not afford to run four Rolls Royces like people do"). John Lennon, author of the last statement and the first of the Beatles, owns one Rolls Royce equipped with folding bed, television set, writing desk and telephone. He also owns a mini-Cooper, a Ferrari, five stationary television sets, innumerable tape recorders and telephones and an 1874 carriage, yellow with wild flowers, drawn by two white horses in front with two more trotting at the rear — a $10,000 toy purchased for his four-year-old son. Like their medieval predecessors, the Beatles are considered subversive by respectable society. Lennon's flip comment about contemporary Christianity ("we're more popular than Jesus now") prompted an Alabama disk jockey to instruct his listeners to burn Beatle records. Mayors across the continent picked up the disk jockey's lead and at the beginning of the group's last American tour, in August 1966, protected citizens by banning Beatles from their cities.

Who would have thought that the pop music of the 1960s would develop into a force as vital as that of the *jongleur* of old? Starting simply as a vehicle for solo performers, rock and roll didn't differ radically from some of the popular music that had preceded it. Out of Negro rhythm and blues and country and western came Elvis Presley. The tunes were predictable, the 12-measure phrases symmetrical, and the lyric content primitive — "You ain't nothin' but a hound dog". When Presley was drafted, relieved adults predicted the end of an unattractive fad. They were wrong. Rock and roll did not die; it only changed. Presley, with his long sideburns, tight pants and suggestive gyrations, reached only one segment of the population, although a large one. The Beatles, bursting onto the scene in the early 60s with Edwardian clothes and English schoolboy haircuts, transformed the original primitive black sound, making it acceptable to the mass of young white people all over the world. They brought to prominence Group Rock, one of the most attractive symbols of our non-private, corporate, thoroughly electronic age. Now literally "armies of minstrels" — the Beach Boys, the Jefferson Airplane, the Grateful Dead, the Who, the

144

The Beatles: Paul McCartney, George Harrison,
John Lennon, Ringo Starr (drums), 1960s
CREDIT: Frank Driggs Collection

Bee Gees, the Doors, the Mothers of Invention, the Buffalo Springfield, and so on — indicate the awesome potential of electronic sound. Even Bob Dylan, who provoked shouts of "traitor" when he plugged his guitar into an electronic amplifier at the Newport Jazz Festival several years ago, committed himself to the medium in which his generation is making its messages.

Meanwhile, although little noticed by the general public, similar developments have been taking place in the serious music of our time. The explosive electronics of the pop field has diverted attention from the fact that technology came to art music well before it came to rock. As early as 1922 the French-American composer, Edgard Varèse, declared that composer and electrician would have to labor together to produce new media of expression. Rejected by musicians and critics alike during the 30s and 40s, when accessibility of music was the keynote, Varèse's views began to gain recognition in the 1950s, and American universities and European radio stations built well-equipped laboratories to experiment with eletronic techniques in sound. This gave rise in Europe to the works of Pierre Boulez and Karlheinz Stockhausen and in this country to the construction of machines such as the RCA synthesizer, a complex, costly apparatus which generates its own sounds, and the Syn-Ket, an instrument which performs "live" electronic music. Columbia University has been in the forefront of the development of the electronic medium. Professors Otto Luening and Vladimir Ussachevsky of the Music Department deposited one of their electronic compositions in the Westinghouse Time Capsule, scheduled to be opened in the 70th century, and the RCA Synthesizer is housed at the Columbia-Princeton Electronic Music Center.

Despite the prestige and backing electronic art music has been given since the end of World War II, its audience has remained sharply limited. In contrast, electronic rock, within a few years, has attracted an audience of staggering size. Contemporary art and rock music share a medium; the crucial differences are stylistic. Art music has

146

abandoned beat; rock has revived it. Art music is essentially abstract — whereas rock has become increasingly verbal and concrete. Finally, electronic art music, aimed at total control of its materials, is at least partly motivated by the desire to eliminate the performer; he is frequently seen as the potential distorter of the composer's idea. Electronic rock propels the performer into the spotlight; he is singer and instrumentalist and recently poet and composer as well. Art music has not yet sought inspiration from rock. Rock, as many writers have pointed out, has drawn upon everything from Gregorian chant to the most far-out techniques of the avant-garde.

Consider the history of the archetype of Group Rock. John Lennon, Paul McCartney, and George Harrison met in 1956 when they were in their mid-teens and, although none of them could read or write music, they began to play guitar together. Drummer Richard Starkey, now Ringo Starr, joined in 1962. The original group, with a few friends moving in and out of it, was one of many unsuccessful "skiffle" bands in Liverpool during the 1950s. They listened to everything from rhythm and blues to contemporary jazz and Presley. In a few years, imitating what they liked and improvising on what they heard, Lennon, McCartney, and Harrison recapitulated much of the current history of pop music, a feat impossible in any but the acoustically equipped society in which we live.

In the spring of 1960 the Beatles, in their first significant club engagement, discovered the value of noise. The group, flat broke, owned four guitars but only two amplifiers and the booking was in a wild club on a noisy street in Hamburg. How were they going to be heard? McCartney recalled: "We didn't worry about arrangements or anything. If we had trouble with our overworked amplifiers — we had to plug two guitars into one — I'd just chuck everything in and start leaping around the stage or rush to the piano and start playing some chords... it was noise and beat all the way." The Germans loved it. When the police evicted the group from one club (they stamped their

147

way through the floor at one point), the audience followed them to the next. Within a year the late Brian Epstein, then a 26-year-old businessman, offered to become their manager, and in the fall of 1961 he became their official disciplinarian in charge of hair, clothes, and manners. *Meet the Beatles,* their first album, appeared in 1964.

Twelve albums have been issued since then, the noise and beat progressively abating. Much as the medieval minstrel picked up artistic techniques from the more sophisticated *trouvère* of the period, the Beatles have appropriated the most artful devices available in their own time. Medieval modes and pentatonic scales apper in the songs of 1964 and 1965, a baroque trumpet sings out "Penny Lane", and a classical string quartet performs the hauntingly beautiful "Eleanor Rigby". George Harrison has studied with Ravi Shankar, the Indian sitar virtuoso, and first used the sitar in a song called "Norwegian Mood". All of his recent music and lyrics show the influence of Indian melody and Indian philosophy. Paul McCartney, studying music now in London, has become absorbed in the avant-garde works of Stockhausen and Luciano Berio. His attitude has changed: "I used to think that anyone doing anything weird was weird. I suddenly realised that anyone doing anything weird wasn't weird at all and that it was the people saying they were weird that were weird." Despite the careful handling of so many diverse musical tools, the legend of how Beatle music is made persists: Lennon whistles to McCartney and McCartney whistles back to Lennon.

In its essence the legend is accurate. But between the initial melodic impulse and the finished product more than cooperative whistling has taken place. When they record the men work a five-day week — from 7:00 P.M. to 2:00 A.M. They spent almost half a year recording their 13th album; it took 12 hours to make *Meet the Beatles.* From 1964 on, they have had the services of a gifted, well-trained musician, George Martin, who translates their unorthodox ideas into recognizable symbols for the regular symphony orchestra musicians who now complement their forces. Within the past year the Beatles have made music

148

for French horn, oboe, clarinet, bassoon, piano, harmonium, tamboura, and sitar. Not long ago Harrison said: "There's much more going on in our minds. There are things past drums and guitars which we must do. In the last two years we've been in a good vantage point inasmuch as people are used to buying our records.... We can do things that please us without conforming to the standard pop idea. We are not only involved in pop music but all music and there are many things to be investigated."

The audience has responded. Today's population is literally turned on to listening; the record business grossed $892 million in 1966 and the greater part of that was from rock. The Beatles' 13th album, *Sergeant Pepper's Lonely Hearts Club Band,* replete with dissonant sounds, unconventional phrasing and advanced electronic techniques had, within two weeks of its appearance, sold a million and a half copies in the United States alone. A salesman at a Manhattan record store compared the response to *Sergeant Pepper* to that which greeted the recording of Horowitz' initial return concert at Carnegie Hall.

Sergeant Pepper is an extraordinary work. It is a work of art that has sprung from unexpected, non-art roots. The salesman's comment was appropriate: *Sergeant Pepper* is to be listened to in the concert context and the Beatles set the tone right away. The beginning of the album simulates the sounds in a concert hall before a performance. Musicians tune instruments, people talk and move around, and an air of expectation prevails.

To the accompaniment of a distorted old-time English music hall sound, the Beatles begin Side I; their business is show business:

It was twenty years ago today,
Sergeant Pepper taught the band to play,
They've been going in and out of style,
But they're guaranteed to raise a smile....

Side I is about illusion. The Beatles sing of particular methods people

149

use to hide the truth from themselves. Ringo wears the stripes. He is Sergeant Pepper, the lonely outsider, the non-intellectual of the group who, as he concedes in the first song following the theme, gets by "with a little help from my friends." In a dialogue between the narrator and the sergeant, Ringo is asked:

> Would you believe in love at first sight,
> Yes I'm certain that it happens all the time.
> What do you see when you turn out the light,
> I can't tell you but I know it's mine.

Drugs are the subject of "I'm Fixing a Hole" and "Lucy in the Sky with Diamonds", an acrostic of LSD. Lavish verbal imagery and tonal distortions obtained by electronic manipulation suggest the visual hallucinations associated with "acid":

> Picture yourself in a boat on a river
> With tangerine trees and marmalade skies
> Somebody calls you, you answer quite slowly,
> A girl with kaleidoscope eyes.

More familiar refusals to face the truth are treated in "Getting Better", a conventional rationalization, and in "She's Leaving Home". After their daughter has fled the house her parents sing:

> We gave her most of our lives
> Sacrificed most of our lives
> We gave her everything money can buy....

While the narrator chants, in contrapuntal fashion:

> She's leaving home after living alone
> For so many years.

Side I concludes with a return to the most obvious fiction of all: show

150

business. The subject of the final song, Mr. Kite, was inspired by an old-time theater poster.

Side II begins with a piece by George Harrison. It is the albums's longest song, built on Indian ragas, and explicitly describes what Side I was all about:

> We were talking — about the space
> between us all
> And the people — who hide themselves
> behind a wall of illusion
> Never glimpse the truth....

The next three numbers treat life without drugs or hypocrisy. The Beatles sing of the sterile, ritualized roles people play. The first song wryly mocks the activities of an elderly couple:

> I could be handy mending a fuse
> When your lights have gone.
> You can knit a sweater by the fireside
> Sunday mornings go for a ride,
> Doing the garden, digging the weeds,
> Who could ask for more.
> Will you still need me, will you still feed me,
> When I'm sixty-four.

The second is a spoof on romantic love. A whore in Liverpool, who procures through her daytime trade as a meter-maid, was the inspiration for "Lovely Rita":

> In a cap she looked much older
> And the bag across her shoulder
> Made her look a little like a military man....

The third describes, in desolate terms, the dissonance of an ordinary day:

Nothing to do to save his life call his wife in
Nothing to say but what a day
how's your boy been
Nothing to do it's up to you
I've got nothing to say but it's O.K.
Good morning, good morning....

There follows a reprise of the Sergeant Pepper theme — with a stunning difference. Sergeant Pepper is no longer the raucous fun man, promising smiles and good times. Avoiding the initial expression of these empty hopes the band starts shouting Hup, two, three, four, pounding out the beat and the ultimate truth of Sergeant Pepper's inner life:

Sergeant Pepper's lonely.
Sergeant Pepper's lonely.
Sergeant Pepper's lonely.
Sergeant Pepper's lonely.

Thus Lennon and McCartney, the group's guiding spirits, commit themselves to the philosophy that Eugene O'Neill expressed in *The Iceman Cometh* — that man cannot live without illusion. The last song, "A Day in the Life", suggests that man cannot live with it either. It is a moving work, a desperate reflection of contemporary life, a song *Newsweek* described as the Beatles' "Waste Land".

The piece is, in a sense, a *roman à clef*. Shortly before its composition a close friend of the Beatles, the 21-year-old son of a prominent British couple, smashed his car in the center of London while high on drugs. After telling of the accident, the narrator cites a film of the English army after it had won the war. In both instances the protagonist is removed from the core of the experience in much the manner of the central character in an Antonioni film. The only links with his friend's death are a news story and a photograph; the only connections with

152

violent war, a film and a book. Lennon's voice, breaking with sadness, invites the listener: "I'd love to turn you on." The last word of this one line refrain leads into an electronic passage in which a large orchestra, recorded on tracks laid upon tracks, builds up to a growling controlled crescendo, simulating a drug-induced "trip". An alarm awakens the narrator who continues his story to the accompaniment of a nervous jazz idiom:

> Woke up, fell out of bed,
> Dragged a comb across my head
> Found my way upstairs and drank a cup,
> And looking up I noticed I was late.
> Found my coat and grabbed my hat
> Made the bus in seconds flat
> Found my way upstairs and had a smoke,
> Somebody spoke and I went into a dream....

High pitched voices intone a series of open, sensuous chords more suggestive of "pot" than "acid", after which John returns, reflects on the emptiness of everyone (the holes in Albert Hall are people), and invites the listener on still another trip. The non-pitched sounds return, increase in volume and duration until they dissolve, with suddenness, into one resonant, depressing, seemingly interminable terminal tonic chord.

At the bottom of the album cover is a burial plot covered with red flowers arranged to spell BEATLES. The original Beatles of the 1950s, joyous and innocent, are dead. Above and to the left are four standing figures in dark ties and dark suits, Madame Tussaud's wax reproductions of Brian Epstein's carefully groomed group of the early 60s. Sergeant Pepper's Lonely Hearts Club Band is pictured in the center of the cover. Its members are adorned with colorful, psychedelic costumes and are devastatingly unsmiling. They are the Beatles of today. Sergeant Pepper's Band, Madame Tussaud's figures, and a host of others, including Shirley Temple, Mae West, Fred Astaire, W. C.

Fields, Marilyn Monroe, Timothy Leary, Edgar Allan Poe, Tom Mix, Bob Dylan, Karlheinz Stockhausen, Tony Curtis, and Lawrence of Arabia look down at the grave below. All mourn the loss of the youthful Beatles, the group Lennon recently referred to as "those four jolly lads".

Dealing with identity, illusion, loneliness, and death, the Beatles represent their generation and its overwhelming sense of anomie. Refusing to accept the status quo and take square places in a straight society, they reach everyone from the Haight-Ashbury section of San Francisco to the Manhattan East Side discotheques. In this respect they differ most dramatically from the art musician of our time. Contemporary art composers are committed to a style of composition that is, in its essence, opposed to a dramatic expressionism that has prevailed in art music for the last few hundred years. Music as drama grew, in part, from tonality, a musical system in which one note, the "key", serves as the focus of an entire work. This single focus is placed into conflict with other keys throughout the course of the piece; the juxtaposition and resolution of the resulting tonal conflict weaves a dramatic, extramusical meaning into the musical fabric of the composition.

During the years in which Picasso and Kandinsky shattered the single focus of perspective in painting, Schoenberg and Varèse shattered the single focus of tonality in music. Schoenberg did it by organizing a new musical arrangement in which all 12 tones of the chromatic scale are equal and Varèse went even farther — by opening his music to all sound, not just pitched sound. Although a number of present-day musicians continue to rely on a traditional, tonal base for composition, the significant musical action of the 1950s and 60s has centered on Milton Babbitt, John Cage, and the musicians working around both men. All make music that is intramusical; abstract, beatless and non-melodic, it reaches only those trained in the highly complex manner of what is referred to as new musical expression.

154

Babbitt's highly structured form and Cage's negation of traditional form have a common base; both are expressions of a belief that
tonality is no longer valid, that there is no *a priori* order, no God-given
frame of reference. The particular tonal-expressive tradition that
began with Monteverdi in the 17th century and culminated in the
dramatic works of Richard Wagner has been virtually overthrown. It
is inevitable that serious art musicians write music the way that they
do. The battle against dramatic expressionism in art music has been
waged and won.

But the Beatles never had anything to do with a war. They replaced
revolution with affable irreverence. Born in Liverpool, they grew up
among the constantly shifting population and extremely high crime
rate of a large seaport, where the standards and taste of bourgeois London mattered little, and local guitar players enjoyed higher repute in
the community than opera singers. Lennon, McCartney, Harrison,
and Starr emerged from this milieu as the antithesis of British tradition, classless kids who began their meteoric rise not musically but so-
cially, by overstating the clothing and hairstyles of the educated Eton
boy. Brashness and confidence have always distinguished their conduct. In Buckingham Palace McCartney criticized the condition of the
carpets. And at a Royal Command Performance in London Lennon
directed the audience: "People in the cheap seats can clap. The rest of
you — rattle your jewelry!"

The Beatles' sense of freedom from the shackles of social tradition
is matched by their freedom from the shackles of the hallowed styles
of musical composition. Lennon, whose mother played the banjo (she
died when he was 13) and McCartney, whose father had a jazz band
30 years ago, never had an awesome musical tradition to fight. At least
ten years younger than the youngest of the recognized art composers
of our day (the oldest Beatle is 27), and a generation younger than Babbitt and Cage, the Beatles grew up with transistor radios next to their
ears. Bach's *Art of Fugue* and Schoenberg's *Method of Composing with 12
Tones* had as little relevance to them as English imperialism and the

White Man's Burden. Despite the use of styles and techniques from various periods throughout the history of music, the Beatles and their youthful colleagues are essentially ahistorical. Born after the social and musical revolutions of the 20th century, able simply to relax and use all the musical tools available, they have created something moving and altogether new.

Are we entering an era in which musical high art, as we have known it, is coming to an end? The medieval poet-musican, who passed on his art through an oral tradition, has a contemporary analogue in the rock and roll performer. He is a central, contributing member of a society that is moving steadily away from notation and inexorably toward the preservation of the musical object on record and tape. No notational system is capable of reproducing the complex texture of a Beatle record or the sophisticated manipulations the sound engineer immobilizes on it. What is preserved in the music is the performance itself; the record is the message. Marshall McLuhan's thesis that the visually oriented and literate society of Western man is being replaced by an acoustically oriented, electronic society receives its firmest confirmation in the most logical field. The compositional tradition associated with notation is being replaced by an overwhelmingly oral tradition — in both art and rock music. Art music, for the moment, has excluded all but the most cerebral, specialized listeners. Rock is all embracing, having absorbed elements of blues, folk, jazz, and the serious avant-garde.

Few other groups are as good as the Beatles, of course. The quality of rock is about as uneven as was the quality of the songs of the *jongleur;* only a small percentage of it is very good. But the best of rock is moving with unprecedented speed into unexpected, more artistically interesting areas. Such a phenomenon has historical antecedents; vital popular forms have anticipated crucial stylistic changes in art music of the past.

A few performers, composers, and scholars of traditional art music

156

have begun to acknowledge that the boundaries between art and rock music are becoming less defined. Cathy Berberian, noted avant-garde singer for whom Igor Stravinsky, John Cage and Luciano Berio have written works, recently recorded an album of 12 Beatle songs, and commented that "Eleanor Rigby" was one of the most beautiful she had heard in years. And Leonard Bernstein called the best of rock "irresistible". From the other end of the spectrum the Beatles, with their drooping Mexican mustaches, lugubrious faces, and increasingly bizarre clothing, are heard exploring progressively more intellectual and artistic frames of reference. Paul told a reporter that he vaguely minds anyone knowing anything he doesn't know and John said he would rather have the attention of 200 people who knew what he was doing than two million who had no idea what was going on.

Despite the similarities, there is a crucial difference between the breeds. Art musicians have reacted to the absence of structure and system in contemporary society by imposing a highly complex structure and system upon their creative work or by annihilating form altogether. The Beatles, on the other hand, have reacted to the same sterility in an extramusical way — by immersing themselves in Eastern mystical theology and experimenting with psychedelic drugs. Because the intramusical aspect of their songs is unaffected by historical considerations, esthetic ideology, or the search for a meaning in life, their lyric buoyancy remains intact. It is in striking evidence in the rollicking single, "All You Need Is Love" — a wild and beautiful distillation of their sole and pervasive antidote to mid-century despair.

POSTSCRIPT: *At the end of 1994 a new album by the Beatles, featuring previously unreleased songs recorded more than 30 years ago, was being sold in record shops. Kevin Howlett, a producer for the BBC, discovered the old Beatles recordings in an archive when he was looking for material for a documentary. "It was like finding Tutankhamen's tomb," Mr. Howlett said.*

IV

U.S. ACADEMICS AND INDEPENDENTS

MILTON BABBITT

ROGER SESSIONS

STEFAN WOLPE

LEON KIRCHNER

CHARLES WUORINEN

JOHN HARBISON

LEONARD ROSENMAN

BETSY JOLAS AND

BARBARA KOLB

Introduction

By the late 1950s, Milton Babbitt and the post-Schoenberg serialists in the United States had displaced the Boulanger neoclassicists, who had by then prevailed for about 30 years. Universities began to give tenure to serialists, and foundations conferred grants. Because the academic community welcomed them, many of these composers had their first chance for financial security. The serialists had more power in the 1960s, 1970s and early 1980s than any other aesthetically connected group.

Leonard Bernstein believed that serialism in the United States began to wane only after Stravinsky died in 1971 because as long as the Russian composer lived and continued to believe in the serial method, his followers would never turn their backs on him. Bernstein celebrated tonality, not only in his compositions and in the music he chose to conduct, but also in the Charles Eliot Norton lectures he delivered at Harvard in 1973. It was Bernstein's belief that Copland stopped composing after his 12-tone work *Inscape*, premiered in 1967, because dodecaphony had destroyed his musical gift

Americans who did *not* reject serialism after Stravinsky died include those composers like Babbitt and Sessions who had adopted the technique long before Stravinsky himself did. Babbitt had been one of the primary figures in the American movement from before World War II, but despite a chair at Princeton and many accolades, he never found the situation promising for what he called the university composer. His views are reflected in several interviews presented here. Charles Wuorinen, born a generation after Babbitt, and serialism's most prolific younger composer, also reveals an increasingly pessimistic tone in conversations I had with him between 1983 and 1993.

Anyone who follows 20th-century music can testify that the *New York Times* worked relentlessly to hasten the end of the serial idea. Harold Schonberg, chief music critic of the *Times* from 1960 to 1980, rarely had a good word for any work indebted to this technique. When he retired his abhorrence of the method was taken up by his succeeding fellow critics.

In 1988 I wrote a piece on Wuorinen's 50th birthday. Because of the occasion I wanted it to convey a celebratory tone. My opening quoted an extremely positive review of his music for a ballet from Anna Kisselgoff's dance column. I ended acknowleding that such music was having a hard time now but reminded the reader that in J. S. Bach's era, his own sons as well as their entire generation were far more famous and fortunate than Johann Sebastian. Gerald Gold, then editor of the Sunday music page, insisted I remove the first paragraph, saying dance critics know nothing about music, and ordered me to "end the piece down." He said if I didn't he would kill it.

The *New York Times*'s position on women in music has always been as "down" as its view of anything associated with the 12-tone technique. In 1973 when the American Academy of Arts and Letters conferred awards on Betsy Jolas and Barbara Kolb, I got permission from the *Times* to interview them. The piece appeared with extremely unflattering photographs and the headline: "Why Can't a Woman Compose Like a Man?" When I complained I was told I had no sense of humor. To date, there has never been a woman on the music staff of the *Times*.

Of the composers discussed here, Roger Sessions and Stefan Wolpe have died. The others, although they survive, seem to me to be less optimistic now than when I interviewed them years ago. It's not as though Babbitt, Wuorinen, Kirchner and Harbison are not receiving performances. They are, and reviews today are often favorable. When Kirchner celebrated his 75th birthday in January, 1994, Richard Dyer, chief music critic of the Boston *Globe*, referred to him as a "living national treasure".

But the fact is that the major record companies show little interest in any of their works so their future looks grim. In March, 1994, Peter Gelb, president of SONY Classical USA, indicated that he was looking not towards them but to Hollywood. In a speech delivered at a trade convention in San Francisco, he said, "Right now most of the best selling recordings have sound-track connections — *The Piano, Schindler's List, Shadowlands.* We will continue to record major artistic events... but I also want to explore more unusual territory. I believe strongly there is a handful of Hollywood composers that is writing orginal, artistically challenging music."

Milton Babbitt
CREDIT: Popsie Randolph / Frank Driggs Collection

1

MILTON BABBITT

I

I expected Milton Babbitt to be serving champagne. The New York Philharmonic, under the direction of Leonard Bernstein, is about to perform his latest work, *Relata II*. It will have its world premiere Thursday night at Philharmonic [later Avery Fisher] Hall. Only once before — in 1955 — when the Cleveland Orchestra played his *Relata I*, written under a Koussevitzky commission, did the composer receive a comparable honor. But Babbitt, the leader of the academic school of composition that has flourished in the United States since World War II, did not appear to be in a celebratory mood. The interview was distinctly low key.

After defining *"relata"* as the traditional word used in logic and philosophy for interrelationships, the composer told the following story:

"*Relata I* started as one work but grew into two large, related movements. I spent 15 months writing *Relata II*, finishing it a full two months before rehearsals, which were scheduled for this past October. The premiere was to have been on October 17. But on the occasion of the first rehearsal, Bernstein introduced it to the musicians with these surprising words: 'Gentlemen, you've probably never played a piece like this before.'

"If this is true — if this is an unfamiliar language to the musicians — look at what the composer is up against: the men could not see the serious mistakes that the copyist had made in writing out their parts. Because of the errors, Bernstein had to stop the rehearsal many times and make the necessary corrections.

Originally published as "The Affair Proved Traumatic" in *The New York Times*, January 12, 1969.

"He was afraid, under the circumstances, that he would be unable to bring the piece up to tempo and asked me, 'Dare we go ahead?' I agreed, of course, that we could not and we decided to postpone further work—and the premiere—until all the parts could be properly checked. I have spent nine weeks doing just that, but I still view rehearsals with trepidation. There are 600 measures in *Relata II*, no two of which are alike. If each measure were to be practiced for only five minutes—a minimal requirement for a Chopin piano piece—we would need 50 hours to rehearse this composition. Instead with luck, we'll manage to find six! So we bang bang, we plow through it, we do it. It's all over within one week—from the first rehearsal to the last performance.

"The piece, of course, is a difficult one. I treat the orchestra as a large ensemble with many octave doublings creating problems of intonation because they occur in intricate rhythmic combinations. There are also questions of relative dynamic projection. With *Relata II* I have tried to exploit the most subtle resources of a most sophisticated orchestra, but rather than flattering the musicians by giving them a challenging score, I managed only to anger them considerably.

"Finally there's the question: who will hear this piece? No one is concerned about my interested musical colleagues, those for whom I really offer it. My associates across the country will not have any opportunity to hear it unless they get to Philharmonic Hall next week.

"On the other hand, the regular Philharmonic audience does not want to hear this piece. And why should they have to? How can it be coherent for them? It's as though a colleague of mine in the field of philosophy were to read his paper on the Johnny Carson show. The milieu is inappropriate for the event.

"Steuermann, Schoenberg's friend and disciple, told me many years ago that music, as we know it, is altogether finished. I did not agree with him at the time, but now I think he was quite correct. I am unable to see who will provide the necessary support. In order for serious music to survive, the people who make it have to survive and the

166

music itself has to survive. Its survival, under the present conditions, appears me to be highly unlikely."

Like Webern and Varèse — two of the most crucial figures to the current generation — Milton Babbitt is the son of a mathematician. From his earliest years in Jackson, Mississippi, Babbitt not only studied mathematics and science but classical Latin and music as well. In 1932, when he was 16, he saw his first Schoenberg scores, which an uncommonly cultivated uncle brought back from a trip abroad; this precipitated his decision to compose. After graduating from NYU in 1935, Babbitt studied privately with Roger Sessions. As early as 1939, when Schoenberg was still the object of intense humiliation — "he was considered more a musical freak than a celebrity," Babbitt recalls — and even the cerebral Sessions opposed the 12-tone technique, Babbitt adopted it for his own use.

"If it had not been for Schoenberg's music and Roger's teaching," Babbitt said, "I never would have stayed in the field." But stay he did and now he is the high priest of what remains in this country of the Schoenberg-Webern serial tradition. Babbitt not only proselytized the method; he also determined its academic tone and, in doing so, found composers a home. For more than 15 years, against bitter opposition, Babbitt fought for a composer's Ph.D. Today Princeton and Harvard are among the universities offering it.

But for Babbitt that is not enough. He claims much can still be done with the large orchestra. He admits that he "jumped at the chance to compose for the New York Philharmonic." But he emphasizes the need for more rehearsal time as well as a chance for a new work to reach everyone."

Babbitt explains why *Relata II* will not reach interested ears and minds: "The performances won't be taped; because it is not being broadcast, taping is against union regulations. It won't be recorded;

recording it would cost at least $20,000. *Relata II* won't even be published.

"The university presses are not publishing music," he said. "I have a chair at Princeton, and no one there thinks of me as a second-class academic, yet Princeton publishes in all other fields, persistently ignoring that of music. My own publisher—a subsidiary of Schirmer—has not published any one of the eight works that I've written for conventional instuments and voice since 1957."

*

"The university—the composer's last hope—turns with delight to the electronic field because it is self-contained, requiring neither performance nor publication. The medium provides a kind of full satisfaction for the composer, too. I love going to the studio with my work in my head, realizing it while I am there, and walking out with the tape under my arm. I can then send it anywhere in the world, knowing exactly how it will sound. My last electronic work, *Ensembles for Synthesizer*, recorded by Columbia Records, has been played hundreds of times in universities. These are the people—the university people—whom we regard as our appropriate colleagues. I feel closer to members of my Philosophy department than to many who regard themselves as musicians."

In Babbitt's frame of reference there are two kinds of composers: "academic" (his kind) and "theater" (those who write for audiences). In his less charitable moments, he dismisses the latter as the "show biz crowd". By thus separating himself from any responsibility to please an audience, he feels he can demand that the world meet him on his own terms, rather than that he give the world the music it wants.

Such an attitude is not as new as it seems. It is reminiscent of the medieval approach in which music, mathematics, geometry and astronomy all were intellectual disciplines in the university, having

168

nothing to do with the public at large. But this position creates a problem today: hardly anyone will subsidize academic music sufficiently. *Relata II*, for which Babbitt collected a scarcely compensatory $3,000, not only fails to reach the academic community for whom it was intended. It also earns Babbitt the performing musicians' antagonism, and probably the hostility of the ticket holder, too.

II

Next Sunday the Sequoia String Quartet, a Naumburg winner and the quartet-in-residence at California Institute of the Arts, will present the New York premiere of Milton Babbitt's Fifth String Quartet. Babbitt, known primarily as a formidable philosopher, father of the American serial school of composition, initiator—on an international scale—of the total organization of a musical work and recondite theorist whose abstruse prose bewilders friend and foe alike, spent much of his early life in pop music.

Yet, in recent years, with the blurring of the traditional distinctions between high art and popular culture, Babbitt continues to avoid the slightest hint of a mix. In fact, as popular culture becomes more popular, his art has become increasingly refined. Today it is virtually inaccessible to any but those with experience in his particular musical language. Babbitt says the piece he writes is the one he most wants to hear. This means that music, if played impeccably, will reveal for the listener with exceptional ears intricate configurations, while the uninitiated won't hear any recognizable patterns.

Perhaps it is his present eminence that moves him now to speak with ease about his early connections to pop music. C. F. Peters has published three songs written in 1946. Here are the lyrics of one, of which Babbitt was the sole author:

First published as "Milton Babbitt—Juggler of Strict Serialism and Pop" in *The New York Times*, October 17, 1982.

Call this a lusty, searing passion
Or just the merest mash in
which we're involved;

While romance burns in other hearts
we'll fiddle and let love's riddle
remain unsolved;

Don't bother naming your intention,
My aim is not prevention,
I'll need to shove to enter any
enterprise you mention
as long as it isn't love.

The song, set in the pop style of the 1930s with a few surprising harmonies, was part of a musical, *Fabulous Voyage,* planned as a vehicle for Mary Martin which never made it onto the stage. Babbitt described the debacle:

"Richard Koch, who went on to become a well-known lawyer and Richard Childs, later the publisher of Modern Age Books, collaborated on the book and lyrics. Everyone wanted to tell us how to write a show. People said it was too elegant, too clever, that it would go in England but not the United States. The experience was very helpful to me. It made it clear I could never be in show business."

*

That Babbitt would even have *considered* show business will come as a shock to those who know him only through his forbidding public persona. Consider, for example, this one passage taken from program notes accompanying his Fifth String Quartet:

"But if there are not extended dimensionally coordinated repetitions creating familiar patterns of putative 'form,' the composition assumes 'form' and 'shape' by the continual, progressive, expanding interplay of recollective and predictive self-references, which should serve comparably the musical memory of the attentive listener."

The demands Babbitt makes on his listener are as uncompromising as those he makes on the reader. This is not to suggest he cannot write a pretty melody. It is rather to emphasize that Babbitt's gratification comes more from the complex structuring of a work than from others saying it is "beautiful" or "great". In fact such compliments fall on deaf ears. "What I find most irresponsible," he says, "is the use of normative terms without any of the analytic sources." The English subtitle of this last remark reads: "What I can't stand is praise or blame unless the listener can describe precisely what he heard."

*

What makes a charming man, a loving grandfather, an avid football fan, a walking encyclopedia of the American pop song, such a veritable Jekyll and Hyde? Whatever the answer, one thing is certain: the dichotomy is not new to him.

Here is a sketch of Babbitt's biography up to the time of World War II. It is the one commonly associated with him and can be found in any number of reference books:

Babbitt grew up in Jackson, Mississippi, as a traditionally trained musician. He began to play the violin at four, and performed a Bach concerto in public at six. At 16 he saw his first Schoenberg score, which an uncle brought back from a trip abroad. In 1938, he joined the music faculty at Princeton and, in 1939, when 12-tone writing was still the object of scorn, he adopted it for his own use. In 1941 he completed *Composition for Orchestra*, a straightforward 12-tone work.

Here is another Babbitt biography covering the same period but selecting different events. The words are Babbitt's own:

"Right after starting to play the violin at the age of four, I switched to clarinet and sax. I was playing gigs at five, and at six spent my time arranging pop music. In Jackson we would get versions of the Broadway shows with their fifth traveling companies. I saw *No No Nanette* when I was seven.

"At 12 I was writing pop songs and at 13 won a song-writing contest that was sponsored by the band leader, Paul Specht. Through high school I was very much into pop and when I started college, at the University of Pennsylvania, I played in the band. Another player was David Raksin, who went on to become one of our finest film composers. I always enjoyed playing around with tunes. I did one movie score, *Into the Good Ground,* which still can be seen on TV."

For Babbitt, the Broadway musical stopped with *Oklahoma!* He prefers an earlier style: "You can't put down *Showboat,*" he says. "And there was *Good News* by DeSylva, Brown and Henderson, and all of those great Irving Berlin revues."

Interestingly, Babbitt's most famous disciple is not Pulitzer Prize winner Charles Wuorinen, whose theories, music and electronic procedures reveal his considerable debt to Babbitt. Rather is it Stephen Sondheim, the composer of *A Little Night Music* and *Sweeney Todd,* among many musicals. Sondheim's school awarded a fellowship that permitted him to study with the composer of his choice and he selected Babbitt. They spent an afternoon together each week for two years.

"We did serious things," Babbitt recalls. "Species counterpoint and Schenker [a modern system of music analysis]. We looked at Mozart and discussed principles of musical structure. We talked a little about pop, too. He is one of the brightest people you'd ever want to meet. He wrote the lyrics for *West Side Story* and whenever he suggested a change in the score, Bernstein rejected it, detecting my influence."

Concerning a life in pop music: "The thing is," Babbitt says, "one gets so quickly bored."

Boring is probably as pejorative a word as there is in his lexicon. Babbitt's serious music is limitless in the interest it provides for those who are able to comprehend what he is doing. Building on

Schoenberg's system, he went on to create an even more stringent technique, one that relies heavily on the intellect.

As his influence grew after the war, Babbitt waged an uphill fight to win for the composer the intellectual status of the mathematician and philosopher. He triumphed for, by the late 1960s, not only did some Ivy League schools grant composers Ph.Ds, but under his aegis, music theory bourgeoned as an intellectual discipline.

No war is won without casualties, and Babbitt is persistently and aggressively charged with being merely a mathematical composer. To this he responds with anger.

"I have no idea what mathematical music is," he says. "Of course there is no set of relations, including musical, that cannot be represented by mathematical relationships. Even a figured bass consists of numbers which are definitions of pitch-class sets. But it is preposterous to call music mathematical because it can be described accurately by the use of mathematical concepts."

Concerning his own purpose in making music, Babbitt says he would call himself a maximalist: "I try to make music as much as it has ever been or as much as it could be. I may try to put too much into a piece. Composing time is slower than real time and that presents a problem. In *Moses and Aaron* Schoenberg stated the processes of the piece in the first few measures. Did he reveal them too fast? It is important to consider the rate at which knowledge accumulates in a piece. The composer reminds the listener of what has happened and adumbrates what will happen. In the most abstruse way, then, there is repetition in this music."

Looking back Babbitt expresses grievances. One is that, at this stage of his career, he is still obliged to copy the parts himself, that commissions do not cover the cost of such a difficult and time consuming chore. Another and more encompassing one is that "there is no publishing or recording of these works and I don't see how they will survive. At least those composers who use the computer will be able to leave their digital tapes behind."

But he acknowledges a silver lining: the large number of sophisticated musicians capable of performing this music brilliantly. One such person is Robert Martin, the cello player of the Sequoia Quartet. Martin not only studied at the Curtis Institute of Music; he concentrated on mathematical logic at Yale where, in 1965, he received his Ph.D. in philosophy. Since then he has divided his time between philosophy and performance. According to Martin, Milton Babbitt should be in a continued state of euphoria.

"He has been a professor at Princeton, an important center for new music, for most of his life, and has held a chair there now for years. He is on virtually all the boards, all the committees, so respected is he as composer and theorist. He shows up at every meeting, every conference. Last month, he gave a paper at the Stravinsky symposium in San Diego; and last year, at the Society for Music Theory meeting, he delivered the concluding lecture, the one for which we played Schoenberg's Fourth Quartet in order to illustrate his points.

"On top of all this, he is still composing, fantastically and prolifically. Every six months I hear about another wonderful new piece. And you say he complains. I can't imagine about what!"

III

Milton Babbitt, William Shubael Conant Professor of Music, Emeritus at Princeton, will be 70 on Saturday. To commemorate the occasion, *Nassau*, the university's weekly newspaper, sent its news editor to interview him. In what must be among the most felicitous assignments in academia in modern times, the interviewer was Randol Schoenberg, grandson of Arnold Schoenberg, the composer and theoretician who has set the tone for Babbitt's compositional life.

*

First published as "Milton Babbitt Has Done It His Way" in *The New York Times*, May 4, 1986.

Babbitt's own identity has been tied to a kind of contemporary music that is very difficult for the uninitiated to understand. To say it is abstruse is not to exaggerate. In a recent interview, the composer said: "On this birthday, one that covers 40 years of creative activity, I have been challenged on my stubbornness, my intransigence, and so on. I am continually being asked, 'Why do you do this thing? Why do you stay with it? You don't make money. There is no real celebrity. Why not admit failure?' All I can say in response is that I'm doing it as self-indulgence, and there's nobody I would rather indulge. If they regard that as immoral, then they have defined immorality in a way with which I do not agree."

No one can intelligently argue against the merit of Babbitt's work, and his steadfastness has a certain validity. Historically, music has moved from simple to complex, and until the newest was made accessible or available, the public did not accept it. Some aspects of Babbitt's position today echo Schoenberg's 50 years ago. In fact, when this writer articulated the following equation to him — Schoenberg was to Carl Orff what Babbitt is to Philip Glass — he said that while he would not make the claim himself, he found it flattering.

When asked why he chose the Schoenberg route over any other, and never made an effort to combine high culture with popular art, Babbitt said: "From the late 1920s, I was aware that these two things were going on but also that they were disjunct domains. I knew that a song like Irving Berlin's 'All Alone' was special. There was no AABA, no literal repetition, and there was a genuinely remarkable development. When I wrote popular songs, I introduced motivic operations I had learned from Schoenberg and Webern and from the reading I had done about them. But I don't see how it could have worked the other way around, what I could have taken from the popular tradition. Songs by Berlin, Jerome Kern, Harry Warren were all identified by their pitch and rhythm. Harmony, instrumentation and dynamics could be changed — and often were — and the piece retained its identity.

"But my colleagues and I were interested in music in which every dimension contributed equally. The first movement of the Webern Symphony, for example, could not have been transcribed for any other instruments. We were accustomed to transcribing Mozart and Beethoven, but we knew that if we were to change any one thing in our music, the piece would become incomprehensible. That is what intrigued us about it."

*

In the years since Schoenberg first exerted an effect upon him, not only the scores but the temperament of the craggy, rigorous, somewhat paranoid Viennese Jew has been so incorporated into Babbitt's own that it is often difficult to know where one ends and the other begins. He says that when he travels by air, and is asked by strangers who he is, "I say Arnold Schoenberg and nobody bats an eye."

No wonder the tie between them is profound: the precocious, intellectually and musically gifted Jew — born in Philadelphia and growing up in WASP-dominated Jackson — must have gone through a childhood far more similar to Schoenberg's than to that of the Eastern European songwriters who settled on Manhattan's Lower East Side. However much Berlin and Gershwin suffered in material terms, both felt themselves to be insiders in a tightly knit world.

Babbitt's own brand of crankiness seems to render him blind to the many honors, tributes and genuine love that have come his way over the years. He answers the question: "If you had to do it all over again, would you do it all over again?" with an immediate "No!"

"There is nothing I like better," he explains, "than writing music. But there is nothing worse than getting along in the world of music. Personal tragedies are everywhere, and people's personalities become transformed. While mathematicians remain interested in their subject, composers increasingly use their pieces as vehicles of contention and competition." There follows the litany of complaints against publishers, record companies and universities. While much of what he says has substance, one can hardly believe it comes from a man who is viewed by the sophisticated public as the avatar of postwar American music and the man who virtually single-handedly conferred on his colleagues, as well as himself, a stature that had eluded them until he appeared on the scene.

Mario Davidovsky and Roger Sessions
Composers Conference at Johnson State College,
Vermont, early 1970s
CREDIT: Clemens Kalischer

2

ROGER SESSIONS

Two major American composers turned 85 during the past few
months. The many celebrations of Virgil Thomson's birthday finally
landed him in the hospital to recuperate. In contrast, Roger Sessions'
85th passed almost unnoticed. Never mind. The celebration is yet to
come. Peter Mennin, director of the Juilliard School where Sessions
has taught since 1966, is giving the composer what may be the best gift
of all. The school's American Opera Center has selected as its contemporary opera of the year the composer's magnum opus, *Montezuma*.

The world premiere of *Montezuma* was presented by the Deutsches
Oper in West Berlin in April 1964, six months after Sessions finished
it. Reviewing it for *The New York Times*, the British composer Peter
Maxwell Davies called it "a masterpiece". Still, it appears to have been
given a poor performance. For one thing, the director, Gustav Sellner,
was an actor who knew virtually nothing about music. Maxwell
Davies reported that the whistles and boos almost drowned out the
applause.

Sessions thinks the audience's minds were made up in advance because they brought whistles to the performance. "Berlin," he goes on,
"was a completely different place than it had been in the early 1930s
when I was living there. It had become totally self-centered; there was
a lot of opposition to *Montezuma* simply because it was an American
work. Still, in the third and fourth performances, the reception was
far less hostile than in the first."

Whatever the performance's inadequacies, the values of the work
clearly came through. Some critics agreed with Maxwell Davies, others
predicted it would become the "great American opera." Sarah

Originally published as "Roger Sessions' *Montezuma* Reaches
New York — At Last" in *The New York Times*, February 14, 1982.

Caldwell, director of the Opera Company of Boston, was in the audience and determined then to bring the work home.

Montezuma is a sprawling work with a cast of 30, a chorus of at least 50, and a 490-page orchestral score that accompanies invasions, rebellions and ritual murders that characterized Cortez's conquest of the Aztec empire. The opera proved so difficult to mount that, during the late 1960s, Caldwell was forced twice to postpone production. Finally it came off in 1976 at the company's theater, a former rock palace that had once been a movie house.

In speaking of that single performance Sessions says: "Having no orchestra pit was a big handicap. The musicians were in a roped-off area on the floor. Naturally it was hard to balance all the forces properly, but Sarah Caldwell's ideas were good. She is a remarkable creature—indefatigable and conscientious. She learned the work well, chose the cast well, and considering all the built-in problems, I thought it worked very well." Andrew Porter was less generous. In *The New Yorker*, he wrote that "for all the magnitude of the Boston endeavor, we have not properly heard and seen" *Montezuma*.

The hope is that the Juilliard production will remedy all that. In his office at the conservatory, Peter Mennin explains why: "Frederik Prausnitz, the conductor, has recorded Sessions' Eighth Symphony and *Rhapsody for Orchestra*. Ian Strasfogel, the director, staged Sessions' other opera, the one-act *Trial of Lucullus*, when we did it here in 1966." And some effort has been made to simplify. "There were spots in the score that not even the most heroic Wagnerian could have possibly gotten through," he says. "We have been working since September with all our efforts in the direction of clarity. Some changes have been made; naturally the composer has the last word on these."

Sessions says: "I am staying out of the way. I don't like to hang around. You get the best results without interference from the composer."

*

180

Having *Montezuma*'s first performance abroad was really not all that odd. Sessions has long ties with Europe. He entered Harvard at 14 and recalls that he planned to spend his junior year in Paris studying composition with Ravel. But World War I aborted that project. After Harvard he enrolled in the Yale School of Music and later studied composition with Ernest Bloch, the Swiss-born composer of Jewish ancestry. In 1920, Bloch was appointed the director of the Cleveland Institute of Music and took Sessions with him as his first assistant. When Bloch left Cleveland, Sessions moved to Italy where he lived for eight years. Then he spent two more in Berlin, "the last two," he says, "before Hitler. I met Schnabel, Stiedry and Klemperer there. During the years I spent in Europe, I also met the best musicians I have ever known — Schoenberg and Stravinsky."

Sessions' music has always reflected a strong predilection for this mainstream modern European movement. There is nothing in his scores that bears even the most remote connection with such idiosyncratic Americans as Gershwin, Cowell, Cage, Partch or even the Aaron Copland of *Billy the Kid* and *El Salón México*. Sessions remains one of the most important Americans tied to contemporary European tradition.

The idea for *Montezuma* came from Giuseppe Antonio Borghese, an Italian anti-fascist writer. In the 1930s, Borghese visited Mexico and became intrigued with the historic confrontation between Spanish explorers and the Aztecs. On his return, he suggested to Sessions, whom he had met while both were teaching at Smith College, that they write an opera on the subject. The basis for the libretto was Bernal Diaz's famous contemporary chronicle; Borghese used Diaz as narrator and chorus.

Sessions says that the opera is "really about fascism, and fascism is something I know a good deal about. I grew up with it. It was strong both in Italy and Gemany when I was there. So although the idea was Borghese's, it was one to which I responded.

Roger Sessions and Efraim Guigui
Composers Conference at Johnson State College,
Vermont, early 1970s
CREDIT: Clemens Kalischer

Borghese asked me questions about writing a libretto, but
then he forgot the most important thing I said, which was
that, roughly speaking, a musical setting takes three times as
long as a reading of the text. In 1941 he gave me a text of
40,000 words, and if I had set what he delivered to me, the
public would have been safely between its sheets only at
about 5 a.m. – and that is without stopping for a drink after
the performance. I spent two or three years cutting the libretto. Several times I read the text aloud in class to get a sense of
the timing, to know what to cut. I did not begin composing
day and night until 1959, and I kept that up until 1962. After
that I spent 15 months orchestrating.

In summing up the opera's story, Sessions says: "It is based on a historical account of two very strong characters, Cortez and Montezuma.
It is also the story of the conflict between these intelligent men and
their young lieutenants, who are warmongers. The fascist element is
contained within the younger men and the violence that erupts is
directly traceable to them. *The Trial of Lucullus* and *Montezuma* are both
cynical about conquest. Let us say they are against conquest."

Sessions himself is something less than a conqueror compared with
his more self-aggrandizing colleagues. A composer's composer, he has
earned the respect of the professionals while walking away with few
of the prizes. The Pulitzer, for instance, has eluded him.* So there exists this paradox of a distinguished and influential composer whose
music remains virtually unknown to the public.

One reason for the few performances of his music including *Montezuma* lies in its difficulties. It is dense and complex. And nobody has
ever walked out of a concert hall humming a Sessions tune. But
rewards are there for meticulous listeners: "There is a craggy quality
to his exterior language," the composer Leon Kirchner explains, "that

* Later in 1982, Sessions was awarded the Pulitzer Prize for his *Concerto
for Orchestra*, composed in 1981.

has often put off even very good musicians. But once you get into the interior of his work, there is a deep dimension that moves the soul."

Despite the paucity of titles and prizes, Sessions has had a gratifying musical life. On the faculty of at least six academic institutions — he taught at Princeton for more than 20 years — Sessions was the principal teacher of Milton Babbitt, David Diamond, Leon Kirchner, Mirian Gideon, Hugo Weisgall, Donald Martino, Andrew Imbrie and John Harbison. He is also the author of several penetrating books on music as well as an important treatise on harmony.

More remarkable, his compositional pace has accelerated with the years. Five of his nine symphonies were composed after he finished *Montezuma*, and that was when he was 66 years old. Sessions' productivity in later years has a famous historical precedent: his own idol, Giuseppi Verdi, was in his 70s when he wrote *Otello* and *Falstaff*.

But while Verdi composed operas and very little else, Sessions, like Beethoven and Debussy, produced only one huge opera. There are other differences. For one thing, Verdi was steeped in tonality while Sessions, in *Montezuma*, uses a free treatment of Schoenberg's 12-tone principle. For another, Verdi's collaborators were better librettists than Sessions' Borghese. Several vocal coaches at Juilliard are reportedly up in arms at the inability of anyone to sing Borghese's prolix text to Sessions' complex music. Consider this one line sung by Cortez's lieutenant: "I saw the hungerers in Tiaxcala with not a sprinkle of salt on the poultice of their lamar dish."

The fate of *Montezuma* depends on whether, given a splendid performance, the opera can transcend such a static libretto. If it does, it will be because of its extraordinary music and that, very often, is all it takes. The prognosis is good because Sessions has been making extraordinary music many years. As early as 1925, in a letter to Romain Rolland, Ernest Bloch wrote about his own reaction to a Sessions piece:

Personally I would give all that I know of Schoenberg and

184

Stravinsky for a few pages of this work, and I think Sessions is an authentic genius. I know him, I have followed him, I have fought for him here in Cleveland where he doesn't fit into this society and doesn't give a hoot for success, money or notoriety....

When I heard *The Black Maskers* played by a miserable orchestra of 35 amateurs in Northampton, Massachusetts, conducted by Sessions himself — he is as bad a conductor as he is a pianist — I was overwhelmed. I could not sleep that night. I wept in my bed. I felt that this man is the only one who could say everything I could not say myself. A spiritual son, closer to me than my own son, and life seemed beautiful after all. For if I had been able to help one human being to develop himself and give this country the immense music that symbolizes its problems and its destiny, well — my sufferings have not been in vain.

Just as the opera, after having been so rarely performed, is about to receive a major production, so one would like to think that Bloch's words, written more than 50 years ago but brought before the public now for the first time, are harbingers of a broad new appreciation and affection for the work of an American master.

185

3

STEFAN WOLPE

Neglect, illness and disaster have marked the life of Stefan Wolpe, who has been something of a legend among the musical avant-garde for the poetry he infuses in the new language. Wolpe applied ten times for a Guggenheim before receiving one, and then he was almost 60 years old. Nine years ago, he was stricken with Parkinson's disease, making it virtually impossible for him to read, write, or talk much of the time. Then, in 1969, just after he moved into his present apartment, a defective lamp wire caused it to go up in flames, damaging his scores and destroying his uninsured Miró, Kline and de Kooning paintings. Students and friends have worked tirelessly to restore his manuscripts and to raise money for a nurse who attends Wolpe every day.

This year the composer will finally receive more wide-spread attention. To commemorate his 70th birthday, several evenings of his music have been planned.

Wolpe lives with his third wife Hilda in Westbeth, a remodeled project for artists in Greenwich Village that formerly housed the Bell Telephone Laboratories. When I visited them one morning at ten o'clock, the living room was dark; a small lamp over a table provided what light there was. A wheelchair dominated the room; bottles of pills lay on tables everywhere. There were, besides some casual furniture, books, paintings and a record player. The composer, with his nurse standing nearby, greeted me with words I was not able to understand.

*

In a second, brighter room, a partition separated us from a bed Hilda Wolpe occupied. As Wolpe posed for photographs, I asked if his wife would pose too. She called out, "No photographs." When I asked

First published as "Stefan Wolpe: A Thoroughly Modern Maverick" in *The New York Times*, February 6, 1972.

186

Stefan Wolpe
CREDIT: Clemens Kalischer

why, she explained that she was not up yet. Then Wolpe spoke the first words that I understood: "Hilda is a very handsome woman."

Blonde, with high cheekbones and a dazzling smile, Hilda Wolpe joined us later when her husband asked her to help with the interview. Throughout the conversation, she prodded him sweetly but with determination to sit forward, use his vocal cords, and articulate better so that I could understand what he said. As time passed, he spoke more clearly. Mrs. Wolpe explained that shyness and inhibition were part of Parkinson's disease, and that the longer I could stay, the better.

I asked the German-born composer how he was drawn into music.

"For my bar mitzvah in Berlin," he began slowly, "I received an electrical toy, a miniature motor that could accelerate the speed of my other toys. This ability to change tempi interested me intellectually. I experimented with my fists on the piano, doing to Chopin and Bach what the motor did to my railroad train or car.

> I studied theory and counterpoint with Alfred Richter in Berlin. The sounds he recommended I found boring and stupid. Finally, he threw me out. This made my father feel righteous. My father wanted me to go into business and my mother wanted only to please my father. My cultural heritage was limited.
> But I met Busoni at his home. Busoni interested me very much. For the first time, I found someone adequate to myself. That was around 1920. At that time, I was friendly with painters at the Bauhaus. They were vehement and expressionistic. Then I wrote music of great exaggeration.

Hilda Wolpe interrupted him: "Exaggeration is still very much a part of his nature." Wolpe added: "Busoni tempered me, warning me against this tendency."

A radical socialist in the 1920s, Wolpe wrote theater music for Bertolt Brecht. In 1933 he was forced out of Berlin by the rise of Hitler. First he went to Switzerland, then to Vienna where he studied composition with Anton Webern. "Webern was a wonderful man. That doesn't say much, does it? He wanted to get rid of a kind of orchestration characteristic of Ravel, a sumptuous orchestration. We studied Mahler and Schoenberg. My purpose was to write atonal music, but atonal music greatly simplified."

*

Wolpe spent time in Russia and Palestine before 1939, when he settled in the United States and went on to become one of our most influential teachers of composition. Two years ago, illness forced his retirement from C. W. Post College, where he taught for 12 years. A maverick, transforming any system he adopts, Wolpe attracted a wide range of students, from avant-gardist Ralph Shapey to the conservative Ezra Laderman. From time to time, Wolpe still composes tonally, but he leans toward a free extension of the serial idea, using small groups of pitches rather than complete 12-note rows. I asked if he ever worked with tape. "When you're my age," he said, "you think a lot before you start with such things. But there is a kind of intermarriage between electronic and non-electronic music. When I compose, I sense a great closeness to this medium. Still I can say: 'This reminds me of a Schubert song.' Music is filled with such moments. Tradition is always there. Like your shadow is always there. When I compose, birds are flying through fire. When I wrote my flute piece, I was deeply engaged in this image. There was a huge space . . . always mobile . . . always active . . . extending and contracting . . . multiple extensions and multiple contractions. I doubt that it's possible to write absolutely 'new music.' "

"Are you critical of that term?"

"Definitely. I find in my work light shadows, traces of Debussy, 13 million Jews being slaughtered." His wife stopped him: "Six million, Stefan, not 13 million Jews." Wolpe went on: "They are all associations, and important, as associations are. The real newness is when you are bored with something and you jump out of it into something else.

189

There are certain immodest composers who keep repeating what they have done. If you're only interested in newness and not with what you can share with others... I am having difficulty formulating a thought. Would you give me time to think it out and come back another day?"

I said I'd be happy to return but suggested he should not prepare a complex statement. Very quietly he said, "I am not dead." I leaned forward to hear better. "Did you say," I asked, "'I'm not dead yet?'" The composer replied: "I didn't say 'yet.' "

*

A few days later I returned at noon. The nurse had just served him lunch, and he was reading *Boulez on Music Today*. "Boulez is brilliant," Wolpe said. "But everything in the book is too climactic. The reader must feel, 'I am not very intelligent.' "

The nurse left for the day. Mrs. Wolpe was still asleep. The composer explained that his wife was a poet, "a marvelous poet. She works at night, lives her life at night, generally sleeping until the late afternoon."

Wolpe tried to pick up the thread. "As long as you can translate a musical situation...." Suddenly he stopped. "Mean disease. Lousy disease. I am having a seizure now. Don't be afraid. You see that I cannot move my leg with my hand. Try to open my fist." I tried but could not. "Some pills relieved the seizures but they made me schizophrenic. I lived in a world of pure fantasy. Do you see that wheelchair? All of a sudden, it would move and I would embrace it as though it were a woman. The seizures are enervating for Hilda. They rob one of light and naturalness. Hilda is a hero."

Then, with a smile, his eyes brightened, and his whole body began to move. Without his cane, he stood up and virtually danced around a small area. "These are the glorious moments," he said. "One feels a sense of hilariousness. During the seizures one cannot move; at these times, one cannot stop moving."

190

During recent years, Wolpe's works have decreased in complexity. Last fall he composed a trumpet piece and I asked if he could notate works today. "At the moment," he answered, "it is difficult for me. This is a tragedy. I have the musical notes in my mind, but I have trouble when they come into competition with other tempi." He began to sing. Then, "Certainly I have new ideas. Now I find I don't need so many densities. All my life I have worked for the reverse of density."

Wolpe talked about the shape of a phrase, its subdivisions and possibilities. He hummed to illustrate his point. He hummed louder and louder, startling me, for he had not yet talked to me above a whisper. "You should have known me at another time," he said. "I never stopped walking, talking, moving. It is very different today. Recently my *Chamber Piece* was played. I was called onto the stage. I got up there, but I couldn't get down."

"In the face of all this," I asked, "you opt for life?"

"Definitely. Otherwise I'd kill myself."

We listened to a recording of the *Chamber Piece Nr. 1,* a beautiful work, clear, direct and full of drama. I asked why he thought he had not received more performances. He answered that performances were not important to him. Hilda Wolpe, who had joined us, disagreed. Performances *were* important to him, she said, but he was not suited to the type of intrigue that made for that particular kind of success.

As I prepared to leave, Wolpe asked if I had enough material. I said that I did. He told me to do a good job. With my coat on, I sat down again and asked what a good job would be — to him? What impression would he like me to give?

Wolpe remained silent for a long time.

"I am a very strange man," he said.

POSTSCRIPT: *Wolpe died on April 4, 1972, less than two months after this interview was published.*

191

Leon Kirchner
CREDIT: John Goldman

4

LEON KIRCHNER

Leon Kirchner, 65 years old this month, is a large, rumpled, soft-spoken man who gives the impression of having just lost his way. Not a prolific composer, he is generally late with deadlines. In fact, he is probably the epitome of what the non-musician thinks of as the serious composer. Self-denigrating and grandiose at the same time, poetic, moody and emotional, his conversations avoid references to technical aspects of music theory and are peppered instead with allusions to Flaubert, Balzac, Artaud and Brahms. Still however audibly he sighs, however pained or bumbling he may appear to be, Kirchner has moved steadily upwards in his career throughout his adult life. As a composer, he has always been his own man; using an advanced 20th-century vocabulary, he has managed to make music that is both lyrical and rhapsodic, a feat that sets him apart from the rest.

In 1977, the opera, *Lily*, the great work of Kirchner's life, was performed for the first time by the New York City Opera. The composer was very unhappy with the outcome. Since he was the conductor as well, he had hoped he would be able to control events, but things got out of hand. Because of his experience with *Lily*, Kirchner decided that for his next work with words he would, as he put it, "choose simpler avenues." Those avenues will be revealed when the Chamber Music Society of Lincoln Center presents Kirchner accompanying Beverly Hoch in *The Twilight Stood*, his antidote to *Lily*. The composer points out that "it uses one singer, no orchestra, costumes or set." Stringing together six Emily Dickinson poems, the composer has created what

Originally published as "Leon Kirchner: For Him, Music Is Its Own Compensation" in *The New York Times*, January 1, 1984.

he calls a "small opera, each poem a scene, with a single character who views a panorama changing at a rate almost beyond control."

*

Recently Kirchner read a biography of Mozart. He says that after he finished it, he cried the rest of the night, so devastated was he by the horrors of Mozart's life. "What right do I have to complain at all," he asked, "when this colossal genius suffered the way he did."

Kirchner's own suffering is due in part to Lily's having failed in the way that it did. It is also due in part to his having lived his entire musical life within the confines of the university with all the jealousies and back-biting that often implies. It is finally due in part to his acknowledgment that the new avant-garde is one with a deeply conservative tonal idiom that attacks those principles in which he most deeply believes.

But he should feel genuine gratification at the remarkable compliments his work has evoked over the years. At the beginning of Kirchner's career, Aaron Copland wrote "Kirchner's best pages are charged with an emotional impact and an explosive power that is almost frightening in its intensity." Twenty years later, in a review of the String Quartet Nr. 3, Paul Hume noted in the *Washington Post* that Kirchner's combining of live and electronic media was "by far the most distinguished marriage of any such attempts he had ever heard." Still later, in 1969, when the composer conducted the New York Philharmonic in his own *Music for Orchestra*, Alan Rich remarked in *New York* magazine that of all the fine composers of that time — and he included Elliott Carter and Roger Sessions on his list — "Kirchner's music is the most immediate, the most powerful in terms of emotional outpouring."

Concerning the act of writing music itself, Kirchner says, "It is a very lonely one. I have worked best when I have not been involved in any activity other than composition. What is difficult is the trial and error process. One has to find the ultimate for that particular moment. Schnabel, whom I respected enormously, felt we should not seek remuneration for the act of composition: he treated it as a deep religious pursuit."

*

Born in Brooklyn, Leon moved to southern California at nine, where his family settled in a small, poor town. Although there were no musicians in his background, Leon began to play the piano at four. At 16, he won honorable mention in an intramural composition contest and, by the time he entered college, he was composing a good deal on his own. In graduate school, Kirchner won the coveted $5,000 George Ladd Traveling Fellowship, better known as the Paris Prize, but because of the onset of World War II, he could not use it for travel abroad. After serving in the Infantry, he went back to the University of California, Berkeley, and in 1947, he composed the *Duo* for violin and piano, his first published work, which drew the attention of Copland who encouraged him at this critical stage of his life. Soon the young musician went on to win, among other distinctions, two Guggenheim Fellowships, two New York Music Critics Circle Awards — the first for his String Quartet Nr. 1 — a Pulitzer Prize, and the Walter Bigelow Rosen Chair at Harvard where he replaced Walter Piston as Professor of Composition. Now, commuting twice a month to Juilliard, he has assumed Roger Session's responsibilities there.

At Juilliard, Kirchner's composition students report he spends quite a bit of time analyzing Haydn works. Former Harvard students who are now professional composers recall him as an excellent teacher, but a harsh taskmaster, hyper-critical, a man who compared them — to their detriment, of course — to the great masters of the past. This piece of behavior, incidentally, is one he repeatedly applies to himself. Analysis of the classics in composition class and downgrading the students' work are habits associated with one formidable composer, the most influential teacher of the 20th century, Arnold Schoenberg. Kirchner did study with Schoenberg when the latter was teaching in Los Angeles and although he later went on to work under Sessions and Ernest Bloch, it was Schoenberg who made the difference.

"At Los Angeles City College," Kirchner recalled, "I was a zoology major. Although I'd been playing the piano all my life, at college I was pre-med. One day the composer Gerald Strang came to give a lecture and spoke of Arnold Schoenberg, a powerful figure, then teaching at UCLA. He played a recording of *Pierrot Lunaire*. In those days we were thinking about Sibelius, but after hearing the Schoenberg work, several of us switched to UCLA. It was awesome. I didn't understand so much of what he said then, but years later, I would often say to myself: 'So this is what he meant.' "

*

In 1959, Kirchner began his opera, *Lily*. The Fromm Foundation gave him a grant that moved the work off the drawing board stage.

"*Lily*," Kirchner said, "was a very big part of my life. It is typical of art in our time that so few of us have the possibility of experiencing the hard cold facts of theater. In the United States there is hardly any way for a composer to try opera."

In *Lily*, based on Saul Bellow's novel *Henderson the Rain King*, Henderson is meant to suggest Lyndon Johnson and the Arnewi tribe the Vietnamese. Kirchner says his message was this: so-called saviors destroy those they set out to free. When *Lily* emerged in 1977, Harold Schonberg used a harsh word: "stillborn."

The work was presented during Julius Rudel's tenure as general director of the City Opera. "Rudel," Kirchner explained "was immensely generous to me. He found me a salary of $30,000 which made it possible for me to take a year off. But things went out of control. The fault lay not with Rudel but with the structure of the company itself.

"I don't like to complain, but one has to have a sense of reality.

196

Opera, after all, is theater. The composer has an image in his mind and there seems to be no pathway by which men and women can realize that image. What appeared on the stage of the State Theater had little to do with my libretto."

Clearly, there was not enough time for the orchestra or singers to become acquainted with the complicated material in this score. Many sophisticated musicians agree the composer got a raw deal. Kirchner compares his situation with Berlioz's *Benvenuto Cellini*. "The first performance," he says, "was traumatic for him. Twelve years later, Liszt mounted a great production and the opera was received with enormous acclaim. But Berlioz was unable to enjoy even that evening, so haunted was he by the memory of the premiere. I've received offers from several opera companies in Europe to produce *Lily*. But I haven't answered them. I'm going to wait" — he smiled — "12 years."

Kirchner's appearance as accompanist in *The Twilight Stood* is not all that unusual. He has performed as piano soloist with the German Radio Orchestra in Baden-Baden under Hans Rosbaud, the Boston Symphony under Erich Leinsdorf, and the New York Philharmonic under Dmitri Mitropoulos and Lukas Foss. In the song cycle, his writing for piano is as virtuosic and demanding as the vocal part. In fact, a look at the score suggests that the piano part could stand alone.

Nor is Kirchner's performing career limited to the piano. Not only has he, for the last ten years, been the director of the highly praised Harvard Chamber Orchestra and Friends; he has also conducted the New York Philharmonic, the Philadelphia, and the Boston Symphony orchestras.

"Would I live my life over again," he says today, "I would take the advice Stravinsky gave me years ago and not tie myself to the university. I would go out there — into the marketplace."

Charles Wuorinen
CREDIT: Anne Dowe

5

CHARLES WUORINEN

I

It is a genuinely unusual occurrence for a living American composer to have five different compositions, two of them world premieres, performed by five different organizations in a period of six days in New York. Yet that is precisely what is happening to Charles Wuorinen whose Trio for Brass Instruments, *Archaeopteryx, Fortune, Arabia Felix* and Horn Trio will be played between April 14 and April 19.

There may have been another occasion when an American composer enjoyed as impressive a week as this. But if there was, that composer did not produce the kind of music Wuorinen does. None of these pieces were composed according to formula. He says his highly chromatic scores have been influenced by Milton Babbitt, Elliott Carter, Stefan Wolpe and the serial pieces of Igor Stravinsky. The serial technique lies at the root of his musical language, and he treats with contempt the minimalist and other styles that have come into fashion during the last 20 years or so. Wuorinen describes his work habits as "obsessive"; composing eight to ten hours a day seven days a week, the New York musician has completed 150 pieces to date.

In a turn-of-the-century brownstone on New York's Upper West Side, the composer's parlor floor work area contains a computer terminal, an eclectic library weighted on the side of Chinese culture, Oriental rugs over parquet floors, an old Mason and Hamlin organ he bought for ten dollars when he was a boy, and a desk adjacent to the piano. Because of the complexity of his technique and his manifest erudition—just consider the titles of some works—Wuorinen was in-

First published as "A Big Week for Wuorinen" in *The New York Times*, April 10, 1983.

itially viewed as a university composer, but that does not hold true anymore. The term, "university composer," came into being in the 1950s and is generally associated with such Ivy League schools as Columbia, Princeton and Yale. Since World War II, the university has been to the composer in the United States what the radio station has been in Germany and the theater has been in France. It guarantees him a steady income.

Wuorinen's own ties are to Columbia University, literally from before he was born. For 40 years, his father taught history there, serving as department chairman for most of that time. From the age of 14, Wuorinen's music teachers were exclusively Columbia professors. In private sessions, he studied harmony with Jack Beeson and species counterpoint with Vladimir Ussachevsky.

Despite pressure from his father to move toward a career in medicine or law, Charles persisted in music and, at 16, won the New York Philharmonic's Young Composers Award with a traditional tonal work, *Song and Dance for Piano*. In his senior year at the Trinity School, he composed a cantata which the glee club performed in Town Hall. The summer he graduated from high school, Wuorinen attended the Bennington Composers Conference: "That was the moment," he recalled, "I became aware of music beyond Bartók, I met other young composers, heard my first Webern, came in touch with Henry Brant who was doing his antiphonal things. All of it proved a powerful influence."

He entered Columbia College and won enough scholarships and private subsidy to attend the Bennington Conference for the next four years. When he moved on to Columbia's graduate school of music, his teacher, the composer Otto Luening, became an ardent supporter.

In 1962, along with fellow student Harvey Sollberger, Wuorinen founded The Group for Contemporary Music, which became a prototype for many university new music ensembles. In 1964 Wuorinen joined the Columbia faculty, and by the late 1960s was lecturing at Princeton and the New England Conservatory of Music.

Meanwhile the prizes kept piling up. When he was only 32 years old, he captured the Pulitzer.

Yet early in 1971, when he came up for tenure at Columbia University, the music department turned him down. "They got rid of me," he said, "as soon as I got the Pulitzer Prize. An editor of the *Times* asked me for an article about what had happened. I wrote that the university was unwilling to support the arts. The conflict was between musicology and composition. It had started with the musicologist, Paul Henry Lang, fighting the influence of the composer Otto Luening. By 1971 both men had retired but a new generation kept the battle alive and the musicologists fought my appointment effectively. Lang replied to my article with one of his own, attributing the department's decision to my arrogance. All kinds of professors wrote letters defending tenure. I was not attacking tenure, just my not being given it. The fight was really between Lang and Luening, and I was Luening's principal surrogate."

There is truth on both sides. Lang believed that the university was a place for learning, not creative activity,[*] and Wuorinen was fiercely arrogant. The denouement was that Wuorinen lost his prime means of support. He says that many of the big universities now seek "the wild and wacky avant-garde. The mixed-media Happening of yesteryear is now ensconced in universities throughout the country." Wuorinen derives his income from a combination of sources: BMI performance fees, royalties from his publisher, commissions from performing groups and foundation grants. Because a substantial grant from the Rockefeller Foundation that had been renewed for three successive years ran out about a month ago, the composer is looking for ways to supplement his income. He expresses interest in film music

---

[*]   I have also written about this in my chapter on Béla Bartók. See pages 49-58 above. — JP (1994).

but has had no experience with it. Conducting is a plausible solution and an activity that has attracted him for more than 20 years.

*

"In 1961," Wuorinen said, "I had no idea of a conducting career. From time to time I conducted the Hartt Chamber Players, performers in the music school attached to the University of Hartford. Then Harvey Sollberger gave a flute recital at Columbia; Joel Krosnick played the cello, and I accompanied at the piano. The event gave us the idea of starting a performing group, and when we did I began to do some of the conducting. The notion was for composers to control performances of their own work. I conducted more and more and became increasingly interested in it. In recent years, I've been fortunate enough to conduct such first-rate players as the Cleveland Orchestra.

"Of course," Wuorinen went on, "I can't *not* compose. If I didn't compose I would be very disturbed. But I also love conducting and, of all activities, it is the nearest to composition. It gives you an instrument you can't play with your fingers and, at the same time, it is abstract. You communicate meaning through gesture and in that sense it is metaphysical."

It is intriguing to note how many composers of this generation were lured by the money and acclaim of conducting to shift gears at some point in their careers. Leonard Bernstein claims he conducted at the start to subsidize his composition. Pierre Boulez reports he went into the field for much the same reason Wuorinen did: to control performances of his own work.

*

Still, it is unlikely that conducting will ever completely displace composition in Wuorinen's life. Unlike many of his composer-colleagues, he is optimistic about the state of his art and deeply convinced

202

of the correctness of his ways. "Contrary to what many people believe," he said, "this is not an age of transition. We are already *in* a new age which is going to be very much remembered, an age comparable to the Periclean period. We *are* Athens, and we don't know it."

Wuorinen has a large ego; he sees himself central to the new era and believes his music will endure. No one knows if he is right or not, and if he is wrong, he may never know it. Meanwhile the fact that five of his pieces will be played in New York in less than a week means at least some people think he is right.

II

Wuorinen, who will be 50 years old on Thursday, is a second-generation 12-tone composer who perceives that his musical universe is being threatened by a burgeoning populism. "I feel what I do is right," he says. "Pluralism has been carried much too far."

Five years ago Wuorinen felt no need to defend his path. Five of his compositions were receiving their New York premières in one week and he remarked then that "contrary to what many believe, this is not an age of transition. We are already *in* a new age which is going to be very much remembered, an age comparable to the Periclean period. We *are* Athens and we don't know it."

Wuorinen saw himself central to this new age and believed that his works would endure. Yet now, in his fourth and last season as composer in residence with the San Francisco Symphony, he finds himself obliged to go along with the programming of the Minimalist works for which he feels no personal enthusiasm.

The dark clouds Wuorinen sees are not figments of his imagination nor aspects of any paranoia. As his kind of music displaced the more openly melodic works of Aaron Copland, Leonard Bernstein, David Diamond, Samuel Barber, Gian Carlo Menotti and many more, so the

Originally published as "A Bleak View of the Future" in *The New York Times,* June 5, 1988.

Minimalism of Philip Glass, Steve Reich, Terry Riley and John Adams has begun to home in on Wuorinen's world. To make it worse, Wuorinen sometimes finds himself appearing to contribute to this development, as with the San Francisco Symphony's programming of Minimalist works. "That is a professional stance," he explains, "not an artistic stance."

When Wuorinen is in full control and not forced to compromise, he faces another kind of trouble. In 1962, he founded the Group for Contemporary Music with the composer-flutist Harvey Sollberger. It went on to serve as a model for many new-music ensembles throughout the United States. Wuorinen's rigorous attitude set the tone, and the group maintained its quality image for 26 years. Yet this spring the board of directors had to cancel the last concert — there was no money to pay the musicians — and the group may have to limits its activities to recordings.

Wuorinen attributes the recent difficulties to cuts made by the New York Council on the Arts.

"There is a great deal of unease in the world of serious music," Wuorinen says. "It expresses itself in ironbound reactions. All of it bespeaks a professional malaise. The big world of serious music is worried about itself, and the manifestation of that worry is conservative reactionism. A dependence on marketing reveals the tendency to view art not for its intrinsic merit but as a tool for social engineering. The public is made the judge. That means we have a world in which the instant response of the untutored becomes the sole criterion for judgment.

"The reactionism," Wuorinen goes on, "had its roots in the Vietnam period, the era of the so-called cultural explosion. That was the turning point. Art became capitalized, a Good Thing, something to be brought to everyone. With that came the promoting, the merchandising, the marketing — the change from art to entertainment. It is not only that serious music is now pop; even Beethoven gets marketed for the masses. A great work like a Beethoven symphony becomes like a

204

CHARLES WUORINEN

blob of toothpaste. There is the bored orchestra. There are the indifferent audiences. They wait it through. They applaud. They leave. The symphony is wrapped in such a way that nobody can find how demanding it is. The Beethoven Fifth is a fierce, not terribly pleasant, work but it is packaged in such a way that it doesn't bother anyone. The same is true of [Bach's] B Minor Mass."

*

Wuorinen's somber view of the current state of his art has been heightened by his realization that some of the people he thought saw new music the way he does — as a continuation of Schoenberg and late Stravinsky — seem to have begun to move away with the crowd. In the fall of 1986 Wuorinen resigned as chairman of the American Composers Orchestra, a group of musicians devoted to the presentation of 20th-century American music. According to Wuorinen, the precipitating cause of his resignation was a remark by one of the orchestra's conductors, Paul Dunkel, that "music in New York would die if it were left in Wuorinen's hands."

The statement wounded Wuorinen, but it also helped crystallize, he says, his feeling that his role with the orchestra had become an "increasingly marginal" one.

Asked what he would do if music in New York *were* placed in his hands, Wuorinen replied, "I would try to change the present relationship of the composer to the public from one in which the composer says, 'Please judge me,' to one in which I say, 'I have something to show you and offer my leadership.' I would do this not through 'music appreciation' but through repeated performance of good new music."

Wuorinen said he would concentrate on presenting "works of genuine merit. I would implement my notion of balanced programming which would reflect the following proportions: one quarter the standard repertory — Beethoven, Brahms and so on; one quarter 20th-century classics — Schoenberg, Stravinsky, Hindemith, Bartók; one

205

quarter present-day established composers — Babbitt, Boulez, Carter, Berio, Martino, Perle; and one quarter the new and untried. The last 80 or 90 years would get a hearing and the young would have a chance to be themselves. I know many serious and honorable composers who are young and continue to advance the art, but nobody pays any attention to them. The current tendency of transmuting art into entertainment will cause serious music to cease to exist."

*

Wuorinen learned of Schoenberg's method during his college years and committed himself to it with passion. He views Minimalism as a return to the old, not only because it relies on tonality, but because it uses repetition, which 12-tone music abjures. To say this is not to suggest that Wuorinen's music has stayed the same over the last 32 years; it has become looser, more intuitive, more accessible. But his commitment to 12-tone composition remains total.

And he continues to move ahead; this year he conducted the San Francisco Symphony in the world première of his first opera, *The W. of Babylon*, and he conducted the New York City Ballet Orchestra in the world première of his first ballet score, *Five*. The recent first performance of his Third String Quartet moved the *New Yorker* critic, Andrew Porter, to write: "This is a poetic — I'd say inspired — composition, representing Wuorinen in an unusually intimate vein, and it strikes me as a major contribution to the string-quartet repertory." In virtually every arena, Wuorinen's first 50 years have been ones of accomplishment. Currently he is the holder of a MacArthur Foundation Fellowship, frequently called the "genius" award, which will bring him almost a quarter of a million dollars over five years.

But institutions lag behind fashion, and the current *haute couture* is definitely not with Wuorinen. Every artist suffers when the art in which he believes looks as if it is being displaced by something else. Johann Sebastian Bach, while he was creating the greatest works of his life, was being eclipsed by the simpler, more "modern" music composed by his own sons. And we all know how it turned out with Bach.

Still, the current tipping of the esthetic scales seems more significant than a temporary shift in style. The question is whether the informedly advanced music in which Wuorinen believes was indeed the fresh start that he and his colleagues thought it to be, or whether it will turn out to have been one in a series of inevitable steps that charted the decay and death of serious music.[*]

---

[*] This last paragraph is the one that I added at the insistence of the *Times* editor, Gerald Gold. See page 162.

John Harbison
CREDIT: Dorothy Littell

6

JOHN HARBISON

John Harbison is an important figure on the musical horizon today although, at 42, he is still not known to the public-at-large. The reason for his relative anonymity may lie in his background, which is academic. Still as a second generation academic, his music is not only less doctrinaire than his predecessors'; it is lyrical, neo-Romantic, sonorous rather than spare, and virtually devoid of contemporary clichés. Harbison appears never to repeat himself; reviewing the world premiere of the Violin Concerto, Richard Dyer wrote in the Boston *Globe* that "each of his works marks an exciting achievement... and for a growing number of knowledgeable people the progress of his music is an important, even defining part of their lives."

Although Harbison is associate professor of music at the Massachusetts Institute of Technology where he teaches composition, plays viola and conducts, he says he rarely writes music there. Instead, when he gets a stretch of at least three free weeks, he goes to a Wisconsin farm where he works in a studio with long windows, an upright piano his mother-in-law chose for him, and a special board on which to compose, one he can easily move around allowing him different points of view. He gives high priority to musical ideas and willingly sits at his board for hours hoping three good minutes will redeem the rest. His Piano Concerto won the Kennedy Center/Friedheim First Prize, the Boston Symphony Orchestra commissioned him to write a centennial piece, and he is the 1981 composer-in-residence at the Santa Fe Chamber Music Festival, now completing its ninth season.

First published as "John Harbison's Continuing Ascent" in *The New York Times*, August 16, 1981.

KUNM-FM in Albuquerque broadcast all of Harbison's recorded music and, in Santa Fe, a number of virtuosos—among them Walter Trampler, Ani Kavafian and Edward Auer—gave first performances of two Harbison works.

Harbison says the new pieces differ strongly from each other: "The Piano Quintet, commissioned by the festival, is an arch 19th-century form; it is straightforward and very direct. The *Mottetti di Montale*, a 35-minute-song cycle based on a complex Italian text, is the most impractical piece I ever wrote. The works represent different sides of myself; the quintet is outward, the motet inward."

Not all of his works can be described as either outward or inward. Generally they suggest an inner turmoil subjected to a rigorous technique. Catastrophic events in Harbison's life may have generated this method of coping with the world. After three years of progressive nervous degeneration, his father died at 51 of Parkinson's Disease. The composer's only two siblings, both younger, suffered the most terrible afflictions and one died, at 38, several months ago. "If you believe as I do," Harbison remarks, "in the psychic as well as physical genesis of illness, you are naturally forced to wonder. There is the selfish anxiety that is inevitable, for with virulent health problems among family members so young, one's own expectations are undermined."

*

Despite the dark aspects of his life, Harbison's career has been marked by continuous ascent. After growing up in the quiet, college town of Princeton, New Jersey, he entered Harvard where he received a B.A. in 1960. Then, while matriculating for a Master of Fine Arts degree at Princeton, he managed also to attend the *Hochschule für Musik* in Berlin and the Salzburg *Sommerakademie*. Over the years, he has accumulated many prestigious fellowships and awards including Harvard's George Arthur Knight Prize for composition, a BMI Composition Prize, Brandeis's Creative Arts Citation, and an Academy of Arts and Letters Award.

Characterizing his background as "post-Calvinist, liberal, Christian," Harbison is critical of his parents for bringing him up in a "permissive haze" that did not help him formulate values at an early enough age. What he did find particularly useful, however, was the musical tradition his father handed down to him.

His father, a history professor at Princeton, wrote pop music. His uncle was a song writer and composed college shows. He himself played jazz through high school and college.

"I've always had an immense respect for Copland and Sessions," he says, "but I have tried to face the fact that in my formative years Ellington, Arlen, Rodgers and Kern also played an important role. I believe there is a kinship among all these composers that has not been adequately recognized. Of course the ambition and structural complexity of Copland and Sessions are completely different from a Richard Rodgers song. But the finish and skill are quite the same."

One thing Harbison is not grateful for is the era in which he came of age musically. "In the early 1960s," he says, "there was tremendous pressure on young composers for instant originality and instant novelty. We got plenty of originality and novelty but very little music. That delayed the emergence of my own voice. It took nerve to go back and compose 'early' music at an advanced age. It may be a risk to make a complex shape but it is also a risk, and I believe a far greater one, to write a very direct and clear melody that you can absolutely stand behind."

Harbison spent part of last spring in Rome where he was composer-in-residence at the American Academy. Rome was not as fruitful as the Wisconsin farm. "I have always been afraid of the MacDowell Colony," he explains, "with all those intense people coming to breakfast. Rome was like that. In addition there was more to see, more to adjust to, and people who could not be ignored."

But the most disconcerting element of his Italian visit was what he

211

perceived to be an imbalance in the attitudes of Italian and American composers towards each other's music: "Italians don't know much about us, and we know a great deal about them. I went over with a fairly typical consciousness of Dallapiccola, Petrassi, Berio, Nono, Donatoni, and even the younger ones like Sciarrino. But conversations with Italian composers reveal their knowledge of American music to be very sketchy. Our scores do not reach them. We print fewer pieces. We don't export our music as a cultural product the way they do. When our orchestras tour they rarely bring our own music; when European orchestras travel, they invariably bring theirs."

Italians are aware, Harbison notes, of only a small segment of American musical activity, such anti-intellectual strains as chance and minimalist composition. "They know Cage, Feldman, Riley and Glass, but they are not really aware of Sessions, Copland and the real Ives. I get very impatient with their characterization of Ives as unfinished, unformed, charming, quirky, with an impish, tinkering quality. The tinkering quality they see in Ives is what they also find in our indeterminate composers and what they finally identify as 'the American thing'. There is great frustration in reading the Italian papers where you find full acknowledgement of Emily Dickinson, Herman Melville, Jackson Pollock and Charlie Chaplin, but no such attitudes towards our composers."

Although Harbison is now working on a commission for the Boston Symphony — "it seems sinful ever to turn down a commission," — he says his first love is opera and that if he had his way he would compose very little else. He began listening to Met broadcasts at ten, subscribed very young to *Opera News* and — when his classmates were awed by Marilyn Monroe — wrote to divas and tenors for their autographs. When asked what he would like to do most in the world, he replies: "Compose a couple of more operas that would have a chance of surviving. Sometimes, when I hear *Pagliacci*, which the cognoscenti, as they walk out, invariably put down, I think 'I'd be glad to get one like that, not just because it is a hit, but because it's a strong, stageworthy opera.'"[*]

One thing he would not like to do is immerse himelf in the computer domain, an arena of interest at MIT. "I know people," he says, "who are in tune with that whole chemistry. Communicating with a machine is not as frightening to them as it is to me. In the laboratory, I get what is known as computer red-eye. It is an actual illness and comes from staring into those fluorescent boxes. Also, I don't have the particular constitution for sitting in small, airless rooms that smell like the insides of someone's socks."

[*] Harbison is currently engaged in a commission from the Metropolitan Opera based on F. Scott Fitzgerald's *The Great Gatsby*.

James Dean in *East of Eden* (1955), directed by Elia Kazan.
Dean, a piano student of Leonard Rosenman, brought his
teacher to the director's attention, as a result of which
Rosenman wrote his first of many film scores.

7

LEONARD ROSENMAN

Leonard Rosenman is a man who is confronting one of the questions of the age: art versus money. Starting as a serious composer, he soon did what used to be called "selling out to Hollywood." After making a fortune writing film and television scores, he is now trying to resume his career as a composer of concert music. His *Chamber Music V* will receive its first New York performance under the direction of Gerard Schwarz at Goodman House.

Art for art's sake or art for profit have always been in conflict. William Faulkner and F. Scott Fitzgerald tried to sell out to Hollywood with little success. Stravinsky tried too, after moving permanently to the United States, but his effort proved useless. Rosenman *did* succeed, and success in movie music means composing it by the minute, by the scene.

In a recent conversation, Rosenman characterized his life as "schizophrenic". He noted that during a two-month stint last spring of teaching composition at the University of Illinois, he had to fly to Florida for a new movie, *Cross Creek*, directed by Martin Ritt and starring Rip Torn. But shifting between Hollywood and academia is not new to him. More than 20 years ago, when Shostakovich, Khrennikov and Kabelevsky were on a visit to Los Angeles, they lunched with ten top American film composers, Rosenman was one of them. Later, that afternoon, the Soviets attended a concert of works by composers on the faculty of the University of Southern California. Rosenman was one of them too. Along with the British composer Richard Rodney Bennett, Rosenman has always had one foot in film and the other in

Originally published as "A Composer Seeks Artistic Prestige After Hollywood: Leonard Rosenman" in *The New York Times*, August 29, 1982.

the concert world. But unlike the facile and unflappable Britisher, Rosenman is torn apart by the dichotomy.

*

Born in Brooklyn in 1924, he grew up with a mother he says was dominating and a father who owned a small grocery store. The older of two boys, he expected to become a painter. But by his early 20s, his musical talent forced him to change his goal.

At Tilden High School, the budding musician met Lukas Foss who recommended he take piano lessons with his own teacher, Julius Herford, who had recently come to the United States from Berlin. Rosenman says Herford was a "monstrous man, a German taskmaster who told me I was not talented, should not go into music, must avoid Dostoyevsky—whom I loved—at all cost, and crossed out notes in my compositions. Although it was a destructive relationship, I studied with him from 16 to 19 when I entered the Air Force."

When he went in the service, Rosenman took with him books on harmony, counterpoint and composition. "I was determined to teach myself to compose," he recalls. "I met Leon Kirchner, the first composer with whom I had a steady intimacy. A kind of osmotic relationship grew, and I got to understand the process of composition. In Hawaii I met Earl Kim. He and Kirchner both had studied with Roger Sessions and suggested I do the same. But first I wanted to try Schoenberg."

Although Rosenman found Schoenberg a "remarkable teacher", he was disappointed with him. Instead of teaching composition, he taught the class 16th-century counterpoint, so within months, Rosenman switched to Sessions. During that same period, he studied musicology with Manfred Bukofzer and piano with Bernhard Abramowitsch, all at the University of California, Berkeley. According to those who knew Rosenman then, he was brilliantly talented both as composer and pianist. Obviously he also had the good sense

216

to know exactly to whom to turn for the various disciplines involved in music.

*

In 1952 Rosenman received a Margaret Lee Crofts scholarship to study with Luigi Dallapicolla at Tanglewood. Luciano Berio, Sal Martirano and George Rochberg were in this group. While there, he received a Koussevitzky commission to compose a one-act opera. In order to stay in New York, he taught piano to support himself. One of his students was James Dean, who had then appeared Off-Broadway and on television. When Dean landed the starring role in the film *East of Eden,* he told the director, Elia Kazan, about his remarkable piano teacher. Kazan listened to Rosenman's music and in what surely was a courageous act — the prevailing movie music was then 19th-century in idiom — invited the young composer to write the score for the film.

As a composer of concert music, Rosenman was thriving in New York. Prestigious concerts included his work, and when Composer's Forum produced a series with each program devoted to an older and a younger man, he shared an evening with Milton Babbitt. But the money was not coming in, and even then Rosenman had expensive tastes.

He says that when he received Kazan's offer he thought: "What an interesting alternative to teaching in a university! I did a fling in Hollywood and then returned to New York, and alternated between the two for a while." *Cobweb,* his second film, was produced by John Houseman who gave him *carte blanche* and Rosenman composed Hollywood's first 12-tone score. In time there were Academy Awards (*Barry Lyndon, Bound for Glory*), Emmys (*Sybil, Friendly Fire*), and BMI performance royalties. Rosenman wrote the music for *The Defenders, Marcus Welby M.D.,* and a variety of other television shows. The work proved lucrative and Rosenman bought land in Malibu where he and

217

his third wife built a house — complete with pool and sauna — and had enough space to raise horses.

In an article published in a 1968 issue of *Perspectives of New Music*, Rosenman claimed it was possible to write the same kind of advanced music for film as for the concert world. In fact, he said, it was easier because "musically unenlightened people comment positively and glowingly on a 'dissonant' score after seeing the film" while the same group will react negatively to the same music when it is presented to them on records without images and words.

But today Rosenman appears less sanguine about his metier: "Film and concert music," he says, "entail entirely different processes. With film one is given an *a priori* construct. It is a very sophisticated version of seeing an array of numbers from one to 100, connecting them and winding up with a picture of George Washington. The point is to fill up space and the work is dictated by literary considerations. With concert music — even in opera, the most literary form — the composer's task is to shape the text into a fundamentally musical work."

Since moving to California in the mid-50s, Rosenman has composed only a handful of serious works and the response to these was not encouraging. He says that during that long period he did not receive a single performance in New York. And when he did receive one in California, the critic, knowing he was a film composer, invariably and automatically judged the work "schmaltzy" — something, he adds, "my music never was." Feeling embattled and artistically paralyzed, Rosenman entered psychoanalysis and went five times a week for the next 12 years. He attributes what he calls his current "visibility" to treatment: "Now I have a grip on myself and although it is late in life, I am motivated and optimistic."

*

Apart from psychoanalytic therapy, several important things have happened to Rosenman since 1966. The most devastating occurred in

218

1970: his second wife died suddenly of a stroke at 43. "Someone," he says, "is literally here one day and gone the next. It makes one reassess life on the basis of its finiteness and fragility. Bill Kraft, a good friend of mine, thought it would be cathartic for me to get busy on something creative, and he suggested to Zubin Mehta to commission me to write a memoriam piece.

"My wife had been a song writer. I made a gigantic harmonic extension of one of her tunes, much like Stockhausen's *Hymnen*. I used a small jazz group playing through ring modulators and called it *Threnody on a Song by K. R.* [Kay Rosenman]. In May, 1971, I conducted the Los Angeles Philharmonic and Mehta was in the audience. He liked the piece, people received it well, it was successful, and I felt a sense of command." The work called for members of the orchestra to rise and cry out the dead woman's name.

The second event took place in the late 1970s. Charles Wuorinen was visiting the California Institute of Arts when Rosenman was teaching there. Wuorinen looked at his music, liked it, and decided to conduct *Chamber Music II* with the Group for Contemporary Music in New York. It was Rosenman's first performance here in more than 25 years.

The third was more of a non-event. In 1980, the Los Angeles Philharmonic played a marathon of works by composers who had been in California when Schoenberg and Stravinsky were living there. Rosenman was not included. Music critic Alan Rich noted the omission in *New West* magazine, and the composer says it was then overwhelmingly clear to him that his fortunes did not lie in Los Angeles. "So, like Willy Loman," he says, "or more to the point like Haydn, when he took off for London, I am now entering the marketplace in New York."

*

It seems ironic that a man who has lived in such high style would now long for his music to be heard by a few hundred people in an unglamorous hall. And this at a time when some of our best composers

219

would be pleased to compose a Hollywood score. John Corigliano, now at work on a commission for the Metropolitan Opera's centennary season, believes our musical repertory has been established and that the need for new music in the concert hall isn't what it was in the past. "In films you are really needed. You don't feel superfluous," he says. "With abstract music, one feels removed from the sense of necessity." Corigliano, who created the sound for Ken Russell's *Altered States*, says that with the right conditions he would welcome another commission in Hollywood.

Wuorinen, who also looks favorably on film music, says he find it "amusing that Rosenman is making this move at a time when so many people in the sphere of serious music are rushing to embrace popular and populist devices. Why is he trying to crash the concert field? Because it is one of the few pockets in the world where the notion of prestige retains its appeal."

Which is only to say that some people want everything. And why not? Messrs. Corigliano and Wuorinen, light years removed from one another in approach, have their reputations firmly in hand as they covet both a sense of usefulness and the big money to be found in Hollywood. Rosenman, on the other hand, is like the protagonist in *L'Histoire du Soldat* — he desires to reclaim the violin he exchanged long ago for worldly riches. While clinging to the present — those lavish accoutrements his money has brought him — Rosenman now devotes virtually all his energies towards finding recognition as a *bona fide* artist.

POSTSCRIPT: *Rosenman has composed many film scores. Among them are* Rebel Without a Cause, The Chapman Report, Beneath the Planet of the Apes *and* Lord of the Rings. *Today Rosenman continues to straddle both worlds. Still living in Los Angeles and writing music for films, he was Composer in Residence at New York University in the fall of 1994, when the University's music department presented a work commissioned years ago by the Schoenberg Institute.*

220

8

BETSY JOLAS AND BARBARA KOLB

Women who do not choose to proselytize feminism as their primary career often find they are eclipsed in the tumult created by those who do. Last month the American Academy/National Institute of Arts and Letters [later the American Academy of Arts and Letters] did its part to redress the damage by calling attention to two women, both of whom have continued to work hard at their metier and still steer clear of all the political brouhaha. In conferring awards to American composers, the Academy/National Institute cited Betsy Jolas and Barbara Kolb.

There are other similarities between the women besides placing composition over any political or social agenda. Each is a lyrical composer, and avoids the angular motion and abrasive sounds currently in vogue with some of the more radical avant-garde. Each is articulate and generous to the other, praising both her character and work. Each moves freely through an interview without mentioning discrimination against her sex. And each acknowledges she took her musical cues from a man to whom she attributes her success. Betsy Jolas names Boulez; Barbara Kolb, Lukas Foss. (Men are not free of such adulation and emulation, either. Webern's tie to Schoenberg is a case in point.) The music and personalities of Boulez and Foss differ enormously, of course, so herein the similarities between the women end.

*

In New York to receive the award, the Paris-based Jolas was staying with friends on Sutton Place. As she smiled genially for the *Times* photographer, a visitor noted that most composers present deadly

Originally published as "Why Can't a Woman Compose Like a Man?" in *The New York Times*, June 17, 1973.

At the 1973 American Academy of Arts and Letters Ceremonial
Composers Aaron Copland (Academy President),
Betsy Jolas (an award recipient), Elliott Carter

serious faces when posing for photographs. Jolas replied: "I look better when I smile."

Betsy Jolas is the first child and older daughter of Eugene and Marie Jolas, an exceptionally cultivated American couple living in Paris when Betsy was born in 1926. Eugene Jolas first published parts of *Finnegan's Wake* in his celebrated literary journal, *Transition*, and Marie Jolas studied singing with the best teachers in Europe. During her childhood years, Betsy Jolas conversed with James Joyce, saw a page of Varèse's *Ionisation*, and accompanied her mother at the piano. "I had a most congenial life," she recalls. "I knew I'd be a dancer, a painter, a musician, that I would have a career in the arts. But I never dreamed I'd be a composer. A composer was a genius — like Beethoven."

When World War II broke out, the Jolases returned to the United States and Betsy attended the Lyçée Française in New York. From there she went to the Dalcroze School of Music where she met Paul Boepple, then director of the Dessoff Choir. Betsy played organ and piano and sang with the Dessoff group. She says her "real masters" date from this period. They are such early composers as Perotin, Lassus, Josquin and Schütz.

After Dalcroze, Jolas went to Bennington College where she studied logic and mathematics and literature with W. H. Auden and managed to write a full-fledged Mass on the side. "It was a modal piece — a combination of Schubert, plainsong and Josquin. I would never have it played today, but the experience was very important to me. Everywhere on campus I heard it being rehearsed. It was then I first thought I would be a composer."

After graduating, Jolas returned to Paris because "my culture was there." At 20, she entered the Paris Conservatoire, studied fugue, then harmony under Olivier Messiaen. At 23, she married a French physician and the following year, 1950, had her first child.

Since then, Jolas has divided her time between her home (she has three children) and her work. When she began to compose seriously, she wrote chromatic music that stood somewhere between the soft official French style and the stringent, uncompromising avant-garde. "It took me a long time to know the kind of music I wanted to write. In 1954, Boulez began the *Domaine Musical* [concerts that presented the most advanced composers of that time: Stockhausen, Berio, Nono and Pousseur]. I went to all the performances. But I couldn't go through that Purgatory — I couldn't do what they set out to do — create a musical language from scratch.

*

"I had met Boulez in the 1950s when I was working at the French radio station, and I was terribly shy with him. I knew how exigent he was. Finally, in 1963, when he was visiting Paris, I determined to show him my work. I was so nervous, but I need not have been. He spent three hours with me. He didn't like everything I did, but he thought I could do better and gave me good technical advice. The following year, I wrote *Quatuor II* for the *Domaine Musical*. Boulez conducted. It was the very best performance. The work was recorded; it was the milestone of my career. Since then I have found my place."

Jolas writes two or three works a year which are highly structured and complex but lovely pieces without any trace of academicism. And today she enjoys significant status in France. Her music is published by Philippe Heugel and when Messiaen leaves Paris to tour, she substitutes for him at the Conservatoire. During her visit to New York, she met with American music publishers in an effort to spread her work to the United States. Asked how her family affected her career, Jolas replied: "It slowed it down. I couldn't go to the avant-garde festivals in Darmstadt each summer because I couldn't be away from home that long. But I wouldn't live my life any differently today."

Barbara Kolb points out that *she* didn't go to Darmstadt either, not because of children at home, but because she never had the money to make the trip. Kolb, 34 years old, lived until recently in a tenement

224

Barbara Kolb

with a rusty bathtub in the kitchen. Today she lives on a nice street on Manhattan's West Side in a neat three-room apartment with a spinet in the living room. There's also a couch, a wrought iron table and chairs, paintings by several of her friends and a parquet floor she sanded herself. She has to use the $3,000 award from the Academy/Institute to help pay performers who recently recorded one of her works.

*

Kolb, who has never been married, concedes she "may be a little jealous of Jolas because Jolas has had an easy life and has a husband and three children she loves. But I don't believe in marriage at all, and most women today feel the way I do. I think marriage can be truly damaging and is rarely beautiful, the way it should be. If a really beautiful relationship didn't exist, marriage would be too horrible for me. Anyway, I ask a lot from a man, and single men in New York are hard to find. Those available play the stock market. They are on Wall Street, decked out in the latest haberdashery. They go to parties all the time, and I am continually bored with them. Then sometimes when I meet some very interesting men — men I adore — they turn out to be homosexuals. I don't try to change them. I'm not Carrie Nation. Homosexuality is so open now that there is no reason they shouldn't be what they choose."

Appearing never to censor her thoughts, Kolb travels in conversation from a moving description of her father's tragic death from cancer to her delight in a *New York Times* review. Harold Schonberg described Kolb's *Soundings*, performed by the Chamber Music Society of Lincoln Center last fall, as "romantic — lyric, personal, inventive. Kolb has, in effect, composed a mood piece and one that is full of color." The fact is that Kolb is replete with color, and brashness is one of her most attractive attributes.

*

After the awards ceremony, Kolb heard composer David Diamond attack Lukas Foss, who was not present to defend himself. Kolb told Diamond he wasn't fit to breathe Foss' name. Diamond retaliated later that week by denouncing Kolb at a party attended by prominent musicians. Learning of this, Kolb offered a scathing denunciation to me:

"Cowell and Copland are the only ones of that era who possessed any imagination at all. With the exception of them and Foss, the rest are parasites, a bunch of real idiots — and you can quote me on that."

Barbara Kolb, an only child, was born and grew up in a small apartment in Hartford, Connecticut. Her mother was "just a housewife who liked to be belle of the ball." Her father, a handsome and meticulous man, was music director of the local radio station and led a few bands in the big-band style of Claude Thornhill. "He was incredible at improvising," Kolb says. "He wasn't a learned musician but a natural talent, completely self-taught. My parents didn't want me to go into music. To them music meant drugs and alcohol, a life filled with debauchery. They knew nothing of the serious music world."

*

Because he refused to mix family with business, Barbara's father would not have a piano in the house. At eleven, Barbara discovered the E flat clarinet and "fell in love with it." After finishing high school, she entered the University of Hartford in its music division, the Hartt School, where she majored in clarinet. Then she studied composition there: "Until then I had written only stupid things — words and music for high school songs. In graduate school, I studied with Arnold Franchetti, who had been a pupil of Richard Strauss. I wrote what he wanted me to write, which is exactly what he himself wrote. I guess you could call it out-of-tune Schumann.

"To make a living, I played E flat clarinet in the Hartford Band and the Hartford Symphony. I hated them both. The Band concerts were held in the summer — every Sunday afternoon! As for the orchestra: being one out of more than 100 players allows no display of individuality."

In 1964 her life took a good turn. She went to Tanglewood as a composition student, met Lukas Foss, and heard his *Time Cycle* and *Echoi:* "I felt an affinity for Foss right away. I was impressed not only by his music but also by his personality. He is always in a state of change. He was impressed by my work and, I guess, by my interest in him. He recommended me for a Fulbright and that started my career."

"In 1965 I moved to New York and have lived on grants and awards since then, supplementing them at first by working as a music copyist. There is nothing as degrading as that — copying other people's scores. You're doing nothing for yourself. A copyist puts down what's in front of his nose. I did awful copying jobs for four years and made between $2,500 and $3,000 a year."

*

In 1968 Foss programmed his protégé's *Three Place Settings* in his concert series at the State University of New York in Buffalo. The following year, Kolb won a Guggenheim and the Prix de Rome. Now her music is published by Boosey & Hawkes, Carl Fischer and Peters and recorded by Vox and Desto. Next fall she will begin her first teaching appointment: composition and analysis at Brooklyn College.

She is pleased about the Brooklyn College job because it will keep her in New York, which she loves. Her Fulbright in 1966 sent her to Vienna: "I didn't like it at all. I found it a boring, backward country. I arrived on September 16, and it was only 38 degrees. I was in a cellar apartment filled with spiders and other insects. On top of that, I could have only one bath a week. Oddly enough, it was the bath problem that upset me most. I left Vienna and gave up the Fulbright."

It is no accident that Kolb hates Vienna and that Jolas chose not to

228

live in New York. Each is the product of a different world. Betsy Jolas'
early acquaintance with Joyce, her knowledge of medieval and
Renaissance composers, her studies with Auden and Messiaen, all led
to the complex and sophisticated work that prompts Kolb to say: "I
respect Betsy Jolas' music. I believe she'll be very important in the
United States in a few years."

Yet it is the very *absence* of High Culture, the freedom from so intellectual a load, that gives Barbara Kolb's work its freshness and
strength. As devoid of gimmicks as of hidden systems, the music she
makes lets her personality shine through in all its uninhibited, asser-
tive splendor.

V

SECOND GENERATION EUROPE

RENÉ LEIBOWITZ

PIERRE BOULEZ

LUCIANO BERIO

HANS WERNER HENZE

KARLHEINZ STOCKHAUSEN

BENJAMIN BRITTEN

Introduction

In 1966 Seymour Peck, editor of the Drama section of the Sunday *Times*, read my article on Marc Blitzstein and called me and asked me to interview Maureen Forrester, the contralto. He followed that with assignments on several well-known sopranos. I did them all, while longing to do what interested me most, living composers.

In the late 60s and early 70s, I spent summers in Sheffield, Massachusetts, a short trip from Tanglewood. Tanglewood is the vacation home of the Boston Symphony Orchestra and of a summer school begun by Serge Koussevitzky. The summer after the Blitzstein piece, I met Luciano Berio, the Italian avant-garde composer who was teaching there. Berio had joined the faculty of the Juilliard School and his newest work, *Passagio*, was to be presented the following season with Berio conducting. I asked Peck if I could interview him.

The *Times* had never printed an interview with a composer, he said, and he was wary about it. Peck agreed to let me do it but warned that if it didn't work, there would be no second time. Soon after the piece appeared, Benjamin Boretz, music critic for *The Nation*, devoted an entire column to it. Peck was so pleased that it provoked serious attention, he gave me the freedom from then on to select the subjects for my interviews.

In his converstions with me, Berio often spoke of Pierre Boulez, the post-Webern composer who had been his friend for more than ten years. I had first learned about Boulez through an essay published in *The Musical Quarterly*.

When I received a press release that Boulez was coming to the United States as a conductor and would preside over four sets of concerts, I asked Peck if I could interview him. Peck looked Boulez up in the *Times* morgue and found nothing. Little was actually known about Boulez in 1968 in the United States. For the only time in my career, I was asked to justify my request with a paragraph about the man.

In my article, I described him as the revolutionary he was. When I asked him if he would consider replacing Bernstein as conductor of the New York Philharmonic, Boulez said no. The orchestra's habits were too bad.

At the time national magazines were publishing lists of contenders for the post. Boulez was not on any of them. Yet within weeks of my article, he was offered the coveted job. There were several reasons for this. George Szell, conductor of the Cleveland Orchestra and principal adviser to the New York Philharmonic, could have had it as his own but he had just learned he had cancer.

Boulez was Szell's principal guest conductor in Cleveland, and the two shared similar musical goals: an attention to detail and a serious-ness of approach. It seemed likely they would work well together again in New York.

The plan was that Szell would conduct the traditional repertoire with which Boulez was not at all familiar and Boulez, in this era of radicalism, would do the 20th-century repertoire he loved.

In 1968 revolution was in the air. On page one of an issue of the *Times*, a student's picture appeared with his feet up on the desk of Grayson Kirk, president of Columbia University. In Paris there was fighting on the streets. My article on Boulez revealed him as an out-spoken rebel, but a rebel who hated what the Philharmonic loved to hate: the American serialists. Boulez was offered the post of music director of the orchestra, and he accepted it. When reporters asked why, only a few weeks earlier, he had said he would never take it, Boulez refused to comment.

As it turned out, Szell died on July 30, 1970, more than a year before Boulez assumed the position in the fall of 1971. So the revolutionary was obliged to conduct the traditional 18th- and 19th-century reper-toire, causing problems for many listeners.

At that time, I was finishing my first book, *The New Music: The Sense Behind the Sound*. In a second edition, published ten years later, the title was changed to *Twentieth Century Music* because by then the term *new music* had come to mean something other than the modern Viennese school.* I sent Boulez galleys with a letter saying I would like my next book to focus on him. I said I intended to report on what happened when a man who believed in an idea confronted the box office realities of the music industry in New York.

The heart of the Boulez drama lay in the programming sessions with Carlos Mosely, then administrative director of the orchestra. Moseley did not want to have me present at those sessions so I knew that the projected book wouldn't work. I suggested a biography instead and Boulez agreed to cooperate.

In preparation for my research abroad, I gave Boulez a list of people I wanted to interview in Europe which included René Leibowitz, his first composition teacher. Boulez said Leibowitz was no friend of his, that he was hiding in Paris, that I would not be able to find him. But I did locate Leibowitz who told me this story: while a student under Leibowitz, Boulez wrote and dedicated the *First Piano Sonata* to his teacher. Leibowitz red-penciled it. When Boulez saw the markings on his meticulously prepared and exquisitely notated score, he became enraged and tore the manuscript to pieces. Then he and Leibowitz sat on the floor and painstakingly glued all the fragments together.

Boulez never forgave Leibowitz. From then on he maligned him in print whenever he had the chance, as composer, conductor and theorist. When I called Leibowitz, almost 30 years had passed. He told me he did not want to talk about Boulez. It was only when I explained

---

*   In 1980 a book with that title would have suggested Philip Glass and Steve Reich. I regret the absence of these composers in the present volume, for their music has attracted a large audience and they have exerted an influence on some composers younger than they are. But at the time I was writing for the *Times*, I thought Glass's Eastern influences and static harmonies and Reich's repetitive patterns far removed from my own musical experience and therefore better left to other writers.

that I needed to know more about *him*, for Leibowitz studied with Schoenberg before the war and later taught Schoenberg to students, that he agreed to meet me.

Leibowitz spoke for more than three hours. He said that he had never before told the story of how Boulez had virtually destroyed his career. Within a week of the interview Leibowitz, 59, who had suffered a heart condition for years, died. I wrote his obituary for the *Times*. That short piece, published here, is a microcosm of a larger story, revealing how those who, like Boulez, followed Webern, rejected Leibowitz whose commitment to Schoenberg was total.

Over the years I have learned that the enmity among members of the same group is far greater than that between opposing camps. This was true about John Cage and his colleague Morton Feldman; each spoke harshly about the other. It is also true of those who worked together in Paris in the 1950s and at Darmstadt and Donaueschingen in the 1960s. Hans Werner Henze, at first close to Karlheinz Stockhausen, later expressed rage at his German colleague.

On the other hand Benjamin Britten, the English composer, remained aloof from such compositional battles. In an interview printed here originally published in the *Times*, Britten says composers talk too much. He himself rarely did interviews. The only reason he agreed to talk to me was to obtain the publicity he needed to raise money for his beloved Aldeburgh, the music festival facility that had burned to the ground. Britten died in 1976. Aldeburgh has survived and will celebrate its 50th anniversary in 1997.

1

RENÉ LEIBOWITZ

Composer and conductor René Leibowitz, who died in Paris on August 28 at the age of 59, remained virtually unknown to all but a small circle of now middle-aged composers. Yet he left an indelible mark on 20th-century music: Leibowitz is the man who revived 12-tone writing in post-war Europe, where it had gone underground during Hitler's war on "decadent" art.

When World War II broke out, Leibowitz went into hiding in Vichy, France, then in an apartment in Paris, where he taught dodecaphony to Pierre Boulez and five fellow students from the Paris Conservatoire. In 1947, he wrote *Schoenberg et Son Ecole*, probably the first book on 12-tone music not written in German, and, in 1948, spent four months with Schoenberg in California. Schoenberg, who was then teaching at U.C.L.A., told Leibowitz of his great disappointment that, though the war was over, the Germans were still not performing his work.

On his return to Paris in 1948, Leibowitz was invited to conduct and teach at the festival in Darmstadt, Germany, which had been founded the year before and had focused on Stravinsky, Hindemith and Prokofiev. Leibowitz accepted, but only on the condition that he could conduct a whole Schoenberg program: the Piano Concerto, the Chamber Symphony Nr. 2 and the *Five Pieces for Orchestra*. He had 20 students that first summer at Darmstadt – among them Hans Werner Henze – and all presented blank faces to him. None had ever heard this music before, but, by the following summer, all of them knew the new literature better than he. Leibowitz had successfully opened the road to European adoption of dodecaphony.

Originally published as "René Leibowitz (1913-1972)" in *The New York Times*, September 10, 1972.

Thus René Leibowitz had one long splendid moment in his life, stretching from Paris in 1944 through Darmstadt in 1948, devoted to the promulgation of Schoenberg's idea. When, in the late 40s and early 50s, Webern displaced Schoenberg as the venerated man and composers applied the serial idea beyond pitch, Leibowitz's time had passed. He refused to follow that path.

René Leibowitz, 1954
CREDIT: Sabine Weiss / Frank Driggs Collection

Pierre Boulez in Cleveland
CREDIT: Don Hunstein

2

PIERRE BOULEZ

I

In 1945, when he was 20, Pierre Boulez led a group booing a performance of Igor Stravinsky's *Four Norwegian Moods* at the Théâtre des Champs-Elysées in Paris. "I was not attacking Stravinsky," he explained, "but the Establishment, which considered him the God, the Idol, the Only Truth. I did it to draw attention to Schoenberg, whose influence was still limited to Vienna and Berlin." A few years later, when 12-tone writing was accepted by the avant-garde, Boulez attacked Schoenberg to bring attention to Webern. And sure enough, post-Webern serialism dominated the 1950s and early 60s.

Boulez played a crucial role in shifting the balance of musical power from Stravinsky and Stravinsky's American disciples, trained in Paris under Nadia Boulanger, back to the Austro-German domain, where it had prevailed from Bach through Wagner. In 1959, he left France and moved permanently to Baden-Baden: "Germany was the most exciting country for contemporary music."

Boulez won the significant battles. Stravinsky, in a famous about-face, adopted the serial technique and hailed Boulez as the best composer of his generation. And after Boulez conducted at Bayreuth, a German critic wrote that he could teach the Germans how to handle Wagner. Today the 43-year-old composer-conductor is in demand all over the world. I spoke to him just after he served as guest conductor for the Boston Symphony Orchestra and before he left for Chicago, his last engagement before New York. Thursday Boulez starts a month-long assignment here conducting the New York Philharmonic.

Originally published as "A Fighter from Way Back" in *The New York Times*, March 9, 1969.

Dressed with the same attention to unusual combinations of color that characterizes his musical work — a dark blue shirt under a brown tweed jacket, with a subtly hued plaid tie — Boulez was restrained for about half an hour. He ate red snapper, drank German beer, and spoke politely about his parents and his teachers. When I mentioned an American composer whose work he dislikes, Boulez suddenly came to life, launching a virtuoso attack on various facets of U.S. music.

Eletronic music: "This same frenzy for technology began in Europe about 1953. By 1958 it had all died down. The idea of electronics as the big future of music is just an American trick of fashion. Next year they'll discover the viola da gamba. Playing Bach on the computer doesn't interest me at all because it's artistically irrelevant. All this indicates a simplistic way of thinking — an appallingly low level of thinking."

As for *Perspectives of New Music,* an avant-garde journal published by the Princeton University Press: "*Perspectives* is similar to *Die Reihe,* begun in Germany about 1953. Its writers think they are great scientists. They are not. I know great scientists and *they* possess invention and imagination. Composers who publish in this journal never discuss important questions of choice and decision. They write only about putting different things together. This is not an esthetic point of view. It's what I call a 'cashier's point of view'."

New Image of Sound, the Hunter College concert series at which Boulez just appeared as composer, conductor and performer, is, says he, "the best series in New York. It is just like the Domaine Musical, which I began in Paris about 1953 — the same kind of programming, the same six concerts a season."

But after a second beer, Boulez relaxed and described how he viewed the gulf that separates the American composer form his European collegue: "There should be no antagonism between the American and European composer. I am always fighting the nationalistic point of view. Americans are jealous — I'm not sure if that's the right word — thinking the Europeans are taking attention

242

away from them. The Americans do operate under a severe handicap, of course; they have no strong personalities in the field. If they were strong enough to establish their personality on the world, they would see that no national favoritism exists.

"After World War II, Europeans were thirsty for all America's creative products—Faulkner, Cummings, Jackson Pollock. Europeans bought, almost without discrimination, anything Steinbeck or Dos Passos wrote. But for an American artist to be exported to Germany he has to be better than the German product. They have no one in America as good as Hans Werner Henze, and that is not setting your sights very high. A composer the stature of Stockhausen they have not."

Boulez diagnosed what he feels is the American malady: "European music is not connected with the university. There is no ivory castle for us. But here, university people and practical musicians ignore each other. It's a very unhealthy state of affairs.

"I do not like this pedantic approach. I do not like scholars who bring only Death to music. The university situation is incestuous. It is one big marriage in which the progeny deteriorates, like the progeny of old and noble families. The university musician is in a self-made ghetto, and what is worse, he likes it there."

I mentioned some Amerian university composers who deny the role of self-expression in new music. Boulez said: "They do so because they are not expressive. It is a type of dialectic I find very childish. Not that I consider expressivity to be the final goal of music. The goal of music is far richer than that. But university composers have no mystery, and music must give a sense of mystery.

"This endlessly, hopelessly academic work reminds me of the Conservatoire. There is no difference between this music and an eight-part counterpoint study. Composers must start with a strong technique, but a technique is just the beginning; it is the means and not the end.

"I have no confidence in those who think they know their goals. You discover your goal as you come upon it. It's out there in front of you; you discover it each day."

Commenting on the unhealthy situation separating intellectual composers from practical musicians, Boulez prescribed his own specific treatment: "An intellectual must use intellectual power to change things not directly related to intellectual affairs. When I compose, I have Debussy, Stravinsky and Berg in my background. For an audience to listen to my compositions, it must have the same background as that. So I conduct early 20th-century music to prepare people to listen to more advanced pieces. The fact of conducting is not exciting to me. I'm not super-happy to conduct a large orchestra. But I feel compelled to bring new creative aspects of music to the whole of musical life everywhere. To go into the crowd without losing my integrity, that is what I want to do.

"It is useless only to complain about the 'degraded' audience. That is why I conduct. In Boston I played Debussy's *Jeux*, which this orchestra played the last time about ten years ago, and the infrequently heard *Three Orchestral Pieces*, by Berg. The job of a conductor is to bring an audience to realize it's as important to hear Berg as to hear Mahler."

Boulez does not think that the United States is beyond all hope. But, he feels, salvation will be difficult. "It must lie with an American who is both intellect and practical musician. What is needed in America is a musical John Kennedy. As long as you have no Kennedy in music, you have no future of music in America."

I mentioned Leonard Bernstein as both intellect and musician. Boulez replied: "Bernstein was not there at the right time. When he arrived at the New York Philharmonic, it was too soon for this activity. Then too, such a figure must be personally involved in the advanced creative thinking of the time. You can't introduce a new work to the orchestra, apologizing for it at the same time."

Boulez denied rumors that anyone had ever approached him with the suggestion he take over Bernstein's present job: "But if anyone had, I could not have considered it. The circumstances of directing the New York Philharmonic are such that you are the prisoner of a frame. I am not American enough to be such a prisoner. Nor do I know enough about New York's musical life to bring about the necessary changes. To change bad habits, one must know them well."

Boulez says that — as director — he would require a much larger orchestra, between 150 and 160 musicians who would play two different kinds of programs. Boulez would do a conservative series featuring big-name soloists as well as a series of avant-garde concerts. "The same musicians," he says, "should be able to do both. A culture center moves in many directions. The money you make with the 'museum' series you must invest in performing new pieces."

II

Pierre Boulez is finally making the New York scene but he is traveling light. With no manager, press agent, secretary, maid or wife — without even a telephone answering service — he lives simply and alone. He says that his aim as musical director of the Philharmonic is "to supply a model of musical life as I conceive it, a musical life that is part of genuine culture — not a kind of second-rate enjoyment."

What he's trying to accomplish with his style, with his pace, and especially with his programming may be hard for Philharmonic audiences to take, and many subscribers have written to the management demanding a return to Beethoven and Brahms. If Boulez cannot find a responsive audience for the major works of the 20th century, he says simply: "I will leave."

His output is formidable; by the time he returned to Europe, Boulez conducted over 60 different works. The musicians performed most of

First published as "Boulez: Bringing 'Em Back to Life" in *The New York Times*, June 20, 1971.

them for the first time. I asked how things were going for him. "Intensely," he replied.

The night before he had conducted Berg and Schoenberg at Alice Tully Hall. That morning he had rehearsed Bartók's *The Miraculous Mandarin* and the rarely performed Schoenberg *Opus 22 Songs*. At 7:30, he would conduct the last performance of the Stravinsky Memorial program. *Pulcinella* and the *Requiem Canticles* were new to the men and he could have simplified his work by using the 1947 version of *Petrushka*, the one they always perform. But he chose the 1911 original. Not all of these are among his favorite works, but Boulez programmed them because he thinks they should be heard.

This refusal to impose his taste on others is consistent with a general sense of mission. During his stay in New York, he rarely was diverted from his work. He attended no films, shows, galleries, or large parties. Here is a typical Boulez day. It is a Tuesday, traditionally a day off for the orchestra:

Boulez awakens early—about five o'clock. Without breakfast, he begins to work. Generally he spends these early hours composing, but this morning he finishes an article on Stravinsky commissioned by the *Saturday Review*. Stravinsky's very recent death does not stop Boulez from criticizing him for using quotations of old music. He concludes with a plea for amnesia in composers. (Later he takes off from Stravinsky's use of the past. "Creators," he says, "must look straight ahead. It is not enough to deface the Mona Lisa because that does not kill the Mona Lisa. All the art of the past must be destroyed.")

At 8:30 he showers—not answering the telephone until he's dry. (He thinks that you get electrocuted if you answer when you're wet.) Then he takes calls. Totally unconcerned with fashion—with no trademark like Bernstein's cape, Ozawa's bell bottoms or Stockhausen's pony tail—he puts on blue suit, white shirt and dark tie and walks a few blocks to Philharmonic Hall to make his first record with the orchestra: the overture to Berlioz' *Beatrice and Benedict* and Ravel's *Tombeau de Couperin*. Still without breakfast, he steps onto the podium at exactly ten o'clock. He takes off his watch, places it on the music stand, takes off his jacket, hangs it by the collar on the podium rail, and says good morning to the men. Boulez does not loosen his tie.

From the sound booth, producer Andrew Kazdin says: "This is the overture to *Beatrice and Benedict*. Take one." Prefacing each direction with "May I take, please, from bar..." Boulez works until 12:50, 30 minutes into overtime, when the telephone next to the podium rings. Kazdin says: "I'm afraid I'll have to stop now." Not yet satisfied with the Ravel, Boulez answers—with intensity—"Please don't." Two minutes pass. Even the usually restless musicians remain still. Then Kazdin gives him the go-ahead. About 1:10 Boulez brings down both his arms (he never uses a baton), puts on watch and jacket and rushes backstage to hear the replay. The musicians file out. Several discuss the overtime; it means $47.50 for each of the 57 men who played the Ravel.

Boulez is laughing as he leaves the sound booth. Obviously he likes what he heard. On seeing me, he remembers our date and puts his hand to his head in a gesture of shock. It's 1:35, he meets with Columbia Records at 2:00. "Let's go to La Crêpe for lunch," he says. "Its faster than the Ginger Man." As we run down the steps (Boulez never walks), he compares himself to Sisyphus: "I push the rock up and it comes down again."

At La Crêpe he talks of the audience's reaction to his first program of Schoenberg, Webern and Berg. "Can you imagine how it feels to see more empty seats each time you come back out on stage?" I ask if it feels bad enough to persuade him to compromise with the audience's taste.

"A free society," Boulez says, "is not very different from a state society. In one case you are dictated to by subscribers; in another case by the government. I know some subscribers have complained that there is too much modern music in next year's programs. But there is very little and I'll reduce it no further. A few days ago I was at a friend's house for dinner and the guests said they had never been able to buy

247

Philharmonic subscriptions. I told them to buy them now. I'm hoping for a younger audience — by that I mean people in their 40s." Boulez adds that he'll leave the bulk of the conventional repertory to guest conductors: "I see no reason why I should conduct Brahms when there are others who do it better."

He says he loves New York. I ask how he knows because he never seems to go anywhere. "That's true," he answers, "but the streets are enough."

Crossing 66th Street, he extends his left hand, bringing an oncoming automobile to a halt. "I love to do that," he beams. "It works — most of the time." After the two o'clock conference with Columbia Records — in which scheduling and promotion are discussed for an hour — he leaves the Board Room for the Green Room of Philharmonic Hall. There he coaches the soloists for *Pulcinella* from the piano until after 5:00. Then back to the apartment to rest.

During his five weeks in New York, Boulez spent only three full evenings with friends. This Tuesday was not one of them. At 7:00, in a rehearsal room at Juilliard, he works with student performers on his own *Marteau sans maître,* part of the New and Newer Music program for that Sunday night. It's the only concert in either Cleveland or New York in which Boulez programmed a work of his own. Later he explains he wants no one to say he is using his position to promote his own work. During the break, he buys a Coke from the machine and talks informally with the performers about Schoenberg's Opus 29 Septet.

Boulez drives everyone as he drives himself. And, on occasion things break down. Two important instruments dropped out of the last bars of the *Requiem Canticles* during the performance. When the conductor spoke to the players during intermission, one said that his mind went blank. This is not hard to understand. Boulez says he needs 20 hours of rehearsal for the kind of programs he conducted this spring. He gets only ten. The problem of time hangs over everything. All his politeness — the pleases, thank you's, I beg your pardons — can-

Pierre Boulez
CREDIT: Don Hunstein

not conceal the time-pressure he feels. He has suggested a rehearsal storage plan: if one program requires only seven hours' work, can we have 13 for the next? The union says no.

What he does at rehearsal is to clean everything up. The musicians played under guest conductors for two years and that is death to discipline. Bernstein had a whole other way: concerned mostly with sweep and thrust, he allowed the instruments a great deal of leeway. But precision claims top priority for Boulez. He'll say to a violinist, "Your rhythm is wrong," and then work with him until his rhythm is right, while the other men shift restlessly in their seats. He concerns himself with balance, not only the balance within one section so that the one horn doesn't stand out over the rest, but balance among the various sections. Above all, he works for correct intonation. During the course of an orchestral passage, Boulez stops: "Third trumpet, your E flat is too sharp." Then he thrusts his right arm out in front of him and brings down the thumb, ever so slowly, until the instrument hits the exact pitch. To close the issue, he whistles it. The performance that results is crystal clear.

This approach to conducting works miracles for 20th-century music; Louise Varèse, widow of the composer Edgard Varèse, told me that Boulez brought out the lyric poetry of her husband's *Ionisation* as no other conductor has ever done. The approach does not always work as well for older music; the sensuous aspects of a melodic line can get lost in Boulez's excessive attention to detail.

Still, at this juncture, there are only two roads for the orchestra to take: it can remain a museum for the presentation of old work, or it can bring to life the music of this century. If Boulez cannot transform the New York Philharmonic into an instrument of "genuine culture", there is little likelihood that anybody can.

One of Pierre Boulez's most striking attributes is his ability to assess himself accurately. He did this in the mid-1970s when, as music
director of the New York Philharmonic, he decided not to consider
another term at the expiration of his contract in 1977. At the time he
remarked that he regarded "the 1970s as an exceptional period in my
life. Now I look forward to what is more myself." What turned out to
be more himself was his post as head of the Institut de Recherche et
de Coordination, Acoustique/Musique of the Centre Georges Pompidou, more commonly known as IRCAM.

Boulez's interest in technology is not new. It goes back to his youth
when, as a student in a Catholic seminary, he graduated before the
minimum age of 16 at the top of his class in physics and chemistry. But
by then Boulez had developed an interest in music, excelling in the
piano and singing boy soprano in the seminary choir.

By late adolescence, music had become the dominating force of his
life. He moved to Paris where, as a composer of the post-war avant-
garde, he helped lead the way to a new musical grammar that was accepted by many talented and aggressive colleagues. In his 30s, Boulez
began to conduct. First he conducted modern chamber music in Paris,
later orchestral music in Germany, England and the United States. In
his mid-40s, science and technology reared their heads again. The Max
Planck Institute in Germany asked Boulez to formulate a plan for an
institute that would incorporate both science and art. Although the
economic recession halted the plan, Boulez had another chance when,
in 1970, he was invited to organize the music at the Centre Georges
Pompidou. Pompidou's invitation came almost stimultaneously with
two others: the BBC and New York Philharmonic orchestras asked

Originally published as "From Wagner's 'Ring' to Computer
Practice" in *The New York Times*, December 7, 1980.

251

him to be their music directors. Boulez, who has said he does not enjoy free time, worked out a schedule so he could accept all three.

In the early 1970s, when Boulez was busy as music director in both London and New York, he also held annual week-long seminars for IRCAM at a 12th-century abbey in the French Alps. This was an appropriate setting because music had been taught along with mathematics in medieval universities. One of Boulez's early decisions was to set up departments headed by composers Luciano Berio, Vinko Globokar, Gerald Bennett and Jean-Claude Risset.

None of them remains at IRCAM today. With such a taciturn figure as Boulez heading an institute that is literally underground — it descends several stories beneath street level and is reached by an entrance that is difficult to find — it is natural for rumors to abound. But the reasons for the disappearance of these men is not difficult to fathom. For one thing why should they be good administrators just because they are good composers? For another, creative men of almost equal stature are bound to generate ego problems. In such a complex and costly operation, one man alone must be responsible for making the right decision at every turn.

Recently two other figures have emerged. Both are American. Tod Machover, a composer, runs the research division. David Wessel, with a Ph.D. in psychoacoustics and psychology, is director of pedagogy. From the beginning, Boulez has drawn on American technology. He visited many research centers in the United States — Stanford, Bell Labs, Cal Arts are a few — and he also consulted Max Mathews, a brilliant computer specialist, long associated with Bell Labs. Mathews began by spending three months a year in Paris.

According to Mathews, Boulez devotes his energies to studying a complex computer language, LISP, and learning to play the most recent computer instruments. Mathews believes Boulez will continue to study until he can compose with the new technology. Tape music has disappeared from IRCAM; everything lies in the computer arena. The particular shift that has taken place is toward the development of new digital instruments such as the 4X machine and the writing of a language with which to play that instrument, the 4XED. Mathews, who calls himself "an instrument maker, not a composer", says Boulez arrives at IRCAM at eight in the morning and generally remains until midnight. Mathews also reports the equipment at IRCAM is the best in the world.

This has cost the French government a lot of money. President Georges Pompidou planned IRCAM and his successors have carried out his wishes. Still, there has been an outcry in the press because IRCAM receives about 40 percent of the total French Government budget for music, and France is not rich in provincial orchestras, opera houses or conservatories.

While it may seem reasonable for the public to clamor for results considering the money they have invested in the institute, it is not possible for IRCAM to come up with *the* piece in its formative years. In fact, if such a pivotal work would appear the outsider would not recognize it as such, for it would not be genuinely new if it were intelligible or congenial to the listener. It is probably because of this that Boulez appears to be trying to placate his critics by turning their attention away from research to public events.

In this domain the visible enterprise is the Ensemble Intercontemporaine which gives concerts concentrating on the contemporary classics: Debussy, the Viennese school and Stravinsky, along with some post-war composers such as Mauricio Kagel, Heinz Holliger, Karlheinz Stockhausen and Berio. This year there has also been the Paris/Moscow Concerts, with performances of Scriabin, unfamiliar 20th-century Soviet music, and new works from Eastern Europe. The concerts are held in a radically innovative hall seating betwen 300 and 400 people. It is an all-purpose hall, often doubling as a theater, laboratory or recording studio, and is capable of being tuned like an instrument. The room consists of panels that can be moved to make it as reverberant as a church or as "dry" as a pop studio. A computer controls every detail taking into consideration the size of the audience.

The institute issues publications. Here are some recent titles:

1. *A Programmable Device for Transforming Sounds in Real-TIme under the Control of a Performer.*
2. *The Use of Linear Prediction of Speech in Computer Music Application.*
3. *Musica, a Program for Encoding Musical Scores.*

At the opening of IRCAM, in January 1977, Boulez said: "The creator's intuition is powerless to provide a comprehensive translation of musical invention. It is thus necessary for him to collaborate with the scientific research worker in order to envision the distant future, to imagine less personal, thus broader choices."

In the early 1970s Olivier Messiaen remarked: "Boulez is a great composer. He is also a very intelligent man. He understands the changes and they make him suffer. There are people who go unperturbed through change. Like Bach. Like Richard Strauss. But Boulez cannot. He thinks that advancing the language is all and he doesn't like what is happening there."

Not liking what was happening there, Boulez turned to technology and convinced a President of France that he was right.

Jacques Barzun predicted: "The new art will not be individual... but communal... will undergo a return to the medieval pattern... a literature of low intensity... a monumental architecture."

If this should come to pass then it is possible for composers of the future to be identified in as anonymous a way as artists of the past: From the School of IRCAM. Those listeners who find little nourishment or delight in today's so-called avant-garde may get some encouragment from the possibility that technology can be successfully harnessed to produce a presently unimaginable, genuinely new art.

POSTSCRIPT: At age 70 Pierre Boulez was recently (1995) named Principal Guest Conductor of the Chicago Symphony Orchestra, for a three year term.

254

Pierre Boulez conducting (top) and with
Olivier Messiaen, Odeon Theatre, Paris, 1966 (bottom)
CREDIT: Don Hunstein (top) / both Frank Driggs Collection

Luciano Berio
CREDIT: Peter Schramek / European-American Music Archive

3

LUCIANO BERIO

I

Luciano Berio is a controversial composer—even among the farthest-out composers around. He has strong feeling about many aspects of music including the relationship between the performers and the audience. His *messa in scena, Passaggio,* puts in the mouths of apparent members of the audience hostile remarks aimed at a woman, the sole figure on stage. Seated throughout the audience, this "speaking chorus" expresses conventional attitudes with which the paying listeners presumably identify. The libretto resembles the contemporary theater of Beckett, Genet and Ionesco. In *Passagio* there is no logical plot but a series of situations in which the lone female figure is confronted by an angry, inept, and conformist world. At the end of the work the woman triumphs, for it is *she* who rejects the audience, not they who reject her. The soprano actually orders the people out of the theater.

Berio is highly experimental and concerns himself not only with pitched sound but with *all* sound, including noise. He investigates different combinations and densities of sound and is particularly interested in the area that exists between the singing and speaking voice. "The traditional singing technique," he observes, "has been to make the voice sound like an instrument—in range, in quality, in all respects. Now we must integrate many more vocal phenomena into the musical structure, particularly those closely related to speech." In *Passaggio,* he uses both singing and speaking choruses to produce varying mixtures of the two.

Originally published as "Soprano to Audience, 'Go Home!' " in *The New York Times,* January 3, 1967.

257

*

His assault on tradition also motivates his complaints about new concert halls. "Philharmonic Hall at Lincoln Center and the Music Center at Los Angeles are national catastrophes. They are based on the old idea of pitting the stage *against* the public. This kind of building is outmoded. With electronic music, for instance, it is absurd for the audience to sit on chairs facing loudspeakers that are placed on a platform. The listener must be totally involved in the sound source.

"New halls should be flexible. In Berlin there is a remarkably beautiful new house which is thoroughly workable in many different ways. It permits a radically different placing of instruments so that the public can surround the stage, or, as in the case of a work like the Berlioz *Requiem*, so that the orchestra can be scattered all around the hall."

Berio attacks the whole idea of the concert as "a deadly ritual. The audience behaves as though it were facing priests in a church. One shouldn't forget that such public performances are of very recent origin. They began at the early part of the 19th century, coinciding with the establishment of museums. The concert hall will never disappear but should co-exist with structures that can accommodate new ideas of music-making."

*

Berio — short, hurried, overbearing, articulate — was born in 1925 in Oneglia, a small town in northern Italy. He heard chamber music in his living room regularly from the time of his birth. At five, he began to study harmony with his grandfather and, after that, learned to play organ and piano. The family's musical heritage goes back centuries; in 1782 one Steffano Berio, an ancestor, composed an oratorio.

Luciano left home at 15 and settled in Milan to study at the conservatory. After graduating, he began to coach and conduct in opera houses throughout Italy. In 1952, still unknown, he visited the United States and went to a concert at the Museum of Modern Art. This was the first presentation of electronic music in this country and the first time Berio ever heard it.* Highly impressed, he returned to Italy. In Milan two years later, Berio founded the Studio di Fonologia Musicale, one of the early centers of electronic music.

About that time he won a Koussevitzky scholarship that took him to Tanglewood to study under Luigi Dallapiccola. He has visited this country on and off since then, but came here to live when he accepted a teaching position at Mills College in Oakland, California in 1963. During the last decade, Berio has composed works for orchestra, large percussion groups, small chamber ensembles and voice, some incorporating electronically produced sounds. He has also written compositions for the electronic medium alone but says of this work that "the products are not so important as the idea and research."

Berio refuses to label his work and is harsh on all journalists who do. "It is fair to say," he concedes, "that my style is 'serial in spirit'. The so-called serial experience, as developed in the work of Webern, has been extremely important and has had an effect on every aware human being, but to formalize it and settle on it is something else. I feel that I can maintain control without submitting to the label of serialism, and control, of course, is the *sine qua non* of composition."

But Berio is not as intolerant of tonal music as some other avant-garde composers: "Because I'm committed to new music, it doesn't follow that I would not teach music from other eras. I *conduct* old music. I love *Bohème*... I hate *Tosca* but love *Bohème*... and I have edited the music of Monteverdi.

"It is true that there is a great distance between new composers and the public, but that is because the economic power has been in the

* A program directed by Leopold Stokowski. See page 335 below.
  —JP (1994)

259

wrong hands until very recently. Now the foundations and universities are helping."

*

Although Berio appears to be thoroughly Mediterranean, both in
his volatile behavior and charming manner, he disclaims nationalism
in his music: "There is no such thing now and it is good. Nationalism
only divides people. It produced Hitler. There is a more global type of
thinking today, a concern with musical processes that has nothing to
do with geography." The composers he mentions as the most significant of his generation — Stockhausen, Boulez, and Henri Pousseur — are not compatriots.

Berio does not deprecate tonal music of the past but he considers
tonality to be outmoded as a principle of contemporary composition:
"In tonal music there were predetermined forms; now we invent form
every time. In tonal music there was a hierarchy, with melody first,
then harmony and finally rhythm taking their places. Now there are
no such components — no melody as such.

"Tonality can still work, of course, for moments of escapism — when
one wants to tickle oneself — like with jazz. But for serious art, absolutely NO!"

II

During the Metropolitan Opera strike, Rudolf Bing delivered a
series of lectures on opera. At the end of one such hour at Juilliard, a
man in the audience asked the subject of the next lecture. "This one,"
he said, "was very disappointing, nothing but gossip and anecdotes.
You treated the subject like a party joke." Startled at the insult, Bing
demanded to know who the man was. "I'm a composer," the man said.

Originally published as "How to Avoid Being in Vogue?" in
The New York Times, February 15, 1970.

A student in the back of the room rose and proudly proclaimed: "That's Luciano Berio!"

Berio not only fights Bing; he persistently fights what he calls a "delayed Beethovian concept of art," the idea that a work of art is a closed object with the genius-musician behind all the controls. In this, the Italian composer has separated from his friend Pierre Boulez. Since 1957, Berio has moved steadily towards a breakdown of both the physical and emotional space between performer and audience. In *This Means That* Berio brings together a number of highly recognizable ingredients: mezzo-soprano Cathy Berberian (the composer's first wife), the Swingle Singers, Charles De Carlo, president of Sarah Lawrence College, and folk songs from Italy, Yugoslavia and Rumania. He has chosen such people and such melodies so that they may project their special identities, interact with each other, and emerge transformed.

"I must transform things," Berio said, "and in order to make a transformation clear, you should deal with familiar objects. I'd use President Nixon if he were available. You can only transform what the audience knows."

*

There is no real score to *This Means That*: it starts with the college president giving a lecture, moves into a musical concept, then into what we might call a happening, and finally into a situation with all of the house lights out. Only the passages between the various episodes have been composed; Berio prepared the tape last spring at the Studio di Fonologia in Milan. The tape serves as a "skeleton" which can integrate, connect, and develop different kinds of behavior — not necessarily all musical.

This Means That was first performed in France with only tape and solo performers. In Brussels, it received a more elaborate treatment and, in Rome, a still more lavish presentation. Berio says, "The piece is open to anything. In Rome we used a symphony orchestra."

*

Berio admits he is politically "to the left". His comments on American life and art are harsh: "There is," he said, in English that is sometimes abstruse, "a fetishism here based solely on money. Rich people tend to reduce what should be a genuine cultural phenomenon into the preservation of an institution. People controlling opera here are really stupid. The good directors are few — you can count them on the fingers of one hand. And the whole of American musical life is controlled by the very rich. I just received a call from the conductor of the Oakland Symphony who will conduct my *Sinfonia* there in two weeks. He said that one of the orchestra's trustees offered a donation of $6,000 to the orchestra if it would just not perform my work. One of the reasons, I guess, is that it's new. Another may be my use of the name Martin Luther King."

Berio went on to say that even the creative aspects of American life are affected by the capitalistic idea. "The automobile industry views people as drivers. All men are viewed in relation to a product. So American music is overwhelmed by a special kind of commercial thinking in which things are separated, broken down, and viewed at incredibly short range. One group of composers attacks another in order to sell its own product. Such measuring according to an arbitrary scale implies that something has gone seriously wrong, that there is a lack of commitment to music. Musicians who participate in this kind of attack do not understand that history is moving them *in spite* of their intentions, that history is actually moving through them."

I asked Berio why, in the light of his hostility to American cultural life, he comes to the United States. "I am here because each of us is responsible for what others of us do. The possibility of transforming things is greater here. I can contribute more here than anywhere else but I could not live in the United States unless I went to Europe every month or two."

262

LUCIANO BERIO

*

Berio, who generally dresses in khaki work clothes, sympathizes with radical youth movements. "The SDS," he said, "consists of just a few thousand kids who tried to compete with a complex institution and found they could not transform it with gestures. The same thing will happen with the female revolution; women do not understand the complexity of the Establishment. Negroes no longer make such mistakes. They are organizing themselves from the inside in a number of very subtle ways. They know that in order to change something, they have to develop something equally complex. One positive thing that came out of Vietnam is the knowledge that a small body of people can compete with and challenge a large and powerful body as long as there is an inner reason."

Despite numerous performances of his work, Berio is depressed. He says that he is filled with "troubles and solitude". He speaks with nostalgia of the 1950s when he, Boulez, Stockhausen and Pousseur were all together in Germany. "There was a common feeling while we were there. We were busy developing a new ground of musical thinking. There was a fight against the Establishment in which all of us were deeply engaged. Today the fight is won and each of us is on his own. The community of feeling no longer exists."

How strange for Berio to be so sad when it appears he has the best of all possible worlds. But his very success may be the cause of his anguish. In a recent note to this writer, he told the following story: "Ravel was offered the Legion d'Honneur. He refused it. Satie commented: 'It is not enough to refuse the Legion d'Honneur; one must not do anything to deserve it."

POSTSCRIPT: *In 1993-94, Berio, who has remained prolific throughout his life, delivered the Charles Eliot Norton Poetics of Music Lectures at Harvard University.*

Hans Werner Henze
CREDIT: Walter Schels

4

HANS WERNER HENZE

Hans Werner Henze is one of the two most significant composers in Germany since World War II, Karlheinz Stockhausen being the other. However, Henze's career has followed quite a different course from Stockhausen's. While Stockhausen has emerged as the leader of Europe's musical avant-garde, Henze writes for the traditional listener. Whether he composes tonally or uses more advanced techniques, whether he writes opera or instrumental pieces, Henze's goal is to make "expressive" music.

Henze came to New York to conduct six composition seminars at the Manhattan School of Music, and to supervise the school's production of his first opera, *Boulevard Solitude*, composed in 1950-51. At 45, Henze is a soft-spoken bachelor — without an apparent trace of arrogance — who speaks openly about himself. He talks of his poverty-stricken childhood and of his addiction to pipe smoking. He says that European journalists are cruel: some write that he turned socialist because he is homosexual and planned to use the movement as a source of boys, while others claim he made the move to counter Stockhausen's radical music with radical politics.

While Henze asserts that both accusations are untrue, he does not deny Stockhausen's power. Henze notes that his own most gifted student at the Mozarteum in Salzburg during the middle 1960s could not get his work performed because he wasn't writing like Stockhausen, and that at Expo 70 in Osaka, the German pavilion played Stockhausen's tapes seven hours a day.

Twenty years ago, Henze and Stockhausen stood on the same side of the esthetic fence, writing 12-tone music in Darmstadt, Germany.

Originally published as "Hans Werner Henze: Where the 'Action' Music Is" in *The New York Times*, July 16, 1972.

Henze first heard Schoenberg in 1946, through broadcasts from the BBC radio. It was the first modern music he had ever heard, for Hitler had suppressed all "deviant" art. Drawn to the sound, Henze became a pupil of René Leibowitz who had studied with Schoenberg in 1932. Henze described Leibowitz: "He analyzed Schoenberg scores so that young people could understand how marvelously the structures were laid out and how this music was related to music of the preceding time. He wanted his pupils to know there was no real gap between Wagner and what happened later."

Henze reminisced about Darmstadt during the early 1950s when his fellow students included not only Stockhausen, but Boulez, Nono and Berio. "It was really quite beautiful then. Here was a group of young friends all working together on a new kind of music. They wanted to bring music forward. Then something happened. The directors of regional radio systems began to play one composer against another. They behaved like 18th-century princes, but it wasn't as harmful in the 18th century because there were many courts then and the competition was among princes, not composers."

The directors of German radio exert formidable control for they not only support orchestras but commission works and produce festivals. Henze commented that Americans who envy the subsidy of music by the German radio do not know the consequences of the monopolies that result.

"What radio directors decide," Henze explained, "depends on individual taste, not on social responsibility. In Germany of the 1950s, composers knew they would have to follow the mainstream of fashion. This was the situation: there were two major festivals, one at Darmstadt and the other at Donaueschingen. This became the guideline for the rest of the composers on how to behave artistically. There was the totally organized serial year, the electronic year, the aleatory year, the not-so-aleatory year. I saw the whole thing becoming a market. Productions were merchandise in the hands of the media. I was horrified by the power civil servants had over the des-

266

tiny of art so, in 1954, I left Germany. Leibowitz left for the same reasons that year.

"At that time radio directors were promoting totally organized serial music, music not supposed to express anything. I found in that musical attitude the beginning of fascism. I hate that word — because it is so over-used — but this was a new, subtle, noiseless fascism, terribly refined, clever and slick. When everything is computerized, when the voice of the creative person is not heard any more because it has been made unhearable by system, then fascism prevails. Art for art's sake is fascistic!"

Turning his back on serialism, Henze moved to Italy and built a villa outside of Rome which is now his permanent home. Between 1954 and 1966 he wrote operas, ballets and orchestral pieces which reveal his facility in any style. Henze is, above all, eclectic, and does not commit himself to one compositional idea. To say this is not to deny his talent but rather to emphasize there is no "Henze sound". Sometimes one senses compromise: the *Elegy for Young Lovers* is solid and tight while *The Young Lord* is often maudlin and loose. But sentimentality never interfered with popular success and, by the mid-1960s, Henze was probably the most prolific and performed composer in Europe working in the traditional idiom. This period culminated in *The Bassarids*, with a text by W. H. Auden and Chester Kallman, produced at the Salzburg Festival in 1966.

It was shortly after this triumph that Henze, who had never engaged in politics, met Rudi Dutschke, the radical student leader in Germany, and became a socialist. He did not, however, give up his villa or his Maserati or alter his life in any apparent way. I asked if journalists question him about the contradiction between his lifestyle and political philosophy. He said they do and added that those questions "bore me to death. If I sold my automobile, I'd be a little saint. I could go into Central Park singing and playing the tambourine. I am a very hardworking man and the comfort I live in is no better or worse than that of any composer in any socialist country."

It may be that Henze embraced socialism because socialist realism provided him with the philosophical support he needed. Though his "accessible" music continued to keep him isolated from his colleagues, an outsider in the world of the avant-garde, now at least he was part of a larger, more important historical movement. "My operas," Henze said, "all written before 1967, were personal complaints about being lonely. I am no longer lonely," he added, "and that is because of socialism."

To announce his new commitment, Henze composed *The Raft of the Medusa*, an oratorio which he himself was to conduct in its first performance in Hamburg in December, 1967. Dedicated to the memory of Ché Guevara who had been killed in Bolivia two months before, the work contains a finale that is an open call to revolution. But the audience learned nothing of the dedication or the end because the piece was never performed. Before it began, revolutionary slogans appeared on stage and radical students waved the red flag, all part of Henze's design. Police were called, the concert canceled and, according to the composer, his rate of performance in Germany plunged.

But his commitment remained intact. Henze not only played an active role in the student upheavals in Germany in 1968, he has also visited Cuba three times since then. Once he stayed more than six months and conducted an original symphony he wrote while he was there.

Henze charted his compositional life: 1948-54, 12-tone music and serialism; 1954-66, freely invented composition without serial parameters; from 1966 on, the displacement of opera by "action music", in which musical instruments are the instruments of action and the musicians are the players on stage.

Henze told me his theater music is autobiographical; his most recent work is no exception to that. *The Tedious Journey to the Flat of Natasha Ungeheuer* traces the difficulties a member of the bourgeoisie encounters on the path to socialism. The work is scored for 17 musicians. The protagonist, a baritone, sings, speaks, and covers the spectrum in between while a percussionist provides a counterpoint. The remaining musicians are divided three ways. A chamber group symbolizes the bourgeoisie; because it is they who made society sick, they wear surgeon's gowns and bloody bandages. Members of a brass ensemble are police officers; they use their horns not only to make music but as instruments of torture as well. A pop group represents the escapist hippie world. There is, in addition, an electronic tape with the voice of Natasha Ungeheuer, "the siren of a false utopia", who tries to seduce the intellectual hero into identifying with and talking about the revolution without committing himself to the class struggle.

I asked Henze how it felt to supervise a production of *Boulevard Solitude*, a piece in a genre he now rejects. "One of the pleasures," Henze replied, "of being a composer is that of hearing an early work. It evokes many memories — where you were when you wrote it, how you felt then, why you did it the way you did.

"But the truth is I don't think I've changed my style very much. I can only recall that after the performance of my Sixth Symphony in Havana in 1970, I felt disappointed because it sounded so much like music I had written before, even if it was more intense, more violent. My emotions are nourished by new motives now, and that makes my handwriting tremble a bit, but what I say and how I say it still comes from the same person."

5

KARLHEINZ STOCKHAUSEN
AND HANS WERNER HENZE

Zubin Mehta will conduct the American premières of two German works: Karlheinz Stockhausen's *Jubilee* and Hans Werner Henze's *Barcarola*. Mehta says he chose the Stockhausen "because it is an interesting score as well as a a festive, contemporary piece, good to open the season with. I came to Stockhausen late in life, performing him for the first time last year. Henze is different. He presents a larger spectrum and I have always admired him."

Stockhausen and Henze have much in common. Born in the late 1920s—each was the first child in his family—they grew up poor in Nazi Germany. Both had schoolteacher fathers who were killed in the war and both, in their mid-20s, got involved in the postwar revolution against musical tradition that centered in Darmstadt, Germany. Because Schoenberg, Webern and Berg were already dead and because the repression and militarism of the 1930s had stunted and driven out many other composers, Stockhausen and Henze, still in their 20s, were the most famous of living German composers. The same can be said of them today. No one on the horizon threatens their position of eminence. Both not only command high fees; they produce prolifically.

All this would seem to indicate they would be close colleagues. But they are not. Nor do they attract the same audiences.

*

Henze has been characterized by Peter Heyworth, the British critic,

Originally published as "Karlheinz Stockhausen and Hans Werner Henze: Contrasts in the Aging German Avant-Garde" in *The New York Times*, September 6, 1981.

270

Karlheinz Stockhausen
CREDIT: Clive Alba / Karlheinz Stockhausen Verlag

as the "principal protagonist of musical conservatism... the main provider of viable new works so desperately needed by the vast network of German opera houses and orchestras." Although, in the early postwar years, Henze participated in the 12-tone movement, he soon abandoned it for a somewhat softer idiom. Convinced that 12-tone writing could never be felicitous for the voice, he chose to compose in more traditional ways and probably did as much to continue opera in this century as the English composer Benjamin Britten did, to whom he once dedicated a work.

During the 1950s and early 60s, Henze turned to Stravinsky-like composition and enlisted as librettists W. H. Auden and Chester Kallman, who had been Stravinsky's collaborators in *The Rake's Progress*. The union resulted in the operas *Elegy for Young Lovers* of 1961 and *The Bassarids* of 1966. Stravinsky was not Henze's sole influence. He says he heard *The Marriage of Figaro* at least 60 times as a boy and kept the score in front of him as he wrote *Elegy*. Henze not only quotes others; often he paraphrases himself. His early opera, *König Hirsch*, finds echoes in his Fourth Symphony while his Fifth contains resonances of *Elegy*.

Although Henze's lyricism and rich orchestral writing drew such collaborators as Auden and Kallman, Margot Fonteyn and the filmmaker and opera director Luchino Visconti, it also heightened his isolation from other composers, especially those who were in the limelight for their avant-garde activities. Henze's music, although popular with audiences, drew little particular attention in the press.

In the fall of 1967, Henze met Rudi Dutschke, the professional student agitator. Dutschke, then in his 30s, was shot in a scuffle with the police. Henze not only paid Dutschke's hospital bills, he also invited him to recuperate in his own house. That was when, according to the composer, his "crisis of conscience" began. Henze's new politics stemmed from this time. In London last week, he expressed his purpose in composing in this way: "To write good pieces that are accessible to the untrained and underprivileged listener." Henze claims that the 1968 unrest achieved two ends: "It brought forth a generation of audiences who demand that music must be satisfactory from a moral and social point of view, and gave rise to new journalists on the left who are sympathetic" to his kind of music.

Since 1968, Henze has composed what he calls "action music", which is connected to his politics. The small theater pieces and dramatic concert works are harder-edged, less sonorous than his early operas. Those same characteristics prevail in the large-scale work, *We Come to the River*, Henze's first opera in ten years. With 126 characters and three separate orchestras, it was given its first performance at Covent Garden in 1976. Although the allegory deals with the harsh regime of Pinochet in Chile, Henze says this work, like all the others, contains many autobiographical references.

Henze's politics may seem seem hypocritical, but his talent and musicianship are very real.

*

If Henze is a principal protagonist of musical conservatism, then Stockhausen is the leader of the radical. Often described as a "tonal architect", Stockhausen has probably done more to move music into untouched areas of sound than any of his European colleagues. By the late 1950s, he was generally recognized as the front runner in the avant-garde.

In 1977, Stockhausen embarked on a seven-evening cycle of operas collectively entitled *Licht [Light]*. *Donnerstag [Thursday] aus Licht*, the first completed work, uses not only such contemporary devices as tape, amplification and electronically generated sound but also a full chorus and orchestra.

Stockhausen explains that he has "composed one formula for *Licht* and that seven sections of that formula will expand to become seven parts of the whole. Every limb represents one day."

The formulas that now occupy the center of Stockhausen's creative life are made up of pitches that appear in fixed orders, a little bit like recurring melodies. The rhythm may change, but the intervals may not. Stockhausen stresses that the formula has nothing in common with the series, so central to new music in the postwar years, for it is not subjected to the various procedures connected to serial composition. It does not appear backwards or with its intervals inverted.

"This is not about an object," Stockhausen says. "It is an integrated form with all the parameters already considered." Just as the pitches of each section of the formula expand to provide the pitch structure of a full evening's work, so do the durations of the notes expand to determine the specific lengths of the same work.

Licht is based, therefore, not so much on musical considerations as on mathematical ones. Its premise is not at all alien to the one behind Stockhausen's *Kontrapunkte* of 1953: "Not the same shape in a changing light," he said then. "Rather this: different shapes in the same light that penetrates everywhere."

*

Stockhausen's self-conviction is awesome. When he delivered a series of lectures in Rome, he berated his audience for not knowing enough of his music and listed his works and the books written about him. "The English," he said, "know every note."

Here is how egocentric he is: in the story behind *Donnerstag*, the hero, Michael the Archangel, is clearly the composer himself. In the last act, Michael is welcomed to Heaven as a Great Being. In a local Italian paper, Stockhausen is quoted as saying that his heroes are the archangel and God *in that order*. Despite this self-adulation, he can be straightforward and direct. The American composer John Harbison, who attended several of his Rome lectures, characterizes Stockhausen's temperament as "an interesting mix of unreasonable arrogance and an urge to communicate."

Stockhausen has six children who are all skilled musicians. Three performed in *Donnerstag*. His second wife supervised the production, and an American woman, Suzanne Stephens, whom he refers to as his "partner", played the basset-horn. Stockhausen's oldest son, Markus, was the soloist for a concerto for trumpet and orchestra that constitutes the entire second act. The composer says he wrote the concerto before the first act and that he wrote it expressly for Markus.

Stockhausen appears to give his trust only to those who commit themselves wholly to him. That includes his principal soloist, a group of 15 performers — four singers, eight instrumentalists and three dancers — most of whom have been with him since 1974. In 1973, he ended his relationship with Universal Edition, his publisher of 20 years, and formed his own Stockhausen Verlag. Stockhausen runs everything: the score to *Donnerstag* lists him as the opera's librettist, composer, choreographer and director.

Throughout history, there have always been two kinds of artists: those who chart new ground and those who sum it all up. Among the innovators are Beethoven, Wagner, Schoenberg and Stockhausen; among the consolidators are Bach, Mozart, Brahms and Henze. Esthetic convictions and matters of ego made Wagner and Brahms enemies. Similar factors keep Stockhausen and Henze from being friends.

POSTSCRIPT: Stockhausen continues to work on Licht *(1994).*

Benjamin Britten
CREDIT: Frank Driggs Collection

6

BENJAMIN BRITTEN

"I have absolutely no feeling that music should go in a certain direction," said British composer Benjamin Britten. "The development of art does not interest me. I am skeptical of those who exaggerate the importance of language. It is what one *does* that interests me."

Britten does a great deal. A composer of immense stature and a distinguished performer as well, he is as prolific today as he ever was. The prodigious invention of the mid-1940s — *Seven Sonnets of Michelangelo* and the operas *Peter Grimes*, *The Rape of Lucretia* and *Albert Herring* — is matched by his compositions of the mid-1960s — the *War Requiem*, a Cello Concerto for Rostropovich and the three Church Parables: *Curlew River*, *The Burning Fiery Furnace* and *The Prodigal Son*.

And he works in a traditional way. Although he was greatly attracted to Schoenberg and Berg during his student days, Britten returned to the tonal fold. He suggests that the Germans and Viennese developed the 12-tone technique because they lived in the shadow of Wagner. "They had to create their own series of rules," the composer said, "in order to break his titanic hold. But that problem did not exist for me. I find I cannot abandon the key idea. There is a tension in a key center that is entirely essential to my work."

Britten compared himself to Mahler, whose music exerted a great influence on him. "Lyricism is my life's blood, too. My use of tonality is different from Mahler's, but that is because we are different people — not because of 50 years that separate us in time."

Britten came to the United States with his long-time associate, the extraordinary English tenor Peter Pears. They came ostensibly to give joint concerts but actually to see philanthropists and representatives

Originally published as "Composers Talk Too Much:
Interview with Benjamin Britten" in *The New York Times*,
November 16, 1969.

of foundations about raising money for the Aldeburgh Festival, a festival they founded on the Suffolk seacoast 22 years ago. Aldeburgh's main concert hall, the Maltings, built in 1967 and frequently acclaimed the best hall in England, was damaged by a fire last summer. To rebuild and enlarge it, Britten and Pears need $200,000.

The composer views the music festival as "the only answer to the recent recession in the concert and opera world. People come to a festival to meet old friends, leave their homes for a while, and enjoy a holiday. At Aldeburgh audiences enjoyed immensely entertaining operas by Harrison Birtwistle and Gordon Crosse. Admittedly the audiences were captive ones. When the works were brought to London, they failed completely because no one came. People in London do not trust new works by composers whose reputations have not yet been made."

Britten's suite at the Essex House was filled with people the morning I called on him. The composer, a slender, graying man was standing inconspicuously in the background. Donald Mitchell, his publisher, was taking telephone calls and arranging business and social events, which included an evening with the poet Robert Lowell. Peter Pears, in a conservative business suit, was armed with publicity on Aldeburgh and immediately spoke of the festival's needs. Camera and sound men from BBC prepared to televise part of our interview and there were a number of others present as well. Britten's notorious reticence with the press obviously does not stem from a need to be alone.

Dressed neatly, British style, in a maroon cardigan, gray slacks, light blue shirt and colorful tie, the composer emerged from the entourage. He appeared modest, almost deferential. Speaking quietly, generally in response to a question, Britten frequently nodded to Pears, suggesting that he reply instead. I asked why he so rarely spoke to journalists:

"Composers are inclined to talk far too much and not let the music speak for itself. I don't enjoy talking very much. One has lots of ideas that cannot be expressed in words. Also one can change one's ideas and then be imprisoned by what one has said.

"Until the 19th century," he explained, "the composer was a servant of society. Mozart tried to please his public in a way to which no composer would admit today. But with the industrial revolution, money fell into the hands of the uneducated. It was then that painters and musicians found themselves out on a limb. In reaction to this situation, they began to blow up their egos and as a result became far too self-important. Now the artist is the glorified mouthpiece of God.

"Beethoven was the first of these — a man who thought he was truly holy. I believe in the reverse of that. I believe in the artist serving society. It is better to be a bad composer writing for society than to be a bad composer writing against it. At least your work can be of *some* use."

Britten identifed his close friends as Aaron Copland, Hans Werner Henze, and Dimitri Shostakovich, all composers who reject "art for art's sake" in favor of art for an audience. Britten frequently visits Russia where he spends time with Shostakovich. He dedicated his *Prodigal Son* to the Soviet artist, who dedicated his 14th symphony to Britten.

*

Within the span of an enormously prolific life, Britten has focused much attention on children. He writes to entertain them (*Let's Make an Opera, Noye's Fludde*) and to educate them musically (*The Young Person's Guide to the Orchestra*). He writes about them (*The Turn of the Screw*) and in response to their specific requests (a highly demanding quartet for flute, violin and two pianos for a pair of gifted, 12-year-old Hungarian twins). Britten writes repeatedly for high boys' voices. I asked him about his involvement or identification with the young. Surprised, the composer paused and replied:

"I try and avoid giving that kind of thing any thought. Do you know the book Sartre wrote on Genet? Genet said that after he read

279

it he found it impossible to work. I do know that violence worries me. I become frightfully angry when children are treated badly. Maybe," the composer smiled, "there is something in my subconscious that gives rise to this, and I am suppressing it."

He began to talk of his early life in Lowestoft, a village in Suffolk very near Aldeburgh. "My mother was a very sweet singer. My father, a dental surgeon, had an open, clear mind and almost a dislike of music. But, as my mother loved music and my father felt that I should do as I wanted, there really was no problem at all. I started to write music when I was five. I just kept putting patterns all over the paper and then asked my mother to play the notes. She couldn't, of course; the music was unplayable. When I was six or seven, the notes became associated with their sounds in my mind."

*

By the time he was 14, Britten had composed ten piano sonatas, six string quartets, three suites for piano, an oratorio and dozens of songs. For several years, he studied in London with composer Frank Bridge and then went to the Royal College of Music. It was then that he became attracted to Schoenberg and Berg.

In 1938, when he was 25, Britten met Pears, then 28 years old. The composer's life assumed a new focus. With Pears in mind, Britten has created ten principal operatic roles, seven song cycles and three canticles. In addition to composing for Pears, Britten accompanies him at the piano on recital tours that take them as far as Eastern Europe and South America.

*

"I began my relationship with Pears," Britten said, "because I wanted to exploit the English language. The relationship has affected my musical life enormously. We share a great love of English vocal music and take pleasure in bringing it everywhere.

"Personal tragedies can go all around one. But not being able to work is the most awful tragedy of all," he went on, recalling the one time in his life when he could not work. It was during the early 1940s. He and Pears had settled in the United States. But World War II broke out, and the composer "felt the tug back to Europe. But unless you were of military importance, you could hardly get out of the United States. I waited six months for passage and during that time was unable to compose. As soon as I stepped on the boat, I started to write and could not stop. I wrote *A Ceremony of Carols*, the *Hymn to St. Cecilia*, and a number of other pieces.

"But events do not generally interfere with my work. When we first arrived back in England in the war, life there was very disturbed. It was then that I wrote *Peter Grimes*, the *Sonnets of Michelangelo* and the quartet. What one writes is the digested result of other experiences recollected in tranquility."

POSTSCRIPT: In June 1976 Britten was elevated to the peerage of Great Britain by Queen Elizabeth II and became a Lord. He died on December 4 of that year.

VI

GROUPS, CENTERS, MEDIA

SYMPHONY OF THE NEW WORLD

THE NEW YORK PHILHARMONIC

LINCOLN CENTER

THE HOPKINS CENTER AT DARTMOUTH COLLEGE

JOHN CROSBY AND THE SANTA FE OPERA

COLUMBIA-PRINCETON ELECTRONIC MUSIC CENTER

VLADIMIR USSACHEVSKY AT BELL LABS

TOD MACHOVER AT IRCAM

Introduction

In the spring of 1961, when my essay on Lincoln Center appeared in *Commentary* magazine, the projected top price for a seat at the new Metropolitan Opera was $13. Today the top price at the Met is about $130. The difference between the two figures indicates some things have changed.

Some things have not. In 1967, when I wrote "The Negro in Search of an Orchestra", there were hardly any blacks in symphony orchestras. The same situation prevails today. To say this is not to suggest no effort was made to turn things around. Rather it is to emphasize that those efforts have come too late.

Here is some of what has happened: in 1966 African-Americans Earl Madison, cellist, and Arthur Davis, bassist, filed a complaint with the New York State Commission on Human Rights against Leonard Bernstein and the New York Philharmonic. They charged discriminatory practices against blacks and cited the refusal to allow behind-the-screen auditions, which would have prevented prejudice in hiring. Bernstein, on the stand, justified his position saying that judges have to be able to see, for example, the bowing technique of a string player to know that performer's capacity for endurance.

After the hearing, the *New York Law Journal* ran this headline: "Philharmonic Ordered to End Racial Bias". It was only then that orchestras held behind-the-screen auditions until at least the final round.

Whitney Young, then director of the National Urban League, called it "shameful for a major cultural institution, one that gives concerts in a beautiful hall financed by public subscriptions, to cling to a color bar.... Behind the red and gold facade of our major cultural institutions is the rotten stench of racism."

Federal laws and conditional funding play a role in reducing manifestations of bias. In 1989 the Detroit Symphony faced losing its state money if it did not conform to appropriate representation in the racial composition of the orchestra. Perhaps 80% of Detroit is black; the Symphony has always maintained high standards. Part of Michigan's demand held that the orchestra could not even hold an audition unless a minority player was applying for the job. Nevertheless, with such requirements imposed from the outside, and apparent good will on the inside, one still sees no more than two or three blacks sitting on that symphony stage. Today, the same conditions apply to the New York Philharmonic. Management claims it wants real change in this arena, but in the summer of 1994, only one black musician was on its permanent roster.

Why? Musicians, like athletes, must start young. Because of hard pressed economic conditions across the country, music education in the lower levels of the public schools is virtually non-existent. Then, too, all orchestras are engaged in the pursuit of good black players so that as soon as Detroit engages one, he or she is often seduced away into a different ensemble. A case in point is timpanist Randall Hicks who left Detroit mid-season to start playing in the New Jersey Symphony.

The elitist tone that has always characterized our major music organizations remains intact. Look at the Sante Fe Opera Company. John Crosby, its founder and director, is the son of parents who owned sugar plantations in Cuba. Crosby created the remarkable opera company that has flourished in New Mexico and, when it burned down, rebuilt it right away. In the summer of 1994, Crosby announced a renovation of the open-air theater that was expected to cost $16.7 million. Similar histories of our largest and most prestigious ensembles dependent on private donors characterize the vicissitudes of the New York Philharmonic as well as of the culture centers that have proliferated across the United States.

Lincoln Center, the first of these, was in the planning stage when I wrote about it in 1960. After it opened it became the model for the Kennedy Center in Washington and literally hundreds of other culture centers. In general, these complexes have generated much that is good. They have helped redevelop run-down areas in their cities, attracted new businesses and galleries and art movie houses, and have brought with them a tremendous upgrading of property values as well as tax revenue for their cities.

But even these material benefits did not come quickly or easily. In 1964 Rudolf Bing, general manager of the Met, said, "Lincoln Center was deteriorating into a free-for-all jungle" and, in June, 1994, the *New York Times*, in an overview of the center, described the five years following Bing's pronouncement as ones during which there were "constant conflicts among the Met, the New York City Opera, the New York Philharmonic and the New York City Ballet.... In 1967 John D. Rockefeller 3rd, the chairman of the Lincoln Center board, reported 'feelings of mistrust, fear, competition and even bitterness' among the center's constituents."

Much of this I predicted in my Lincoln Center article. But I also expressed two concerns that were far more important than those battles generated by jealousies. One was that New York's lively, decentralized musical life would become less lively when it became centralized into 14 acres of real estate in the west Sixties. Intentions at that time included the disappearance of Carnegie Hall, on 57th Street and Seventh Avenue, the Metropolitan Opera house on 38th street and Broadway, and the deterioration through disuse of the many smaller halls around the city. As it turned out, only the old Met came down, and everything else remained in place as art organizations in the United States continued to flourish.

My second concern was that Lincoln Center, particularly as it represented itself in its advance publicity, would exude a show business panache that would exact as its price an atmosphere that would diminish creativity. Whether, as I suggested at the beginning of this book, the period of Western musical art is at its end and Lincoln Center and the other centers merely reflect that fact, or whether these polished complexes helped bring this state about, is difficult to say with certainty.

What happened, however, to the Congregation of the Arts at Dartmouth's Hopkins Center, suggests the inevitability theory is the one that rings true.

Everything seemed right at Hopkins Center, both in the generous funding and in the bold concept. Nelson Rockefeller, a Dartmouth alumnus, contributed heavily to Hopkins and arranged that the same team of architects who designed Lincoln Center also design Dartmouth's art buildings. John Dickey, president of Dartmouth, selected conductor Mario di Bonaventura to head the program and gave him a professorship. It was di Bonaventura's notion to invite every significant European, American and South American composer to spend two weeks playing, conducting and supervising performances of as much of his own music as was humanly possible. In 1969, Witold Lutoslawski, the Polish composer, was quoted as saying that di Bonaventura was "the brain and the heart of the festival... one of the figures whose very existence in our time lets us think with optimism about the future of musical life in the world."

Yet after seven years the program was no more. President Dickey retired and his successor, John Kemeny, who had worked at Los Alamos, and was Professor of Mathematics at Dartmouth, succeeded him as president. Kemeny had no interest in the program, and he let it go.

Kemeny, who was ultimately responsible for the death of this program, which, more than any other at that time, concentrated on the composer, was a computer expert. Among other contributions, he created the computer language known as Basic. In 1987 Dartmouth built a $1 million computer-music amphitheater that allows students to "write" and play back orchestrated compositions at the keyboard not of a Steinway but an Apple Macintosh.

The pieces here dealing with electronic music go back to its earliest days—the beginning of the Columbia-Princeton Electronic Music Center and the explorations in computer-music technology at Bell Labs in Murray Hill, New Jersey. The question that follows is whether

288

INTRODUCTION

electronic music will finally provide the impetus needed to keep art music growing in the West. To be generous all one can say at this time is that it is still in an experimental stage. What Bell Laboratories' Max Mathews told me—that "computers will be smaller, cheaper, more available... compositional rules will be built into them... they will be used as performing instruments"—has all come to pass. Still, the innovations we have so far seen that are removed from the hands of ordinary people are more in evidence in the technology of stage productions than in music that is designed for the concert hall. Tod Machover, a 38-year-old composer who worked at IRCAM, Boulez's computer music institute in Paris, for seven years and is now in charge of the Media Laboratory at Massachusetts Institute of Technology, said in June, 1994, "The danger of electronic music today lies in the degrading of music itself."

Machover's remark would not surprise Charles Wuorinen. In 1993, in a conversation with me designed to provide liner notes for a Koch recording of his works, Wuorinen said:

"From the earliest time that I can remember having any thoughts about the world of composition and the meaning of the tremendous changes that have taken place in the 20th century, I had the uneasy feeling that innovation could not continue forever and that changes that had been initiated before World War I were far more profound than the seemingly more radical changes introduced into the world by, say, electronic music. I have been proved right in that respect because we now see tremendous electronic sophistication used to produce diatonic burblings. So the underlying musical ideas have in fact regressed. Everyone used to say that electronic music was the most radical thing yet. And those of us who were involved in it always said, 'It's just another instrument; it's just a tool.' "

A point of interest is that it was someone whose field was outside music who played a crucial role in nourishing the electronic medium in its early years. Cultural historian Jacques Barzun, whose long and distinguished teaching career was spent at Columbia, fought for the

289

money and space to get the Electronic Music Center going in the basement of Low Library, and then fought again to keep it going and keep the equipment up-to-date. Barzun took part in the negotiations that led to the joint Columbia-Princeton Center, the struggle at that point being to accept an unheard-of association with another university. Finally Barzun helped arrange the first campus concert in McMillin Theater, presiding over it and speaking to the audience to calm its fears.

1

SYMPHONY OF THE NEW WORLD

"If you're black, they think you can't read music. But if you *can* read music, they're sure you can't swing."

Thus Warren Smith, percussionist with the Symphony of the New World, characterized the somewhat schizophrenic position of the black who aims at being an "art" musician. To be a musician of any color in the United States is to have chosen — from a financial standpoint — something less than the best of all possible worlds. To be a black musician in search of a symphony orchestra may well be to have chosen the worst.

Prejudice against blacks in the field of instrumental art music appears to continue unabated. Apart from one black player in the New York Philharmonic, one in the Cleveland Orchestra, and three in the Pittsburgh Symphony, such major orchestras as those of Philadelphia, Boston and Chicago currently have no black musicians in any of their chairs. Conductors of the topflight ensembles claim that nonwhite musicians with professional experience are impossible to find. Blacks answer that the lesser orchestras refuse to provide the "necessary" experience.

The Symphony of the New World, now in its fourth year, was designed to put an end to this disheartening pattern. Of its 88 members, 36 are black, many of whom have had no previous professional work in this field. Now they are playing in the orchestra with such well-known instrumentalists as Mischa Gusikoff, former concertmaster in the Philadelphia Orchestra, and Elias Carmen, who was first bassoonist in the NBC Symphony under Toscanini.

Originally published as "Symphony of the New World: The Negro in Search of an Orchestra" in *The New York Times*, November 26, 1967.

The plan has begun to work. Instrumentalists with the orchestra have been hired by the Baltimore, Syracuse, Denver, Quebec, North Carolina, Richmond, Minneapolis and Milwaukee Symphonies and four of its members are among the five black players in Stokowski's American Symphony Orchestra in New York. Benjamin Steinberg, director of the Symphony of the New World, hopes that one solvent day—when his orchestra is giving a minumum of 20 concerts a year—they will all come to him. He may be right. Steinberg—who is white—is one of their true friends.

But friends have been hard to find. The blacks in his organization relate—with passion—incidents of a discriminatory nature to which they say they are continually exposed. Many cite Donald White, the only black in the Cleveland Orchestra, who has been sitting in the last stand of the cello section for nine years. Last year, his tenth with that orchestra, he was promoted to next-to-last stand. They attribute this position not to inadequate talent, but to racial prejudice. And they speak of flutist Harold Jones who, after auditioning successfully for the conductor of the St. Louis Symphony and settling on a salary with that orchestra's manager, was asked to appear for an extra audition before a select group of musicians in order to prove, one of his colleagues said, "that he was a good enough Negro to get the job." Jones refused to comply.

*

The Symphony of the New World, by its very nature, removes the specter of discrimination from the unqualified pleasures of first-rate music-making. The genesis of the organization can be traced directly to the social conscience of the 51-year-old Steinberg, who made his Town Hall debut as a violinist before he was 12, and played with the Pittsburgh and NBC orchestras. Steinberg, with the black conductors Dean Dixon and Everett Lee, began to work for the establishment of an integrated orchestra as early as 1940 but, because of insufficient funds, the dream never materialized. Disillusioned, Dixon and Lee went to Sweden — Dixon became conductor of the Gothenburg Symphony — but Steinberg stayed on, interrupting his crusade from time to time to conduct such ensembles as the Leningrad, Yalta and Moscow Symphonies and our own Ballet Theater. In 1964 he crystallized his previous efforts by setting up a steering committee of 14 musicians, 12 of whom were black, and thus formed the nucleus of the present orchestra.

A gift of $1,000 from the Equitable Life Assurance Society and many small donations from black supporters provided the initial financial backing for the Symphony of the New World. The Martha Baird Rockefeller Fund offered a $5,000 grant to be matched two for one; with the help of $1,000 from American Airlines, Friends of the New World Symphony raised the required $10,000. This year the National Foundation for the Arts contributed $25,000 and the New York State Council on the Arts agreed to subsidize several concerts in low-income areas of the city. However, the Ford Foundation, by far the largest of all foundations, has refused Steinberg's repeated requests for money.

The secret of Steinberg's success in establishing and maintaining this orchestra is two-fold. The first reason is concrete: he hired a black artist, Harry Smyles, a graduate of Western Reserve University, who was once described by Serge Koussevitzky as an oboist "perfectly qualified to take a position in any orchestra in America." The second reason is less tangible. Some say it is that Steinberg was committed to this particular struggle well before the integrationist movement became fashionable. A black social worker, who is active with the Friends of the Symphony, was more explicit: "We love him. This is the only organization I support that is headed by a white man."

To the question of how he has kept the faith of black musicians in a time of such hostility against the white liberal, Steinberg replied: "I'm not a white liberal. I'm a white radical." But Steinberg's radical beliefs have had to be tempered by considerable diplomacy, for apart from

293

coping with the mammoth problems of any ordinary orchestra, he has to handle an imposing variety of complicated people.

To begin with, although symphony orchestras today generally have few women, there are 30 women in the Symphony of the New World. Steinberg's expansiveness knows no bounds. Of the 52 white musicians in the group, some are there for the same reason Steinberg is; some others have come for the extra money. As for the black players, they embody a wide spectrum of attitudes ranging from a certain compliance with the *status quo* to a more aggressive, separatist ideal.

James DePreist, guest conductor for the orchestra's concert at Philharmonic Hall, is not a militant man. He grew up on the same street in Philadelphia as his famous aunt, Marian Anderson, studied pre-law at the Wharton School of the University of Pennsylvania, and became a student of composer Vincent Persichetti at the Philadelphia Conservatory of Music. DePreist says that, as a child, he felt nothing was closed to him — everything was possible. Indeed, it seemed to work out that way. DePreist was sponsored by the State Department for tours of the Near and Far East in 1962, won a first place in the Dimitri Mitropoulos Competition in 1964, and as a result of that success, served as Bernstein's assistant with the New York Philharmonic for the following two years. Most guest conductors with the Symphony of the New World have offered at least one work by a black composer: DePreist, for his concert with the Symphony, chose Wagner, Beethoven and Shostakovich. And unlike most members of the orchestra who believe in bringing performances up to Harlem, DePreist has pressed for eliminating neighborhood concerts in favor of bringing black audiences down to Philharmonic Hall.

*

In a different position along the spectrum is Lucille Dixon, double-bass player, who trained under the late Frederick Zimmerman of the New York Philharmonic and played under Steinberg with the National Youth Association Orchestra during the early 1940s. With the advent of World War II, the orchestra disbanded and Dixon's white colleagues were placed with other symphonies. She was not. First she joined Earl Hines' band. Then, forming her own jazz group, Dixon began to work at the Savannah Club and did not pick up her bow again—in a serious capacity—until she began to play with the Symphony of the New World. Dixon, actively involved with the black cause, speaks with pride not only of her black colleagues in the orchestra but of audiences in Harlem which she characterizes as consistently loyal and attentive.

Finally, in a position removed from both DePreist and Dixon, there is a small corps of young, talented, bearded radicals. They are grateful to Steinberg for "making it possible to play music we love with well-trained members of our own race." Nevertheless, their appreciation is qualified. Ronald Lipscomb, 24-year-old cellist singled out by Bernard Greenhouse for a scholarship at the Manhattan School of Music, spoke quietly about the values at stake: "We are happy to be here. But this should be seen for what it is: a middle-class operation with integrationist ideals, having no relation whatever to the mass of black people." Several colleagues agreed: "Only a white man could have found the money and backing to make this orchestra work. But what we want now is a black orchestra: black owned, black operated and black controlled."

The audience for the concert was, as Lipscomb predicted, middle class. The first floor of Philharmonic Hall appeared to be dominated by white people while blacks filled the less expensive seats in the balconies. Steinberg estimates that of this almost full house, 60 per cent was black, whereas less than one percent of the orchestra's Harlem concerts are attended by white listeners. All who came to Philharmonic Hall—even those with children and infants—responded enthusiastically. In contrast to the early mass exodus of white matrons every Friday afternoon, when the New York Philharmonic subscription audience rushes for taxi cabs and suburban trains while the con-

295

cert is still in progress, all these listeners sat through the entire performance of the hour-long Symphony Nr. 11 by Shostakovich.

Black Americans have made great strides in the field of sports, theater, and government. Why have they not been able to move at a more rapid pace into the world of the present day symphonic organization? DePreist suggests that the reason lies in the traditional concept of the orchestra as a "plaything for the rich — a problem-free toy."

POSTSCRIPT: *The Symphony of the New World disbanded at the end of the 1976-77 season.*

2

THE NEW YORK PHILHARMONIC

In his *Philharmonic: A History of New York's Orchestra* Howard Shanet profits from America's love of record-keeping to tell his story with such particularity that his book should prove extremely useful for a long time to come.

The reader learns everything he ever wanted to know about the New York Philharmonic and—possibly—a little bit more. He learns not only the names of the musicians who played in concerts more than 100 years ago, but what they played, how they played, and how much they earned for their services. Shanet lists many in the audience as well, distinguishing those who purchased subscriptions from those who bought individual tickets. Concerning the opening concert, facts abound: that it was postponed for exactly one month and why, that it was held at the Apollo Rooms, "410 Broadway (east side of the street between Canal and Walker)," that it was 27 degrees outside but stale and stuffy inside, that between 600 and 650 people were seated in the house which could have accommodated about 700, that three conductors presided over the event and that none of them received as much as the "Porter-Messenger". Shanet tells us a ticket cost 83 cents and that this would have bought 15 pounds of mutton or six hours of a skilled carpenter's work.

The author describes the early days well. We learn that in 1839, three years before the opening Philharmonic concert, *Fidelio* ran 14 nights in a row in a 2,000 seat house and that the city had a population of only 312,000 at that time. Similarly, we learn of orchestras that came and went, the nature of the competition each represented, and

Review of "Philharmonic: A History of New York's Orchestra" by Howard Shanet in *The New York Times Book Review*, January 26, 1975.

the minor scandals that occurred from within: in 1843 the Philharmonic secretary stole $100 from the till and was impeached in April,
1844. Many intriguing facts emerge: until 1853 the musicians stood up
while they played, the better looking ones doubling as ushers; in 1901
millionaire Andrew Carnegie took over as president and contributed
$456. The appendix is almost as long as the text, including all the
programs between 1942 and 1971. The index is impeccable.

Shanet's book is clear, orderly and agreeable to read. But it is more
a chronicle than genuine history. At its most complex, history is not
only the story of past facts but an examination, an assessment of these
facts, a search into the various power struggles in an effort to determine why things moved as they did. In this particular history, the
author never pierces the surface, never tries to uncover the drama
below.

When Shanet introduces Arthur Judson, once the most powerful
man in American music, he does so by listing Judson's achievements
as though he were presenting him for membership in the Century
Club. We never get the feel of this man who, during the period between 1915 and 1956, managed the Philadelphia and New York Philharmonic Orchestras and held both jobs simultaneously for 13 years,
who represented virtually all the leading conductors, was adviser to
the Cincinnati Symphony, and brought together five competing agen-
cies into what is now Columbia Artists Management Inc. Thus Judson
was the principal source of supply of soloists and conductors to the
very orchestras he ran, a flagrant conflict of interest. Yet Shanet concludes: "Since Judson's flair for making money out of music led him
constantly to seek expanding audiences, he could honestly combine
profit-making with democratic ideals of public service and reconcile
his private business interests with his administration of the New York
Philharmonic."

And so it comes as a complete surprise when, several chapters later,
in the middle of the 1946-47 season, Artur Rodzinski resigned from the
post of musical director and pointed the finger directly at Judson: "The

298

three pillars of a soundly run orchestra," Rodzinski told reporters, "are the board, the manager and the musical director. As the New York Philharmonic is run, these pillars are not of equal importance, as they must be. The board and musical director revolve around the manager as if they were satellites." Shanet reports that the press sided with Rodzinski; otherwise he leaves it at that.

The author's reluctance to investigate the balance of power between management and artistic leadership in the Judson-Rodzinski affair gives a clue to the cautious tone of the book. Presenting large numbers of facts, Shanet rarely hazards bold comments or conclusions. Mahler and the Guarantor's Committee are a case in point. Shanet reports that a confrontation took place between the conductor and the "strong-willed ladies" who were chosen to supervise the selection of music after Mahler's advanced programming had displeased their group. Shanet assumes no stance. Instead, he describes Mahler as a "difficult man, tense and high strung," and later charactarizes the women's committee of that time as a group of "rich, hard-working, intelligent, loyal, and public spirited women... willing to give their time and money for the good of the city's musical life."

What moved Shanet to write this book? Now chairman of the music department of Columbia University and conductor of the University Orchestra, Shanet's first bona fide job was as assistant conductor under Leonard Bernstein with the City Symphony in 1946-47. When Bernstein became musical director of the New York Philharmonic in 1959, he brought in Shanet as program annotator. That same year the idea of a Philharmonic history came up and Bernstein suggested Shanet abandon his post in favor of this far more challenging enterprise.

At the outset the author defines what he hopes to prove: "I am determined to do what I can to combat the vast and largely unjustified, inferiority complex that has oppressed American music and continues to do so today." Considering the two men at the helm — Bernstein, the first American to become music director, and Carlos Mosely, who in a

State Department post had built up the country's first library of American music — Shanet's auspices and purposes were in perfect harmony. Virtually everyone acknowledged that. The first chapter was presented to Mrs. Lytle Hull when she was made honorary chairman of the society, and the book's publication was initially planned to coincide with the opening of Philharmonic Hall in 1962. When Shanet did not make that, it was planned to coincide with the opening birthday. So although the author claims this is not "official" history, it is very nearly that: when he takes Toscanini to task for not playing American music or hiring American soloists and guest conductors, he knows he isn't treading on very dangerous ground.

But Shanet's bias of time and place interferes most with detachment and good judgment when he deals with his own period. A chapter entitled "The Spectacular Conductor" is one long lyrical song of praise of Bernstein. If ever a qualifying statement intrudes on Bernstein's sloppiness or excessive sentiment, it is put into the mouths of critics and then repudiated seconds after that. Everything of the 60s is treated with superlatives. On the music director: "There was always a story or a picture in Leonard Bernstein because the musical love that flowed out of him sought and found people." On the high brass: "One of the strongest administrative-managerial teams that [the Philharmonic had] ever enjoyed — individually inventive yet accustomed to working together." On the still troublesome acoustics in Avery Fisher Hall: "Science, art, patience and money — and apparently voodoo — had triumphed."

To say Shanet is biased in favor of those to whom he is in debt is not to deny the book's very great value. Shanet loves facts — as do most Americans — and here he has produced the encyclopedic ideal: a fat book jammed with facts. As for his *idée fixe*, Shanet should take heart in the notion that America is not alone in its self-deprecatory ways. Sir Thomas Beecham used to say he could never understand why England imported so many third-rate conductors when it had so many second-rate ones of its own.

3

LINCOLN CENTER

After a year-long "public participation program", last September, a professional survey sponsored by the Lincoln Center for the Perform- ing Arts revealed the following bit of information: "AS MANY PEOPLE KNOW ABOUT LINCOLN CENTER AS KNOW ABOUT THE GREAT PYRAMIDS." This comparative statistic was presented in the September 13 issue of *The Performing Arts,* one of the numerous publications which the Lin- coln Center office puts out. Left unanswered, however, was the ques- tion: What is it that people know about Lincoln Center?

There are many facets to this vast project which is now being developed in New York City – and surely destined to have a major im- pact not only on the cultural life of the city but on the cultural life of the nation as well. There is a good deal which still remains unknown about the project's various monetary resources, the real estate trans- actions its development has involved, and its potential effect, not only on the neighborhood of the West Side of New York where it is being erected, but on the architecture of the city as a whole.

The Lincoln Center for the Performing Arts, which, according to present plans, will be completed around 1964, hopes to bring together a major part of New York's various performing arts into one super-or- ganization, on an area of 14 acres. Lincoln Center's officials have en- visioned their plan as creating a single formidable "culture symbol" for the entire country; issuing a preliminary statement of aims, the direc- tors declared: "Lincoln Center will stand as a symbol of America's cul- tural maturity, affirming for the... world our nation's faith in the life of the spirit." Over a million handsomely designed book covers, for use by high school students, carry the message that "Lincoln Center

Originally published as "Lincoln Center: Planning for Music" in *Commentary,* May 1961.

will make our city the capitol of the performing arts just as the United Nations makes it a capitol for world affairs." Yet in all this euphoric anticipation, the question of what effect such a concentration might have on the vitality of the arts themselves has received surprisingly little attention. Surely, the importance of this question goes almost without saying. Here I propose to discuss what — as things look now — would seem to be the likely results which Lincoln Center will bring forth so far as the musical arts of the city of New York are concerned — and therefore, to a certain extent, the musical life of the whole country.

When it opens, Lincoln Center will comprise the following organizations: the Metropolitan Opera, the New York Philharmonic Orchestra, the City Center of Music and Drama, the Juilliard School of Music, the High School of Music and Art, the School of Performing Arts, the New York Public Library's Music Division and Music Library. In general, these organizations will have their own facilities — auditoriums, storage space, rehearsal rooms. In addition, one of Juilliard's halls will be used for chamber and solo recitals, and Philharmonic Hall will serve to house visiting orchestras from other cities and from abroad. (The summertime schedule of events may shift the popular open-air Lewisohn Stadium Concerts to the Center's Philharmonic Hall, which will have removable seats for "Pops" concerts; and the Guggenheim Band Shell in Damrosch Park — in Lincoln Center — will probably take under its auspices the Goldman Band Concerts now given on the Mall in Central Park.) Athough the constituent organizations will of course always have first call on their own auditoriums, Lincoln Center intends to book any particular hall whenever the primary tenant is not using it. "In this way," the 1959 Progress Report states, "the Center will be able to plan wisely the total of musical and art services to be presented in the several halls of the Center."

The advantages of belonging to Lincoln Center will, obviously, be varied and numerous. Each hall is to have near-perfect acoustics* and

---

* After many months of studying 30 of the world's greatest halls, several air conditioning. For the further pleasure and convenience of patrons, performers, and students, there will be spacious lounges, lovely gardens, promenades, terraces, roomy elevators, connecting ramps between buildings, fountains, snack bars; ingeniously designed wheel chairs will be available for disabled music lovers. Every hall will boast seats measuring between 22 and 24 inches wide.* The Philharmonic's great hall will be equipped with a movable apron that can be used in at least four different ways: as an elevator to bring up grand pianos; or, sunk part way down, as a pit for small orchestras; or, resting at floor level, to accommodate extra seats; or, raised to stage level, to provide an additional ten feet of stage space whenever it is needed. The Met will have four push-button stages and a "theater-box" for tourists: its removable glass wall and a speaker system to pipe in the sounds will allow the curious visitor who passes through during the day to see and hear the performers practicing—undisturbed.

The Juilliard School of Music, now situated in the Morningside Heights section of New York City, and which has for 56 years functioned as one of the country's great musical conservatories, will be the major institution in a vast educational compound to include also the New York City's High School of Music and Art, and School of Per-

---

"chief acoustical consultants" hired by the Center decided that 700,000 cubic feet was the optimum number of cubic feet for a hall and that the optimum reverberation time—the time it takes for a sound to decay into unaudibility—was between 1.8 and 2 seconds. This information is related in a film, *Design for Music,* which recounts in detail the acoustical research and preparation by Bolt, Beranek, and Newman. The Public Relations department estimates that the film will be seen by over five million people.

---

* A serious study of seat widths was made by the American Seating Company, public seating consultant to Lincoln Center. R. L. Knowland, its representative, found that Americans have become so accustomed to sitting in front of their television sets that they demand the same kind of ease and comfort in an auditorium. (La Scala's seats, for Milan's lovers of opera, measure 18 inches in width.)

303

forming Arts. Harold Schonberg, music critic for the *New York Times*, recently has said that if he were a Juilliard student he would be "delirious with joy at the opportunity of being right next to the musicians of Lincoln Center—being able to attend rehearsals and learn how things are done professionally, not theoretically."

The desire to create a "culture symbol", to provide each hall with television equipment so that millions of people can look in from coast to coast, to establish for New York City the prestige that the Center will thus bring to it, are all part of the vision of the people at the offices of Lincoln Center. The Center is taking full responsibility for raising the money to turn this vision into reality. It has bought the land, hired the architects, employed the acoustical tests, measured bottoms, and suffered through all of the big and little conflicts that naturally occur when experts and committees of experts are at work. The Center will serve as landlord, leasing halls to the constituent organizations (and renting them out when they are not being used); and it will also do the general housekeeping. But "the whole is greater than the sum of its parts"—this is the motto of Lincoln Center, and it is meant to indicate that each member organization will retain its autonomy. Beyond assuming "continuity and financial stability", no group is asked to sacrifice anything—in the way of artistic integrity, educational values, or public service. On top of all this, the First Progress Report states that Lincoln Center will "pass on to the constituents any benefits of large-scale, year-round operation and of the Center's tax exemption." To most of the musical organizations that have joined Lincoln Center, resigned as they were to an existence of comparative penury, all these advantages, and the talk of "benefits", must surely sound like a miracle from a more efficient, more organized, and much richer world than the one to which they had quite inured themselves.

Shortly after its inception in 1955, Lincoln Center announced its decision to include in its project drama and dance, as well as music. An Advisory Council, consisting of several very distinguished men and women in the field of the dance, was formed to establish a theater

304

Lincoln Center for the Performing Arts
CREDIT: Stephanie Berger

for "Dance and Operetta". In the April 1958 issue of *Dance Magazine*, Walter Terry speculated at length as to which New York company would be fortunate enough to be picked. The choice finally fell upon the New York City Ballet; and it is a choice that begins to suggest some of the unanticipated consequences that may result from the creation of Lincoln Center. The City Ballet is part of the City Center of Music and Drama, an organization formed by Mayor LaGuardia in the early 40s to offer the people of New York tasteful artistic production at popular prices. The opera company was its first unit, and the Center gradually acquired ballet, drama, and light opera groups. The question now is—in the move of the ballet company to Lincoln Center, which of the other groups will live and which will die?

The answer is by no means clear at the present time. One of the public relations men at Lincoln Center seemed quite startled to hear that the City Center even had an opera company. "All of the opera is to be in the Met," he said. On the other hand, the Women's Guild for the New York City Opera is now trying to raise $20,000 to provide the company with a new production when, in fact, "it opens at Lincoln Center"; informal statements from several members of the City Center's board of directors—to the effect that "we move only as a group, as an entity"—lead these women to believe that their activities are entirely justified. Somewhere between these contradictory predictions of things to come is a fairly casual comment by William Schuman, president of the Juilliard School of Music and a member of the Lincoln Center Council (which should be distinguished from the Lincoln Center *Board of Directors*, the Lincoln Center *Officers*, and the Lincoln Center *Committee Chairman*): "It is possible that there may be *some* opera in that building [the City Center's "Dance and Operetta" hall] and some operetta at the Met. As for maintaining a separate [opera] company in the Dance theater...?" —a comment that leaves the whole situation quite unresolved.

But if New York is to lose the City Center's opera company, what would such a loss mean? A little over a mile away, downtown, from where the City Center now stands is the Metropolitan Opera House, whose patrons can afford high prices but whose stage is rarely graced by either indigenous or new European works. The Met's uncharacteristic commitment to perform a new opera by Gian-Carlo Menotti in 1963 is — characteristically — a well-protected venture, for the management will have an opportunity to see the opera and to study its critical and box-office response when it is performed next year in several European houses. On the other hand, the New York City Opera during the last few seasons has produced not only over a dozen American operas and such challenging contemporary "international" pieces as Dallapiccola's *Prisoner*, Stravinsky's *Oedipus Rex*, Orff's *Carmina Burana*, Eck's *Inspector General*, and Britten's *Rape of Lucretia*, but it has also proved to be the sole company in New York City that provides new ideas in performing the standard repertory *and* an opera house for patrons who cannot afford luxury prices. The purpose and philosophy of these two professional opera companies — the Met's and the City's — are obviously different. But if both were to be ensconced at Lincoln Center, it is not hard to understand why the Metropolitan might not care to look through its graceful arches and see the New York City Opera, with its current $3.95 top, staring at it from across the plaza.*

Northwest of the City Center at its present location on 55th Street near Carnegie Hall is the Juilliard School of Music, the city's largest conservatory and certainly one of the greatest in the world. At Lincoln Center, it will offer its usual symphonic and choral concerts, chamber and solo recitals, new and repertory works in the fields of the dance, chamber music, and full-scale operas. To all this it will add performances of the spoken drama, for the conservatory plans now to be a training school for the repertory theater. It has also decided to

---

* The projected top for the new City Center Theater at Lincoln Center is tentatively set at $4.95. This is still a far cry from the tentative $13.00 top for the Met.

discard its undergraduate school, and consequently all these numerous activities will be undertaken with considerably less than half of its present student body. Under conditions of such pressures, it seems unrealistic to expect from Juilliard any great amount of risky, pioneering effort in the field of the lyric theater — particularly in view of the school's productions during the last 15 or so years. Since 1945, of more than 70 operas which the school has produced — in class, seminar, or as full-dress productions — only two have been written by American composers. In short, the New York City Opera would seem to be indispensable: separated from the Met and Juilliard by several miles, with an operative philosophy of its own and with its own board of directors, it has served both American composers and the city well.

Yet if the entire City Center — its ballet, opera, and "light opera" companies — moves to Lincoln Center, the conflict that would seem to inhere in the principle of constituent autonomy plus Lincoln Center's super-organizational control may then become evident. If, as seems likely, Lincoln Center's board of directors is motivated primarily by the desire to please its wealthier, more generous trustees — those by chance who happen to support the Metropolitan Opera and the Juilliard conservatory — and motivated as well by its rule regarding individual "continuity and financial stability", it may certainly decide to do without the City Center's opera company. This prophecy is not so speculative that it cannot be spelled out a little. Lincoln Center could supplement the New York City Ballet with visiting troupes like the Bolshoi Ballet, England's Royal Ballet, and the Royal Danish Ballet, and it would present, on its own, such "operettas" as *Brigadoon* and *Finian's Rainbow*. (I have it on good authority that the name "Theater for Dance and Operetta" does not refer to such gems as Mozart's *Schauspieldirektor* or Rossini's *L'inganno felice;* this genre is too limited to name even half a house after it.) In the process of transferring the City Center from its present location to Lincoln Center, the people of New York will not only lose 510 seats but the city may also lose its

308

only source of experimental and inexpensive opera. And finally, of course, the whole country will suffer from the loss.

When Lincoln Center decided to include within its 14 acres an "educational institution for training in the arts", it first asked Columbia University, in 1955, to join. For more than half a century Columbia has had a distinguished music department which offers undergraduate courses in theory, history, literature, and applied music — and graduate courses in musicology and composition; and for many years now, the university has been trying to raise funds to build an art center where the classroom work can be shown to the rest of the university. Yet when Lincoln Center asked Columbia to transfer the performance work of its music department, the university refused — and without any dissenting voice among its faculty.

One reason for its refusal was the Center's inconvenient location: students of the humanities would have had to travel almost three miles to take a course in music. The more significant considerations, however, were outlined by Douglas Moore, chairman of the Music Department and MacDowell Professor of Music (as well as a noted composer in his own right). Mr. Moore believes that "university performances are free from certain pressures which limit experimentation in the professional market, and it is perhaps better to keep the two separate"; that while "failure should be one's frequent companion in an educational institution," it is unpalatable in a public, commercial world; and, finally, that student performers should serve their own artistic and intellectual communities, and not be placed in an isolated 14 acres of the city, several hundred yards from the Metropolitan. There was no disagreement at Columbia with Mr. Moore on any of these points.

Columbia having said no, Lincoln Center then invited the Juilliard School of Music to come in. Juilliard officials studied the project carefully for a year and a half. On February 7, 1957, the school accepted. The directors of the school and the trustees of the Juilliard Musical Foundation thereupon agreed to make two major changes in the

309

school's operation when it became part of the Center: (1) to train only advanced students; and (2) to include, among its courses, training in drama along with music and dance.

The first of these decisions will affect something like 700 students. In January of this year, Juilliard had 1,563 students. Of these, 691 were in the regular graduate division (which encompasses both music and dance), 169 were in the extension division, and 703 were in Juilliard's preparatory school. A Lincoln Center-Juilliard press release lists the new criteria for acceptance: "The students will be those giving promise of becoming leaders in their respective branches of the art as performing musicians, actors, dancers; as composers, playwrights, choreographers; as stage directors, designers for the theater; and as artist-teachers in this field."

The number of students to be enrolled finally is still undecided, but there is no doubt that those in the preparatory and probably many in the extension division will be forced to study elsewhere. The same press release states that "although there will undoubtedly be a number of exceptions involving younger students, it is anticipated that in general the student body will be in the 18 to 28 age range." (Composers, according to William Schuman, will most likely be in the 25 to 35 age range.)

Mr. Schuman is aware of the "serious void" that these changes will create, but is "optimistic of rescuing the preparatory division." He hopes to preserve both the faculty and student body in a separate institution to come into being somewhere near Lincoln Center—but not under the auspices of Juilliard. If that should prove impossible, Mr. Schuman believes that in any event training in the performing arts has already advanced to the point where "preparatory education can really be left in the hands of others."

Juilliard's emphasis, then, will be on the practical, working situation. Early training for the young composer, the gifted child, the youthful dancer will be sacrificed by one of America's leading conservatories of music. As opposed to this loss, the gain is peculiarly

310

American: technique and polish. But there are other losses as well — more subtle ones — and Mr. Schuman (who is also a distinguished and well-known composer) seems to recognize them. He speaks with pride of the fact that Juilliard has had no public relations department; he sees no reason for anyone's serving as mediator in his communications. He also refers to the large number of the school's musical offerings to which the press is not invited because of the special nature of the work done in a conservatory. He tells of his personal dissatifaction with the part played by Juilliard in the *Omnibus* program on Lincoln Center presented on television on January 1, 1961 — attributing the school's poor showing to the last-minute notification from the Center's main office. Mr. Schuman must know, then, that in a few short years he will be in something like a large fishbowl, placed conspicuously on a table made of travertine marble, stared at continually and curiously by tourists and critics alike. Thus, in the circumstance of Columbia's rejection and Juilliard's acceptance, there has been revealed another element of what it is that the musical world in New York City will lose as soon as Lincoln Center is completed — the nurturing quiet that the academy provides.

The decision to include a library-museum has been the last in the plans of Lincoln Center, which have come to encompass a "trilogy of education, creative scholarship, and performance."

The New York City Public Library system contains two music branches. (There is also a fairly new department for circulating records.) One of the two branches, called the Music Division, is a research library located in the main building at Fifth Avenue and 42nd Street; the other, the Music Library, housed in a separate building on East 58th Street, circulates musical scores and books about music. As of now, the decision is to move both of these branches eventually to Lincoln Center.*

* It is a fact worth noting — though, of course, difficult to assess — that

The Music Division is one of the finest research libraries in the world. Its holdings of scores, manuscripts, books, and microfilms have been collected over a period of years for the benefit of the interested student of music. Precisely for this reason, Paul Henry Lang, professor of musicology at Columbia University, devoted a fairly lengthy column in the New York *Herald Tribune* to plead that the decision to move the library be reversed. Its holdings, he said, were not collected for professionals in an opera company, symphony orchestra, or conservatory. Mr. Lang quite rightly went on to point out that musical scholarship always straddles at least two fields. If the scholar is concerned with troubador music, it is obvious that he must also have French literary and historic references at hand. The same overlap occurs in studying the German song, Italian cantata, English ballad opera, any of the Renaissance madrigals, and all of church music. But Lincoln Center would house only a music library. Mr. Lang wondered what could possibly "be gained by this costly transfer of a great research library into an empire devoted exclusively to the cultivation of music readily available in print...?"

The operating procedures of the second music branch, the Music Library, are quite different, but the purpose is essentially the same: public service. Demands for material are directly related to the programs being performed in the city. When Handel's *Messiah* is scheduled for Carnegie Hall, the library is deluged with requests for the score; otherwise, it is rarely asked for. When the Philharmonic is performing Vivaldi's *Concerto Grosso in D Minor*, then private teachers throughout the area (as well as those working in music schools and conservatories) assign the Vivaldi. But will this be possible when the Music Library is transferred? It seems right to suppose that if Leonard Bernstein, say, wanted 15 copies of Vivaldi's *Conerto Grosso in D Minor*,

---

several people, trustees simultaneously of the New York Public Library, the Metropolitan Opera, and the New York Philharmonic Orchestra, are also on the Lincoln Center board of directors.

312

the scores would be more readily available to him than to some student who had to first get to the Center by subway. Will the Lincoln Center Library, in other words, be able to serve a wider public than the professional Lincoln Center "neighborhood"?

A rather interesting reason seems to lie behind the transfer of the Music Library and the Music Division to Lincoln Center. If all the Center had wanted was an excellent library, it already had one. Any university or conservatory would envy Juilliard's magnificent library — and, after all, only a small fraction of Juilliard's student body will be there to use it in 1964. Without the two city libraries, however, a tourist coming through Lincoln Center during the day might see only an empty concert hall, an empty opera house, an empty dance theater, an empty chamber music hall.* Of course, tourists will, if they wish, be able to see a variety of groups practicing. But several officials seemed to feel that the Center should be represented by something in its "finished" state. If what at least a dozen people attached to Lincoln Center have told me is true — that the men and women who visit Radio City today will include Lincoln Center on their tours tomorrow — then such tourists should be given as much as possible to "see". This is the reasoning, it seems, which has led to the inclusion of "creative scholarship" — that is, New York City's two public libraries devoted to music — in the trilogy of Lincoln Center's musical complex.

*

Her life has been sold for an old man's gold,
She's a bird in a gilded cage.

Lincoln Center may be built of glass and travertine marble, but gold

---

* Guided tours are being planned. A great room beneath the central plaza will be the meeting place; its walls will be decorated with bronze plaques bearing the names of those who contributed money to Lincoln Center.

313

will also be there — and is naturally bound to make a difference to the trustees, the directors, the administrators. For it is the trustees, directors, administrators, and real estate dealers who are responsible for this new center which will "affirm for the entire world our nation's faith in the life of the spirit." In truth, between the anonymous committees somewhere, remote and authoritarian, and the men and women who daily will be performing or teaching at Lincoln Center, or providing a variety of other services, there has been remarkably little communication.

For example, the head librarian of neither the Music Division nor the Music Library were consulted about changing locations. One was informed personally of the decision; the other only read about the move in the newspaper. Moreover, since the press issued the original notices, the librarians have heard little more.

The history of Lincoln Center contains other such examples of gaps in communication. On December 12, 1958, William Schuman advocated the merger of the High School of Music and Art with the School of Performing Arts (two public high schools in New York) in a "logical location next to Lincoln Center" — so that the students of these schools might benefit from the activities at the Center. The proposal was announced in the press (somewhat later because of a newspaper strike), and by now the merger has gone through; the schools will eventually be moved to the Lincoln Center area. Yet until the merger — and possibly since then — neither of the principals of the two schools heard about these plans from any source other than the press. Neither of them has received any communication either from Lincoln Center or the New York City Board of Education. One principal told me that if I wanted information about the merger I should refer to a recent article written by Harold Schonberg in the *New York Times Magazine,* for that was where he had received all his information and he assumed that Mr. Schonberg had been in touch with someone who knew. The other gentleman said: "Everything about Lincoln Center is so nebulous. What I hear is through the grapevine, hearsay, rumor."

The principals, librarians, performers — few of them have been asked for their opinions.

At the same time, it is also true that those people who *are* in charge of the Lincoln Center for the Performing Arts seem to have had very little involvement in any of the arts. The New York *Herald Tribune*, announcing the appointment of General Maxwell Taylor as president of Lincoln Center, stated quite specifically that the General had "never been known as a patron of the arts." A public relations official has said that General Taylor's chief credential was that of being chairman of Mexican Light and Power, "the largest private enterprise in Mexico." (General Taylor is, of course, the retired Army Chief of Staff.) It would be more than a little naive to think that a man with such administrative experience — or a man like Colonel William Powers, now the executive director of the construction of Lincoln Center, and best known for his construction of "housing, warehouses, bridges, dams, and operational military installations such as the first Bomarc Guided Missile Installation at Maguire Air Force Base" — that such men have nothing to contribute to the building of a complicated, expensive project like the Center. They have their special talents, surely. But it also seems more than a little perturbing that, amid all the plans — no one telephoned the principal of the High School of Music and Art.

In December, shortly after the National Cultural Center in Washington issued an elaborate report concerning "America's cultural needs," Professor Lang of Columbia, writing in the New York *Herald Tribune*, argued that the trustees of the Washington Center [later Kennedy Center], like those of Lincoln Center, had been imprisoned by the net of concepts they had themselves engineered. He concluded: "The sheer weight of steel and concrete stands in the way of the artistic and social implications. Such a basic error would not have been made had these plans been entrusted to persons more familiar with the problems of culture and readier and hardier in their search for truth."

As a reporter searches for the truth about Lincoln Center, questions

315

abound. Why, to ask a small question, is this complex of education, creative scholarship, and performance to be called "Lincoln Center for the Performing Arts" rather than "Lincoln Center for Music, Drama, and Dance"? And why has the Met been placed so conspicuously in the very center of the Center, with its great imposing tower? Why, too, is the Met's the only auditorium which has had its seating capacity increased and been able to retain even its "boxes"? (Some women who work for and attend the Philharmonic regularly are quite unhappy that Lincoln Center took away their boxes. "Mezzanines," one has said, "are for the movies.") All of these and other questions begin to be answered if one recognizes that what underlies the whole project of Lincoln Center — all of its activities — is the adulation of the performer, which has been symbolized in America's musical culture by the deification of the prima donna.

On the *Omnibus* program devoted to Lincoln Center previously mentioned, Wallace K. Harrison, the Center's chief architect, commented that the Center would be a place "where a child can come and meet all of the great artists of the world." Of course this hardly means that the child will see Stravinsky lolling on the plaza benches or Hindemith grabbing a quick hamburger. But the child may, on the other hand, see Rise Stevens jump into a taxi with her television make-up still on. Lincoln Center's artist will be the interpreter, the virtuoso; it is this symbol which places severe limits on the Center's cultural significance. Is it unreasonable to worry about the effect of this attitude upon the youngsters of the High School of Music and Art and on the climate of the musical life of the country in general? Mr. Harrison's expectations to one side, wouldn't this overemphasis on the glamorous world of performance tend to turn students away from other aspects of musical expression — particularly composition?

Music in this country has always been treated as a sport, or a contest in high fidelity. Van Cliburn reigns while Roger Sessions is hardly known. The architect for the Center's Philharmonic Hall, Max Abromovitz, recognized this implicitly when he gave his reasons for using glass walls: "Having people on the outside looking in and on the inside looking out is an exciting kind of *game*." Mr. Abromovitz hopes the glass will be part of the "pageantry of the hall as audiences converge upon it." Like many others at Lincoln Center, Mr. Abromovitz seems not to have realized that the pageantry of glass and the maximum reverberation time of a tone finally has very little to do with one's love of music and with the essential beauty of it.

When James Johnson Sweeney recently resigned as the director of the Solomon R. Guggenheim museum, the growth of fine arts was not critically foreshortened by the actions of either the museum or Mr. Sweeney, whatever the particular issues involved — for there are other museums and other directors. But when Lincoln Center was conceived, its planners assumed that there would be little musical activity in New York outside it. If this were to be the case, the people of New York City would be the immediate sufferers. For if the musical activity in the three and a half blocks that go to make up Lincoln Center is geared to the principle of "continuity and financial stability," to the taste of nationwide TV, to tourists, and to the glorification of the star, then the entire musical life of the nation will suffer accordingly. Technique and polish can be guaranteed where there is plenty of money; vitality needs more care.

It might be well to glance at what once happened: during the baroque era, the singer was the thing. Opera died then; and it took a popular, middle-class form of the lyric theater to breathe life into it again. It seems to me that the one workable response to Lincoln Center is an off-Lincoln Center — which will act for music as off-Broadway does for the theater. Perhaps one should think about finding a really unusual neighborhood in New York, far away from the new center of things in the West 60s. Fifty-seventh Street and Seventh Avenue might be a good place to start, in a building like — well, like Carnegie Hall.

POSTSCRIPT: *Immediately after this essay appeared, William Schuman telephoned me. He was enraged I had revealed not only that Juilliard had been*

Lincoln Center's second choice, but also that he had had reservations about Lincoln Center's methods and goals. But instead of my article causing trouble for Schuman, he soon was named the Center's President.

A few weeks after his appointment Schuman and I met. He told me that at the Board of Directors' meeting that followed my Commentary *piece, copies of it were placed on the conference table in front of each director. Schuman said many changes were being made, some stimulated by what I had written. One such change could well have been his own appointment; I had attacked General Maxwell Taylor's presidency and had concentrated my attention on Schuman because he was the only practicing musician among the heads of the various constituent organizations.*

Some good things have happened, most notable among them the operas presented by the New York City Opera Company under the recent direction of Christopher Keene. These include Schoenberg's Moses und Aron, Ferrucio *Busoni's* Doktor Faustus, *Bernd Alois Zimmerman's* Die Soldaten, *Hugo Weisgal's* Esther, *Ezra Laderman's* Marilyn, *and Lukas Foss's* Griffelkin. *In February 1995, the company announced it will open its 1995-96 season with Hindemith's rarely performed* Mathis der Maler *and will follow that with American premieres of Toshiro Mayazumi's* Kinkakuji *in October and Jost Meier's* Dreyfus Affair *in April.*

Mr. Keene's commitment to adventurous programming is the exception. It is inarguable that glamor and glitz have transcended virtually all other concerns throughout the first 30 years of Lincoln Center's life.

4

THE HOPKINS CENTER
AT DARTMOUTH COLLEGE

Hanover, New Hampshire
Hopkins Center at Dartmouth College does for today's composers
what Prince Nicolaus Esterhazy did for Haydn: it commissions compositions and sponsors performances. These may appear to be trifling
deeds in a large and complex world, but they are crucial ones for the
creative musician. Unlike the painter who sees his finished canvas or
the writer who reads his completed manuscript, the composer cannot
even hear his work until performers play it.

*

The present alienation between composer and listener began early
in the 20th century. Schoenberg and Webern did not write to please;
the new esthetic grew out of a more mystical idea of the path music
should follow. Since that time, composers have found it increasingly
difficult not only to make a living but also to hear their pieces played.
The major musical organizations neglect them because the mass
audience that displaced private patronage in the 19th century does
not like the new sound.

Foundations first tried to fill the void created by the lack of public
support, but those in charge generally made conservative decisions.
In 1945, the then 70-year-old Arnold Schoenberg applied to the Guggenheim Foundation for a grant to enable him to finish *Moses und*

Originally published as "Prince Esterhazy Is Alive and Well in
New Hampshire... Sort Of" in *The New York Times,* August 25,
1968.

319

*Aron** and *Die Jakobsleiter*, two works at the core of his creative life. Although he specified that he was living on a monthly pension of $38
from U.C.L.A. and had a wife and three young children to support,
the request was denied. The Koussevitzky Foundation also turned its
back on those who looked to the future, favoring those who looked
to the past. Igor Stravinsky, at the helm of "neoclassicism" and a close
associate of Koussevitzky from the earliest days of his career, recently acknowledged that the conductor "established a nationalist movement that insured his popularity but probably retarded the course of
new music."

In the 1950s, when many composers accepted the legacy that
Schoenberg and Webern left them, they were desperately in need of
help. Although universities welcomed them into their faculties, few
could guarantee frequent, first-rate performances; they had no large,
hand-picked group of performers on hand.

*

That is why Hopkins is unique: living composers hear well-trained
musicians perform a large number of their works. In the first six summers of its life, Hopkins has presented more than 300 contemporary
pieces, 32 of which it commissioned. (Seventy of these works have
been United States or world premières.) During this period the Center has sponsored ambitious retrospectives of Elliott Carter, Carlos
Chavez, Easley Blackwood, Boris Blacher, Peter Mennin, Alberto
Ginastera, Witold Lutoslawski, Andrew Imbrie, Hans Werner Henze,
Walter Piston, Ross Lee Finney, Ernst Krenek, Aaron Copland, Henry
Cowell, Zoltán Kodály, Frank Martin, Vincent Persichetti and Niels
Viggo Bentzon, all of whom have been on hand to supervise perfor-

* Schoenberg's original title, *Moses und Aron*, demonstrates the
  composer's obsessive treatment of numbers, for the absence of the
  second "a" in Aron gives him a total of exactly 12 letters, avoiding the
  dreaded number, 13.

320

mances. Composers of electronic music are absent from the list — not for any esthetic bias, but because they need no performers.

The physical setting is luxurious. The Center includes a large and elegant concert hall, smaller recital halls, practice rooms, listening rooms and rehearsal rooms. In addition to the musical facilities, Hopkins houses two theaters, four art galleries, an outdoor garden, an outdoor sculpture court, terraces, social lounges and banquet halls.

*

The genesis of Hopkins took place in the 1920s with a plan for a theater, but it didn't get under way until the 1950s, when trustees decided they needed facilities for music, art and film as well. The history of Hopkins Center is remarkably similar to that of Lincoln Center. Rockefeller money supported both ventures (Nelson Rockefeller went to Dartmouth), architect Wallace K. Harrison worked on both complexes (both Hopkins and the Met have the same five vaulted arches), and both opened their doors to the public in the fall of 1962.

One striking difference distinguishes the two: nothing of a corporate nature determines music at Hopkins. Because Dartmouth is an educational institution, independent of box-office pressures and critical acclaim, the Center put its musical life into the hands of one man with a vision: Mario di Bonaventura. In an era in which culture centers glorify the performer, di Bonaventura courageously set out to focus on the creator.

*

His experience in the field has been first-hand. After making his performing debut at the age of 14 as a violinist in Town Hall in 1938, di Bonaventura studied composition with Nadia Boulanger and Igor Markevitch, both of whom were devoted to Stravinsky's style of writing, and with Luigi Dallapiccola, who adopted Schoenberg's 12-tone

321

technique. In 1959 the West Virginia-born musician became conductor of the Fort Lauderdale Symphony Orchestra and, when Hopkins Center began to rise, he visited Dartmouth as guest conductor. Administrators were so impressed that they hired him as music director of the Hopkins summer "Congregation of the Arts" and gave him enough money to make it work. One composer visiting Hopkins this month summed it up: "It's Mario's baby. He runs the whole show."

*

During the winter di Bonaventura does little in the way of scheduled teaching. Although he has a few composition students at Dartmouth, most of his time is spent recruiting young musicians for the eight-week festival. After personally auditioning them or listening to their tapes, the conductor chooses about 90 performers. Di Bonaventura claims that even the best-trained musicians from well-known conservatories are remarkably out of touch with the current musical scene. His purpose is to educate them: "I allow students to remain at Hopkins for only two seasons. When they arrive, most have heard nothing more recent than early Stravinsky. After they leave, I count on them bringing to performers and audiences all over the country the lessons they learned here."

*

The fee for each student is $700, but generous scholarship funds defray the cost for most. Warner Bentley, the director of Hopkins Center, reports that financial donors do not criticize the far-out nature of the music performed. "They know that we don't want to be just another Tanglewood." (Apart from one week in August devoted to contemporary music, Tanglewood still relies heavily on the traditional repertory. Ernst Krenek, Tanglewood's present composer-in-residence, received a performance of only one of his works during the

322

Mario di Bonaventura (left) and composer Witold Lutoslawski
at the Hopkins Center, Dartmouth College.
Lutoslawski died in February 1994. His music has had
considerable staying power. In November 1994, Esa-Pekka
Salonen conducted the Los Angeles Philharmonic in
Lutoslawski's Fourth Symphony at Avery Fisher Hall.
CREDIT: Heinz Kluetmeyer

entire summer season. More than 20 of his pieces have been played at Hopkins.) Bentley points out that the enlightened nature of the Hopkins program not only educates music students but the community; programs including Beethoven and Bach expose New Hampshire and Vermont audiences to Lutoslawski and Skalkottas as well.

*

But those who benefit most are neither students nor listeners but the composers who are given money, performers, audiences and the freedom to write as they will. Di Bonaventura does not play favorites. The eclecticism of his selection not only reveals the diversity of his own training, but indicates a belief that the contemporary composer is not heir only to Schoenberg, or Webern, or Stravinsky, or Ives, but has taken something of consequence from each.

Despite the lavish facilities at Hopkins, there is nothing camp about the proceedings. During a rehearsal of a world première by the advanced Polish composer Krzysztof Penderecki, di Bonaventura interrupted the reading to instruct the cellists: "In this section you must hum the first four measures and whistle the last — in the octave of your choice." A girl in dungarees, sandals and long blonde pony tail giggled effusively. Di Bonaventura rapidly clicked the baton on his music stand and reprimanded her. "We'll have none of that here," he said sharply. "There has never been a more serious man than Penderecki."

If Nicolaus Esterhazy had mistreated Haydn, the composer would have abandoned him for another rich and tasteful prince. But it is a blessing that di Bonaventura is good to his composers for, today, to whom could they turn?

324

5

JOHN CROSBY AND THE SANTA FE OPERA

As John Crosby watched his handsome modern opera theater in Santa Fe, New Mexico, burn to the ground at dawn one morning, he says he experienced three distinct emotions: a sense of shame because of his inability to deliver the next performance as planned, a fear of recrimination by those who would assume that only a negligent man could be at the helm of an opera house going down in flames, and a need to understand the nature of the fire and the manner in which it was spreading so that a similar disaster could not destroy the new house which he was certain — even then — he would build.

As it turned out, 36 hours after the fire a stage had been built in the local high school gymnasium and the company put on a splendid performance of *Barber of Seville* (it was the only production whose costumes had escaped the fire). Within 24 hours the community of less than 40,000 contributed, unsolicited, $12,045, and today, in place of the completely timbered old theater, there is a new one of masonry largely covered by redwood, with a water storage and sprinkler system more costly than the entire original structure.

It took Crosby only three weeks to plan and budget his new Santa Fe Opera amphitheater. Figuring increased backstage space and a proscenium as large as the Met's, he assured his backers it would cost $1,755,000, and that it would be ready by the opening of the 1968 season. He delivered the goods — under budget and ahead of schedule.

*

Originally published as "Phoenix Rises at Santa Fe: John Crosby and the Santa Fe Opera" in *The New York Times*, June 2, 1968.

In the mid-50s Crosby, then in his 20s, conceived the idea behind the Santa Fe Opera Company: a perfect theater, high quality performances and contemporary works against a backdrop of the ravishing natural beauty of the Southwest. Not his national heritage, family background or inborn talent can account for the strength behind this idea or the force and efficiency with which he has carried it out. For Crosby's early years were not spent to the accompaniment of Puccini on the organ grinder or Wagner in the opera house. The New York-born, 41-year-old impresario and bachelor spent much of his youth in New England, at Hotchkiss and Yale, and studied piano and violin on the side. Absorbing the generally eclectic influences of such liberal northeastern institutions, he finally focused his interest on the popular musical theater. But it was not until he began postgraduate work at Columbia that he knew his field was opera.

There he met Rudolf Thomas, director of the opera workshop, with whom he developed what he refers to as the "ultimate in teacher-pupil relationships." He would go to Thomas's house in Connecticut at ten in the morning and "we would spend the day at the piano, playing and conducting and talking about everything from Wagner in particular to the history of opera in general." The spirit of the Santa Fe Company grew out of these sessions; its realization was implemented by Crosby's association with Leopold Sachse, a director with the Hamburg Opera in the 30s and, more recently, with the Met. Armed with Thomas's faith, Sachse's counsel, his parents' money and his own recently discovered desire to conduct, Crosby built a beautiful outdoor theater in the mountains just outside of Santa Fe.

Crosby the conductor projects no image at all; Crosby the business man is everywhere apparent. In an elegant townhouse in Manhattan, he maintains the winter offices of the Santa Fe Opera, engages artists for the summer in Santa Fe, and sees an occasional interviewer. There he sits, a collegiate-looking young man (of pre-hippie days) with cropped hair, tweed jacket, buff pants and desert boots. The same dichtomy of style pervades his repertoire: along with *Butterfly*,

Traviata, Magic Flute, Rosenkavalier, and *Elixir of Love,* this season Crosby is presenting the American premiere of Hans Werner Henze's *The
Bassarids,* as well as Stravinsky's *Persephone,* and Schoenberg's first experiment in 12-tone composition, *Die Jakobsleiter.*

The choice of Santa Fe was fortuitous: asthma first brought Crosby
to New Mexico when he was an adolescent. Transferring from
Hotchkiss to Los Alamos Ranch School, he spent a year in the foothills
of the Jemez mountains where the Atomic City now stands. Crosby
points out that he is not alone in his addiction to the area: John Sloan,
D. H. Lawrence and Georgia O'Keefe settled there almost half a century ago because they too found something "timeless, of old Spain"
about Santa Fe and its surroundings. Crosby attributes the current
sophistication of the city to its age — it was founded by the Indians in
1610 — and adds that 30 per cent of his audiences are Santa Fe residents.
The rest come from as far away as Vietnam; the repertoire is that special.

During its first eleven years, the Santa Fe Opera Company has
given American stage premieres of Alban Berg's *Lulu,* Stravinsky's *Persephone,* Hindemith's *News of the Day* and *Cardillac,* Shostakovich's *The
Nose,* Strauss' *Daphne,* Henze's *The Stag King* and *Boulevard Solitude.* It
has also produced world premieres of operas by the young American
composers Marvin David Levy and Carlisle Floyd. In between Crosby presents not only the standard repertoire but also those pieces not
too often performed: Stravinsky's *Rossignol, Mavra, Renard, Rake's
Progress,* and *Oedipus Rex;* Poulenc's *Dialogues of the Carmelites,* Berg's
Wozzeck, Honegger's *Joan at the Stake,* and Donizetti's *Anna Bolena.*

Despite the sophisticated audiences of which Crosby speaks, he has
a hard time selling 20th-century opera and it is expensive for him to
produce. *Lulu* required 50 hours of orchestral rehearsals against 12 for
Butterfly; yet *Butterfly* sells out six performances while *Lulu* cannot
even fill two.

Why, then, does he pursue this particularly difficult path? Crosby
gives only the most high-minded of reasons: "In Europe musicians zip

327

from city to city, conveniently hearing works by Hindemith, Stravinsky, Henze and Berg. Could a young student of composition at Columbia do that here? American composers have no way to learn the craft of the theater. And they would like to. I receive at least 30 unsolicited manuscripts each year; many of them are based on librettos about the Rio Grande. But what can you expect? How can anyone learn how to write opera if he is not exposed to the good works by the great composers of the previous generation?"

POSTSCRIPT: *John Crosby continues to maintain a balance between material concerns and adventurous programming. Work on reconstruction of the Santa Fe Opera Theater is scheduled to begin in January 1996 and is expected to be completed in May 1998. At the same time commissions for the next three years include operas by composers who have never before tackled the genre: David Lang, Tobias Picker, and Peter Lieberson.*

6

COLUMBIA-PRINCETON ELECTRONIC MUSIC CENTER

In a tiny room crowded with electronic equipment that virtually surrounded him, composer Mario Davidowsky was at work on a new
piece. What was the next step?

"I am about to trigger these two envelopes," he said. "One sharp attack and short decay using a high band of white noise very loudly will
combine with one sharp attack and very long decay on a high 3,000
cycle per second sine wave."

Thus Davidowsky, an Argentinian musician, associate director of
the Columbia-Princeton Electronic Music Center, was shaping a note.

The year 1955 was important for electronic music. RCA
demonstrated the Olson-Belar sound synthesizer, and the Rockefeller
Foundation gave the studio a grant of $12,000. When the gatekeeper's
cottage was about to be destroyed, Jacques Barzun arranged for a permanent home: the small room in the cellar of the McMillin Theater
where Davidowsky still likes to work.

In 1958, Milton Babbitt, who had no interest in tape, began to work
with the Mark II—an improved version of RCA's first sound synthesizer—in an RCA laboratory in New Jersey. Babbitt considers pitch
the most important aspect of music while Luening and Ussachevsky,
relegating pitch to a lower position, focus on sound *per se*. With the
synthesizer, Babbitt codes information in advance and controls every
millisecond of his work while the others, working with their hands,
like painters, splice pieces of recorded tape together.

In 1959, the Rockefeller Foundation announced a grant of $175,000
to set up the Columbia-Princeton Electronic Music Center, with Ussachevsky, Luening and Babbitt as its directors. What had seemed to

---

Originally published as "Can the Mark II Sing 'Happy
Birthday'?" in *The New York Times*, May 3, 1970.

Composer Milton Babbitt at the RCA Synthesizer,
Columbia-Princeton Electronic Music Center
Courtesy Milton Babbitt / Frank Driggs Collection

some observers to be just a harmless experiment suddenly became the bulwark of a new academic establishment. RCA rented its Mark II to the Center that year for $16,600. And Columbia allotted the Center three rooms in an old converted building on 125th Street, west of Broadway. One room became a tape studio, the second a laboratory and the third a home for the formidable Mark II. Soon after another tape studio was set up in Princeton.

In 1960, the musical action began. A Rockefeller grant brought Davidowsky from Argentina and a Guggenheim grant brough Bulent Arel from Turkey. These five men, ranging in age from 35 to 70, all of whom have composed for traditional instruments, form the hard core membership of the electronic family group. Alice Shields and Pril Smiley are technicians and composers as well.*

*

In 1961, the Center presented its first public concert. Columbia Records recorded it, and Leonard Bernstein proved sufficiently impressed to commission a piece for tape and orchestra to be played at the Young People's Concerts of the New York Philharmonic. Controversy began to reign in the press: would the machine kill music?

Many composers who have worked at the Center—Charles Wuorinen, Harvey Sollberger and Charles Dodge—subscribe to the Center's traditional artistic values of musical structure and discipline; they teach in the universities' music departments and also give performances of new works, not all of which are electronic. Many others benefit from what they have learned at the Center and go on to set up studios at other schools: Jon Appleton established one at Dartmouth, Morton Subotnick at Mills, and Mel Powell at Yale.

But sometimes the directors feel let down. Talented composers such

---

*   Both women remain at the Center today (1994), the only members there from the original group.

as George Perle and Peter Westergaard try the equipment and abandon it to return to work with traditional instruments. Other composers become overly captivated with technology. Walter Carlos, at the Center for more than two years, recently used the Moog synthesizer to produce his *Switched-On Bach*. Both his teachers—Ussachevsky and Davidowsky—are uncomfortable when his name comes up. They view the success of this record, which has sold over a million copies, as something of an artistic sell-out, an exploitation of the medium for the sake of gimmickry.

Babbitt, on the other hand, takes a more tolerant view: "There is no single way to electronic music. The medium is vast and flexible, imposing the least amount of structuring." Babbitt does not think the medium is maligned when it is used to make such transcriptions as *Switched-On Bach*. "One would not invalidate the symphony orchestra because of Stokowski's orchestral transcriptions of Bach. Then why invalidate electronic music because of Carlos's transcriptions of Bach? One must not approach the Carlos transcriptions except as a transcription of Bach. Why focus on the medium and challenge it? The medium is *not* the message."

*

A larger source of concern to the Center is the number of electronic composers who are drawn to mixed media, to Happenings or "total theater" in which chance plays a prominent role. Such men as John Cage, Salvatore Martirano, Lejaren Hiller and Luciano Berio seek an uncontrolled situation, allowing things to happen as they will. The Columbia-Princeton group despairs of this. Davidowsky says, "Here, as composers, we try to organize an artistic object, to establish relationships, hierarchies and so forth. Some involved with 'total theater' are not creating an artistic object but instead are creating an actual process that provides them with psychological—not intellectual—stimulation. This gives them a sense of participation in some unidentifiable

332

kind of thing. In this sense, it's a poor man's group therapy, a symptom of the collapse of all values. God is dead and there is nothing to replace Him. But artists have a moral and intellectual responsibility not to play ball with the market."

7

VLADIMIR USSACHEVSKY AT BELL LABS

Not far below the surface of Vladimir Ussachevsky's contemporary psyche lies a genuine romantic Russian soul. The composer's apartment tells the story: photographs of his father — a bearded captain in the Czar's army and an honorary Mongolian Prince — a grand piano, Persian rugs; original paintings, oriental scrolls and medieval music manuscripts hang on the walls.

Yet the composer stepped out of this old, cultivated atmosphere and into the shining, corporate world of the Bell Telephone Laboratories in Murray Hill, New Jersey. There, as "composer in residence", he moves around Input, Output, and Digital Magnetic Tape Rooms, focusing his energy on a multi-million-dollar computer that needs 20 people to attend it and costs $645 an hour to run. The men with whom he works are both mathematicians and composers; they are young, conventionally dressed and show none of the traditional signs of conflict and neurosis that for the past 150 years have been the trademark of creative musicians.

*

Ussachevsky is the "old" man in the computer field, which he came to indirectly. Most of his European contempories experimented with a variety of new musical sounds and compositional systems between the two world wars. But until Ussachevsky was 40, he composed in a consistent, traditional style which he characterizes as "pseudo-roman-

---

Originally published as "Seven Times the Computer Said No: Vladimir Ussachevsky at New Jersey's Bell Telephone Laboratories" in *The New York Times*, March 3, 1968. Vladimir Ussachevsky died on January 4, 1990.

tic Russian—very melodic, very harmonic and modestly dissonant."
Even Varèse's radical work for percussion, *Ionisation,* which he heard
at a Hollywood Bowl concert in 1933, left him unaffected. After World
War II the composer's course suddenly changed: recognizing the
potential that the tape recorder held for the manipulation of sound,
Ussachevsky began to work in the new medium.

In 1951, while Ussachevsky was teaching "traditional" music at
Columbia University, Peter Mauzay, the student engineer at
Columbia's radio station WKCR showed him how sound could be
manipulated with tape. The composer began to experiment and discovered that, by superimposing sounds, he could produce complex
and interesting sonorities. With tape one can record conventional
sound, cut it up, slow it down, or erase it at any point. Ussachevsky
experimented with these techniques until he produced something
"musical".

*

His first piece for tape recorder was performed at a Columbia concert in May, 1952. Immediately afterward, another Columbia music
professor, Otto Luening, became interested in the medium. During
the same year Leopold Stokowski learned of their experiments and included a tape work by each of them for the first electronic concert ever
held in this country, at New York's Museum of Modern Art. Since then
Ussachevsky's electronic pieces have been performed in concert and
on radio and television. He has appeared as tape recorder soloist with
many orchestras in performances of his own works, and has produced
electronic scores for both theater and films. (He composed the score
for the film adaptation of Sartre's *No Exit* and an electronic score for a
45-minute abstract film by Lloyd Williams, *Line of Apogee.*) Ussachevsky gives numerous demonstrations of the tape medium both
here and abroad and, with Milton Babbitt and Otto Luening, directs
the activities of the Columbia-Princeton Electronic Music Center, the
oldest studio for electronic music in the United States.

While Ussachevsky was improving his tape music techniques, scientists and engineers were going even further, producing a machine that not only manipulates sound but generates it electronically. In 1955 the first RCA Olson-Belar electronic sound synthesizer was developed. With the synthesizer, now installed at the Columbia-Princeton Center, the composer is directly in touch with the sound-making process: he manipulates switches, actually hearing the results, before punching the code on the paper tape controlling the oscillators, filters and other electronic mechanisms that structure the sound he wants.

*

But soon he was moved a step further away. In 1957 Max Mathews, who had a Ph.D. in electric engineering from MIT and was director of behavioral research at Bell Labs, while attending a piano recital devoted to Schoenberg's 12-tone works began to think about generating musical sound by computer. He set up the following system: a computer is fed instructions by the composer. These instructions describe what musicians refer to as the various "parameters" of a musical tone. The parameters not only include pitch, but such other attributes of a tone as its attack, duration, decay and instrumental timbre. The instructions cause the computer to transmit a series of numbers from the computer memory to a "converter"; they become a sequence of electronic pulses that vary according to the original values the computer generated. These pulses are smoothed by a filter and come out as sound through an ordinary loudspeaker.

One of the reasons Bell Telephone Labs sponsors this work is to learn more about those special aspects of a sound wave that give an instrument or voice its distinctive qualities. Another reason is altruistic: according to executive John Pierce, "Technology has a responsibility to bring new developments to the attention of artists." Pierce's idea has a most appropriate history. In 1927 Edgard Varèse began dis-

336

cussions with Harvey Fletcher, who was then director of acoustical research at Bell Labs, concerning the development of electronic instruments for composition. With Fletcher's recommendation, Varèse repeatedly applied to the Guggenheim Foundation for a fellowship to "pursue work on an instrument for the producing of new sounds" and to prove the "necessity of closer collaboration between computer and scientist." The foundation rejected his application each time.

*

Forty years later Bell invited Ussachevsky to try their GE 645. Although he has not given up tape, he has a number of reservations about the tape medium and has embraced the computer with enthusiasm: "Both the permissiveness of our time and electronic popular music have contributed to considerable vulgarization and bastardization of tape composition. There is a preoccupation today with gadgetry that results in a general indifference to standards and a lot of mediocre music.

"But the computer has wonderful potential as a total music production tool. The music can be composed by computer — the University of Illinois has done much work in that area — and its sound production synthesized by computer — Princeton, along with Bell Labs, has concentrated its efforts in this area. There are still a lot of bugs in the system, of course. After all, there are still bugs in Lord and Taylor's billing....

"When the composer wants to be in total control — as I am in the tape studio — the computer offers a great deal. If you want to be that kind of composer with the computer as your tool, then you have to know much that is outside the average musician's experience."

The specialized knowledge the computer requires has discouraged many musicians from entering the field. Alice Shields, Ussachevsky's assistant at the Columbia-Princeton Center, adds other reasons for her avoidance of computer-generated sound: "I like to work with my hands and to experiment for dramatic effects. Through complex transpositional devices, which I control with knobs and dials, I can find new results that are hard to calculate scientifically. With the computer you have to know exactly what you want in advance and then be able to program it."

The computer is a potent machine. It is not only composer and performer but critic as well. Ussachevsky's first piece written at Bell has been rejected by the computer seven times; he has not yet heard the complete work — from beginning to end. The composer attributes the rejections to the complexity of sounds he programmed it to generate. Two of Bell's mathematician-composers, Steve Johnson and Richard Moore, defend the machine and attribute the rejections to ordinary, human error in the programming. Johnson points out that a performer, upon noticing a missing note in the middle of a measure, will automatically fill it in but that a computer is unable to take such initiative. Moore adds that it is not unusual for a man to spend three months on a work which the computer will either absorb or interpret or more often reject in less than a second.

Despite its technical difficulties, the computer can open a formidable new world of sound for the musician who knows how to use it. Jean Claude Risset, a French physicist and composer at Bell, created a computer-trumpet sound which professional musicians could not distinguish from the real thing. The logical extension of this achievement is that composers will no longer be inhibited by the technical limitations of a traditional instrument or the human limitations of the performer. The man behind the program can produce flute-like trills indefinitely and complicated rhythmic patterns impossible for an instrumentalist to execute.

*

Because of the specialized knowledge computer music still demands, work in the field is just beginning to emerge. But Max Math-

338

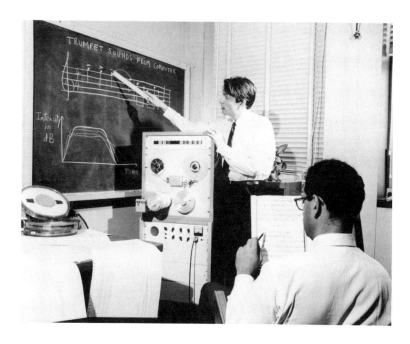

Jean-Claude Risset with electronic equipment at
Bell Labs, Murray Hill, New Jersey
CREDIT: Frank Driggs Collection

ews sees a more democratic if distant future: "Today the computer is
something like the car in the 20s; it is fine to fool around with but you
wouldn't want your wife and kids to use it. All this will change. Computers will be smaller, cheaper, more available. Compositional rules
will be built into them. They will be used as performing instruments
and become commonplace in the average American's home. A tired
plumber, after a hard day's work, will settle down with his computer
to compose music."

Although he claims that in 20 years 90 per cent of the serious
musicians in this country will be using the computer, Mathews
refused to comment on the computer's relevance to the production of

339

high art: "I'm not sure I know what 'high art' is. I know what I like and I know what bores me."

In a room at Bell there is a small green plant which bears an identification tag: "Crassula (jade plant). Give full sun. Keep soil on dry side. Likes good ventilation." When I asked how the plant could thrive in the absence of windows, the public relations officer replied: "The unchanging and thoroughly controlled environmental conditions are far more beneficial to the plant than sun and air." A technician supported him. She had not gotten out into the sunlight, she said, since working at Bell. And she has never been in better health.

In what way will music blossom — away from the dusty garrets of Bohemia, implanted in an academic-industrial world?

8

TOD MACHOVER AT IRCAM

Composers' Forum and the American Center in Paris will present a concert of works including some by an American associated with IRCAM, the Institut de Recherche et Coordination Acoustique/Musique in Paris, founded and directed by Pierre Boulez.

Tod Machover, the American composer who is an IRCAM director of musical research, was born to the combination of technology and music; his father is a computer scientist, his mother a professional pianist. He not only learned computer language young; he began to play the piano at two, developed considerable skill on the cello, composed seriously as a teen-ager and went on to study composition first under Luigi Dallapiccola in Florence, then under Milton Babbitt and Elliott Carter at the Juilliard School in New York.

In 1978, when he was 26, Machover became IRCAM's first American composer-in-residence. On January 1, 1980, he got his present post. That he not only survived but prevailed during a period when five figures of international stature then heading various IRCAM departments—Gerald Bennet, Luciano Berio, Michel Decoust, Vinko Globokar and Jean-Claude Risset—virtually disappeared from the Paris scene, probably testifies not only to Machover's musical talent and scientific know-how, but also to his instinct for diplomacy.

Completely at ease in front of a computer screen, Machover manipulates dials, pushes buttons and pulls levers until he finds the exact sound he wants. How he alternates between manipulation and listening calls to mind the way Stravinsky is said to have sat at the piano and played a chord, then listened and changed one note in the

Originally published as "American Technology Thrives in Paris: Directed by Tod Machover and Others at Pierre Boulez's IRCAM" in *The New York Times*, May 6, 1984.

chord, listened and changed another note until the chord was what he wanted.

Composers who work at IRCAM are there either because they were invited or because they applied and were accepted. Either way, insofar as Americans are concerned at least, the composers are paid a stipend. In addition to Machover, American composers recently at IRCAM range from Barbara Kolb, who wrote what Machover describes as a "straightforward piece for tape and instruments", to the jazz tombonist George Lewis. Lewis, educated at Yale, directed the musical activities at The Kitchen, the center of experimentation in downtown Manhattan, before going to IRCAM as a visiting composer. Two of his works are included on the Symphony Space program. Frank Zappa, the pop star who has described Boulez's Ensemble InterContemporain as "the primo creamo of the contempo worldo" also spent five or six days at IRCAM making a recording.

*

Machover spoke about his String Quartet Nr. 1 and *Chanson d'Amour*, Part II, for piano. Both, he says, were composed during a period when he wrote "lots of instrumental music while digesting all the experience of electronic instruments. The quartet, written first, was a real reaction against all the electronics I had been doing."

When asked about the reference to love in the title of the piano music, Machover quickly replied: "I won't talk about that." When pressed on whether his own secrecy owes a debt to Boulez, the young composer answered: "Personality-wise, I am pretty different. Private yes; secret no." And as though to confirm that assessment, he began to explain in what way the two pieces that comprise *Chanson d'Amour* deal with romantic love.

"They were written in 1982," he said. "What I wanted to write were two little sketches of romantic love. What I did was something larger. In the first of these pieces there is an image of a passionate, disruptive love. The subtitle is *'La Vita nuova'* taken from Dante. I had fallen in love with an Italian girl when I didn't want to. That experience completely imposed itself on an otherwise ordered life. This first piece will not be performed. The second of the pair alone lasts 30 minutes.

"It is subtitled," Machover went on, "*'Zwischen Himmel und Erde'* — between heaven and earth — and reflects an attempt to come to earth with a much more sane kind of love, one that has its limits. In this instance the girl is German. There are two sets of variations. Little by little they turn into one element. In its micro-activity, the piece recalls Beethoven's Opus 111. I intended that reference and people do hear it." As for the women behind the works, Machover explained, "I don't try to portray people or situations in music. But my pieces are always dramatic. Although I respect those who see in music only abstract relationships, those who view music in a purely formal way, music has to do with meaning for me and that is what I find wonderful about it. If the piece is successful, the listener should recreate something of the experience of the composer as he was writing it."

Machover, who thinks it a "real danger to wait for the next advance in this incredibly fancy and seductive [electronic] technology in order to write your next piece," is planning to fulfill a Koussevitzky Foundation commission with a piece for chamber orchestra without electronics.

He also expects to complete a multi-media opera, a co-production of IRCAM and the Pompidou Center for a Paris premiere. A spectacle with live performers, computer music, and multi-screen video projections, it will tie together, the composer says, "all my various compositional and technological interests and reintegrate the human voice and dramatic forms." The text is based on the novel, *Valis,* by the American science-fiction writer Philip K. Dick, and is, according to Machover, "a wild fable about the fine line between psychological disturbance, mystical awareness, and technological manipulation."

POSTSCRIPT: Valis, *with a rock-influenced score, received its premiere in 1987 at Paris' Pompidou Centre.*

VII

ON STAGE AND BEHIND THE SCENES

SEIJI OZAWA AT 35

NINA BEILINA

ROBERT MANN

HARVEY SOLLBERGER

JOSÉ QUINTERO

RICHARD TUCKER

MARIA CALLAS

EVELYN LEAR AND

MARIE COLLIER

THE NEW YORK PHILHARMONIC

CODA

PARENTS AND GENIUS CHILDREN

JEROME LOWENTHAL AND THE

JEWISH COMPOSER

Introduction

In 1974, Jacques Barzun, the scholar, teacher and author who had helped electronic music gets its footing, was president of the Institute of Arts and Letters. On its 75th anniversary, he addressed the group, emphasizing that institutes are not populated exclusively by giants.

"Literature and the arts are kept alive by the concurrent energies of a great variety of talents, and not by geniuses alone. It is an illusion to suppose that the great genius, who by definition is unique, isolated and infrequent, could by himself insure the continuity of culture. It is therefore foolish to look askance at the coming together of the lesser geniuses and the higher talents in institutes and academies. These groups exist, not to create and revolutionize — no group can do that — but to connect and sustain."

I also place lesser talents along with major artists to convey the essence of the culture. In music there is still another dimension with which the Institute does not concern itself. This dimension does not exist in literature, painting or sculpture. It consists of the performer who acts as an interpreter between the creator and the listener.

This section deals with those people who occupy center stage as well as those who are not so visible. There is the current conductor of the great Boston Symphony Orchestra, a violin virtuoso from the Soviet Union, the first violinist of a great quartet, and a flutist who specializes in experimental performance. There is the opera director who had staged memorable performances of Eugene O'Neill's spoken dramas during the peak years of his career.

There is the tenor, Richard Tucker, and the one and only Callas as well as several other sopranos whose careers have followed altogether different courses. In reading the stories of these singers, one can try to answer the question that has mystified me: the origins of drive, that particular energy that allows nothing to stand in one's way.

Some clues to that question may be found in a lecture I delivered to the Phi Beta Kappa students and their parents at a commencement exercise in May, 1984. It is the first of the last two pieces here, neither of which has ever before been published, that form the last part of this volume. This talk draws on material from my first three biographical books. There can be no doubt that the discipline of psychoanalytic psychology—now under such widespread attack—has provided me with the thread that leads me out of the labyrinth of a creative artist's life. This is no less true for the biographical sketches that appeared in some of the articles reprinted here than it is for the full length biographies.

The discipline does not answer all the questions, of course, but it provides considerable help. In May, 1933, when Marie Bonaparte's study of Edgar Allan Poe was published in Paris, Freud wrote in his foreword: "Such studies do not claim to explain the genius of creative artists, but they show the factors that awakened it and the type of material fate has imposed on it."

As for the final piece: it was written for the Arts and Leisure section of the *Times*. Then I was told it would appear in the news section of a daily edition because it was so provocative. Finally I learned the editors there thought it too provocative to publish anywhere in the paper. The subject: the Jewish composer.

1

SEIJI OZAWA AT 35

Lenox, Massachusetts

Seiji Ozawa, born 35 years ago in Manchuria, is a rising star in the western musical world. Ozawa not only treats music of the past with care and musicianship, but he also conducts contemporary works by Messiaen and Ligeti in a clean, yet interesting way. Clean performances of this music are often dry; interesting ones are frequently sloppy. Ozawa's ability and diplomacy have earned him very prestigious jobs at a remarkably young age.

*

I interviewed the conductor one afternoon in the Green Room of Tanglewood's Shed and learned above all else that he is an aloof, controlling man.

This was the sequence of events:

I arrived at Tanglewood's Main Gate and was greeted by Marvin Schofer, the Boston Symphony Orchestra press officer; David Levenson, a member of the press staff; and Clemens Kalischer, the photographer assigned to the story. To the right of us was the cafeteria, to the left the Tanglewood Shed. Schofer left us to go to the cafeteria where Ozawa was having lunch in order to escort him to the Shed. Kalischer suggested we remain where we were because the two men would have to pass us. Levenson blanched. "Ozawa wants you waiting in the Green Room," he said. We acquiesced to the formal conditions and walked over by ourselves.

Outside the Green Room we met Mary Smith, concert manager of the B.S.O. I told her I needed one hour and a half to interview Ozawa

Originally published as "Ozawa: 'I DO NOT LIKE INTERVIEWS' "in *The New York Times,* August 23, 1970.

and had just learned from Levenson that only one hour had been set aside. Smith said Ozawa would never have agreed to an hour and a half and objected even to an hour, but she added that his afternoon was free and that if the interview went smoothly, she was certain he could be persuaded to stay.

Levenson, Kalischer and I were talking in the Green Room when the door was flung open; Ozawa, accompanied by Schofer, rushed into the room. He seemed out of breath, smiled pleasantly, and kept running his fingers through his mass of long black hair. He was dressed like an American swinger: tight black cotton pants, black turtleneck shirt, navy blue blazer and espadrilles without socks. He said he had just finished hot dogs for lunch.

A few minutes later and not a bit out of breath, Vera Ozawa glided into the room. The conductor's wife sat down in a corner, picked up a book from a nearby table, and flipped through its pages during her husband's interview. Her skin was adorned with heavy eye make-up, her fingers with several oversized rings. She wore black patent shoes with chunky heels, black turtleneck sweater with a leather belt slung low around her waist and a lightweight suede jacket over slightly flared dungarees. Mrs. Ozawa identified herself as a writer. Her husband added proudly that she was a poet. She's also known as a model who owns a boutique in Tokyo.

*

The thin, agile conductor sank into the only large, comfortable chair in the room. Schofer said that, in accordance with Ozawa's wishes, Levenson would stay throughout the interview. I objected to this, explaining that both Ozawa and I would be inhibited by Levenson's presence. But the conductor would not budge. I asked him why he was so adamant. Schofer quipped: "That's the first question of the interview." Then he left the Shed; Levenson, the photographer and Mrs. Ozawa stayed. Ozawa and I proceeded to embark on a singularly guarded, superficial interview. We went through a formal ritual — comparable to a Noh drama — in which the conductor recited many facts before his seemingly uninterested wife, a Tanglewood-oriented publicity man, the *Times*'s photographer and myself.

"I do not like interviews," Ozawa began, as though he were telling me something I did not know. "Musicians," he added, "can not talk well." I disagreed and cited several recent interviews I have had with exceptionally articulate men: Boulez, Babbitt, Berio, Carter and Britten. "But they are composers," the conductor explained, "not musician musicians — performers like myself." Ozawa said he can communicate musical directions to members of the orchestra but that when he wants to compliment them, he finds it difficult. "I wish I could talk to them like Bernstein does."

Leonard Bernstein has exerted an enormous influence on Ozawa. Ten years ago, Ozawa sought out and found Bernstein in Berlin. That summer he enrolled at Tanglewood where Bernstein had studied and taught. In 1961 Ozawa became one of Bernstein's three assistants with the New York Philharmonic and accompanied him that spring to Japan. A few years later Ozawa was appointed Bernstein's only assistant. Ozawa opened Tanglewood's festivities this summer with a devoted performance of Bernstein's *Chichester Psalms*. The composer was on hand — in white suit and long black cape — to embrace the conductor and exchange congratulations all around.

There is much of Bernstein in Ozawa's personal style: both dress flashily, fashionably (Ozawa wears bell bottoms on the podium). Both use the left hand during a performance to control dramatically unruly hair. Both expend themselves before the public to the point of physical exhaustion and both generate a frenetic audience response. Vera Ozawa, whom the conductor married a few years ago after a divorce from his first wife, a concert-pianist, is thin, chic, and elegantly cool, superficially similar to Felicia Bernstein.

But, as Ozawa himself confessed, he does not communicate like Bernstein. He even refuses to answer questions.

351

"Why," I asked him, "have you cancelled the performance of Xenakis' *Eonta?*"

"I will not answer that."

"What recent films or plays have you seen?"

"None."

"When did you marry Mrs. Ozawa?"

"Look it up in City Hall. If the *Times* is interested in my personal life, they should have sent someone from the Women's Page. Then I would not have granted an interview."

I told the conductor that people were interested in him as a man and asked whether he ever read Rex Reed's highly personal interviews on the *Times*'s movie page. Mrs. Ozawa finally looked up. "We saw him," she said, "in *Myra Breckinridge.*"

*

Hot dogs, Messiaen and *Myra Breckinridge!* Why did a Japanese man commit himself so vigorously to the West?

Ozawa does not think in psychological terms. He answered — with resignation — that *all* interviewers ask him that question and then delivered what appears to be his standard response:

"Before the war the Japanese people were interested in the West but at that time the channels were closed. Then all the money went into the war. Afterwards — with the Japanese culture dying — all eyes and ears turned to the West — to Western music, art, architecture and writing."

But the Ozawa family's adoption of the West started well before World War II. Kalsumi, the oldest of the boys, played accordion and harmonica when he was young, at a time when such instruments were rare in Japan. He pressed his father to buy a piano and all of the boys learned to play it well. Ozawa speaks with reverence of the instrument: "A pianist can do anything by himself. A pianist can make all music alone."

352

*

Western thought appears to have been introduced to the children through their mother, a convert to Christianity. "Although she never had us baptized," Ozawa said, "she did sing us Christian hymns and, when I was 15, sent me to live in a church for a year. We were poor and, in exchange for playing organ for services, I received my room and board. That was when I learned all the Protestant hymns and all of Bach's keyboard music. At 19, playing rugby, I broke two fingers" — Ozawa held up his index fingers — "and that stopped my piano career." Piano was replaced by composition which was soon replaced by conducting. In 1959, at 24, Ozawa conducted the Japan Radio Orchestra (NHK) and the Japan Philharmonic and was named outstanding musical talent of the year.

Ozawa then set his sights on the West and persuaded a Japanese firm to lend him a motor scooter in return for promoting it on a tour of Europe. In Besançon he won first prize in the important International Competition for Young Conductors for which Charles Munch was a judge. That was shortly before he met Bernstein in Berlin.

*

During the early 1960s, when he was in New York and Tanglewood, Ozawa says he was emotionally torn. "I did not know where I wanted to be. I kept thinking of Japan as such a *sweet* country. But in 1962 I went back to conduct the NHK orchestra, this time as a professional. Then I had a big problem. The musicians were accustomed to taking orders only if they came from conductors with a German accent or Russian name. I was the first Japanese conductor in its 50-year history. I thought I was doing good — cleaning up sections of the orchestra. But the night of the first concert, not one musician came. *I* came but the orchestra did not. The management had cancelled the show. This was good for me to see. This was good for me to find out. Japan was really not *that* sweet. Now I could easily leave my country. I no longer had any choice."

As I left Tanglewood, I felt I had elicited little material on which to base a good article. Ozawa had not revealed himself at all. Was my failure due to the fact that I am a woman and Ozawa will not talk seriously to women about musical politics or music itself? (I asked which contemporary composers were his favorites. Mentioning the most disparate musicians, he carefully touched all practical bases: Xenakis, Ives, Bernstein and Schuller.) Or was my failure due to my inability to understand a Japanese man with the open, smiling face he presents to the public and the closed, tight self he holds from the world?

Later, checking some points about Ozawa's career, I came upon an account of the incident with the NHK orchestra: the musicians broke their contract with the conductor, complaining of his "arrogant attitude".

Two important questions remain: Is arrogance a defensive mask for tension and insecurity? And does Ozawa's reluctance to communicate with words suggest anything regarding his communication with music?

POSTSCRIPT: *No one will deny that Ozawa has had a brilliant career, holding the post of Music Director of the Boston Symphony Orchestra for more than twenty years. At 58, he has enjoyed the longest tenure of any music director of a major symphony orchestra.*

But the aspects of his temperament I noted still remain very much in evidence. In a 1994 New York Times article, "Seiji Ozawa: 20 Years in Boston and Still Passing Through", the writer, after quoting musicians in Boston to the effect that the conductor has made no real contact either with them or Boston itself, goes on to say: "When an Ozawa performance is unsuccessful, and many are, it is usually not that the playing is poor, and certainly not that it is dangerous. To the contrary, it is likely to be accomplished but per-

Seiji and Vera Ozawa at Tanglewood, 1970
CREDIT: Clemens Kalischer

functory, played as if out of obligation, be the work a Beethoven symphony or a Boston premiere."

Nevertheless Ozawa conducts those premieres well. As he treated Messiaen and Ligeti years ago, so he treats Messiaen and Sir Michael Tippett today. But of the various 20th century composers he conducts, none receives the intense and exciting interpretation that Ozawa gives Leonard Bernstein, the man who was his model from the beginning of his career.

2

NINA BEILINA – ÉMIGRÉ ARTIST IN AMERICA

Nina Beilina, the prize-winning Soviet violinist who immigrated to the United States eight years ago, will give what Omus Hirschbein, the performing arts director of the 92nd Street Y, calls her "comeback performance".

Considering her accolades, why should Beilina be giving a comeback? She is a winner of the Tchaikovsky, Enesco and Long-Thibaut Competitions, among the most prestigious instrumental contests in the world. And after her American debut in January 1978, Harold Schonberg wrote in *The New York Times:* "Beilina did not make a false move anywhere. She is an important instrumentalist and a first-class musician to boot. Whatever she touched came out with incredible polish, assurance, and when needed brilliance.... Russia's loss is our gain."

The following September, in a *Times* article entitled "How American Culture Has Been Shaped by the Artist in Exile", Donal Henahan grouped Beilina with Mstislav Rostropovich, Galina Vishnevskaya and Vladimir Ashkenazy. Nobody in the music world registered surprise.

Despite all that, her career went into a tailspin. Michael Scammell, the author of the recently published biography of Aleksandr Solzhenitsyn, believes defectors and émigrés generally suffer from what he calls "excessive expectations" of American life and that "everything that was negative in Russia they paint in positive colors here."

Like the dancers Valery and Galina Panov and Aleksandr Godunov, the pianist Oxana Yablonskaya and the writer Solomon Volkov, Beilina was originally feted and fussed over and her expectations of America seem to have been fulfilled. But, again, like some of

---

Originally published as "Émigré Artists and Great Expectations: One Violinist's Tale" in *The New York Times*, December 9, 1984.

Nina Beilina
CREDIT: Steven Speliotis

her Russian colleagues, she soon suffered a setback in her career. While she attributes her professional difficulties in the Soviet Union primarily to the prejudice against "ethnic minorities" there – Beilina is a Jew – the problems she ran into in the United States had more to do with an inability to deal effectively with the kind of career decisions that had always been made for her by Soviet authorities.

There was much that Beilina cites as negative about musical life at home. She made records for the Melodya label but they were never sent to the United States. She was not permitted ever to record Bach. Authorities determined her programs, and once, when she requested permission to play a small piece by Alfred Schnittke, a living Russian composer, she had to go through what she described as interminable red tape.

*

Not permitted to play in Western European and North American capitals, Beilina was limited to touring South America and Eastern European countries. Not assigned as soloist-with-orchestra in the big cities, she played concertos in the outlying areas. Not allowed to teach violin in the Moscow Conservatory, she traveled hours each month to hold classes in the school at Gorky. Although the government made it impossible for her to have the career to which she aspired, it took pretty good care of her. She concertized frequently, lived comfortably and enjoyed the benefits of a nursemaid for her young son.

But that did not make for the gratifying professional life she sought. "To make a good career in Russia," Beilina says, "you have to be a Communist, preferably a member of the K.G.B. Every third person in the big orchestras is an informer. The other way to make a great career in Russia is to be in bed with someone. When I was 18, I played at a competition and met Tikhon Khrennikov, the powerful composer who had been Secretary General of the Union of Soviet Composers since

1948. I played his Concerto and he became an admirer, wanting me to be his lover. I never did anything like that for my career, but there are those who were close to me who thought it would have been less corrupt for me to sleep with Khrennikov than to leave Russia."

In the mid and late 1960s, Beilina's mother and father died. In 1970 her husband, the Leningrad conductor Israel Chudnovsky, contracted cancer; their only child was then two months old. During her husband's illness and her own emotional recuperation after his death, Beilina played nothing but Bach, who she says she has come to think of as "standing alone on a mountain peak". Having no ties left in Russia, she applied for an exit visa and received it. This was 1976.

*

Bringing neither money, nor papers nor her own violin, Beilina arrived in New York penniless. A wealthy woman for whom she played offered to be her personal representative.

Placed by a social agency in a hotel on upper Broadway, she met other musicians; word spread that Nina Beilina was here. A manager of her South American tours arranged for an audition at Carnegie Hall with an American manager. On that audition day in March 1977, Carnegie Hall was filled with many more people than one interested American manager. One of the listeners was Avery Fisher, who told Beilina to do nothing without him. He said she should throw away her "awful black dress" and that he would open all the doors. Fisher arranged for an audition with Omus Hirschbein who launched her with a debut at the 92nd Street Y.

The violin-dealer Jacques Francais lent Beilina a del Jesu Guarneri, and the community of critics shared Harold Schonberg's assessment. ICM, a powerhouse in the concert management industry, took Beilina on as a client and she was celebrated in music circles.

But the "expectations" soon caused her to shift managements and representatives in a frenetic effort to gain the recognition that had

360

eluded her at home. Before her second concert, less than one year after her first, Beilina had left ICM because, she says, "it didn't move quickly enough. Even with those great reviews I never got to play with a great conductor or was invited to a great festival. I was never asked, for example, to perform at the 'Mostly Mozart' [festival in New York]. Even if you play well, it doesn't mean a thing." Despite this remark, she acknowledges that leaving ICM was the biggest mistake of her career.

Playing well *had* meant something, and ICM had not done badly. Contacting the Oria Management in Milan, it served as a conduit for her first performance ever of the Mendelssohn concerto with the Santa Cecilia Orchestra in Rome. ICM was also behind the benefit concert for Share Zedek, a hospital in Jerusalem, that Beilina played with an orchestra at Carnegie Hall, a performance with the Tulsa Symphony and several recitals. Still, Beilina characterizes this period as one of frustration and misery.

However, there is no cinematic *Moscow on the Hudson* ending here. Beilina did not throw in the towel, sell frankfurthers or get a hack license. But just as she refused to submit to Khrennikov in Russia, so she seemed unwilling to yield to the necessities of performance here — getting rid of her black dress, smiling for the audience. Despite the initial support and recognition of Avery Fisher and ICM, and a luxury apartment in a rent-subsidized complex for artists in New York, she never seemed to learn how to manipulate the U.S. system any better than the one she left at home, for the fact is she never *did* get to play with a great conductor nor was she invited to a great festival.

Disenchantment took its toll and Beilina began to give uneven performances. At a Carnegie Hall recital, Donal Henahan critized her performance of Bach's Unaccompanied Sonata Nr. 3 in C. She determined, then, to play the same work in New York at least once again. After nearly five years, she got her chance when, last March, Beilina shared the stage of Merkin Hall with a colleague from the Mannes College of Music where she has a few students. In his review of the concert John

Rockwell wrote that in the Bach piece "Beilina reached the peak of her artistry. The music flew by fleetly and sweetly, building to climaxes with no hint of Romantic heavy breathing. Everything was as formally correct as could be, yet the music actually gained thereby in expressivity."

*

When the photographer who took her picture for this story asked Beilina to play for him, she closed her eyes. When he asked her to open them and look at him she said: "I always play with my eyes closed."

Then she stopped and smiled — as if she was now going to try to do what she had formerly been unwilling to do. Eight years after her entrance into this alien world, Beilina put her instrument back up under her chin, began playing, and did what she never did before: she opened her eyes.

3

ROBERT MANN

Cynics believe there isn't a musician alive who would choose as a career that of being a member of a chamber-music group — except by default. They say that the fame, money and power that come with a virtuoso life are so intoxicating that every performer would be a soloist if he could. But Robert Mann, the first violinist of the Juilliard String Quartet and the only original member still in the group, refutes this assertion.* He is the quintessential chamber-music artist, involved not only with the composer of the work but with each musician on stage.

Mann is held in the highest regard by demanding professionals. Itzhak Perlman recently told an interviewer that he relies on Mann the way a boxer relies on a trainer. And last month, Donal Henahan, in his *New York Times* review of Mann's performances of Beethoven violin and piano sonatas with Emanuel Ax, noted the "high serious-ness and authority" of the playing as well as the "warmth and affec-tion" rare in Beethoven performances. Mann's ability to excel as soloist is not new: in 1941 he won the Walter W. Naumburg Award.

Robert Mann was born in Portland, Oregon. When he was nine years old, his father — at various times a grocer and tailor — asked him whether he wanted to play the piano or violin. Mann cannot recall why but he chose the violin and began lessons that cost only $1.50 each. When he was eleven, his violin teacher, whom he describes as an alcoholic Belgian, was shot and killed. Two years passed without music. Then, at 13, he began to study with someone who taught him

---

*   Today (1994) Mann continues as first violinist of the Juilliard String
        Quartet.

Originally published as "Robert Mann's Life in Chamber Music" in *The New York Times*, July 6, 1980.

Robert Mann
CREDIT: Charles Abbott

"what musical language meant in terms of felt phrase and structure, of all the things that go into the making of music." It was then that he met a group of young people who banded together to perform chamber music and madrigals. At 18, Mann won a scholarship to the Institute of Musical Art in New York. The next year was emotionally turbulent — "high living, pining after girls, staying up all night unproductively." At his final examination one teacher remarked that he had never seen so promising a student deteriorate so rapidly.

At 19, Mann began to study with Edouard Dethier. "Dethier was hooked on chamber music," Mann says. "He needed a fix once a week. In those sessions — and they lasted five years — we came to grips with the essence of music. The point was to get inside a phrase, to make that phrase really exist, and that has been a lifelong involvement for me."

*

Two days after Pearl Harbor, Mann made his solo debut at Town Hall. In 1943 he entered the army with violin in hand and three pieces under control: "The Flight of the Bumble Bee", "Smoke Gets in Your Eyes", and the title song from *Intermezzo*, the Leslie Howard movie. A soldier challenged him on the world-record performing time of the "Bumble Bee" and Mann ripped through it in one second short of the world record. He confesses he left out a four-bar repeat. The performance succeeded in keeping him off KP and in music.

Discharged from the army in 1946, Mann returned to Juilliard. William Schuman, then president, interviewed Mann on the subject of a resident string quartet that would travel and concentrate on contemporary music. The Juilliard String Quartet was born and has performed more than 350 20th-century pieces over the past 34 years. Thus it became identified with new music, but Mann says that is only because so few other groups were performing it. In fact, the quartet devoted at least as much time to bringing the standard repertory to

365

life and did so in a way that sometimes startled listeners: fast tempos, athletic and sometimes violent interpretations. The four members presented a disreputable appearance: sloppy clothes, scuffed shoes, unmatched socks, the very antithesis of the formal white-tie-and-tails that had come to be the earmark of the renowned older quartets.

In 1947 Mann met Lucy Rowan, then concert manager of Juilliard, and they began to date. They lived together before marriage at a time when it took courage to do that. Then, when they married, they kept it a secret because Lucy Mann says she feared the marriage wouldn't work and so decided not to announce it at all.

Lucy, Robert and two other members of the quartet were all getting some kind of psychological treatment. In fact, what changed Mann, he says, was really the Reichian analysis he received from a therapist in the late 40s and early 50s and even, on occasion, from Wilhelm Reich himself. He characterizes the process as directed towards arriving at the "original, vulnerable state of the new-born, before the body has begun to close, before the muscles have begun to lock up, before opportunism has had a chance to set in."

Mann recalls that in the early 1960s William Schuman invited him and his wife to his New Rochelle home. Sitting around the swimming pool Schuman said: "I'm almost certain your answer will be negative, but I want to start a chamber society at Lincoln Center and would like to have you as its director." Schuman was correct; Mann turned the opportunity down. Because the Juilliard travels as much as it does, it would have been impossible for Mann to stay with the group.

Now, Mann is 60 years old and has achieved recognition from colleagues all over the world. It is particularly ironic that at this moment, when chamber music has the greatest audiences in its history, he should be so articulate a critic of standards of chamber-music performance and performers.

"For years I devoted all my energies to developing certain elements of chamber music—its sophistication, complexity, elegance, vitality—in order to make it viable for audiences. And I succeeded. Then, all of a sudden, in the last seven or eight years, everyone is getting into the act. People are now mesmerized by cosmetic overlay, surface presentation, and temperamental veneer. You can either knock people over with sound and virtuosity, or you can communicate something significant. Unfortunately those who are successful today strive primarily for sound and virtuosity. I adhere to a more Zen-like approach; in chamber music the virtuoso principle doesn't work."

Despite these dissatisfactions., Mann has an enviable life. He has sustained a marriage of nearly 30 years, fathered two talented children—he recently performed a duo-violin recital with his son—composed more than 70 works, and helped develop at least a dozen of the world's leading young quartets. In 1962 he realized a dream that began when he listened to broadcasts of the Budapest Quartet from the Library of Congress; the Juilliard became the Library's quartet-in-residence.

One of Mann's closest friends is Dudley Moore, the actor and musician who is now in New York making a film. When asked why he thinks Mann—with his attractive looks and brilliant musicianship—never became a celebrated virtuoso, Moore said: "He loves playing chamber music so much. And he is embarrassed discussing finances. Finally it may be like it is in the theater: to be a great star, there has to be some lack of heart."

4

HARVEY SOLLBERGER

Although he considers himself both a composer and a performer, it is as an experimenter with the flute that Harvey Sollberger is now making his mark. Sollberger has expanded the potential of the traditionally pure-toned flute into an instrument capable of producing new kinds of sounds.

Composers seem to be writing more music for the "new" flute than any other instrument, and Sollberger will display some of these unusual sounds at a concert given by the Group for Contemporary Music. The program, entitled "Explorations of the Contemporary Flute", will feature six compositions, all written in the past 25 years, including one of his own works: *Riding the Wind* for amplified flute, violin, cello and piano.

The concert at Alice Tully Hall will be the first downtown performance for the Group, one of the earliest ensembles in the United States devoted to 20th-century music. The Group, which Sollberger codirects with the composer Charles Wuorinen, began in 1962 as a means for graduate composers at Columbia University to hear well-played performances of their own compositions. Until now Sollberger has lived his professional life in the shadow of Wuorinen, who earned a Pulitzer Prize in composition in 1970, and whose aggressive attacks on people in high places have always made journalistic copy.

Sollberger's training was conventional, and he is not sorry: "One should not bypass traditional training. But there are more alternatives than the tradition suggests. Students are generally exposed to 50 fingerings to handle the combinations of the diatonic and chromatic scales. Yet there are close to 16,000 combinations, so many thousands

Originally published as "Harvey Sollberger: New Sounds from an Old Instrument" in *The New York Times*, March 28, 1976.

Harvey Sollberger
CREDIT: Arne Svenson

of possibilities that have not yet been explored. C above middle C, for instance, is generally an open note on the flute. There are at least a dozen other fingerings which would obtain the same pitch but alter the sound in clearly recognizable ways. One can render a sound narrow and tight; another can make it wide and fuzzy. Each has its own very striking ambiance."

Born in Iowa in 1938, Sollberger began to study the flute at 12, but he remained untouched by contemporary music until, at the University of Iowa, he first played Samuel Barber's Second Symphony. Then Luciano Berio visited the school and brought a tape of his own *Sequenza* for flute, played by Severino Gazzeloni. "I'd been waiting for that work without knowing it," Sollberger says. "It was unlike anything I had ever heard. It involved modes of playing, a continuity of articulation that was different from anything I'd ever known. Gazzeloni was a catalyst for a whole generation. He did more than any other flutist to stimulate composers of his own time."

Many virtuosos have turned away from the new. Jean-Pierre Rampal commissioned Boulez's Sonatina for Flute (composed in 1946) but never played it. Indeed, it was not performed until 1954, when Gazzeloni played it in Darmstadt. Here the pitch range extends up to the hard-to-reach high F. Sollberger says that chromatic fingerings up to high F sharp are possible and that musicians wishing to play the recent literature must become familiar with them.

Sollberger teaches at the Manhattan School of Music (where the Group moved when Columbia withdrew its support). There, he says, it is possible for a student majoring in the flute to receive his degree without ever playing 20th-century music. The traditional repertoire, Sollberger points out, requires an "ideal sound" which contains virtually no variety in the vibrato. "There is a uniformity, a homogeneity in the sound in which the vibrato is used indiscriminately, like a pastry chef putting whipped cream on everything he makes. This kind of playing is encouraged everywhere. Conservatories press for required pieces in the tradition of 'The 50 Great Melodies'. Flute students must play the Mozart concertos, the Prokofiev and Bach sonatas, the Schubert variations and so forth."

Sollberger acknowledges that "avant-garde" techniques can be used in a banal way—but that, of course, is not what he has in mind when he teaches his students how to produce accurate microtones (anything less than a half-tone), how to make several notes sound simultaneously (it has to do with fingerings and embouchure), how to work the key clicks Varèse first required in his *Density 21.5* and Berio asked for later in the *Sequenza*, how to generate the buzz tones at the low end of the register, and how to change the timbre of a pitch by "altering the balance of air pressure and embouchure."

Why is Sollberger abandoning the Manhattan School tomorrow night in favor of Lincoln Center, the "Establishment" complex he has always professed to abhor? "The key word is extension," he says. "I believe in extension as a flutist, as a composer, and in the geographical-social sense as well."

POSTSCRIPT: Sollberger is currently (1995) on the faculty of the University of California, San Diego.

José Quintero
Courtesy: José Quintero

5

JOSÉ QUINTERO

"Last year, when I was in Indianapolis with the National Company of the Metropolitan Opera, the first Gemini flight was being conducted. A television set was on near the rehearsal area, but the singers kept walking briskly by it—vocalizing all the time—never glancing at the screen. They were totally absorbed in their art. Opera is a world unto itself. It has its own boundaries—more so than theater or dance."

Thus José Quintero, the director most responsible for the renaissance of the Off Broadway theater, described his reaction to working in opera. "The absorption is impressive, of course; still, I don't quite understand it. A serious actress preparing for a role visits galleries, reads poetry, listens to music. I don't think that one out of 99 singers does this kind of thing to help her in the crystalization of her conception. One of the most instructive experiences I ever had was going out to lunch with a group of opera people. The only subject discussed was opera. It is like entering a foreign country and not knowing the language."

The slender, attractive director is an expert at entering foreign countries without knowing the language. Quintero cannot read a note of music, yet he managed to move from straight plays into musical comedy and opera. Working on and off in the operatic medium since 1958, he is polishing *La Bohème* for the Metropolitan Opera National Company.

But such long steps from one form of theater to another are nothing at all compared with Quintero's very choice of career. The whole idea of theater was alien to him during his boyhood in Panama; there was little theater there. When he was 17 his wealthy father sent him

Originally published as "José Quintero Revisits 'A Foreign Country' " in *The New York Times*, January 1, 1967.

to study medicine at the University of Southern California. The results were disastrous. Failing all of his first-year science courses, the young man switched to a liberal arts program, with a major in speech. Here Quintero took courses in theater history and, for the first time in his life, met actors.

This experience was a revelation; he found he liked his new environment. After graduating, he was offered a job as business manager of a theater group in Woodstock, New York. Quintero used his last $33 for a bus ticket to the East Coast — his father had withdrawn support because of his son's interest in theater — and the week he arrived, the company folded. But the "business manager" stayed on, teaching Spanish to artists in the community throughout the winter.

*

Quintero managed to save a little money, and in 1950 he invested it in a former Greenwich Village nightclub, which he and a few friends converted into a theater. They opened Circle in the Square with a revival of *Dark of the Moon* by Howard Richardson and William Berney. Off Broadway, a flourishing medium in the bygone days of Eugene O'Neill and the Provincetown Playhouse, was dead by this time, but Quintero's venture spurred its revival. *Dark of the Moon* was followed by imaginative productions of Truman Capote's *The Grass Harp* and Tennessee Williams' *Summer and Smoke*. Brooks Atkinson, drama critic for the *Times,* made his first trip downtown for *Summer and Smoke.* He reviewed it in eloquent terms, and the Off Broadway revival was launched. His interpretation of Eugene O'Neill's *The Iceman Cometh* established Quintero as one of the most important directors of the late 1950s, bringing a new kind of recognition that far exceeded Greenwich Village and its image.

"What we did gave others courage to do the same," Quintero said. "We had emerged at the same time that a new generation of actors was emerging. Katharine Cornell and the Lunts were ready to retire. Jason

374

Robards, George C. Scott, Geraldine Page and Colleen Dewhurst all came out of Circle in the Square.

"Pretty soon, though, Off Broadway regressed and became just a little Broadway. Big names started to come down to the Village and the theater no longer served its purpose. Plays would run over a year; we had become nothing but landlords. Running a play for over a year was not a healthy thing. Since Circle had acquired its reputation by the efforts of so many people, I felt we should run it as a nonprofit venture, giving certian people a chance to do their own special projects—like Thornton Wilder's one-acters, *Plays for Bleecker Street*. My partner, Ted Mann, did not see it the same way, so I left Circle in the Square."

Quintero's childhood may have been lived without theater, but not without high drama. He recalls that his father, a successful politician, "was extremely dramatic in his political presentations and in his person. But the real drama training in my youth came from the Catholic Church, one of the most highly theatrical institutions in the world. In the Mass we see the same tragedy, the Crucifixion, lived over and over again, yet kept remarkably alive. The Church taught me a sense of pageantry, a sense of ritual, a sense of the value of color—blue for purity, purple for royalty, white for virginity and black for death. It also taught me how to give life to inanimate things. A religious statue was alive for me; I could talk to it. Perhap that is why I never had to do 'Method exercises'. I had no trouble believing that a loosely strung piece of gauze on a stage set was really a tree. I had *that* training from the day I was born.

*

"Although I have often been accused—if that is the right word—of being a 'method director', the fact is that I never went to the Actors Studio. One of the most important elements in the theater is the personalization of experience—the equalizing of the character's ex-

375

perience with your own. If believing *that* makes me a method director, then I am one."

Quintero denies that he is "slumming" when he enters the opera house. He had succeeded brilliantly on Broadway with O'Neill's *Long Day's Journey into Night* shortly before accepting his initial challenges in the lyric theater—the New York City Opera's *Lost in the Stars*, by Kurt Weill, and Norman Dello Joio's *The Triumph of Saint Joan*, and the Metropolitan Opera's *Pagliacci* and *Cavalleria rusticana*. Since staging these operas in 1958, Quintero has directed a wide variety of works, ranging from the Off Broadway production of Genêt's *The Balcony* to the movie based on Tennessee Williams' *The Roman Spring of Mrs. Stone* and even to episodes of the television series *The Nurses*. He has also had considerable experience on Broadway, "some of it good, some very painful."

Pousse Café was Quintero's *bête noire*. Producers of the musical comedy called him in at the last moment to save the play. But despite Quintero's hurried efforts, *Pousse Café* died quickly and violently. The Broadway axiom — you're as good as your last job — applied; the director lost his commitment to stage *A Joyful Noise*. He has not worked on Broadway since.

In 1965, for the first time in nearly a decade, Quintero returned to opera to direct the newly formed Metropolitan Opera National Company's *Susannah*, by Carlisle Floyd. He likes working with the company, comparing it to Off Broadway. "The average age of the singers is 26, so each of them has a sense of freedom and enthusiasm that comes from not being too settled in the repertory. If an established star has sung *Bohème* or *Carmen* 200 times, she sees no reason to alter her conception of the role — no matter what you, as a director, may be trying to do. Young people are far more flexible. They have not created steel corsets for themselves, and improvement and growth are still possible."

Quintero hopes to direct some contemporary musical work — maybe Berg's *Lulu* or Britten's *A Midsummer Night's Dream*. The idea of doing a work by a living composer is especially appealing. He feels that it would bring about a "closer collaboration between the component parts" — conductor, director, designer — than is usually the case. He looks longingly at the big scenes in opera, pointing out that, on Broadway, plays are sometimes limited to as few as two characters and rarely do they exceed ten. With awe, and some envy, he mentioned that British theater director Peter Hall staged Schoenberg's *Moses and Aaron* in Covent Garden with 75 people on stage for the bacchanal.

Bohème is no *Lulu*, no *Moses and Aaron*. There are no orgies, no philosophy, and certainly no serial music. But that doesn't seem to bother Quintero. He is delighted with the job: "I love all opera. Music can express such intense emotion; in the spoken theater there is much more restraint. And the climate for working in opera is now a good one. The performer is beginning to regard himself as an 'actor-singer'. In the 30s, 40s and 50s, opera was a concert stage paying lip service to the drama. It has only been during the past ten years that impresarios have called in real directors to direct opera.

"As for *Bohème* — I love it! Can you believe that this is the first time in my life that I have directed a completely romantic love story?"

6

RICHARD TUCKER

In an afterword to *Richard Tucker*, the radio producer George Jellinek writes that Tucker, who died in 1975, was the greatest tenor America has produced. He was also the only one able to encompass the entire range of the tenor repertory with the exception of the *Heldentenor* roles. Tucker planned his career carefully, husbanding his voice for the right role at the right time. Thus in his 60s, he was able not only to continue to sing at a remarkable pace and with a stunning intensity but also to tackle the role he had coveted for years — Elézar in *La Juive* by Jacques Halévy, the story of a heroic and vengeful Jew. It was the last role Enrico Caruso sang, and Tucker sang it in concert at Carnegie Hall and in staged productions in New Orleans and Barcelona. Early in 1975, under much pressure from Tucker, the Metropolitan Opera finally began planning its own production. But Tucker died before it was announced.

If his voice was remarkable, as an actor Tucker was limited. An exasperated Arturo Toscanini reminded him that "Aida is a woman, not a building. Put feeling in this. Better you put your *pants* into this!" Once Ezio Pinza pleaded with him to actually kiss Marguerite in a scene from *Faust*. According to his biographer, James A. Drake, Tucker replied, "Aw, hell, I'm a married man and the father of three kids.... I'll feel like an idiot." Hardly the material for a juicy biography here.

Yet the surprising fact is that there is considerable juice. Embedded in the detailed and often fascinating information about backstage goings-on, the tidbits that make for splendid operatic lore, is the story of a man blessed first of all with a great instrument. In addition, he had an adoring mother, a father who recognized the potential in his

---

Originally published as "Canny and Gifted: Review of *Richard Tucker* by James A. Drake in *The New York Times Book Review*, March 25, 1984.

Richard Tucker as "Canio" in Leoncavallo's *I Pagliacci*
CREDIT: Frank Driggs Collection

young voice and steered him precisely the right way, a family thoroughly devoted to God, and his own uninhibited aggression, which allowed nothing to stand in his way. Romantic love seems pale indeed when confronted with the passion that nourished Tucker's drive to be first.

Drake has written an authorized biography, with the assets and limitations that genre implies. On the one hand, the author has had access to stories only friends and relatives can provide. On the other, Tucker's ego has been soft-pedaled, and not a single unsavory aspect of his life emerges.

As for his lifelong feud with his brother-in-law, Jan Peerce, the author identifies entirely with his subject, who once attributed the difficulties to "one word—jealousy. This man can't take it when anybody surpasses him." The price of authorization here is, for example, that Drake never explains to the reader that Toscanini, who appears throughout the book, favored Peerce over every other tenor and what consequences that had for Tucker's career.

Born to immigrant parents in the Williamsburg section of Brooklyn in 1913, Tucker was raised in an Orthodox Jewish home and sang in a synagogue choir from the age of six. Except for the Caruso records he heard, secular music held no interest for the young Rubin Tucker. He went from a $5-a-day job in the fur market to a distinguished career as a cantor to a career as an internationally acclaimed opera star with an annual income of $300,000.

Tucker was short, weighed close to 200 pounds and was conceited in the extreme. He never displayed a trace of stage fright and in radio and television interviews presented the cockiest of attitudes. Drake says that when he was not on stage, he always "made it a point to return to Great Neck by six-thirty, in time for the evening meal." At the height of his career, Tucker earned $70,000 for serving as cantor on the High Holy Days in a Chicago synagogue. Always out to make a still better financial deal, the tenor once flipped a coin to try to move Rudolf Bing, then the general manager of the Metropolitan Opera, from a fee of $700 per performance to one of $750 and lost. Later Tucker estimated the outcome cost him $2,600 that year.

POSTSCRIPT: Barry Tucker, the tenor's son and president of the Richard Tucker Foundation which awards prizes to young singers, displays the same competitive attitude in regard to Tucker's career as his father did.

Responding to a request from John Cardinal O'Connor to "do a concert" in St. Patrick's Cathedral in 1994, Barry Tucker selected January 15th which just happened to be the cardinal's 75th birthday. As part of the concert a film clip of Tucker's performance of "Vesti la guibba" from I Pagliacci on "The Ed Sullivan Show" was shown. The New York Times reported that, as the younger Tucker look out at the sea of people in the cathedral, he told the cardinal: "See? Richard Tucker can still get standing room only."

Maria Callas

7

MARIA CALLAS

Maria Callas's life is eloquent testimony to the truth of Erik Erikson's observation that "when artists go under, it is not as slaughtered lambs, but as the vanquished in the struggle for power." Callas's formidable personality and temperament gave her insight into the larger-than-life heroines of many 19th-century operas. With the tools of her musicianship and remarkable technique, she translated this identification into performances that could transform people's lives. Her style was at one with the Romantic period and altogether alien to our own time. No one knew this better than she. Even at the end of her career, when a director of Covent Garden asked her to narrate *L'Histoire du soldat*, she refused: "I'm not very keen on Stravinsky. I don't really like modern music.... I don't really even approve of Puccini. Mine is the nineteenth century."

The 19th century also marks the style of Arianna Stassinopoulos, Callas's most recent biographer. The author, who never met her subject and attended only one of Callas's performances (when Stassinopoulos was ten years old), was the choice of British publisher George Weidenfeld. And an interesting choice it was. Stassinopoulos has produced a biography loaded with detail, high on hyperbole and lacking in objectivity. *Maria Callas* contains the elements of a juicy libretto, complete with malevolent mother, opportunistic husband and sadistic lover, all bent on exploiting a vulnerable female.

Stassinopoulos is best known abroad for her book *The Female Woman*, in which she attacks the feminist emphasis on career and celebrates the traditional womanly virtues. In this biography, she

---

Review of *Maria Callas: The Woman Behind the Legend* by Arianna Stassinopoulos in *The New York Times Book Review*, March 15, 1981.

portrays Callas as a tragic figure for whom Aristotle Onassis was a necessity because he awakened her sexuality and womanhood: "Aristo had brought love, frivolity, passion and tenderness to the life of a dedicated nun.... He had opened the way for a host of feelings never before experienced and impressions never before sensed.... Onassis made her aware of her sensuality, and he was her first real lover. Maria discovered sex at 36 and she discovered it through Onassis."

However frivolous this book may be, Callas was in no way frivolous. Even one note alone of hers was unmistakable; that cannot be said of anyone else. Her voice ranged from a low dramatic soprano to the highest coloratura and she could articulate virtuoso runs and trills with impeccable accuracy. Her timbre was unique, something like an English horn, and in her recordings her voice conveyed emotion as few others ever did. Callas was an extraordinary artist and one of the most electrifying personalities of our time. What caused her to subjugate herself and her art to years of degradation with Onassis, a man who "belittled her constantly: 'what are you? Nothing. You just have a whistle in your throat that no longer works' "? This is a reasonable question for any Callas biography to raise, but it is not one that is answered adequately here.

To paint a faithful portrait of her subject, the author need only have listened carefully to the central figures in the story; instead she follows their every comment with angry refutations. Callas's husband, Giovanni Battista Meneghini, a millionaire in his 50s when she married him, told a reporter when she left him for Onassis: "This man has billions, you must understand." Then Stassinopoulos undermines him: "It was the rich man's impotent envy of the superrich, the stingy millionaire's resentment at the extravagant multimillionaire." Callas's mother backs up Meneghini: "I was Maria's first victim. Now its Meneghini.... Maria would [like to] marry Onassis to further her limitless ambition." But here again Stassinopoulos argues: "She could not have shown less understanding of her daughter. Ambition was the last thought in Maria's mind when... she was at the Milan airport, boarding the private plane Onassis had sent for her."

Both literally and figuratively, Callas had an enormous appetite, and it manifested itself in behavior that Stassinopoulos repeatedly refers to in her narrative: "As was her lifelong habit, [Callas] picked what she wanted from everybody else's plates." It was not enough for her to thrill millions, to have her fans break down doors or yell themselves hoarse. Callas had to be Number One and she demanded more money than anyone else only because, as she readily admitted, she had to have the most. "I'm not interested in money," she told the Vienna State Opera, "but it has to be more than anyone else gets."

Her voraciousness knew no limits; no challenge was too much to attempt. Callas began her career singing Wagner, but she soon moved into coloratura roles and almost singlehanded revived the entire *bel canto* repertoire. She even went so far as to sing Donizetti's *Anna Bolena*, a role that the born coloratura Beverly Sills claimed took five years off her own operatic life. Callas's challenges were not merely vocal. In 1952, when she weighed 180 pounds, she set Audrey Hepburn as her model and lost 62 pounds in less than two years. By 1954 she was thin, rich, beautiful, famous. Around this time her voice began to falter and she turned her attention elsewhere. She moved into Elsa Maxwell's circle, met Aristotle Onassis and made every effort to marry him.

Unlike many sopranos, for whom the voice is an end and not a means, Callas used hers as a tool, a source of revenge, a way of thumbing her nose at the gods for a wretched childhood. Fat, ugly, acned, she lived in awe of her sister, "tall, slender, beautiful Jackie with chestnut hair and brown eyes" who was her mother's expressed favorite. All Maria ever had was her voice, and she could work wonders with it: "Only when I was singing did I feel loved." Later Callas remarked: "If you live, you struggle. It is the same for all of us. What is different are the weapons you have and the weapons that are used against you." When her mother was on welfare and appealed to her for help, she replied with a letter later published in *Time* magazine: "If you can't make enough money to live on, you can jump out of the window or drown yourself."

All of this can be gleaned from Stassinopoulos's book, which contains large doses of information, some of it useful, some of it cheap. We learn that Callas's mother, who wanted a boy to replace the son she had lost to typhoid fever, would not look at Maria when she was born. During her marriage to Meneghini, Callas was in love with the Italian film director Luchino Visconti, described by Stassinopoulos as "largely homosexual." When Callas was 43 years old, she became pregnant and, at Onassis's insistence, aborted the baby. After Onassis married Jacqueline Kennedy, Callas relied on tranquilizers and sleeping pills and attempted suicide.

The material is presented with little nuance, and conclusions are seldom drawn even when the facts cry out for some. Consider, for instance, Callas's weight loss. Stassinopoulos writes that following Callas's 1954 appearance as Queen Elizabeth of Spain in Verdi's *Don Carlo*, it was an "ironic tribute to her transformation that the rave reviews were reserved for her physical appearance" and not for her voice. Nowhere does the author suggest that the weight loss may have affected the instrument.

Stassinopoulos claims that, in contrast to Callas's passion for Onassis, her relationship with Meneghini was loveless from the start and that she married him because his wealth allowed her to be more "selective" in accepting engagements without suffering financially. "She liked his stability," the author continues, "she liked the way everyone deferred to him, and above all she liked the way he liked her."

But surely Onassis, too, appealed to her in those ways. The point is that by 1957, with a triumphant career behind her, she required a man ten times more powerful than the one she had needed ten years before. As for the matter of selectivity in accepting engagements: with Onassis as her lover, Callas became so selective that during 1963 she did not appear in a single opera. And she was then only 40 years old.

Callas claimed that there is no such thing as concidence, that "the patterns, large and small, of every aspect of her life" all had some clearly defined meaning. Unlistening, her biographer ignores the fact that the name of the sister Callas hated in her youth was the same as the woman who finally married Onassis. Nor does Stassinopoulos mention that 2-1/2 years after Onassis's death, Callas died during the very week that Jacqueline Onassis won a $20 million suit against her late husband's will. Mrs. Onassis's victory may well have been for Callas the last in a series of grotesque defeats.

To say that Callas's acquisitive purposes were outside the realm of art is, as Erikson suggests, to misunderstand art. Stassinopoulos's major error is to separate the human being from the artist: her subtitle is "The Woman Behind the Legend". In portraying the soprano as "Maria... suffocated by La Callas", Stassinopoulos has produced a lively but superficial biography. The awesome artist who is her subject deserves a more insightful evaluation.

8

EVELYN LEAR AND MARIE COLLIER

On stage the two women playing mother and daughter could hardly be more alike. Marie Collier, Australian soprano making her Metropolitan Opera debut in the world premiere of Marvin David Levy's *Mourning Becomes Electra*, is the mirror image of Evelyn Lear, American soprano making her Met debut in the same work. The striking physical resemblance is not an accident.

When the Met signed Lear for the role of Lavinia over two years ago, a search began for a mezzo-soprano who would be visually acceptable as Christine, her mother. This proved to be more difficult than anticipated. Finally composer Levy and director Michael Cacoyannis interviewed and auditioned Marie Collier, principal soprano with the Royal Opera House, Covent Garden. Collier fulfilled many crucial physical requirements: she was the same height and had the same high cheekbones and slender hips as Lear. There was only one problem: she was not a mezzo-soprano. The decision was made to alter the score, converting Christine into a soprano, the appropriate range for Collier.

The emphasis on drama and the de-emphasis on musical structure that this decision implies is consistent with the current operatic ideology: the play is, very much, the thing. Lear and Collier endorse this principle, attributing the recent focus on dramatic action to the influence that television has had on the operatic genre. In independent interviews Lear referred to herself as a "singing actress", and Collier called herself an "operatic performer". Each said that, when she is presented with a new work, she considers the libretto at least as im-

Originally published as "This *Electra* Has Two Brilliant Sopranos: Evelyn Lear and Marie Collier at the Metropolitan Opera" in *The New York Times*, April 9, 1967.

388

Evelyn Lear and Marie Collier in Marvin David Levy's *Mourning
Becomes Electra* – Metropolitan Opera production
CREDIT: Louis Melancon / Metropolitan Opera Archive

portant as the score. And each insisted that, despite some disappointing reviews in New York, *Mourning Becomes Electra* based on Eugene O'Neill's play would be well received anywhere in the world. They should know; both have made headlines through extraordinary performances in the contemporary repertoire.

*

This is where all similarities between the two brilliant and beautiful sopranos end. Evelyn Lear is succinct in characterizing the differences: "Marie is charming and sweet. I'm charming and not sweet. I'm charming and honest."

Lear reminisced, with obvious pleasure, about the vicissitudes of her life. "My grandfather, Savel Kwartin, was one of the great cantors of the world and my mother, Nina Kwartin, one of the great singers of all time. But her career was thwarted by the family. One of my most vivid recollections is of an evening on which she was to give a Town Hall recital. Can you believe that she had to cook dinner *first* — for my father, brother and myself. We were all too selfish."

Nina Kwartin's daughter resolved to realize her mother's ambitions. "I knew I wanted to be a singer from the time I was three years old," she added. "But my parents were very smart and insisted that I study music first. I took piano lessons — for a time with Ray Lev — and also studied the French horn."

The young musician had a hard time from the start. An early marriage to a young doctor ended in divorce after seven years. During this period, she began to study voice seriously and made a number of abortive attempts to establish a career. "Finally," she said, "I came to the realization that I would never make it."

Yet, in 1953, Lear reaffirmed her decision to sing and enrolled in the Opera Workshop of the Juilliard School of Music. There she met Thomas Stewart, baritone from San Saba, Texas, and "the most divine man there ever was." Within a year the two singers were married.

390

"Everything was against it," she recalled. "He was younger than I, not Jewish, and a baritone at that! On top of everything, I had two children." Lear's son was six and her daughter four, when she married Stewart.

*

Despite the hazards, the marriage proved a good one and Lear's career began to improve. She won a Concert Artist's Guild Award, gave a Town Hall recital, and sang with Thomas Scherman and the Little Orchestra Society in a performance of Ravel's *L'Enfant et les sortilèges*.

There were good reviews out of town for her work in Marc Blitzstein's musical *Reuben, Reuben* but the show folded before it reached New York.

Still ebullient over her own notices, Lear applied for the role of Maria in *West Side Story*. But Cheryl Crawford, who at that time had the option on *West Side Story*, wired Lear that she was too old for the role. Attempting to recover from this assault, the soprano auditioned for the New York City Opera Company but was rejected there, too. Thomas Stewart was also suffering. Having sung with the City Opera for one season, he was not rehired for a second. The couple decided to act on the advice of the late Frederick Cohen, director of the Juilliard workshop, and go to Europe.

Within two years, both husband and wife became members of Berlin's Deutsche Oper and since that time have become the most formidable of European stars, with Lear making headlines in performances of demanding contemporary German works and achieving global fame with her portrayal of Alban Berg's corrupt Lulu: "I love to do Handel, Mozart and Strauss, and I love to do my neurotic modern heroines too. I am never afraid to make an ugly sound on stage because it is *real* and reality is never ugly."

Reality is not ugly for Evelyn Lear today, she has reached the goal she set for herself when she was three. "I'm not the crazy, ambitious, scratching-for-any-job girl that I was a few years ago. A combination of recognition and inner security has made me the way I am now — with a real sense of inner peace. I have two healthy children, a wonderful marriage, and if I gave up my career tomorrow, I would still know I have done what I set out to do."

Marie Collier, on the other hand, insists she never set out to do anything at all: "I had no determination. I have no determination. Everything has happened to me as a result of accident and circumstance. Not one person have I ever approached. Not one move have I ever made in my own behalf."

Collier poured scotch over ice as she spoke — in careful, whispered tones — about her entrance from Australia into the international world of music. "My parents had nothing to do with music," she said. "I was interested in science. I used to take piano lessons, of course, and sing in the church choir and in amateur productions of Gilbert and Sullivan. But I didn't see my first opera until I was 19."

After finishing her education, Collier worked as a pharmacist's assistant, but was pressed into operatic service by a voice teacher who told her, "You have a gift; you must use it." The young soprano accepted the dictum and made her debut as Santuzza in *Cavalleria rusticana* with the National Theater Movement in Melbourne. She toured Australia for two years, performing in *The Tales of Hoffmann* and singing the role of Magda Sorel in Menotti's *The Consul* 75 times. Her teacher persuaded Collier's husband, Victor Borwerg, a civil engineer, that his wife could not benefit from any more Magda Sorels and that they should go to Europe.

The couple settled in Milan where Collier began to study, and within two years Lord Harewood, one of the directors of the Royal Opera House, Covent Garden, invited her to audition. Collier signed a contract in 1956. During the following eight years the soprano sang major roles in both traditional and contemporary opera, but did not reach international stardom until she replaced Maria Callas, on short notice, in a sold-out performance of *Tosca* at Covent Garden. Although Collier had sung the role there about a dozen times, this occasion provoked a 20-minute ovation and an offer of a contract with La Scala.

Collier's feat has been a heroic one. While running a house in a London suburb and raising three boys and a girl, she has managed to build a phenomenal career. Now, she looks forward to a future that is thoroughly committed. She will sing the only role in Schoenberg's monodrama, *Erwartung*, in London and follow that with a performance of the Verdi *Requiem* in addition to six Maries in *Wozzeck* at La Scala. Moreover, B. B. C. will devote a documentary program to her career, filming her at work in five countries. Despite these manifestations of worldly success, Collier suffers from anxiety and was hospitalized for three weeks last year for a condition doctors diagnosed as "nervous exhaustion". She attributes the cause of her anxiety to a lack of adequate training: "This is my specific path and I am insufficiently prepared for it. I *hate* to be insufficiently prepared."

The agony and anguish before the recent premiere of *Mourning Becomes Electra* were considerable. The cast had the benefit of only one three-hour rehearsal before the public dress rehearsal and at that time they worked only on Act I; Acts II and III were never rehearsed on the big stage. (Revisions, corrections and cuts were being made even after several performances.) In addition to the technical and musical problems with which both sopranos had to cope, they were gripped in a Eugene O'Neill drama of murder and incest which is as intense as it is relentless. That Marie Collier and Evelyn Lear could maintain a dignified working relationship as well as a cordial personal one is a feat to note in the annals of the prima donna.

POSTSCRIPT: *Marie Collier died four years later, on December 7, 1971, from a fall from a window.*

9

THE NEW YORK PHILHARMONIC
BETWEEN MEHTA AND MASUR

During a recent lunch at the Century Club, music philanthropist Avery Fisher told a friend that Zubin Mehta, director of the New York Philharmonic, had not given the management enough time to find a replacement when he told it two years in advance that he would leave at the end of the 1990-91 season.

On the surface Fisher was right; major conductors today are booked many seasons in advance. But in a larger sense he is wrong because when something seductive comes along that any one of them wants to do, he manages to work things out. When Herbert von Karajan resigned from the Berlin Philharmonic in April of this year, the orchestra's administration had no difficulty at all in finding guest conductors of the first rank to fill in all of his remaining dates.

It is one thing, of course, to rearrange one's schedule in order to be able to guest-conduct an orchestra widely regarded as the world's preeminent ensemble. It is quite another to cancel advance obligations to take on the formidable task of serving as music conductor of the New York Philharmonic, a huge and byzantine machine imbedded in a great media center. Any conductor offered the post has to ask himself whether he could make a difference.

Pierre Boulez, Mehta's predecessor, was the music director from 1971 to 1978. He came to New York with a mission: to convert a very large audience to the 20th-century music in which he believed. Considering the orchestra a part of high culture, Boulez thought he could play an important role in influencing the direction new music would take. He had history on his side; Mozart and Haydn heard their works almost as soon as they wrote them.

Originally published as "Who Cares Who Conducts the Philharmonic Museum?" in *Newsday*, August 20, 1989.

But the situation is not at all the same today and the post-Schoen-berg music Boulez favored did not go over well with the listeners. There is some irony here. The major symphony orchestras have achieved all they are ever likely to achieve in precision, virtuosity and responsiveness. Moreover they bring more music to more listeners with each passing year. Yet now the concept of the orchestra as an in-strument that fulfills a limitless range of composers' demands is in-creasingly under challenge.

The orchestra no longer serves contemporary music, but it still is extraordinarly useful as a museum, one that mounts masterpieces from the past and occasionally presents a contemporary work. It follows that the selection of a music director in New York is even more criti-cal than the selection of the head of the Metropolitan Museum of Art. The music director not only has the final word on the choices of pieces presented, but as conductor he himself must bring them to life. A con-ductor cannot hang a Beethoven score on a wall in Avery Fisher Hall. He knows his audience is unable to translate the printed notes into imagined sounds.

Julius Baker, principal flute under Leonard Bernstein, the remark-able American musician who preceded Boulez at the Philharmonic, believes the next music director should be "an inspiring man of music, a consummate musician with a skillful baton technique." There are still such men of the right age—Claudio Abbado, Carlos Kleiber, Klaus Tennstedt, Charles Dutoit, Sir Colin Davis. Rumor has it that Sir Colin, the 62-year-old English conductor, and Abbado, the 53-year-old Italian, have been offered the post, but turned it down. Chances are the others, if approached, would do the same to one of the most pres-tigious positions in the music world. Here are a few of the reasons why:

First, the orchestra members in New York are famously contentious with conductors. They are fiercely independent because the city of-fers them so much free-lance musical income. Second, the audience is surly. Listeners leave if a work is unfamiliar or if they have to catch a train. Third, the critics are not merely tough. There has been a virtual tradition dating back to the Philharmonic's earliest days for the major reviewers to test their power by seeing how long it takes them to bring the orchestra's music director down.

Another problem is rehearsal time. It is, of course, crucial to the quality of performance. But the musicians' union prohibits flexible schedules. If there is a conventional program one week and a difficult one the next, rehearsal cannot be diverted from one period to the other.

The cost of extra rehearsal time is prohibitive, and money is at the root of other problems as well. The New York Philharmonic used to derive considerable royalties from the sale of its records, but, because its records do not sell, the orchestra has not recorded under Mehta for some time. Any music director the Philharmonic chooses today will almost certainly have to be one a record company wants to record. At this instant, the talk is of Giuseppe Sinopoli, who has conducted the New York Philharmonic and records for Deutsche Grammophon. Sinopoli is not just a conductor. He is also a composer, a surgeon and a psychiatrist. He claims to use Freudian principles when he deals with musicians, whatever that means.

Recordings of Sinopoli's performances reveal a musician who can be mannered, even eccentric. But it is possible that those who make the final choice of music director of the New York Philharmonic will give greater consideration to his other talents and to his connection to Deutsche Grammophon. And Sinopoli, at 42, may be young enough, and possibly psychoanalyzed enough, to have the courage to say yes.

POSTSCRIPT: *As this book is going to press, Sinopoli is director of the Dresden Staatskapelle while Kurt Masur is in his fourth season with the New York Philharmonic. Covering the opening concert, Edward Rothstein, chief music critic of the* Times, *wrote that the orchestra has become "a conservative institution in the best sense. One does not look to Mr. Masur for leadership in the performance of new music. One looks to him for restorative, sometimes inspired interpretations of the great orchestra tradition."*

coda

10

AN IDIOSYNCRATIC BALANCE:
PARENTS AND GENIUS CHILDREN

It is obvious that every student here tonight is not only exceptionally bright but has flowered intellectually. So it might appear
presumptuous of me to address you on the subject of what makes the
gifted succeed or fail. But the years just ahead are critical ones in terms
of the crystallization of careers. So I thought it might be useful if I were
to share with you some information not generally known about the
lives of a few remarkable musicians. Because I believe in multiple intelligence — a theory that holds that basic intelligence is a pool that can
go in any direction — into art, science, mathematics, business — it follows that I think the lessons learned in music are equally valid in any
other field.

Music, incidentally, generally lags behind the other arts. The
Renaissance in fine arts predates that in music; the Impressionistic
painters Cezanne and Renoir predate the Impressionist composers
Debussy and Ravel. Even in societal aspects music lags. I say this to
explain why there are no women in my examples. Still, it must be emphasized that this is not a scientific study. I am merely reporting here
observations I have made based on the lives of the small sample of men
who are the subjects of my biographies.

Now I would like to take you back to a church in San Francisco in
the spring of 1978. A 75-year-old Hungarian pianist is playing the two
St. Francis Legends by Liszt to raise money to pay his wife's medical
bills. The Liszt pieces are long and very difficult yet many in the
church that day say they think they are listening to Liszt himself. A
music lover tapes the performance and sends it to the head of the International Piano Archives who is stunned by what he hears. The per-

---

For the Phi Beta Kappa Society, New York University, May 22,
1984.

former is Erwin Nyireghazi, a phenomenal prodigy of the turn of the century, described as second only to that greatest of child prodigies Josef Hofmann. Erwin Nyireghazi has not been heard from in 50 years.

His story is a remarkable one. At three he was discovered to have perfect pitch. At six he began to play the piano almost every evening for the British aristocracy. At eight he played for Queen Mary, who conversed with him in English, then in German. He also played in public, performing a piano concerto under the direction of the legendary conductor Arthur Nikisch. From the age of six, Erwin heard himself referred to as a genius by his mother who alerted a Hungarian psychoanalyst, Dr. Gesa Revesz, to his special gifts. For six years Dr. Revesz spent a few hours a day several days a week with the boy and wrote a book, *The Psychology of a Musical Genius,* in which he published some of the child's compositions and compared him to the young Mozart.

Possessed with the ability to memorize a complicated score after only one or two performances, Erwin also sightread scores in a breathtaking way. Yet this extraordinarily gifted man dropped out of public view for 50 years. Between the late 1920s and the late 1970s, when he was living in California, Nyireghazi occasionally played the piano for a small fee at parties attended by Hungarians. His single claim to fame during that time was an anonymous one: he had his hands filmed so that they could appear as if they were those of Cornell Wilde, the movie actor who played Chopin in the biographical film, *A Song to Remember.* Most important, according to his own account, Nyireghazi continued to compose every day of his life, completing more than 800 scores which are on microfilm in a vault in a San Francisco bank.

But alcoholism and an insatiable sexual appetite characterized the years between prodigy and rediscovery. He did not own a piano during that period. Yet that day, in that San Francisco church, Nyireghazi set the music world on its ears. Critics, managers, publicists alike all responded with uncharacteristic zeal.

400

Harold Schonberg, then chief music critic of the *New York Times*, thought that in Nyireghazi he had found a living representative of the return to romanticism he had been promoting for years. Schonberg wrote repeatedly of Nyireghazi, claiming his playing was like — and I quote — "nobody else's." Most of the critical community agreed; and the outside world responded. The Ford Foundation, committed to funding institutions alone, broke all precedent and set aside $38,000 to help Nyireghazi get back on his feet. Baldwin provided free pianos, one on the west coast, one of the east. CBS Records signed Nyireghazi to a lucrative contract, and started by issuing a two-record album and one single disk, which many people in the audience may have on their shelves. An agent arranged a three-part deal: an author would write Nyireghazi's biography which would be published by Random House. The book would serve as a vehicle for a Hollywood film and a TV movie-of-the-week.

Through all of this I remained reserved, a stance that is out of character for me. When my colleagues asked why, I replied I thought it unlikely that a man who had so successfully failed for so long would turn himself around just to please them. Clearly there had been something far more gratifying to him in his absence from the concert stage than in his presence there.

But what that something was I did not yet know and I went to San Francisco to try to find out. Nyireghazi told me he would need four double scotches to free himself from his inhibitions so he could begin to speak truthfully to me. I provided the alcohol and he told me his story over a period of several days.

His parents were born in Budapest. His father, a tenor in the Royal Opera House, had loved music. Erwin adored his father and says the man wanted nothing more than to inculcate a love of music in his son. He died when Erwin was only eleven years old. "It was then," Nyireghazi said, "that I began to hate giving concerts. I was entirely in my mother's hands. It was she who drove me into a career. She wanted both the money and the fame and was not interested in music

401

for its own sake. My mother exercised complete authority over me. Once she broke an umbrella over my head. Because she wanted people to think of me as a precocious prodigy, she had me wearing short pants and long curls until I was well into my teens. I fought with her bitterly and constantly. During the war she was killed in a concentration camp. I am grateful to Hitler for that."

At 17 Nyireghazi had left Europe for the United States. Although he made the move primarily to break with his mother, it was she who arranged for a concert management here to organize three Carnegie Hall recitals soon after his arrival, in the fall of 1920. The first was sold out, but the second and third were not. Critics complained of the liberties that Nyireghazi took with the scores, even to the point of changing notes. Within a few years he was a Times Square shuttle vagrant. Fifty years later, in 1978, when the critics were looking for a single cause for this dramatic downfall, they came up with "malicious management". While it is true that Nyireghazi's initial reluctance to make piano rolls for mechanical pianos, as called for in his contract, angered his management, it is unlikely that any single confrontation with a business associate could have brought about the degrading decline that characterized Nyireghazi's adult life. Motives for human behavior are, of course, infinitely complex, but my intelligence and intuition both suggest that one motive transcends all the rest: Nyireghazi's determination to undermine his mother's will at all cost.

For even after the church performance, after all the brouhaha, Nyireghazi disappeared once again from the spotlight. Alcohol, irresponsible behavior, the abuse of those who were working with him, all played a role in this decline as they must have half a century before. He continued to compose every day — he is said to write in a style that is a mix of Tchaikovsky and Brahms — he still consumed large quantities of Scotch, and he lived in the same dollar-a-day flophouse that he had been in when the International Piano Archives, the Ford Foundation, Baldwin Pianos, CBS Records, Random House *et al.* invaded his life.

402

It is, of course, nothing new to say that the so-called stage mother, a woman who uses her child as a tool for money or her own ego gratification, is a destructive phenomenon. Everyone probably would agree to that. In fact most observers of the human condition — psychologists and sociologists — say that the best approach to young genius is that of gentle nurturing. Their belief is that many geniuses never fulfill their promise because their need for nurturing goes unheeded.

My experience suggests something else, something, in fact, that is strikingly different: the father whose genius-son succeeds has insistently insulted the child's gifts in that area and put every possible obstacle in his way. Too much parental involvement in a particular field — whether the aggressive exploitation suffered by a Nyireghazi or the kind support offered in other quarters — tends to dull the child's own natural competitive instinct and create a good degree of indolence. On the other hand, persistent doses of harsh resistance seem to goad the young person's resolve to do precisely what his father says he cannot.

From Erwin Nyireghazi to Leonard Bernstein is a long road. Bernstein [in 1984] is an achieved composer, conductor, pianist, teacher, television personality, author, probably the most exciting living musician, surely the most visible one.

Bernstein's father was not a tenor in any Royal Opera House. Sam Bernstein was the oldest child in a Chassidic family in Beresdiv in the Ukraine and fled to America when he was 16. He started to work in the Fulton fish market in New York. Through strength of character and ambition, he built up a beauty supply business that, in the early 30s, provided his family with a winter and summer house, two cars, a succession of maids and a butler/chauffeur.

Leonard, the oldest of his three children, never liked his father's business. In fact he so wanted to separate himself from his father's ways that, at the age of ten, the year he touched a keyboard for the first time in his life, he started both a secret culture and a language shared by close friends and siblings which kept his father at a considerable distance. That private language persists among the siblings today.

The upright piano, left by an aunt moving out of Boston, captivated Leonard immediately and, by the time he reached his teens, he was playing very well. Father fought son bitterly in this. Sam's only experience with musicians had been in the shtetls of the old country where they played for weddings and bar mitzvahs in exchange for a few kopeks, some food or a night's lodging. Sam refused to give Leonard money for lessons and warned him repeatedly that if he persisted in his ways he would end up under a palm tree in a cocktail lounge. Leonard earned money for lessons playing in a local jazz band.

Through a series of then unimaginable events, at the age of 25, Leonard Bernstein took over the New York Philharmonic in a performance that was broadcast coast to coast. A front-page story appeared in the next day's *New York Times* along with a photograph of the bow-tied young man. Offers from orchestras poured in and interviews abounded.

Burton Bernstein, Leonard's younger brother, has described their father's reaction to these heady events in his book *Family Matters:*

"Our new neighborhood in Brookline [Massachusetts] was abuzz with the news that Lenny Bernstein's family was moving in. Sam was more dazzled and confused than anyone else by Lenny's fame and the attention being paid to him and his family. After all he had made no secret of his unhappiness with Lenny's artistic bent. Indeed, he had used his considerable power to obstruct it. Could he now take credit, in part, for the miracle? At first he tried. In his initial interviews with the hungry press, his statements were of the 'I-knew-he-had-it-in-him-all-the-time' variety. One multi-column interview, with photographs on the feature page of the Boston Sunday *Post* prompted general wincing. Its headline read: 'Father in Tears at Boy Conductor's

Triumph. Boston Merchant calls Son's Accomplishment: "My contribution to an America that has done Everything for Me".' "

But Sam Bernstein was subscribing to clipping services then and
read the interviews his son was giving: "Lenny was uncommonly
frank about his father," Burton Bernstein writes, "describing him as
something of an ogre who had done all he could to prevent Lenny
from becoming a musician."

This upset Sam a great deal. He developed ulcers and shingles. He
even consulted a Boston psychoanalyst. At 25, Leonard Bernstein had
triumphed over a tough and rejecting father in a remarkable and
potent way. (I would like to add, parenthetically, that Sam's strength
returned and he lived until the age of 77.)

It is important to note that Leonard's sister, Shirley, was an ally with
her brother from the earliest years. In fact, in my relatively small
sample, I have found that when gifted sons have had sisters, those
sisters, talented and strong in their own right but without the promise
of distinguished careers for themselves, have channelled their own
energies and skills into helping their brothers achieve the fame that
they did. Whether this works in reverse — with the brother helping
the endowed sister — I cannot even hazard a guess.

Let us look at Pierre Boulez. Boulez was Bernstein's successor as
music director of the New York Philharmonic. He is also a fine composer and a brilliant theorist. Throughout his teens, according to his
sister, she interceded with their father in support of a career in music
for Boulez. It was, she said, referring to his choice of music as a career,
a "clear-cut decision *against* his father." In reconstructing the battle to
me, Boulez characterized it in the following way: "Our parents were
strong. But finally, we were stronger than they."

And so it goes, at least in the 20th century, where rebellion informs
so much of our culture. Stravinsky's father, insulting his son's musical talent, insisted the young man attend law school. It was not until
the elder Stravinsky died that Igor was able to leave law school and
embark on an organized path of study in music. Stravinsky's mother

was equally negative. She did not hear *Le Sacre du printemps*, Stravinsky's pathbreaking work of 1913, until its 25th anniversary performance and then she told friends she did not expect to like it, that he did not compose "her" kind of music. Edgard Varèse, perhaps the most revolutionary composer of the 20th century—his vision led directly to electronic music—described his father as a "kind of Prussian sergeant, the drill-master type." Henri Varèse, an engineer who wanted his son to follow in his own path, was so agitated by Edgard's interest in music that he locked the grand piano, covered it with a shroud, and kept the key hidden from his son. When the boy finally did go to the conservatory for lessons in harmony and counterpoint, he did it in absolute secrecy. Varèse's biographer writes: "As soon as any man established a relationship with Varèse involving authority over him—Rodin, the renowned sculptor, or d'Indy, the composer, for example—that relationship was bound to fall apart very quickly. Behind the face of a d'Indy lurked the features of his father, hated since birth. Because of this it took very little—a simple criticism which Varèse disliked intensely—to make all his aggressiveness, his willfulness, and his violence burst through to the surface."

Clearly these harsh and controlling fathers did not succeed in crushing their genius-sons. For the sons possessed enough ego strength—in addition, of course, to their gifts—not only to resist but resist brilliantly. The hostile aggression, however, seems to be an important component of each of these people's temperaments when they were young.

But the other part of the equation—of the peculiar balance I referred to in the title of my talk, is that for the child to survive such unrelenting harsh treatment, there had to be support somewhere. With Bernstein and Boulez it was provided by ever-adoring mothers and sisters. With Stravinsky an uncle; with Varèse a grandfather. The idiosyncratic balance appears to be this: large doses of criticism and oppression of the son from the father in combination with unconditional love from somebody else. In any event it is academic: even the

406

knowledge of the precise formula cannot translate into families delivering it.

There are two points with which I would like to end this talk. The first is that whatever you are doing now—and here I address the parents—clearly it cannot be all wrong. You have produced Phi Beta Kappa students. The second is that, when in the future your child's career turns momentarily sour, your *last* reaction should be one of guilt for the angry remarks you may have made in the past. For it is probably those very occasions when you withheld sweet encouragement that you made the most crucial contributions to the great successes I know these men and women will achieve.

11

JEROME LOWENTHAL AND THE JEWISH COMPOSER

After Jerome Lowenthal's Alice Tully Hall concert last month, people from the audience waited to greet the pianist in the Green Room. Among them was the Arab wife of Edward Said, the Columbia professor and Palestinian activist, who asked Lowenthal what he was playing at his next New York recital. Lowenthal replied that on February 11th he would perform works by Mendelssohn, Meyerbeer, Milhaud, Gershwin and the contemporary composer, George Rochberg. "What an interesting program," Mrs. Said remarked. "You can be certain I'll be there."

Lowenthal mentioned this reaction to a guest at a supper party given for him by Itzhak Perlman after the Tully Hall concert. His point was that the February program was valid musically, would attract the music-loving public, and did not need any extra-musical thread. But the fact is that there is such a thread and one bound to generate controversy, for all the composers Lowenthal is performing were at least *born* Jewish.

One must emphasize the word "born" for until recently conversion was not uncommon among Jews working outside their religious traditions. Mahler had himself baptised at 37 to be eligible for the directorship of the Vienna Opera. Schoenberg, also for pragmatic reasons, converted to Lutheranism at 24. Gertrude Schoenberg, the composer's widow, explained that conversion was "quite a usual procedure for educated Jews as the belief in assimilation at this time flourished." Mozart's great librettist, Lorenzo da Ponte, converted. So did Jacques Offenbach, who became a Catholic. And so, of course, did Felix Mendelssohn. And even in the case of this awesome prodigy, the cultivated were not beyond prejudice. Carl Freidrich Zelter, the German com-

---

Written for *The New York Times*, February 1981.

poser, conductor, and teacher of Mendelssohn, wrote to Goethe about Felix: "The pupil is a good, pretty boy, lively and obedient; to be sure he is the son of a Jew but no Jew himself.... It would really be something if the son of a Jew turned out to be an artist."

In contrast to past times, the Hebrew Arts School of the Abraham Goodman House invited Lowenthal to participate in its "Heritage Concerts" series. Lowenthal, a slightly built, soft-spoken intelligent man, described what led to this particular event.

"I received a call from the director of the Hebrew Arts School who asked me to give a recital of music by Jewish composers. Without thinking, I said no. The woman was very nice and asked: 'Why not think about it?'

"I have many ties to Israel," Lowenthal went on. "I lived there from 1958 to 1961, played at the home of the President, and performed repeatedly with the Israeli Philharmonic. Whenever I played conventional recitals in synagogues, someone would come to me afterwards and say: 'All my life my mother talked to me about Jewish *lieder* and I came hoping for something like that." I would answer that I was sorry but *that* was not what I did. The person would invariably comment: 'Ah, these Americans.' "

Lowenthal not only has memories of Israel; he maintains strong and important ties. At ten, when his father died, he became a protégé of the Philadelphia music patron, Frederick R. Mann. Mann has a large concert hall named after him in Tel Aviv. And Lowenthal's deceased wife, Romit Amir, also a pianist, was born and raised in Israel. These associations may have played at least some role in what followed the call from Goodman House, for Lowenthal reports that the program had its origins in what he calls a "series of visions".

"First Mendelssohn's *Variations serieuses* appeared as the opening, 'beautiful' piece, then George Rochberg's *Partita-Variations* for the big, serious work, the one that fills the second half of the first part of a program. The Rochberg work possesses the kind of aesthetic strength an audience wants at the center of a concert. For the second part,

Milhaud's rarely heard *Saudades do Brazil* came to mind, then Gershwin's *Three Preludes,* so loved abroad, and finally the mandatory virtuoso 'Liszt' piece; this was my great inspiration: Meyerbeer through a Liszt transcription, *Grand fantaisie dramatique sur Les Huguenots.*"

Lowenthal said he asked the school to consider the program. "I said that if they wanted a program that would emphasize Jewish elements in music, this most assuredly was not it. For my program emphasizes Jewish eclecticism. And that is not a pejorative word with me. All art is eclectic. Artists are bees who gather their honey from every flower that attracts them. So to be eclectic is not specifically Jewish but it is my belief that Jews are more receptive to finding their sources in any and every place than the artist in general is.

"From a technical point of view," the pianist went on, "none of the music I am playing has any specific Jewish elements in it. There is no preponderance of augmented seconds or of minor tonalities. But from a spiritual point of view the situation is far more complex. If we say that something of Jewishness is essential to the character of the Jew, then, almost by definition, there is something Jewish in all this music. Still, I want to emphasize that the six composers whose works I am playing represent six different aesthetic visions. The fact that they are Jewish is simply a source of pride to me."

George Rochberg does not share Lowenthal's point of view. He says that when he first learned of the recital, he fired back a note to the pianist: "I am delighted you are playing my music — but under such strange circumstances!"

In a telephone conversation, Rochberg explained:

"I don't really respond to this whole approach. It's a narrowing, parochial idea. It deprives you of the broader context of the world in which you grew up. Sure, I'm the son of immigrant parents but music, to me, is not the product of this. And at this late date it seems foolish to me to identify works of composition by biologically inherited con-

410

nections or self-affiliated loyalties. What *is* Jewishness? The whole question is a quagmire; but one thing I am certain of is that the Jewishness I don't want to be associated with is the Jewishness of the early decades of this century—the Lower East Side of New York, the accents, the Jew afraid of the world around him."

Rochberg believes that the less attention to the issue the better. "I cannot help but believe," he explains, "that there is an indelible connection between Orthodox Judaism and the Holocaust. I prefer to feel free of all those traditionalisms and I do. I am absolutely free of them."

Lowenthal's concert is not an isolated case of the grouping together of Jewish composers. Judith Raskin gave a recital of explicitly Jewish music—songs based on Yiddish, Hebrew and liturgical texts—composed by five living Jewish composers: A. W. Binder, Lazar Weiner, Miriam Gideon, Hugo Weisgall and Ezra Laderman. And a Conference of Contemporary Music at the Y included a panel of composers that was comprised entirely of Jews.

The question of separatism in music attracts attention today what with the proliferation of concerts of music by women and blacks. But in such instances these composers often have difficulty being heard in any context other than this separatist one. That, of course, can hardly be said of Mendelssohn, Meyerbeer, Milhaud, Gershwin, Rochberg or any members of the Y panel. To some it seems ironic that at a time when Jewish composers hold so eminent and solid a position as they do in international art, these three particular events should occur.

Reaction among musicians to the Lowenthal concert has been predictably varied. On the one hand Elie Siegmeister says: "What could be the objection to it? I think it's an interesting program and one that has never been done. Even in my so-called American pieces, there are some basic Hebraic elements." On the other hand Morton Gould, generally cool and unflappable and a man rarely heard to speak harshly about anyone or anything, was passionate in his denunciation:

411

"For us to add ammunition to people who tend to think there is something special about being Jewish — other than getting our brains blown out from time to time — is very dangerous. It's the other side of the Hitler coin. Such a program does imply there is something special about Jewish composers and that simply is not so.

"If one were to do a concert of liturgical music, that would be understandable. Or a concert of music played only in Minsk, a Jewish ghetto, that, too, would be understandable. Or if one were to do a program of Jewish composers who have never been exposed, were short-circuited in some way or disappeared for some reason, that would be a viable idea.

"But to do a concert of Mendelssohn, Meyerbeer, and the others is wrong from every point of view. In the future programs may appear with asterisks after each of their names. Instead of 'Steinway Piano' on the bottom of the page, we may read 'Jewish composer' instead."

In a *New York Times Book Review* of *Voices Within the Ark: The Modern Jewish Poets*, Harold Bloom raises the notion of Jewish sensibility and asks if it can be defined in any way that is not strictly thematic. To that question Lowenthal and Siegmeister would say yes and Rochberg and Gould would answer no. Bloom then goes on to suggest that the price of feeling deeply at home may well be cultural extinction and that the "repressed motive" behind such anthologies as this is the need to reassert profound and mysterious ties at a time when they are becoming frighteningly tenuous.

Which could also explain the Jewish concerts.

412

SELECTED COMPOSITIONS
BY 20TH-CENTURY COMPOSERS CITED IN THE TEXT
INCLUDING GUIDE TO EDITIONS AND RECORDINGS

ABBREVIATIONS:

C / Chamber	PE / Performing Edition
Chor / Chorus	PS / Piano Score
Ens / Ensemble	SS / Study Score
O / Orchestra	VS / Vocal Score
P / Philharmonic	
Pl / Players	Cass / Cassette
R / Radio	CD / Compact disc
S / Symphony	LP / Long-playing record

PUBLISHERS / LIBRARIES / ASSOCIATIONS:

Amberson: *see G. Schirmer*

American Composers Alliance (ACA): *see American Composers Edition Inc.*

American Composers Edition Inc. / 170 West 74th Street / New York NY 10023 / (212) 362-8900

American Music Center (AMC) / 30 West 26th Street – Suite 1001 / New York NY 10010 / (212) 366-5260

American Musicological Society (AMS) / 201 South 34th Street / Philadelphia PA 19104 / (215) 898-8698

American Society of Composers, Authors and Publishers (ASCAP) / 1 Lincoln Plaza / New York NY 10023 / (212) 621-6329; 7920 Sunset Boulevard – Suite 300 / Los Angeles CA 90046 / (213) 883-1000

Amphion Editions Musicales, Paris: *see Theodore Presser*

Arrow Music Press: *see Boosey & Hawkes*

Associated Music Publishers: *see G. Schirmer Inc.*

Belmont Music Publishers / P.O. Box 231 / Pacific Palisades CA 90272 / (310) 454-1867

Belwin-Mills Publishing Corp.: *see Theodore Presser (rental); CPP/Belwin Inc. (other)*

Boelke-Bomart Publications: *see Jerona*

Boosey & Hawkes Inc. / 52 Cooper Square / New York NY 10003 (212) 979-1090 (rental/sales)

Broadcast Music Inc. (BMI) / 320 West 57th Street / New York NY 10019 / (212) 588-2000

Chappell Music Co.: *see Theodore Presser (band rental); Warner/Chappell (other)*

Chester Music New York Inc.: *see G. Schirmer*

Colfranc New York: *see Boosey & Hawkes*

Cos Cobb Press: *see Boosey & Hawkes*

CPP/Belwin Inc. / 15800 NW 48th Street / Miami FL 33014 / (305) 620-1500

413

Elkan-Vogel Inc.: *see Theodore Presser*
ECS Publishing / 138 Ipswich Street / Boston MA 02215 / (617) 236-1935
Eulenburg Miniature Scores: *see European American*
European American Music Distributors Corp. / P.O. Box 850 / Valley
    Forge PA 19482 / (610) 648-0506
Faber Music Inc. / 50 Cross Street / Winchester MA 01890 / (617) 756-0323
Carl Fischer Inc. / 62 Cooper Square / New York NY 10003 / (212) 777-
    0900
Galaxy Music Corp., Boston: *see ECS Publishing*
H. W. Gray Co. Inc.: *see CPP/Belwin Inc.*
Edition Wilhelm Hansen: *see Music Sales Corp. (sales), G. Schirmer (rental)*
Henmar Press: *see C.F. Peters*
Heugel & Cie., Paris: *see Theodore Presser*
International League of Women Composers / Southshore Road / Box
    670 / Point Peninsula / Three Mile Bay NY 13693 / (315) 649-5086
International Music Co. / 5 West 37ht Street / New York NY 10018 / (212)
    391-4200
Jalni Publications: *see Boosey & Hawkes*
Jerona Music Corp. / P.O. Box 5010 / Hackensack NJ 07606 / (201) 488-
    0550
Edwin F. Kalmus & Co. Inc. / 6403 West Rogers Circle / Boca Raton FL
    33487 / (407) 241-6340
E.C. Kerby Ltd.: *see Boosey & Hawkes (rental); Hal Leonard (other)*
League of Composers: *see American Music Center*
Hal Leonard Publishing Corp. / P.O. Box 13819 / 7777 West Blue Mount
    Road / Milwaukee WI 53213 / (414) 774-3630
Library of Congress Music Division / James Madison Memorial Building
    – Room 113 / Washington DC 20540 / (202) 707-5507
Margun Music Inc./Gunmar / 167 Dudley Road / Newton Centre MA
    02159 / (617) 332-6398
E.B. Marks Music Corp.: *see Theodore Presser (rentals), Hal Leonard (other)*
McGinnis & Marx Music Publishers / 236 West 26th Street – Suite 11-S /
    New York NY 10001 / (212) 675-1630
Merion Music Inc.: *see Theodore Presser*
Mills Music Inc.: *see CPP/Belwin Inc.*
Music Sales Corp. / 225 Park Avenue South / New York NY 10003 / (212)
    254-2100 / distr. ctr: 5 Bellvale Road / Chester NY 10918 / 914) 469-2271
National Endowment for the Arts (NEA): *see National Endowment for the
    Humanities*
National Endowment for the Humanities (NEH) / 1100 Pennsylvania
    Avenue NW / Washington DC 20506 / (202) 606-8438
New Music West / P.O. Box 7434 / Van Nuys CA 91409 / (818) 840-0730
Oxford University Press / 200 Madison Avenue / New York 10016 / (800)
    334-4249
New York Public Library Music Division / 40 Lincoln Center PlAza/
    New York NY 10023/ (212) 870-1625

414

Peermusic (Peer International Corp.) / 810 Seventh Avenue / New York NY 10019 / (212) 265-3910

C.F. Peters Corp. / 373 Park Avenue South / New York NY 10016 / (212) 686-4147

Theodore Presser Co. / Presser Place / Bryn Mawr PA 19010 / (610) 525-3636

PWM (Polskie Wydawnictwo Muzycne): *see Theodore Presser*

G. Ricordi & Co.: *see Boosey & Hawkes*

G. Schirmer Inc. / 5 Bellvale Road / Chester NY 10908 (rental); *see also Hal Leonard (sales)*

Schott Music Corp.: *see European American Music*

Southern Music Publishing Co., Inc.: *see Peermusic*

Stockhausen-Verlag / Kurten (Germany)

Universal Edition: *see European American*

Warner/Chappell Music Inc. / 10585 Santa Monica Boulevard / Los Angeles CA 90025 / (310) 441-8600

SELECTED VOCAL MUSIC

Choral

BARTÓK: *CANTATA PROFANA (THE NINE ENCHANTED STAGS)*(1930). Pub (SS/PE): Universal. Pub (VS): Boosey & Hawkes
●Aler, Tomlinson, Boulez, Chicago SO & Chor [Deutsche Grammophon CD 435863-2 GH]

BERIO: *A–RONNE* (radiophonic documentary for 5 actors; concert vers. for 8 voices)(orig. on tape)(1975)
●Berio, Swingle II [London CD 425620-2]

BERIO: *CORO* for Chorus & Orchestra (1976)
●Berio, Cologne RSO & Chor [Deutsche Grammophon LP 2531270; CD 423 902-2]

BERIO: *SINFONIA* for 8 Voices & Orchestra (1968-69)(30m). Pub (PE): Universal
●New Swingle Singers, Boulez, O National de France [Erato/Warner CD 2292 45228-2]

BERNSTEIN: *CHICHESTER PSALMS* for Chorus & Orchestra (1965)(18m). Pub: Boosey & Hawkes
●Bernstein, Camerata Singers, New York P [Columbia LP MS 6792]
●Bernstein, Vienna Youth Chor, Israel PO [Deutsche Grammophon CD 415 965-2 GH]

BERNSTEIN: *SONGFEST* (Cycle) for 6 Singers & Orchestra (or Piano) (1977)(41m). Pub (VS): Amberson/Boosey & Hawkes, Jalni (corrected ed.)
●Dale, Elias, Williams, Gramm, Reardon, Rosenshein, Bernstein, National SO [Deutsche Grammophon CD 415 965-2 GH]

BERNSTEIN: *SYMPHONY 3:* see Orchestral Works (Symphonies)

BLITZSTEIN: *THE AIRBORNE SYMPHONY:* see Orchestral Works (Symphonies)

BOULEZ: *LE SOLEIL DES EAUX* (cantata) for Soprano, Chorus & Orchestra (radio play vers. 1948; cantata vers. 1958, 1965)(8m)
●Bryn-Julson, Boulez, BBC SO & Chor [Erato CD 2292-45494-2]
●Nendick, McDaniel, Devos, Boulez, BBC SO & Chor [EMI CD 63948-2]
●Also vers. with Boulez, BBC SO & Chor [Angel LP]

BRITTEN: *A CEREMONY OF CAROLS,* Op 28 (1942). Pub (VS): Boosey & Hawkes
●Guest, St John's College Choir [London CD 430097-2 LM; Argo cass KCSP 164]

BRITTEN: *SPRING SYMPHONY:* see Orchestral Works (Symphonies)

BRITTEN: *WAR REQUIEM* for Soprano, Tenor, Baritone, Chorus & Orchestra, Op 66 (1962). Pub (SS/VS): Boosey & Hawkes
●Vishnevskaya, Pears, Fischer-Dieskau, Bach Choir, Britten, London SO & Chorus [London 2-CD 414383-2 LH2; cass 5-1255]
●Harper, Langridge, Shirley-Quirk, Hickox, London SO & Chor [Chandos 2-CD CHAN 8983/4; cass DBTD 2032]

HARBISON: *THE FLIGHT INTO EGYPT* for Soprano, Baritone, Chorus & Insts (1986)(48m). Pub: Associated/Hal Leonard; 1987 Pulitzer Prize
●Anderson, Sylvan, Hoose, Cantata Singers & Ens [New World CD 80395-2]

HENZE: *DAS FLOSS DER MEDUSE (THE RAFT OF MEDUSA)* (oratorio) for Speaker, Soprano, Baritone, Chorus & Orchestra (1968)
●Moser, Fischer-Dieskau, Regnier, Henze, Nordeutschen Rundfunks O & Chor [Deutsche Grammophon 2-LP DG 139428-139429]

LEIBOWITZ: *CHANSON DADA* for Children's Chorus & Instruments (1968)

McCARTNEY & DAVIS: *LIVERPOOL ORATORIO* (1991)
●Te Kanawa, Burgess, Hadley, White, Davis, Royal Liverpool PO & Chor [Angel 2-CD CDQB 54371; 2-cass 4D2Q 54371]

SCHOENBERG: *GURRELIEDER* (1901-13). Pub (SS): Universal
●Jerusalem, Dunn, Fassbaender, Brecht, Haage, Hotter, St Hedwig Chor, Chailly, Berlin RSO [London 2-CD 4330321-2 LH2]
●Norman, Troyanos, McCracken, Klemperer, Ozawa, Boston SO, Tanglewood Chor [Philips 2-CD 412 511-2 PH2]

SCHOENBERG: *DIE JAKOBSLEITER (JACOB'S LADDER)* (oratorio) (1922; completed W. Zillig)
●Boulez, BBC SO & Chor, Ens InterContemporain [Sony CD SMK 48462]

SESSIONS: *WHEN LILACS LAST IN THE DOORYARD BLOOM'D* (cantata) for Soprano, Mezzo-Soprano, Baritone, Orchestra & Chorus (1970) (40m). Pub (VS): Merion Music/Theodore Presser
●Hinds, Quivar, Cossa, Ozawa, Boston SO, Tanglewood Fest Chorus [New World LP; CD NW-296-2]

STOCKHAUSEN: *STIMMUNG* for 6 Vocalists (1968)(72m). Pub: Universal
●Collegium Vocale Köln [Deutsche Grammmphon LP]
●Flowers, Walmsley-Clark, Long, Covey-Crump, Rose, Hillier [Hyperion CD CDA 66115]

STRAVINSKY: *SYMPHONIE DE PSAUMES:* see Orchestral Works (Symphonies)

THOMSON: *5 SONGS TO POEMS OF WILLIAM BLAKE:* see Voice(s) and Instrument(s)

WEBERN: *CANTATA 1* for Soprano, Chorus & Orchestra, Op 29 (1939). Pub (PE): Universal

417

WEBERN: *CANTATA* 2 for Soprano, Bass, Chorus & Orchestra, Op 31 (1943). Pub (SS): Universal

WOLPE: *CANTATA ABOUT SPORT* (1952)

WUORINEN: *GENESIS* (oratorio) for Chorus & Orchestra (1989). Pub: Peters
● De Waart, Minnesota O & Chorale [Koch CD]

Stage & Dramatic Works

BARTÓK: *DUKE BLUEBEARD'S CASTLE* (1-act opera), Op 48 (1911). Pub (VS): Universal/Boosey & Hawkes
● Troyanos, Nimsgern, Boulez, BBC SO [CBS]
● Marton, Ramey, Fischer, Hungarian State Opera [CBS/Sony CD MK 44523]
● Ludwig, Berry, Kertesz, London SO [London CD 414167-2]
● Also LPs [Columbia LP M34217 & MS 6425]

BERIO: *PASSAGIO (messa in scena)* for Soprano, 2 Choruses & Orchestra (1962)

BERNSTEIN: *CANDIDE* (comic operetta)(1956). Pub (VS): Schirmer
● Anderson, Ludwig, Jones, Hadley, Gedda, Green, Ollman, Bernstein, London SO (composer's final rev. vers. 1989) [Deutsche Grammophon 2-CD 429734-2; cass 429734-4]
● Mills, Eisler, Lankston, Mauceri, NYC Opera (1985 opera house vers) [New World 2-CD NW 340-41-2; 2-cass NW 340/41-4]
● Stadler, Baker, Brennan, etc. [Columbia 2-LP S2X 32923]
¶ OVERTURE. Pub (SS): Schirmer, Jalni
● Bernstein, New York P [CBS/Sony 3-CD SM3K 47154]
● Mehta, Los Angeles PO [London cass 5-7031]
¶ OVERTURE & EXCERPTS
● Cook, Adrian, Rounseville, Krachmalnick (orig Broadway cast 1956) [CBS/Sony CD SK48017; cass ST 48017]

BERNSTEIN: *ON THE TOWN* (musical show)(1944). Pub: Schirmer
● Martin, Walker, Comden, Green, Murray, Tutti Camarata Orch, Leonard Joy (orig 1945 Decca recording) [MCA Classics CD MCAD 10280]
● Also vers. with Comden, Green, Alexander, etc. [Columbia LP OS 2028 / LP S 31005]
¶ BALLET MUSIC
● Bernstein, New York P [CBS/Sony CD SMK 47530]
¶ 3 DANCE EPISODES. Pub: Jalni

BERNSTEIN: *A QUIET PLACE* (opera). Pub: Jalni
● White, Ludgin, Morgan, Brandsletter, Kazaras, Vocal Ens, Bernstein, Austrian RSO [Deutsche Grammophon 2-CD DG 419 761-2]

418

BERNSTEIN: *TROUBLE IN TAHITI* (1-act opera)(1952 – incl. in *A Quiet Place*, 1983). Pub: Schirmer, Jalni (corrected ed.)
●Williams, Patrick, Vocal Trio, Bernstein, Columbia Wind Ens [CBS/Sony 3-CD SM3K 47154]

BERNSTEIN: *WEST SIDE STORY* (musical show)(1957). Pub (VS): Schirmer / Chappell
●Lawrence, Kert, Rivera, Goberman [Columbia LP OS 2001]
●Te Kanawa, Troyanos, Carreras, Ollmann, Bernstein cond. O & Chor [Deutsche Grammophon 2-LP 415253-1; 2-CD 415253-2 GH2; cass 415253-4 GH2]

BERNSTEIN: *WONDERFUL TOWN* (musical show)(1953)
●Russell, Adams, Gaynes, orig. cast [Decca LP MCA 1528E]
●Russell, Chaplin, McKeever (1958 TV recording) [Sony CD SK 48021; cass ST 48021]

BLITZSTEIN: *THE CRADLE WILL ROCK* (10-scene play in music)(1937). Ms: Witmark
●Orig. cast (da Silva etc.), Blitzstein [American Legacy LP T 1001]
●Bova, Peters (1964 prod.) [CRI 2-LP SD 266; also on MGM LP]

BLITZSTEIN: *I'VE GOT THE TUNE* (1-act radio song-play)(1937). Ms: Univ WI

BLITZSTEIN: *NO FOR AN ANSWER* (2-act opera)(1941). Pub: Chappell
●Channing, Conway, orig. cast, Blitzstein [Theme Records LP AEI 1140]

BLITZSTEIN: *REGINA* (musical play in prologue & 2 acts)(1949). Pub: Chappell
●Ciesinsky, Réaux, Greenawald, Ramey, Mauceri, Scottish Opera & Chor [London 2-CD 433812-2 LH2]
●Lewis, Carron, Brice, Hecht, Krachmalnick, New York City Opera O & Chor [Columbia/Odyssey 3-LP]

BLITZSTEIN: *REUBEN, REUBEN* (2-act musical play)(1955)

BLITZSTEIN: *SEND FOR THE MILITIA* (theater sketch) for Speaker & Piano (1935)

BRITTEN: *BILLY BUDD* (2-act opera), Op 50 (1951, rev. 1960). Pub (VS): Boosey & Hawkes
●Glossop, Pears, Langdon, Shirley-Quirk, Wandsworth Schl Boys' Ch, Ambrosian Opera Ch, Britten, London SO [London 3-CD 417428-2 LH3]

BRITTEN: *DEATH IN VENICE* (opera), Op 88 (1973). Pub: Faber
●Pears, Shirley-Quirk, Bowman, Bowen, Lemming, Bedford, English CO [London 2-CD 4-25669-2 LH2]

BRITTEN: *PETER GRIMES* (3-act opera), Op 33 (1945). Pub (VS): Boosey & Hawkes
●Pears, Watson, Pease, Watson, Nilsson, Brannigan, Evans, Britten, Covent Garden [London 3-CD 414577-2 LH3; Decca (UK) cass K 71 K 33]

419

●Vickers, Harper, Summers, Bainbridge, Allen, Robinson, Davis, Covent Garden [Philips 2-CD 432 578-2 2PM; cass 7699 089]

¶4 *SEA INTERLUDES*, Op 33a. Pub (SS): Boosey & Hawkes
●Previn, London SO [EMI CD CDM 64736]

BRITTEN: *THE TURN OF THE SCREW* (2-act opera), Op 54 (1954). Pub (VS): Boosey & Hawkes
●Pears, Vyvyan, Hemmings, Dyer, Cross, Mandikian, Britten, English Opera Group [London 2-CD 425672-2 LH2]

COPLAND: *THE TENDER LAND* (3-act opera)(1954)(106m). Pub (PE): Boosey & Hawkes. Pub (VS): AMC
●Brunelle, Plymouth Music (Soloists, O & Chor) [Virgin 2-CD 59207]

¶SUITE (20m)
●Copland, Boston SO [RCA LP]

GERSHWIN: *GIRL CRAZY* (musical show)(1930)
●Blazer, Luft, Carroll, Korbach, Mauceri [Elektra-Nonesuch/Warner CD 7559 79250-2; cass 7559 79250-4]

¶OVERTURE
●Tilson Thomas, Buffalo PO [CBS cass 40 76632]

GERSHWIN: *OF THEE I SING* (musical show)(1931). Pub (VS): Warner Bros
●Gilford, Kert, McGovern, O'Hara, Garrison, Tilson Thomas, O of St Luke's [CBS/Sony 2-CD M2K 42522]

¶OVERTURE
●Tilson Thomas, Buffalo PO [CBS cass 40 76632]

GERSHWIN: *LET 'EM EAT CAKE* (musical show)(1933)
●Gilford, Kert, McGovern, O'Hara, Garrison, Tilson Thomas, St Luke's O [CBS/Sony 2-CD M2K 42522]

GERSHWIN: *PORGY AND BESS* (opera)(1935). Pub (VS): Chappell
●White, Mitchell, Boatwright, Quivar, Henricks, Clemmons, Thompson, Maazel, Cleveland O & Chorus [London cass 5-13116]
●White, Haymon, Blackwell, Clarey, Evans, Rattle, Glyndebourne Opera, London PO [Angel 3-CD CDCC 49568]

HARBISON: *FULL MOON IN MARCH* (2-act opera)(1977)(32m). Pub (PE): Associated. Also: AMC (score, tape); MIT Library, WGBH (Boston) Record Library (reels)

HENZE: *DIE BASSARIDEN (THE BASSARIDS)* (1-act opera)(1965). Pub: Schott
●Tear, Schmidt, Armstrong, Lindsley, Wenkel, Burt, Murray, Albrecht, Berlin RIAS Chamb Chor, RSO [Koch Schwann 2-CD 314 006-12]

HENZE: *BOULEVARD SOLITUDE* (7-scene lyric drama)(1951). Pub: Universal

HENZE: *ELEGIE FÜR JUNGE LIEBENDE (ELEGY FOR YOUNG LOVERS)* (3-act opera)(1961). Pub: Universal

HENZE: *DIE ENGLISCHE KATZE (THE ENGLISH CAT)* (opera)(1982). Pub: Universal
●Stenz, Parnassus O [Wergo 2-CD WER 6204-2]

HENZE: *DER JUNGE LORD (THE YOUNG LORD)* (2-act opera)(1964). Pub: Schott / Universal
●Dohnányi, Deutsche Opera Berlin [Deutsche Grammophon 3-LP SLPM 139257-139258-139259]

HENZE: *KÖNIG HIRSCHE (THE STAG KING)* (opera)(1955). Pub: Universal

HENZE: *DER LANGWIERIGE WEG IN DIE WOHNUNG DER NATASCHA UN-GEHEUER (THE TEDIOUS JOURNEY TO THE FLAT OF NATASHA UN-GEHEUER)* (stage work). Pub: Universal

KIRCHNER: *LILY* (opera) (1976; vers. for soprano, tape & chamber ens. 1973)
●1973 vers. [Columbia LP M 32740]

MACHOVER: *VALIS* (opera).
●Azéma, Felty, Mason, Edards, Machover [Bridge CD BCD 9007; cass BCS 7007]

MOORE: *THE BALLAD OF BABY DOE* (2-act opera)(1956). Pub (VS): Chappell. VS, disc: AMC
●Sills, Cassel, Buckley, New York City Opera [Deutsche Grammophon 3-LP 2709 061]

MOORE: *CARRIE NATION* (2-act opera)(1966). Pub (PE): Galaxy. Pub (VS): AMC

MOORE: *THE DEVIL AND DANIEL WEBSTER* (1-act opera)(1938). Pub (PE): Boosey & Hawkes
●Winters, Aliberti, Festival O & Chor [Desto LP]

SCHOENBERG: *ERWARTUNG* (monodrama) for Soprano & Orchestra, Op 17 (1909). Pub: Universal
●Silja, Dohnány, Vienna PO [London 2-CD 417348-2 LH2]

SCHOENBERG: *MOSES UND ARON* (opera)(1930-32). Pub (SS): Belmont (Edition Schott)
●Bonney, Zakai, Langridge, Mazura, Haugland, Solti, Chicago SO [London 2-CD 414264-2 LH2]

SESSIONS: *MONTEZUMA* (3-act opera)(1947-63). Pub (PE/SS): Marks

SESSIONS: *THE TRIAL OF LUCULLUS* (1-act opera)(1947)

STOCKHAUSEN: *LICHT (LIGHT: THE SEVEN DAYS OF THE WEEK)* (opera cycle)(1977-   )
¶*MONTAG AUS LICHT (MONDAY FROM "LIGHT")* (Nrs. 55-59)(1984-88)
¶*DIENSTAG AUS LICHT (TUESDAY FROM "LIGHT")* (Nrs. 60-   )
(in progress)

¶*DONNERSTAG AUS LICHT (THURSDAY FROM "LIGHT")* (Nrs. 48-50)(1978-1980)
●Soloists, Cologne RSO Chor, Stockhausen, Ens InterContemporain [Deutsche Grammophon LP 2740272; 4-CD DG 423 379-2]

¶*SAMSTAG AUS LICHT (SATURDAY FROM "LIGHT")* (Nrs. 51-54)(1981-83)
●CD vers. [Deutsche Grammophon CD 4233956]

STRAVINSKY: *OEDIPUS REX* (opera-oratorio)(1927; rev. 1948). Pub: Boosey & Hawkes
●McCowen, Pears, Meyer, McIntyre, Dean, Davies, Luxon, John Aldis Choir, Solti, London PO [Decca (UK) cass KCET 616]

STRAVINSKY: *THE RAKE'S PROGRESS* (3-act opera)(1951). Pub (VS): Boosey & Hawkes
●Pope, Walker, Langridge, Dean, Rameye, Chailly, London Sinf & Chorus [London 2-CD 411644-2 LH2]
●Young, Raskin, Sarfarty, Reardon, Garrard, Sadler's Wells Chorus, Stravinsky, Royal PO [CBS/Sony 2-CD SM2K 46299]

THOMSON: *FOUR SAINTS IN THREE ACTS* (3-act opera)(1928, orch 1933). Pub (VS): Schirmer
●Soloists, Thome, O of Our Time [Elektra/Nonesuch 2-CD 79035-2]

¶ABRIDGED VERS.
●Robinson-Wayne, Matthews, Thomson [RCA LP LM 2756]

THOMSON: *THE MOTHER OF US ALL* (2-act opera)(1947)(90m). Pub (PE): Theodore Presser, Schirmer. Also: AMC (VS/disc)
●Leppard, Santa Fe Opera [New World 2-LP; 2-CD NW 288/89]

WUORINEN: *THE W. OF BABYLON, OR THE TRIUMPH OF LOVE OVER MORAL DEPRAVITY* (2-act Baroque burlesque)(1975)

Voice(s) & Instrument(s)

BABBITT: *PHILOMEL* for Soprano & Tape (1964)(19m). Pub: Associated
●Beardslee [New World LP]
●Bettina [Neuma CD 45074]

BABBITT: *VISION AND PRAYER* for Soprano & Synthesizer (1961; also 1954 vers. for soprano & piano). Comp. at Columbia-Princeton Electronic Music Ctr
●Beardslee [CRI CD 521]

BEATLES: SONGS
●*The Beatles—20 Greatest Hits* [Capitol LP C11H-12245; cass C41H-12245]
●*The Beatles Collection* [EMI/Capitol BC-13 — 12 orig. LPs & "Rarities" LP]
●*Sgt. Pepper's Lonely Hearts Club Band* (12 nrs) [Capitol LP C11H-46442; CD C212-46442; cass C41H-46442]

422

BERIO: *CHAMBER MUSIC* for Soprano & 3 Instruments (1952). Pub: S-Z
●Berberian, Juilliard Ens [Philips CD 426 662-2]

BERIO: *CIRCLES* for Soprano, Harp, 2 Percussion Ens (1960)(18m). Pub
(PE): Universal
●Berberian, Pierre, Drouet, Cassadesus [Wergo CD WER 6021-2]
●Also LP [Candide LP]

BERIO: *RECITAL 1 (FOR CATHY)* for Soprano & 17 Instruments (1972)
●Berberian, Berio, London Sinfonietta [RCA LP ARL 1 0036]

BERIO: *SEQUENZA 3* for Solo Female Voice (1963)(9m). Pub (PE):
Universal
●Berberian [Philips CD 426 662-2]
●Berberian [Wergo CD WER 6021-2]
●Also LP [Candide LP]

BERNSTEIN: *SYMPHONY 1* for Mezzo-Soprano & Orchestra: see Orchestral Works (Symphonies)

BOULEZ: *LE MARTEAU SANS MAÎTRE (THE HAMMER WITHOUT A
MASTER))* for Alto & 6 Instruments (1952-54, rev. 1957)(32m). Pub
(SS/PE): Universal
●Minton, Boulez, Ens Musique Vivante [Columbia LP M 32160]
●Deroubaix, Boulez with Ens. [Columbia LP ML 5275; also Turnabout LP]
●Also LPs [Columbia LP MK 42619, Odyssey LP 32 16 0154]

BOULEZ: *PLI SELON PLI* for Soprano, Piano, Guitar, Mandolin & Orchestra (1962)(69m). Pub: Universal (portions)
●Bryn-Julson, Boulez, BBC SO [Erato LP NUM 75050-75051; CD ECD 88074]
●Lukomska, Bergmann, Stingl, d'Alton, Boulez, BBC SO [Columbia LP M
30296]

BRITTEN: *LES ILLUMINATIONS* (song cycle) for High Voice & Or-
chestra, Op 18 (1939)
●Pears, Britten, English CO [London CD 417153-2 LH]
●Harper, Marriner, Northern Sinfonia O [Angel LP S 36788]
¶VERS. FOR VOICE & PIANO. Pub (PE): Boosey & Hawkes

BRITTEN: *SERENADE* for Tenor, Horn & Strings, Op 31 (1943). Pub:
Boosey & Hawkes
●Pears, Tuckwell, Britten, English CO [London CD 417153-2 LH]
●Tear, Civil, Marriner, Northern Sinfonia O [Angel LP S 36788]
¶VERS. FOR TENOR, HORN & PIANO. Pub (PE): Boosey & Hawkes

BRITTEN: *7 SONNETS OF MICHELANGELO* for Tenor & Piano, Op 22
(1940). Pub (PE): Boosey & Hawkes
●CD vers. [Hyperion CDA 66209]

CARTER: *A MIRROR ON WHICH TO DWELL* (6 Poems of Elizabeth
Bishop) for Soprano & Chamber Ensemble (1981)(20m). Pub
(PE): Associated

●Bryn-Julson, Boulez, Ens InterContemporain [Erato CD 2292-45364-2]
●Schadeberg, Palma, Speculum Musicae [Bridge CD BCD-9014]
●Wyner, Fitz, Speculum Musicae [Columbia LP M 35171]

CARTER: *SYRINGA* for Mezzo-Soprano, Bass-Baritone & Chamber Ensemble (1978). Pub: Associated
●Ciesinsky, Opalach, Purvis, Speculum Musicae [Bridge CD BCD-9014]
●De Gaetani, Paul, Sollberger, Speculum Musicae [CRI cass ACS-6003]

COPLAND: *12 POEMS OF EMILY DICKINSON* for Voice & Piano (1950) (20m). Pub (PE): Boosey & Hawkes
●Schneiderman, Russell Davies, O of St Luke's [MusicMasters CD 01612-67101-2]

FOSS: *SONG OF SONGS* (cantata) for Soprano & Orchestra (1946)
●Tourel, Bernstein, New York P [CBS/Sony CD 47533]

GERSHWIN: SONGS
●*Crazy for Gershwin* (orig. vers. of songs with various artists] [Memoir CD CDMOIR 502]
●Morris, Bolcom [Elektra/Nonesuch CD 79151-2]

HARBISON: *MIRABAI SONGS* for Soprano & 8 Instruments (1982). Pub: Associated/Hal Leonard
●Felty, Harbison, Collage New Music Ens [Northeastern CD NR 230-CD]
●Upshaw, Zinman, O of St Luke's [Elektra/Nonesuch CD 79187-2; cass 79187-4]

HARBISON: *MOTETTI DI MONTALE* (song cycle) for Soprano & Piano (1980)(35m). Pub: Associated

JOLAS: *QUARTET* 2 for Soprano, Violin, Viola & Cello (1964). Pub: Heugel
●CD vers. [CDC 7 499042]

KIRCHNER: *THE TWILIGHT STOOD* (song cycle) for Soprano & Piano (1983). Pub: Associated/Hal Leonard

KOLB: *3 PLACE SETTINGS* for Narrator, Clarinet, Violin, Double Bass & Percussion (1968). Pub: Fischer
●LP vers. [Desto DC 7143]

LEIBOWITZ: *L'EXPLICATION DES MÉTAPHORES (EXPLANATION OF METAPHORS)* for Speaker, 2 Pianos, Harp & Percussion, Op 15 (1947). Pub: Boelke

LUTOSLAWSKI: *LES ESPACES DU SOMMEIL* for Baritone & Orchestra (1975)
●Fischer-Dieskau, Lutoslawski, Berlin P [Philips LP 416387-1 PH; CD 416387-2 PH; cass 416387-3 PH]
●Shirley-Quirk, Salonen, Los Angeles PO [CBS 2-CD M2K 142271]

ROREM: *THE NANTUCKET SONGS* (10) (1979). Pub (PE): Boosey & Hawkes
●Bryn-Julson, Rorem [CRI LP 485 SD; CRS CD 657; cass ACS 6007]

ROREM: *POEMS OF LOVE AND THE RAIN* (17-number cycle) for Voice & Piano (1963). Pub (PE): Boosey & Hawkes
•Sarfaty, Rorem [CRI LP]

ROREM: *POÈMES POUR LA PAIX* (6-song cycle)(1953; arr. medium voice & orchestra 1956)

ROREM: Song recitals (various titles, incl. selections from cycles)
•Bressler, Gramm, d'Angelo, Curtin, Sarfaty, Rorem [New World LP NW 229]
•Curtin, Wolff [CRI cass C 238]
•Rees, Rorem [Premier CD PRCD 1035]

ROREM: *6 SONGS* for High Voice & Orchestra (1953) [Pub (PE, PS): Henmar, Peters

¶VERS FOR VOICE & PIANO. Pub (PE): Peters

ROREM: *14 SONGS ON AMERICAN POETS.* Pub (PE): Peters

ROSENMAN: *CHAMBER MUSIC 2* for Soprano, 10 Players & Tape (1968)

SCHOENBERG: *GEDICHTE AUS DAS BUCH DER HÄNGENDEN GÄRTEN (BOOK OF THE HANGING GARDENS,* Op 15 (song cycle)(1907). Pub (PE): Universal
•Bryn-Julson, Oppens [Music & Arts CD 650-1]
•DeGaetani, Kalish [Elektra/Nonesuch CD 79237-2-ZK]

SCHOENBERG: *PIERROT LUNAIRE* , Op 21 (1912). Pub: Universal
•DeGaetani, Weisberg, Contemporary C Ens [Elektra/Nonesuch CD 79237-2-ZK; cass 71251-4]
•Minton, Boulez, Zukerman, Debost, Pay, Harrell, Barenboim [CBS/Sony CD SMK 48466; cass MT-42072]
•Schoenberg, Schoenberg Ens [CBS CD MPK-45695]

STRAVINSKY: *L'HISTOIRE DU SOLDAT (THE SOLDIER'S TALE)* for 3 Actors & Orchestra (1918). Pub: Chester
•Gielgud, Moody, Courtenay, Boston SCPl [Deutsche Grammophon LP 2530 609]
•Nureyev, MacLiammoir, Jackson, Zalkowitsch with Ens [Argo cass KZNC 15]

THOMSON: *LE BERCEAU DE GERTRUDE STEIN OU LE MYSTÈRE DE LA RUE DE FLEURUS (THE CRADLE OF GERTRUDE STEIN)* for Soprano & Piano (1928). Pub (PE): Hugnet, Peer International

THOMSON: *5 SONGS TO POEMS OF WILLIAM BLAKE* (1951)(also arr. for male chorus & piano). Pub (PE): Peer International
•Soloists [CRI LP SD 398]

VARÈSE: *ECUATORIAL* for Bass & Chamber Orchestra (1933-34). Pub: Ricordi
•Paul, Weisberg, Contemporary C Ens [Elektra/Nonesuch cass 71269-4]

VARÈSE: *OFFRANDES* for Soprano & Chamber Orchestra (1921)

●Yakar, Boulez, Ens InterContemporain [Sony CD SK 45844]
●DeGaetani, Weisberg, Contemporary C Ens [Elektra/Nonesuch cass 71269-4]
WUORINEN: *A WINTER'S TALE* for Soprano & 6 Instruments (or Piano)
(1991). Pub: Peters
●Bryn-Julson, Wuorinen, Chamber Mus Ens of Lincoln Center (6 insts)
[Koch CD 7272]

SELECTED CHAMBER MUSIC
(10 or Fewer Instruments)

General Chamber

BABBITT: *ALL SET* for Jazz Ens (8 players)(1957)(8m). Pub (SS): As-
sociated
●Weisberg, Contemporary C Ens [Elektra/Nonesuch CD 792222 J]
BARTÓK: *SONATA* for Violin. Pub (PE): Boosey & Hawkes
BERIO: *SEQUENZA 1* for Flute (1958)(5m)
●Nicolet [Wergo CD WER 6021-2]
BERIO: *SEQUENZA 6* for Viola (1967). Pub (PE): Universal
●Recorded vers. [RCA RK 1150/1-2]
BERIO: *SEQUENZA 7* for Oboe (1969). Pub: Universal
●Holliger [Philips CD 426662-2]
BRITTEN: *6 METAMORPHOSES AFTER OVID* for Oboe, Op 49 (1951). Pub
(PE): Boosey & Hawkes
●Mack [Crystal CD CD 323; cass C 325]
BRITTEN: *NOCTURNAL* for Guitar, Op 70 (1963). Pub: Faber
●Kraft [Chandos CD CHAN 8784; cass ABTD 1419]
DAVIDOVSKY: *SYNCHRONISM 9* for Violin & Tape (1988).
Comp. at Columbia-Princeton Electronic Music Ctr & MIT Media Lab.
Pub: Peters
●Computer Music Currents [Wergo CD WER 2022-50]
SEE ALSO: *Synchronism 1* for flute & tape (1962), *Synchronism 2*
for flute, clarinet, violin, cello & Tape (1964), *Synchronism 3*
for cello & tape (1964), *Synchronism 4* for chorus & tape (1966),
Synchronism 5 for percussion & tape (1969 – see below),
Synchronism 6 for piano & tape (1970 – see below), *Synchronism
7* for orchestra & tape (1974), *Synchronism 8* for wind quintet
& tape (1974)
JOLAS: *FIGURES* for 9 Instruments (1965)

KOLB: *LOOKING FOR CLAUDIO* for Guitar & Tape (1975). *SPRING RIVER FLOWERS MOON NIGHT* for 2 Pianos, Percussion Ens & Tape (1975)(19m). Pub: Boosey & Hawkes
●Starobin (*Looking for Claudio*); Phillips, Renzulli (pnos), Kobb, Brooklyn College Perc Ens (*Spring river flowers moon night*) [CRI LP SD-361; CD 576]

ROSENMAN: *CHAMBER MUSIC 5* for Piano & 6 Players (1979)
●Fussell, Collage [CRI LP SD 486]

SCHOENBERG: *SUITE* for 2 Clarinets, Bass Clarinet, Violin, Viola, Cello & Piano, Op 29 (1926). Pub (SS): Universal
●Boulez, Ens InterContemporain [Sony CD SMK 48465]

SOLLBERGER: *RIDING THE WIND* 2-4 for Flute (1973-74)(7m/4m/7m). Pub (PE): ACA
●Sollberger [Neuma CD 450-81]

STOCKHAUSEN: *KONTRA-PUNKTE* for 10 Instruments (1953). Pub (SS): Universal
●LP vers. [RCA LP VICS 1239]

STOCKHAUSEN: *ZYKLUS* for Percussionist (1950). Pub: Universal
●LP vers. [Columbia MS 7139; Erato STU 70603; Heliodor Wergo 2549016; Mainstream 5003]

STRAVINSKY: *OCTET* for Winds (1923). Pub (SS): Boosey & Hawkes
●Boston SCPl [Deutsche Grammophon LP 2530 551]
●Stravinsky, Ansermet, Straram [EMI 2-CD 2DCB 54607]

STRAVINSKY: *SEPTET* for Piano, Winds & Strings (1953). Pub (SS): Boosey & Hawkes
●Boston SCPl [Deutsche Grammophon LP 2530 551]

VARÈSE: *DENSITY 21.5* for Flute (1936)(4m). Pub (PE): Colfranc/E. C. Kirby, New Music
●Ens InterContemporain [Sony Classical CD SK 45844]

VARÈSE: *OCTANDRE* (octet) for Flute, Winds & Brass (1923-24)(7m). Pub (SS): Colfranc/E. C. Kirby
●Boulez, Ens InterContemporain [Sony CD SK 45844]

Duets

BABBITT: *SEXTETS* for Piano & Violin (1966)(13m). Pub (PE): Peters
●Schulte, Feinberg [New World CD NW 364-2]

BARTÓK: *RHAPSODIES* (1-2) for Violin & Piano (1928). Pub (PE): Boosey & Hawkes
●Szigeti, Bartók (1) [Vanguard CD OVC 8008]

BERNSTEIN: *ELEGY FOR MIPPY 1* for Horn & Piano. Pub (PE):
Schirmer, Jalni

BERNSTEIN: *ELEGY FOR MIPPY 2* for Trombone Solo. Pub (PE):
Schirmer, Jalni

BERNSTEIN: *SERENADE* for Violin & Piano (1954)(33m)(also for Violin,
String Orchestra, Harp & Percussion). Pub (PS): Schirmer

BERNSTEIN: *SONATA* for Clarinet & Piano (1942)(10m). Pub (PE): Wit-
mark
  ●Ma (cello arr.), Kahane [Sony CD SK 53126]
  ●Russo, Ignacio [CRS CD 8949]

BERNSTEIN: *WALTZ FOR MIPPY 3* for Tuba & Piano. Pub (PE): Schirmer,
Jalni

CARTER: *SONATA* for Cello & Piano (1948). Pub: Associated
  ●Greenhouse, Makas [Desto LP]
  ●Krosnick, Jacobs [Nonesuch LP; Elektra/Nonesuch CD 79183-2]

GOULD: *SUITE* for Cello & Piano (1981). Pub: Schirmer/Hal Leonard

LUTOSLAWSKI: *PARTITA* for Violin & Piano (1984)(also for Violin &
Orchestra). Pub: Chester/Music Sales
  ●Sareder, Strobel [Pavane CD ADW 7283]

MANN: *DUO* for Violin & Piano (1972). Score & tape: AMC

MANN: *DUO* for Violin & Tape (1975). Score & tape: AMC

ROREM: *PICNIC ON THE MARNE (7 WALTZES)* for Saxophone & Piano
(1983)

SCHOENBERG: *FANTASY* for Violin & Piano, Op 47 (1949). Pub (PE):
Peters
  ●Menuhin, Gould [Sony CD SMK 52688]

STRAVINSKY: *DUO CONCERTANTE* for Violin & Piano (1932). Pub (PE):
Boosey & Hawkes
  ●Perlman, Canino [Angel LP S 37115]

STRAVINSKY: *PASTORALE* for Violin & Piano (1933). Pub: Schott
  ●Boston SCPl [Deutsche Grammophon LP 2530 551]

WOLPE: *SONATA* for Violin & Piano (1949). Pub (PE): McGinnis & Marx
  ●Fleezanis, Ohlsson [Koch CD KIC 7112]

Electronic

AREL: *STEREO ELECTRONIC MUSIC 1* (1964)(10m)
  ●[Columbia LP MS-6566]

AREL: *STEREO ELECTRONIC MUSIC 2* (1970)(14m). Comp. at Columbia-Princeton Electronic Music Ctr
- •[CRI LP SD 268; CRI CD 611; Finnadar Quadraphonic QD 9010]

BERIO: *THEMA (OMAGGIO A JOYCE)* on tape (1958)(8m)
- •Based on voice of Cathy Berberian [Turnabout LP TV 34177 S]

BERIO: *VISAGE* on tape (1961)
- •Based on voice of Cathy Berberian & electronic sounds [Turnabout cass KTVC 34046]

DAVIDOVSKY: *ELECTRONIC STUDY 1* (1961)(6m). Comp. at Columbia-Princeton Electronic Music Ctr
- •[Columbia LPs ML 5966 & MS 6566]

  SEE ALSO: *Electronic Study 2* (1962), *Electronic Study 3* (1965)

DAVIDOVSKY: *SYNCHRONISM 5* for 5 Percussion Players & Tape (1974)(9m). Pub (PE): Marks
- •Fitz, Heldrich, Marcone, des Roches, van Hyning (perc), Sollberger cond. [CRI LP SD 268; CD 611]

LUENING: *FANTASY IN SPACE* (3m). *INVENTION IN 12 TONES* (4m). *LOW SPEED* (4m). *MOONFLIGHT* (3m)
- •[Desto LP DC 6466; CRI CD 611]

LUENING/USSACHEVSKY: *INCANTATION* (3m)
- •[Desto LP DC 6466; CRI CD 611]

POWELL: *NO SONG, NO DANCE*

SHIELDS: *TRANSFORMATION OF ANI* (9m). Comp. at Columbia-Princeton Electronic Music Ctr
- •[CRI LP SD 268; CD 611]

SMILEY: *KOLYOSA* (7m). Comp. at Columbia-Princeton Electronic Music Ctr
- •[CRI LP SD 268; CD 611]

STOCKHAUSEN: *GESANG DER JÜNGLINGE* on tape (1956)
- •Realized at Studio für Elektronische Musik, WDR Köln [Deutsche Grammophon LP; CD 13881]

STOCKHAUSEN: *HYMNEN* (Anthems for Electronic and Concrete Sounds) for tape and/or instruments (see also General Orchestral)(1969)
- •Realized at Studio für Elektronische Musik, WDR Köln [Deutsche Grammophon 2-LP 2707039]

USSACHEVSKY: *COMPUTER PIECE 1* (4m). *PIECE FOR TAPE RECORDER* (6m). *SONIC CONTOURS* (7m)
- •[CRI CD 611]
- •[CRI LP SD 268 (*Computer Piece 1*)]
- •[CRI LP SD 112 (*Piece for Tape Recorder*)]
- •[Desto LP DC-6466 (*Sonic Contours*]

429

USSACHEVSKY: *2 SKETCHES FOR A COMPUTER PIECE* (3m)
●[CRI LP SD 268]
USSACHEVSKY (with Alice Shields & Pril Smiley): *LINE OF APOGEE*
(film score) (1967). Comp. at Columbia-Princeton Electronic Music Ctr
●[New World CD 80389-2]
USSACHEVSKY: *SUITE FROM "NO EXIT"* (film score)(1962). Comp. at
Columbia-Princeton Electronic Music Ctr
●[New World CD 80389-2]
WUORINEN: *TIME'S ENCOMIUM* on tape (1969). Comp. at Columbia-Prin-
ceton Electronic Music Ctr; 1970 Pulitzer Prize
●[Nonesuch LP H-71225]

Organ

THOMSON: *ORGAN VOLUNTARIES* (1986). Pub: Schirmer
THOMSON: *VARIATIONS ON SUNDAY SCHOOL HYMNS* (1926). Pub (PE):
H. W. Gray

Piano solo

BABBITT: *3 COMPOSITIONS* (1947)
●Taub [Harmonia Mundi 905160]
BABBITT: *REFLECTIONS* for Piano & Tape (1974). Pub: Peters
●Taub [Harmonia Mundi 905160]
BARTÓK: *MIKROKOSMOS* (1926-39). Pub (PE): Boosey & Hawkes
●Bartók (31 selections) [Sony CD MPK 47676]
●Helffer [Harmonia Mundi 2-CD HMA 90968/9]
BARTÓK: *SONATA*. Pub (PE): Boosey & Hawkes
●Damerini [Etcetera CD KTC 1129]
BERNSTEIN: *7 ANNIVERSARIES* (1943). Pub (PE): Witmark
●Bernstein [RCA CD 09026-60915-2; cass 09026-60915-4]
●Also CD [Pro Arte CCD 109]
SEE ALSO: *4 Anniversaries* (1948), *5 Anniversaries* (1954), *2 Anni-*
versaries (1982) [all on Pro Arte CCD 109]; *13 Anniversaries* (1988)
BOULEZ: *SONATA 1* (1946). Pub: Amphion
●Aimard [Erato CD 2292-45648-2]
●Henck [Wergo CD WER-60121-50]
BOULEZ: *SONATA 2* (1948)(32m). Pub (PE): Heugel
●Henck [Wergo CD WER-60121-50]

●Pollini [Deutsche Grammophon CD 419202-2 GH]

BOULEZ: *SONATA 3* (1957). Pub: Universal
●Henck [Wergo CD WER-60121-50]

CARTER: *NIGHT FANTASIES* (1980)(21m). Pub: Associated
●Oppens [Music & Arts Programs of America CD 604]
●Rosen [Etcetera LP ETC 1008]

CARTER: *SONATA* (1946, rev. 1982)(22m). Pub (PE): Mercury, Theodore Presser
●Jacobs [Elektra/Nonesuch CD 79248-2-ZK; cass 79248-4-AW]
●Rosen [Etcetera LP ETC 1008]
●Webster [Desto LP]

COPLAND: *PIANO FANTASY* (1957)(30m). Pub (PE): Boosey & Hawkes
●Masselos [Columbia/Odyssey LP 32 16 0040]

COPLAND: *PIANO SONATA* (1941)(21m). Pub (PE): Boosey & Hawkes
●Bernstein [RCA CD 09026-60915-2; cass 09026-60915-4]
●Somer [CRI LP 171]

COPLAND: *PIANO VARIATIONS* (1930)(12m). Pub (PE): Boosey & Hawkes
●Masselos [Columbia/Odyssey LP 32 16 0040]

COWELL: *THE BANSHEE. THE TIDES OF MANAUNAUM*
●Cowell (with 17 other pieces) [Smithsonian/Folkways CD SF 40801]

DAVIDOVSKY: *SYNCHRONISMS 6* for Piano & Electronic Sound (1970)(8m). Pub (PE): Marks; 1971 Pulitzer Prize

GERSHWIN: *PRELUDES* (3)(1926). Pub (PE): New World/Warner Bros
●Gershwin [Pearl 2-CD PEAS 9483]
●Kahane [Sony CD SK 53126]
●Levant [CBS/Sony CD MLK 39454; cass PMT 39454]

KOLB: *APPELLO* (1976)(13m). *TOCCATA* for Harpsichord & Tape (1971)(4m). Pub: Boosey & Hawkes (*Appello*), Henmar/Peters (*Toccata*)
●Gottlieb (*Appello*), Kipnis (*Toccata*) [CRI LP 537; CD 576]

MACHOVER: *CHANSONS D'AMOUR* (1982)

SCHOENBERG: *SUITE*, Op 25 (1923). Pub (PE): Universal

STOCKHAUSEN: *KLAVIERSTÜCKE (PIANO PIECES)* (1-4 [1952], 5-10 [1954-61], 11 [1956], 12 [1978-79, from *Donnerstag aus Licht*], 13 [1981, from *Samstag aus Licht*], 14 [1984, from *Montag aus Licht*]. Pub (PE): Universal
●Nrs. 1-11 [Columbia CBS 72591-2]
●Henck (Nrs. 1-11) [Wergo 2-CD WER 60135/36-50]
●Wambach (Nrs. 1-8) [Koch CD 310016]
●Wambach (Nrs. 9-11) [Koch CD 310009 H1]
●Wambach (Nrs. 12-14) [Koch CD 310015]

STRAVINSKY: *SONATA* in F Sharp Minor (1904) Pub: Faber
●Crossley [Philips LP 6500 884]

431

●P. Serkin [New World CD NW 344-2; cass NW 344-4]

THOMSON: *PORTRAITS* (various, publ. in 7 vols. 1948-1983)

WEBERN: *VARIATIONS,* Op 27 (1936). Pub (PE): Universal
●Pollini [Deutsche Grammophon CD 419202-2 GH]

Piano(s) — 2 players or more

BOULEZ: *STRUCTURES* (Bks 1 & 2) for 2 pianos (1952, 1961)). Pub (PE):
Universal
●A. & A. Kontarsky [Wergo LP WER 60011; CD WER 6011-2]

GERSHWIN: *RHAPSODY IN BLUE* for Piano & Orchestra (1924) (2-piano
vers)
●K. & M. Labècque [Philips CD 400022-2 PH]
●Also LP [Columbia LP MK 42619]

STRAVINSKY: *CONCERTO* for 2 Solo Pianos (1935) Pub: Schott
●Ashkenazy, Gavrilov [London CD 433829-2 LH]

STRAVINSKY: *3 PIÈCES FACILES* for Piano 4-Hands (1915). Pub (PE):
Chester
●A. & A. Kontarsky [Wergo CD WER 6228-2]

STRAVINSKY: *5 PIÈCES FACILES* for Piano 4-Hands (1917). Pub (PE):
Chester
●A. & A. Kontarsky [Wergo CD WER 6228-2]

STRAVINSKY: *SONATA* for 2 Pianos (1944). Pub (PE): Boosey & Hawkes,
Chappell
●Ashkenazy, Gavrilov [London CD 43829-2 LH]
●A. & A. Kontarsky [Deutsche Grammophon CD 437 027-2 GG]

WOLPE: *ENACTMENTS* for 3 Pianos (1953). Pub: Peer/Southern
●Continuum [Elektra/Nonesuch cass 78024-4]

WOLPE: *THE MAN FROM MIDIAN* (ballet suite) for 2 pianos (or orchestra (1942). Pub: McGinnis & Marx *(Suite 1)*

Quartets (for strings unless otherwise specified)

BABBITT: *QUARTET 4* (1970)(16m). Pub (PE): Peters
●Juilliard String Qt [CRI CD 587]

BABBITT: *QUARTET 5* (1982). Pub: Peters
●Composers String Qt [Music & Arts Programs of America CD 606]
SEE ALSO: *Quartet 2* (1954), *Quartet 3* (1970)

BARTÓK: *QUARTETS* (1-6) (1909-39). Pub (SS/PE): Boosey & Hawkes

432

●Emerson Qt [Deutsche Grammophon 2-CD DG 423 657-2]

BERNSTEIN: *FANFARE FOR BIMA* for **Trumpet, Horn, Trombone &** **Tuba.** Pub (PE): Schirmer

BRITTEN: *PHANTASY* for **Oboe, Violin, Viola & Cello, Op 2** (1932). Pub (SS): Boosey & Hawkes
●Zubicky, Tønnesen, Tomter, Mork [Simax CD PSC 1022]

CARTER: *8 ETUDES AND A FANTASY* for **Flute, Oboe, Clarinet & Bassoon** (1950)(23m). Pub (SS/PE): Associated
●Aulos Wind Qnt [Koch Schwann CD 3-1153-2]

CARTER: *QUARTETS 1* (1951)(38m), *2* (1959)(20m), *3* (1972) & *4* (1986). Pub (PE/SS): Associated; 1960 Pulitzer Prize, New York Music Critics Circle Award (Nr. 2); 1973 Pulitzer Prize (Nr. 3)
●Composers Qt (Nrs. 1-2) [Nonesuch LP H71249]
●Composers Qt (Nr. 4) [Music & Arts Programs of America CD 606]
●Juilliard String Qt (Nrs. 1-4) [Sony 2-CD S2K 47229]
●Juilliard String Qt (Nr. 2) [RCA LP LSC 2481]

CARTER: *SONATA* for **Flute, Oboe & Cello & Harpsichord** (1952). Pub (SS): Associated
●Sollberger, Kuskin, Sherry, Jacobs [Nonesuch LP; Elektra/Nonesuch CD 79183-2]

DIAMOND: *QUARTETS* (1-10) (1940, 1944, 1946, 1951, 1960, 1962, 1964, 1964, 1966, 1968). Pub: Southern
●[CRI LP S-294 *(Quartet 9)*]

JOLAS: *QUARTET 2*: see **Voice & Instrument(s)**

JOLAS: *QUARTET 3*. Pub: **Heugel**
●Concord String Qt [CRI LP 332]
SEE ALSO: *Quartet 1* (1956)

KIRCHNER: *QUARTET 1* (1949). Pub: Associated/Hal Leonard
●American Art Qt [CRI LP SRD 395E]
SEE ALSO: *Quartet 2* (1958) [Columbia CBS MQ 32740]

KIRCHNER: *QUARTET 3* with **Electronic Tape** (1966)(16m). Pub: Associated; 1967 Pulitzer Prize

LEIBOWITZ: *MARIJUANA* for **Violin, Trombone, Vibraphone & Piano** (1960)

LUTOSLAWSKI: *QUARTET* (1964)(24m). Pub (PE/SS): Chester, PWM
●Varsovia Qt [Olympia CD OCD 328]

POWELL: *QUARTET* (1982)
●Composers String Qt [Music & Arts Programs of America CD 606]

SCHOENBERG: *QUARTETS* (1-4) (1936-65). Pub (SS): Kalmus (1), Universal (2, 3), Schirmer (4)
●LaSalle Qt [Deutsche Grammophon 4-CD 419994-2 GCM4]

433

STRAVINSKY: *DOUBLE CANON* (1959). Pub (PE): Boosey & Hawkes
●Alban Berg Qt [Angel CD CDC 54347]
STRAVINSKY: *3 PIECES* (1914). Pub (PE): Boosey & Hawkes
●Alban Berg Qt [Angel CD CDC 54347]
WEBERN: *5 MOVEMENTS, Op 5* (1909). Pub (SS): Universal
●Alban Berg Qt [Telefunken]
●LaSalle Qt [Deutsche Grammaphon 4-CD 419994-2 GCM4]
WUORINEN: *QUARTET 3*
●Hudson, Zeavin, Martin, Sherry [New World CD 385-2]
SEE ALSO: *Quartet 1* (1971), *Quartet 2* (1979)
WUORINEN: *TASHI* for Clarinet, Violin, Cello & Piano (1975)(also for orchestra). Pub: Peters
●Group for Contemporary Music [Koch CD 7242]

Quintets

BERIO: *DIFFÉRENCES* for 5 Instruments & Tape (1959)(15m). Pub: S-Z
●Castagner (fl), Lewis (cl), Pierre (harp), Trampler (vla), Barab (vc), Berio cond. [LP Series 2000]
●Juilliard Ens [Philips LP; CD 426 662-2]
CARTER: *QUINTET* for Winds (1948). Pub (SS/PE): Associated
●Aulos Wind Qnt [Koch Schwann CD 3-1153-2]
COWELL: *BALLAD* for Winds (1956). Pub (PE): Associated
HENZE: *QUINTET* for Winds (1952). Pub (SS): Schott
●LP vers. [Candide, Philips LPs]
POWELL: *QUINTET* for Winds (1985). Pub: Schirmer/Hal Leonard
●New York Woodwind Qnt [New World CD 80413-2]
SOLLBERGER: *RIDING THE WIND 1* for amplified Flute, Clarinet, Violin, Cello & Piano (1974). Pub (PE): ACA
●Soloists [CRI LP SD 352]

STOCKHAUSEN: *ZEITMASSE* for Flute, Oboe, Clarinet, English Horn & Bassoon (1956). Pub (SS): Universal
●Gleghorn, Muggeridge, Leake, Christlieb, Ulyate, Craft cond. [Columbia LP ML 5275, Odyssey LP 321 60154]

434

(SELECTED COMPOSITIONS)

Sextets

COPLAND: *SEXTET* for Piano, Clarinet & Strings (arr. of *Symphony 2*, 1937)(15m). Pub (PE/SS): Boosey & Hawkes
●Boston SCPl [Elektra/Nonesuch CD 79168-2; cass 79168-4]

SCHOENBERG: *VERKLÄRTE NACHT (TRANSFIGURED NIGHT)* for String Sextet (or Orchestra), Op 4 (1899). Pub (SS/PE): International. Pub (SS): Birnbach, International, Kalmus
●La Salle Qt, McInnes, Pegis [Deutsche Grammophon CD 423250-2 GC]
●Talich Qt, Najnar, Bernasek [Calliope CD CAL-9217]

Trios

BARTÓK: *CONTRASTS* for Clarinet, Violin & Piano (1938)(15m). Pub (SS/PE): Boosey & Hawkes
●Goodman, Szigeti, Bartók [Sony CD MPK 47676]
●Shifrin, Bae, Doppmann [Delos CD 3043]

KIRCHNER: *TRIO* for Violin, Cello & Piano (1954). Pub: Associated/Hal Leonard
●Kirchner, Boston SCPl [Elektra/Nonesuch CD 79188-2]

SCHOENBERG: *TRIO* for Strings, Op 45 (1946). Pub (SS): Bomart
●Juilliard String Qt membs [Sony CD SK 47690]
●LaSalle Qt membs [Deutsche Grammophon CD 423250-2 GC]

WOLPE: *ENACTMENTS* for 3 Pianos: see Piano(s)–2 Players or More

WUORINEN: *TRIO* for Brass Instruments (1981)
●Taylor, Braynard, Palma [Koch CD KIC 7123]

WUORINEN: *TRIO* for Horn, Violin & Piano (1981). Pub: Peters
●Purvis, Hudson, Feinberg [Koch CD KIC 7123]

SELECTED ORCHESTRAL MUSIC

Ballet

BERNSTEIN: *DYBBUK* (1974)
●Johnson, Ostendorf, New York City Ballet O [CBS/Sony 3-CD SM3K 47158]
●Also LP [Columbia LP M 33082]

435

BERNSTEIN: *FANCY FREE* (1944)(24m). Pub (PE): Schirmer, Jalni (corrected ed.)
- ●Bernstein, New York P [CBS/Sony CD SMK 47530]

CARTER: *THE MINOTAUR* (1947). Pub: Associated
- ●Schwarz, New York CS [Elektra/Nonesuch CD 79248-2-ZK; cass 79248-4-AW]
- ¶SUITE (24m). Pub: Associated
- ●Hanson, Eastman-Rochester SO [Mercury LP]

COPLAND: *APPALACHIAN SPRING* for 13 Instruments (1944; rescored 1970)(56m). 1945 Pulitzer Prize
- ●Bernstein, New York P [CBS CD MK 42265]
- ●Copland, London PO [CBS CD MK 42430; cass 40-72872]
- ●Mehta, Los Angeles PO [London cass 5-7031]
- ●Slatkin, St Louis SO [Angel CD CDMB 64315]
- ¶SUITE for 13 Instruments (20m). Pub (SS): Boosey & Hawkes
- ●Copland, Boston SO [RCA LP]

COPLAND: *BILLY THE KID* (1938). Pub: Boosey & Hawkes
- ●Bernstein, New York P [CBS CD MK 42265]
- ●Copland, London SO [CBS MK 42430]
- ¶SUITE (20m). Pub (SS): Boosey & Hawkes
- ●Copland, London SO [Everest LP]

COPLAND: *RODEO* (1942). Pub: Boosey & Hawkes
- ●Bernstein, New York P [CBS CD MK 42265]
- ●Copland, London SO [CBS CD MK 42430]
- ¶SUITE. Pub (SS): Boosey & Hawkes

GOULD: *FALL RIVER LEGEND* (1947)(74m)
- ●Peters, Rosenstock, National P [Albany Records CD TROY 035-2]
- ¶SUITE (20m). Pub: G & C Music/Chappell
- ●Gould, others [RCA LP]
- ●Hanson, Eastman-Rochester O [Mercury CD 432016-2]

GOULD: *I'M OLD FASHIONED (ASTAIRE VARIATIONS)* (1983)

GOULD: *INTERPLAY* for Piano & Orchestra (1943). Pub: Mills
- ●Gould, Gould O [RCA CD 09026-61651-2]

SCHUMAN: *JUDITH* (A Choreographic Poem)(1949)(24m). Pub (SS/PE): Schirmer
- ●Schwarz, Seattle SO [Delos CD DE 3115]

STRAVINSKY: *L'OISEAU DE FEU (THE FIREBIRD)* (1910). Pub: Boosey & Hawkes
- ●Boulez, New York P [CBS CD MK-42396]
- ●Dorati, Detroit SO [London 2-CD 421079-2 LH2]
- ●Haitink, London PO [Philips 2-CD 438350-2; cass 7300 353]
- ●Stravinsky, Columbia SO [CBS CD MK 42432]

STRAVINSKY: *PETRUSHKA* (1911; rev. 1947). Pub (SS): Boosey & Hawkes, Kalmus, Norton Critical Scores
- •Bernstein, New York P (1947) [Deutsche Grammophon CD MYK-37221; cass MYT-37221]
- •Boulez, New York P (1911) [CBS CD MK-42395]
- •Dorati, Detroit SO [London 2-CD 421079-2 LH2]
- •Dutoit, London PO [Deutsche Grammophon cass DG 3300 711]
- •Haitink, London PO [Philips 2-CD 438350-2]
- •Stravinsky, Columbia SO [CBS CD MK-42433]

STRAVINSKY: *LE SACRE DU PRINTEMPS (THE RITE OF SPRING)* (1913). Pub (SS): Boosey & Hawkes, International
- •Abbado, London SO [Deutsche Grammophon cass 3300 635]
- •Dorati, Detroit SO [London 2-CD 421079-2 LH2]
- •Haitink, London PO [Philips 2-CD 438350-2]
- •Karajan, Berlin PO [Deutsche Grammophon cass 3300 884]
- •Solti, Chicago SO [London CD 417704-2 LM; cass 5-6885]
- •Stravinsky, Columbia SO [CBS CD MK-42433]

WOLPE: *THE MAN FROM MIDIAN* (ballet suite) (1942)(also for 2 pianos). Pub: McGinnis & Marx (*Suite 1*)

Band (Symphonic or Other)

COWELL: *CELTIC SUITE* (1939). Pub: Schirmer

COWELL: *HYMN AND FUGUING TUNE 1* (1944)(4m). Pub (SS): Leeds

GOULD: *CENTENNIAL SYMPHONY* (1983)

GOULD: *DERIVATIONS* for Clarinet & Band (1956). Pub: G & C Music/Chappell
- •Goodman, Gould, Columbia Jazz Combo [CBS/Sony CD MK 42227; cass MT 42227]

GOULD: *PRISMS* (1962). Pub: G & C Music/Chappell

GOULD: *SYMPHONY 4 (WEST POINT)* (1952)(20m).
- •LP vers. [Mark LP 21360]

Concertos, etc.

BABBITT: *CONCERTO* for Piano & Orchestra (1985)(26m). Pub: Universal/Boosey & Hawkes
- •Feinberg, Wuorinen, American Composers O [New World LP 346-1; CD 346-2]

BARTÓK: *CONCERTO FOR ORCHESTRA* (1943). Pub (SS): Boosey & Hawkes
●Ancerl, Czech PO [Sound CD 3439; Decca (UK) cass KSXC 6212]
●Dohnányi, Cleveland O [London CD 425694-2 LH]
●Dutoit, Montreal SO [London CD 421443-2 LH]
●Jansons, Oslo PO [Angel CD CDC 54070-2; cass EL 54070]
●Karajan, Berlin PO [Angel LP S 37059]
●Mehta, Israel PO [London cass 5-6949]
●Reiner, Chicago SO [RCA CD 60175-2 RG; cass 60175-4 RG]
●Solti, London SO [London CD 417754-2 LM]

BARTÓK: *CONCERTOS* (1-3) for Piano & Orchestra (1926, 1931, 1945)
●Ashkenazy, Solti, London PO London 2-CD 425573-2 LM2]
●Pollini, Abbado, Chicago SO (1, 2) [Deutsche Grammophon CD 415 371-2]

BERNSTEIN: *SERENADE AFTER PLATO'S "SYMPOSIUM"* for Violin, String Orchestra, Harp & Percussion)(33m)(also for Violin & Piano). Pub (PS): Schirmer, Jalni (corrected ed.)
●Francescatti, Bernstein, New York P [Columbia LP; Odyssey LP Y 34633]
●Kremer, Bernstein, Israel SO [Deutsche Grammophon CD 423583-2 GH]
●Stern, Bernstein, S of the Air [Sony 3-CD M3K 45956]

BLITZSTEIN: *CONCERTO* for Piano & Orchestra (1931)
●Barrett, Foss, Brooklyn P [CRI CD 554]

BRITTEN: *CONCERTO* for Piano & Orchestra, Op 13 (1938, rev. 1945)
●Richter, Britten, English CO [London CD 417308-2]

BRITTEN: *CONCERTO* for Violin & Orchestra, Op 15 (1939). Pub: Boosey & Hawkes
McAslan, Bedford, English CO [Collins CD 1123-2; cass 1123-4]
●Haendel, Berglund, Bournemouth SO [EMI CD CDM 64202; HMV (UK) cass TC-ASD 3483]

BRITTEN: *SYMPHONY* for Cello & Orchestra, Op 68
●Wallfisch, Bedford, English CO [Chandos CD CHAN 8363; cass ABTD 1126]
●Rostropovich, Britten, English CO [Decca (UK) 425 100-2]

CARTER: *CONCERTO* for Orchestra (1969). Pub: Associated
●Bernstein, New York P [Columbia LP M 30112]
●Knussen, London Sinfonietta [Virgin CD CDC 59271]

CARTER: *CONCERTO* for Piano and Orchestra(1965)(26m). Pub (SS): Associated
●Lateiner, Leinsdorff, Boston SO [RCA LP]
●Oppens, Gielen, Cincinnati S0 [New World CD NW 347-2; cass NW 347-4]

CARTER: *DOUBLE CONCERTO* for Harpsichord, Piano & 2 Chamber Orchestras (1961). Pub (PE): Associated
●Jacobs, Kalish, Weisberg, Contemporary C Ens [Elektra/Nonesuch CD 79183-2; cass 71314-4]

COWELL: *CONCERTO* for Harp & Orchestra (1965)

COWELL: *RHYTHMICANA* for Rhymicon & Orchestra (1931)

GERSHWIN: *CONCERTO* in F for Piano & Orchestra (1925). Pub (SS):
New World, Warner Bros
●Levant, Toscanini, NBC SO [Hunt Productions CD 534]
●Siegel, Slatkin, St Louis SO [Vox 2-CD CDX 5007]
●Szidon, Downes, London PO [Deutsche Grammophon CD DG 427 203-2 GR;
cass 427 203-4 GR]

GERSHWIN: *"I GOT RHYTHM" VARIATIONS* for Piano & Orchestra (or 2
Pianos)(1934). Pub: New World
●Levant, Gould, Gould O [CBS CD MK 42514; cass FMT 42514]

GERSHWIN: *RHAPSODY IN BLUE* for Piano & Orchestra (1924). Pub (SS):
New World, Warner Bros
●Gershwin (from 1925 piano roll), Tilson Thomas, Columbia Jazz Band [CBS
CD MK-42516; cass FMT-42516]
●Siegel, Slatkin, St Louis SO [Vox 2-CD CDX 5007]

GERSHWIN: *SECOND RHAPSODY* for Piano & Orchestra (1931). Pub:
New World
●Siegel, Slatkin, St Louis SO [Vox 2-CD CDX 5007]

GOULD: *CHORALE AND FUGUE IN JAZZ* for 2 Pianos & Orchestra (1934)

GOULD: *THE JOGGER AND THE DINOSAUR* (concert piece) for Rapper &
Youth Orchestra (1992)

GOULD: *TAP-DANCE CONCERTO* for Orchestra (1952)
●LP vers. [Columbia LP]

HARBISON: *CONCERTO* for Double Brass Choir & Orchestra (1988).
Pub: Associated, Hal Leonard
●Previn, Los Angeles PO [New World CD 80395-2]

HARBISON: *CONCERTO* for Cello & Orchestra (c.1990)

HARBISON: *CONCERTO* for Piano & Orchestra (1978)(24m). Pub: As-
sociated/Margun
●Miller, Schuller, American Composers O [CRI LP SD 440]

JOLAS: *3 RECONTRES* for String Trio & Orchestra (1972)

KOLB: *VOYANTS* for Piano & Chamber Orchestra (1989)

LUTOSLAWSKI: *CHAIN 2 (DIALOGUE)* for Violin & Orchestra (1984).
Pub: Chester
●Mutter, Lutoslawski, BBC SO [Deutsche Grammophon CD DG 423 696-2 GH]

LUTOSLAWSKI: *CONCERTO* for Cello & Orchestra (1970)(23m). Pub
(PE): Chester
●Rostropovich, Lutoslawski, O de Paris [Angel LP S 37146]

LUTOSLAWSKI: *CONCERTO* for Orchestra (1950-54) (30m). Pub (SS):
Chester
●Dohnányi, Cleveland O [London CD 425694-2 LH]

LUTOSLAWSKI: *CONCERTO* for Piano & Orchestra (1987)(25m)
●Zimerman, Lutoslawski, BBC SO [Deutsche Grammophone CD 431 664-2]

LUTOSLAWSKI: *DANCE PRELUDES* (5) for Clarinet & Orchestra (Harp,
Piano, Percussion & Strings)(1955)(7m). Pub (SS): PWM
●King, Litton, English CO [Hyperion CD CDA 66215]

LUTOSLAWSKI: *PARTITA* for Violin & Orchestra (1988)(also for Violin
& Piano). Pub: Chester
●Mutter, Lutoslawski, BBC SO [Deutsche Grammophon CD DG 423 696-2 GH]

POWELL: *DUPLICATES (CONCERTO)* for 2 Pianos & Orchestra (1989).
1990 Pulitzer Prize
●Feinberg, Taub, Miller, Los Angeles PO [Harmonia Mundi CD HMU 907096]

SCHOENBERG: *CONCERTO* for Piano & Orchestra, Op 42 (1942). Pub
(SS): Schirmer, Universal
●Gould, Mitropoulos, New York P [Memories 2-CD HR 4415/16]
●Brendel, Kubelik, Bavarian RSO [Deutsche Grammophon CD 431 740-2]

SCHOENBERG: *CONCERTO* for Violin & Orchestra, Op 36. Pub (SS):
Universal
●Zeitlin, Kubelik, Bavarian RSO [Deutsche Grammophon CD 431 740-2]

SCHUMAN: *CONCERTO* for Violin & Orchestra (1947, rev. 1954, 1959).
Pub: Merion
●Zukofsky, Tilson Thomas, Boston SO [Deutsche Grammophon CD DG 429
860-2 GC]

SESSIONS: *CONCERTO* for Orchestra (1981). 1982 Pulitzer Prize
●Ozawa, Boston SO [Hyperion CD CDA 66050; cass KA 66050]

SESSIONS: *CONCERTO* for Piano & Orchestra (1956)(18m). Pub: Marks
●Taub, Dunkel, Westchester P [New World CD 80443-2]

SESSIONS: *CONCERTO* for Violin & Orchestra (1935)(35m). Pub (PE):
Marks
●LP vers. [CRI LP S-220 USD]

STRAVINSKY: *CAPRICCIO* for Piano & Orchestra (1929, rev. 1944)(19m).
Pub (PS): International
●Koussevitzky, Boston SO [Pearl CD PEA 9020]
●Stravinsky, Ansermet, Straram O [EMI 2-CD ZDCB 54607]

STRAVINSKY: *CONCERTO* for Piano & Wind Instruments (1924, rev.
1950) Pub: Boosey & Hawkes (1950 vers.)
●Crossley, Salonen, London Sinfonietta (1950 vers.) [Sony CD SK 45797]
●Stravinsky, Ansermet, Straram O [EMI 2-CD 2DCB 54607]

STRAVINSKY: *CONCERTO* in D for Violin & Orchestra. Pub (SS): Schott
●Chung, Previn, London SO [London CD 425003-2 LM]

STRAVINSKY: *EBONY CONCERTO* for Clarinet & Jazz Ensemble (1945)
●Goodman, Stravinsky, Columbia Jazz Ens [CBS MK 42227; cass MT 42227]

440

STRAVINSKY: *MOVEMENTS* for Piano & Orchestra (1959). Pub (SS):
Boosey & Hawkes
●Crossley, Salonen, London Sinfonietta [Sony CD SK 45797]
WUORINEN: *CONCERTO 3* for Piano & Orchestra (1983). Pub: Peters
●Ohlsson, Blomstedt, San Francisco SO [Elektra/Nonesuch CD 79185-2]
SEE ALSO: *Concerto 1* (1966) [CRI LP 239], *Concerto 2* for ampl. piano
& orchestra (1974)
WUORINEN: *FIVE* (concerto) for amplified Cello & Orchestra (1987)
●Sherry, Wuorinen, O of St. Luke's [Koch CD 3-7110-2]
WUORINEN: *THE GOLDEN DANCE* for Piano & Orchestra (1986)
●Ohlsson, Blomstedt, San Francisco SO [Elektra/Nonesuch CD 79185-2]

General Orchestral

BABBITT: *RELATA 1 & 2* (1965, 1968). Pub: Associated
●Zukofsky, Juilliard O (1) [New World CD 80396-2]
BARTÓK: *MUSIC FOR STRINGS, PERCUSSION AND CELESTA* (1936). Pub
(SS): Boosey & Hawkes
●Karajan, Berlin PO [Deutsche Grammophon CD]
●Reiner, Chicago SO [RCA CD 60175-2 RG; cass 60175-4 RG]
BERNSTEIN: *ON THE WATERFRONT* (film music)(1955)
¶SYMPHONIC SUITE (rev. 1960). Pub: Schirmer
●Bernstein, Israel PO [Deutsche Grammophon 2-CD DG 415253-2 GH2]
●Bernstein, New York P [CBS/Sony CD SMK-47530]
BLITZSTEIN: *FREEDOM MORNING* (symphonic poem)(1943)
BOULEZ: *ÉCLAT* (1964)/*MULTIPLES* (1970). Pub: Universal
●Boulez, Ens InterContemporain [CBS/Sony CD SMK 45839]
●Also LP [Columbia LP M 37850]
BRITTEN: *VARIATIONS ON A THEME OF FRANK BRIDGE* for String Or-
chestra, Op 10 (1937). Pub: Boosey & Hawkes
●Britten, English CO [Decca (UK) cass KSXC 6450]
●Britten, London SO [London CD 417509-2 LH]
●Marriner, Acad St. Martin-in-the-Fields [Argo LP ZRG 860]
●Menuhin, Bath Fest O [HMV (UK)]
BRITTEN: *THE YOUNG PERSON'S GUIDE TO THE ORCHESTRA (VARIA-
TIONS AND FUGUE ON A THEME OF HENRY PURCELL)*, Op 34 (1946).
Pub (SS): Boosey & Hawkes
●Britten, London SO [London CD 417509-2 LH; Decca (UK) cass KSXC 6450]
●Previn, London SO [Angel LP S 36962]

441

CARTER: *VARIATIONS FOR ORCHESTRA* (1955)(24m). Pub (PE/SS): Associated
●Gielen, Cincinnati S0 [New World CD NW 347-2; cass NW 347-4]
COPLAND: *EL SALÓN MÉXICO* (1936)(10m). Pub (SS): Boosey & Hawkes
●Copland, New Philharmonia O [CBS CD MK 42429]
COPLAND: *QUIET CITY* for Strings, Trumpet & English Horn (1940)(10m). Pub (SS): Boosey & Hawkes
●Foss, Buffalo PO [Turnabout LP]
●Marriner, Acad St. Martin-in-the-Fields [Argo cass KZRC 845]
COWELL: *HYMN AND FUGUING TUNE 3* (1944)(7m). Pub: Associated
COWELL: *HYMN AND FUGUING TUNE 10* for Oboe & Strings (1955)
●Nicklin, Marriner, Acad St Martin-in-the-Fields [Argo CD 417 818-2 ZH; cass KZRC 845]
COWELL: *SINFONIETTA* for Chamber Orchestra (1928)
●Whitney, Louisville O [Louisville LP]
COWELL: *SYMPHONIC SET,* Op 17 (1939)(12m). Pub: Arrow. Pub (PE): New York Public Library
DIAMOND: *ROUNDS* for String Orchestra (1944)(12m) Pub: Elkan-Vogel; 1944 New York Music Critics Circle Award
●Schwarz, Los Angeles CO [Elektra/Nonesuch CD 79002-2; cass D1-79002]
DIAMOND: *SUITE 1* (from ballet *Tom*) (1936)
DIAMOND: *THE WORLD OF PAUL KLEE* (1957)
●Avshalomov, Portland Youth PO [CRI CD 634]
FOSS: *BAROQUE VARIATIONS* (1967)
●Foss, Buffalo PO [Nonesuch]
GERSHWIN: *AN AMERICAN IN PARIS* (1928). Pub (SS): Warner Bros, New World
●Mehta, Los Angeles PO [London CD 436570-2; cass 5-7031]
●Slatkin, St Louis SO [Vox 2-CD CDX 5007]
●Toscanini, NBC SO [RCA LP; Hunt Productions CD 534]
GERSHWIN: *CUBAN OVERTURE* (1932). Pub: New World
●Mehta, Los Angeles PO [London CD 436570-2]
●Slatkin, St Louis SO [Vox 2-CD CDX 5007]
GOULD: *AMERICAN BALLADS* (6)(1947)(34m). Pub (PE): Schirmer
●Klein, London PO [Angel CD CDC-49462; cass 4DS-49462]
GOULD: *AMERICAN SYMPHONETTE 2* (1935). Pub: Kalmus
●Klein, London PO [Angel CD CDC-49462; cass 4DS-49462]
SEE ALSO: *American Symphonette 1* (1933), *American Symphonette 3* (1937)
GOULD: *JEKYLL AND HYDE VARIATIONS* (1955). Pub: G & C Music/Chappell
●LP Vers. [RCA LP]

442

GOULD: *LATIN AMERICAN SYMPHONETTE* (1940)(21m). Pub: Mills
● Abravanel, Utah SO [Vanguard CD OVC 4037]
● Hanson, Eastman-Rochester SO [Mercury LP]

GOULD: *LINCOLN LEGEND* (1942)

GOULD: *SOUNDINGS* (1969)(16m)
● Gould, Louisville O [Louisville LP; Albany 2-CD TROY 013-14-2]

GOULD: *SPIRITUALS* (1941)(19m)
● Hanson, Eastman-Rochester O [Mercury LP MG 50016; CD 432016-2]

HENZE: *BARCAROLA* (1979)
● Rattle, City of Birmingham O [EMI CD 54762]

JOLAS: *TALES OF A SUMMER SEA* (1977). Pub: Heugel

KIRCHNER: *MUSIC FOR ORCHESTRA* (1969)(13m). Pub (PE): Associated

KOLB: *SOUNDINGS* for 11 Instruments & Tape (2 conds.) (1972; rev. 1975, 1978)(19m). Pub (PE): Boosey & Hawkes
● Tamayo, Ens InterContemporain [CRI CD 576]

LUTOSLAWSKI: *CHAIN 2:* see Concertos

LUTOSLAWSKI: *CHAIN 3* for Orchestra (1986)(12m)
● Lutoslawski, BBC SO [Deutsche Grammophon CD 431 664-2]
● CD Vers. [Polski Nagrania PNCD 044]
SEE ALSO: *Chain 1* for chamber orchestra (1983) [Polski Nagrania PNCD 044]

LUENING: *SYMPHONIC FANTASIAS* (1-2)(1924, 1949)
● Adler, Vienna O (Nr. 1) [CRI LP 103; cass ACS 6011]
SEE ALSO: *Symphonic Fantasias 3-10* (1969-81, 1969-81, 1948-85, 1985, 1986, 1986, 1989, 1990)

POWELL: *MODULES (AN INTERMEZZO)* for Chamber Orchestra (1985). Pub: Schirmer/Hal Leonard
● Miller, Los Angeles PO [Harmonia Mundi CD HMU 90796]

ROREM: *AIR MUSIC* (1974). 1976 Pulitzer Prize
● Leonard, Louisville O [Louisville LP LS 787; Albany CD TROY 047]

ROSENMAN: *THRENODY ON A SONG BY K.R.* for Jazz Ensemble & Orchestra (1971)

SCHOENBERG: *ORCHESTERSTÜCKE (5 PIECES)*, Op 16 (1909, rev. 1949). Pub (SS): Eulenburg, Peters
● Boulez, BBC SO [Sony CD SMK 48463]
● Levine, Berlin P [Deutsche Grammophon CD 419781-2 GH]
● Rattle, City of Birmingham SO [EMI CDC 7 49857-2]

SCHOENBERG: *VARIATIONS* for Orchestra, Op 31 (1928). Pub (SS): Universal
● Karajan, Berlin P [Deutsche Grammophon CD 415326-2 GH]
● Solti, Chicago SO [London 2-CD 425008-2 LM2]

SCHOENBERG: *VERKLÄRTE NACHT (TRANSFIGURED NIGHT)* for String

443

Orchestra (or Sextet), Op 4 (1917, rev. 1943) Pub: Universal (1917), Associated (1943)
●Ashkenazy, English CO [London CD 410111-2 LH]
●Karajan, Berlin P [Deutsche Grammophon CD 415326-2 GH]
●Marriner, Acad St Martin-in-the-Field [London CD 43002-2 LM]

SCHUMAN: *NEW ENGLAND TRIPYTCH* (1956)(13m). Pub (PE): Merion, Theodore Presser
●Schwarz, Seattle SO [Delos CD DE 3115]

SCHUMAN: *VARIATIONS ON "AMERICA"* (after Charles Ives) (1963)(8m). Pub: Merion/Theodore Presser
●Schwarz, Seattle SO [Delos CD DE 3115]

SESSIONS: *THE BLACK MASKERS* (incidental music)(1923)
¶SUITE (1928)(22m). Pub (SS): Marks, Cos Cob Press/Arrow Music
●Hanson, Eastman-Rochester SO [Mercury LP Olympian series]

SESSIONS: *RHAPSODY* (1970)
●Batea, Columbia SO [New World CD NW 345-2]
●LP vers [Argo LP ZRG-702]

STOCKHAUSEN: *HYMNEN* for tape and/or 4 players and/or orchestra and/or colored lights (1969). Pub: Universal

STOCKHAUSEN: *JUBILÄUM (JUBILEE)* (1977). Pub: Stockhausen-Verlag

STOCKHAUSEN: *PUNKTE* (1952, rev. 1962, 1967). Pub: Universal

STRAVINSKY: *CONCERTINO* for 12 Instruments (1952). Pub: Hansen
●Boston S C Pl [Deutsche Grammophon LP 2530 551]
●Craft, O of St. Luke's [MusicMasters CD 01612-67103-2]

STRAVINSKY: *RAGTIME* for 11 Instruments (1918). Pub: Chester
●Boston S C Pl [Deutsche Grammophon LP 2530 551]
●Craft, O of St. Luke's [MusicMasters CD 01612-67110-2]

THOMSON: *THE PLOW THAT BROKE THE PLAINS* (film music)(1936). Pub (SS): Schirmer
●Kapp, Philharmonia Virtuosi [ESS.A.Y. CD 1005]
¶SUITE (13m). Pub (PE): Music Press
●Marriner, Los Angeles CO [Angel CD CDM 64306]
●Stokowski, S of the Air [Vanguard CD VBD-385]

THOMSON: *THE RIVER* (film music)(1937)
●Kapp, Philharmonia Virtuosi [ESS.A.Y. CD 1005]
¶SUITE (1942)(23m)
●Marriner, Los Angeles CO [Angel CD CDM 64307]
●Stokowski, S of the Air [Vanguard CD VBD-385]

VARÈSE: *AMERIQUES* (1918-22). Pub: Colfranc
●Boulez, Ens InterContemporain [Sony CD SK 45844]

VARÈSE: *ARCANA* (1927)(16m). Pub: Colfranc
●Boulez, Ens InterContemporain [Sony CD SK 45844]

444

●Mehta, Los Angeles PO [London LP 6752]

VARÈSE with Bülent Arel: *DÉSERTS* for 14 Winds, Percussion & Tape
(1949-54/1960-61). Comp. at Columbia-Princeton Electronic Music Ctr
●Definitive vers [Columbia LPs ML 5762 & MS 6362; CRI CD SD 268]

VARÈSE: *HYPERPRISM* for 9 Winds & 7 Percussion (1923)(4m). Pub:
Colfranc

VARÈSE: *INTÈGRALES* for 11 Winds & 4 Percussionists (1924-25)(12m).
Pub: Colfranc
●Boulez, Ens InterContemporain [Sony CD SK 45844]
●Mehta, Los Angeles Percussion Ens, Los Angeles PO [London LP 6752]
●Weisberg, Contemporary Chamber Ens [Elektra/Nonesuch cass 71269-4]

VARÈSE: *IONISATION* for 11 Percussionists (1929-31)(6m). Pub (PE):
New Music
●Boulez, Ens InterContemporain [Sony CD SK 45844
●Mehta, Los Angeles Percussion Ens, Los Angeles PO [London LP 6752]

WEBERN: *5 MOVEMENTS* for String Orchestra (or String Quartet), Op
5 (1909)
●Karajan, Berlin P [Deutsche Grammophon CD 423254-2 GC]

WEBERN: *PASSACAGLIA,* Op 1 (1908). Pub: Universal
●Karajan, Berlin P [Deutsche Grammophon CD 423254-2 GC]

WEBERN: *5 PIECES* for Orchestra, Op 10 (1913)
●Dorati, London SO [Mercury LP 432 006-2]

WEBERN: *6 PIECES,* Op 6 (1910). Pub: Universal
●Karajan, Berlin P [Deutsche Grammophon CD 423254-2 GC]

WEBERN: *VARIATIONS,* Op 30 (1940). Pub: Universal
●Abbado, Vienna PO [Deutsche Grammophon CD 431774-2 GH]

WOLPE: *CHAMBER PIECE 1* for 14 Instruments (1964). Pub:
Peer/Southern
●LP vers. [New World LP 306]

WOLPE: *CHAMBER PIECE 2* for 13 Instruments (1967)(4m). Pub:
Southern
●Korf, Parnassus Ens [New World LP]

WUORINEN: *MOVERS AND SHAKERS (CELEBRATING THE PLAYERS OF THE
CLEVELAND ORCHESTRA)* (1984). Pub: Peters (engraved score)

WUORINEN: *TASHI* (1975)(also vers. for clarinet, violin, cello &
piano). Pub: Peters

445

Symphonies

BERNSTEIN: *SYMPHONY 1 (JEREMIAH)* for Mezzo-Soprano & Orchestra (1944)(26m). Pub: Harms, Jalni (corrected ed.); New York Music Critics Circle Award
●Ludwig, Bernstein, Israel SO [Deutsche Grammophon CD 415964-2 GH]
●Tourel, Bernstein, New York P [Columbia LP]

BERNSTEIN: *SYMPHONY 2 (AGE OF ANXIETY)* for Piano & Orchestra (1949)(30m). Pub (PE): Schirmer, Jalni (corrected ed.)
●Entremont, Bernstein, New York P [Columbia LP]
●Foss, Bernstein, Israel SO [Deutsche Grammophon CD 415964-2 GH]

BERNSTEIN: *SYMPHONY 3 (KADDISH)* for Speaker, Solo Voice, Chorus & Orchestra (1963). Pub (PE/VS): Amberson (rev. vers.)/Schirmer
●Bernstein (F), Tourel, Camerata Singers, Bernstein, New York P [Columbia LP]
●Caballé, Wagner, Jeunesse Chor, Berlin Boys' Chor, Bernstein, Israel SO [Deutsche Grammophon CD 423582-2 GH]

BLITZSTEIN: *THE AIRBORNE SYMPHONY* for Speaker, Tenor, Bass, Male Chorus & Orchestra (1946)(55m) Ms: Univ WI
●Welles (Orson), Velis, Watson, Bernstein cond. [Columbia LP M 34136; CD]

BRITTEN: *SIMPLE SYMPHONY* for Strings, Op 4 (1934). Pub: Oxford
●Britten, English CO [London CD 417509-2 LH]

BRITTEN: *SINFONIA DA REQUIEM*, Op 20 (1940). Pub: Boosey & Hawkes
●Britten, New Philharmonia [Decca (UK) CD 425 100-2]

BRITTEN: *SPRING SYMPHONY* for Soprano, Mezzo-Soprano, Tenor, Chorus & Orchestra, Op 44 (1949). Pub: Boosey & Hawkes
●Vyvyan, Proctor, Pears, Emmanuel Sch Chorus, Britten, Covent Garden [London]
●Armstrong, Baker, Tear, St Clement Dane's Sch Boys' Choir, Previn, London SO & Chorus [EMI CD CDM 64736; HMV (UK) cass TC-ASD 3650]

CARTER: *A SYMPHONY OF THREE ORCHESTRAS* (1978)(17m). Pub (SS): Associated
●Boulez, New York P [Columbia LP M 35171]

COWELL: *SYMPHONY 13 (MADRAS)* (1958)

DIAMOND: *SYMPHONY 5* (1951, rev. 1964). Pub: Southern
●Keene, Juilliard O [New World CD 80396-2]

DIAMOND: *SYMPHONY 6* (1954)

DIAMOND: *SYMPHONY 7* (1959). Pub: Southern
SEE ALSO: *Symphony 1* (1941), *Symphony 2* [Delos 3093] *Symphony 3* (1945), *Symphony 4* (1945) [Delos 3093], *Symphony 8* (1960), *Symphony 9* (1985)

GOULD: *CENTENNIAL SYMPHONY*: see Band

446

GOULD: *SYMPHONY 4 (WEST POINT):* see Band

GOULD: *SYMPHONY OF SPIRITUALS* (1975)
- ●Klein, London PO [Angel CD CDC-49462; cass 4DS-49462]
- ●Smith, Louisville O [Albandy 2-CD TROY 013-14-2]
- ●Susskind, London SO [Bay Cities CD BCD 1016]

SEE ALSO: *Symphony 1* (1942), *Symphony 2 (Symphony on Marching Tunes* (1944), *Symphony 3* (1948)

HENZE: *SYMPHONIES 1-5* (1947 rev. 1963, 1949, 1950, 1955, 1962). Pub (SS): Schott
- ●Henze, Berlin PO [Deutsche Grammophon 2-LP; 2-CD 429 854-2]

HENZE: *SYMPHONY 6* (1969). Pub: Schott
- ●Henze, London SO (Nr 6) [Deutsche Grammophon LP; 2-CD 429 854-2]

HENZE: *SYMPHONY 7* (1984). Pub: Schott
- ●Rattle, City of Birmingham SO [EMI CD CDC 54762]

HENZE: *SYMPHONY 8* (1993). Pub: Schott

LUTOSLAWSKI: *SYMPHONY 3* (1972-73)
- ●Lutoslawksi, Berlin PO [Philips LP 416 387-1 PH; CD 416 387-2 PH; cass 416 387 3-PH]
- ●Salonen, Los Angeles PO [CBS 2-CD M2K 42271]

SEE ALSO: *Symphony 1* (1947), *Symphony 2* (1967) [Polski Nagrania PNCD 041]

SCHUMAN: *SYMPHONY 3* (1941)(30m). Pub (PE): Schirmer
- ●Bernstein, New York P [Deutsche Grammophon CD 419 780-2 GH]

SCHUMAN: *SYMPHONY 5 (SYMPHONY FOR STRINGS)* (1943). Pub: Schirmer
- ●Schwarz, Seattle SO [Delos CD DE 3115]

SEE ALSO: *Symphony 4* [Louisville LP S 692], *Symphony 6* (1948) [Columbia CML 4922; CRI LP SD 477], *Symphony 7* (1960) [Turnabout LP TVS 34447], *Symphony 8* (1962) [Columbia Odyssey LP Y 34140], *Symphony 9 (Le Fosse ardéatine)* (1968) [CRI LP SD 477], *Symphony 10 (American Music)* (1975)

SESSIONS: *SYMPHONY 2* (1946)(26m). Pub (SS): Schirmer
- ●Mitropoulos, New York P [CRI LP; CD CD 573; cass ACS-6002]

SESSIONS: *SYMPHONY 4* (1958)(24m). Pub (PE): Marks
- ●Badea, Columbia S [New World LP 345-1; CD NW-345-2]

SESSIONS: *SYMPHONY 5* (1964)(18m). Pub: Marks
- ●Badea, Columbia S [New World LP 345-1; CD NW-345-2]

SESSIONS: *SYMPHONY 8* (1968)
- ●LP vers [Argo LP ZRG-702]

SEE ALSO: *Symphony 1* (1927) [CRI CD 573], *Symphony 3* (1957) [CRI CD 573; cass ACS-6002], *Symphonies 6, 7, 9* (1966, 1967, 1978)

STRAVINSKY: *SYMPHONY* in C (1940). Pub: Schott
- ●Stravinsky, Columbia CO [CBS]

STRAVINSKY: *SYMPHONIE DE PSAUMES (SYMPHONY OF PSALMS)* for

Chorus & Orchestra (1930, rev. 1948).
Pub (SS/VS): Boosey & Hawkes, Kalmus
●Toronto Fest Singers, Stravinsky, Columbia CO [CBS]

STRAVINSKY: *SYMPHONY IN THREE MOVEMENTS* (1945). Pub (SS): Associated, Schott
●Craft, O of St. Luke's [MusicMasters 2-CD 01612-67078-2]
●Dutoit, O Suisse Romande [London CD 414272-3]

WEBERN: *SYMPHONY* for Chamber Orchestra, Op 21 (1928). Pub (SS): Universal
●Karajan, Berlin P [Deutsche Grammophon CD 423254-2]

WUORINEN: *PERCUSSION SYMPHONY* for 24 Percussion (1976)
●Wuorinen, New Jersey Perc Ens [Nonesuch LP H 71353; Elektra/Nonesuch CD 79150-2]

448

INDEX

Bold figures indicate listing in
Appendix ("Selected Compositions")

449

42, 47; *Hymn and Fuguing Tune 1*, **437**;
Hymn and Fuguing Tune 3, **442**; *Hymn
and Fuguing Tune 10*, **442**
Hymn to St. Cecilia (Britten), 281
Hymnen (Stockhausen), 219, **429, 444**
Hyperprism (Varèse), 37, 40, **445**
"I Got Rhythm" Variations (Gershwin),
97, **439**
IBM 7094 computer, 113
Iceman Cometh, The (O'Neill), 152, 374
ICM: see International Concert Manage-
ment
Idiots First (Blitzstein), 117
Igor Stravinsky: The Recorded Legacy, 24
"I'll Build a Stairway to Paradise"
(Gershwin), 101
Illuminations, Les (Britten), **423**
"I'm Fixing a Hole" (Beatles), 150
I'm Old Fashioned (Astaire Variations)
(Gould), 132, **436**
Imbrie, Andrew, 184, 320
Incantation (Luening/Ussachevsky), **429**
Indiana University (Bloomington IN), 12,
49
Indy, Vincent d', 39, 406
inganno felice, L' (Rossini), 308
Inspector General (Eck), 307
Institut de Recherche et de Coordina-
tion, Acoustique/Musique
(IRCAM)(Centre George Pompidou,
Paris), 251 *ff.*, 289, 341-343
Institute for Studies in American Music
(Brooklyn NY), 89
Institute of Musical Arts, (New
York)(see also Juilliard School), 128,
130, 365
Intégrales (Varèse), **445**
Intermezzo (film), 365
International Competition for Young
Conductors, 353
International Composers Guild, 40
International Concert Management
(ICM), 360, 361
International Piano Archives, 399, 402
International Society for Contemporary
Music, 20, 50, 72
Interplay (Gould), **436**
Into the Good Ground (Babbitt), 172
Invention in 12 Tones (Luening), **429**
Ionesco, George, 257
Ionisation (Varèse), 223, 250, 335, **445**
Iowa, 370

IRCAM: see Institut de Recherche et de
Coordination, Acoustique/Musique
Israel, 122, 409
Israel Philharmonic Orchestra, 120, 409
Italy, 181, 211, 212, 258, 261, 267
I've Got the Tune (Blitzstein), 419
Ives, Charles, 12, 46-48, 61, 74, 108, 128,
212, 324, 354
Jackson (MI), 167, 171
Jakobsleiter, Der (Schoenberg), 320, **417**
Japan, 122
Japan Philharmonic, 353
Japan Radio Orchestra (NHK), 353, 354
Jazz Sonata (Antheil), 92
Jefferson Airplane, The, 144
Jekyll and Hyde Variations (Gould), **442**
Jellinek, George, 378
Jerusalem (Israel), 361
Jeux (Debussy), 244
Joan at the Stake (Honegger), 327
Jogger and the Dinosaur, The (Gould), **439**
Johnny Johnston (Weill), 108
Johnson State College (VT), 178, 182
Johnson, Lyndon, 196
Johnson, Steve, 338
Jolas, Betsy, 162, 221-226, 228, 229, **426,
433, 439, 443**
Jolas, Marie, 223
Jones, Harold, 292
Josquin des Prez, 223
Joy of Music, The (Bernstein), 122
Joyce, James, 223, 229
Jubiläum [Jubilee] (Stockhausen), 270, **444**
Judith (Schuman), **436**
Judson, Arthur, 298, 299
Juilliard Musical Foundation, 309
Juilliard School of Music (New York)(see
also Institute of Musical Arts), 81, 84,
89, 128, 179, 180, 184, 195, 233, 248,
303, 304, 306, 307, 309-311, 313, 317,
341, 365, 390, 391
Juilliard String Quartet, 363 *ff.*
Juive, La (Halévy), 378
Julius Caesar (Blitzstein), 111
Jumping Hare, 143
junge Lord, Der [The Young Lord] (Henze),
267, **421**
Juno and the Paycock (O'Casey), 115
König Hirsch (Henze), 272
Kabalevsky, Dmitri, 215
Kagel, Mauricio, 48, 253
Kalischer, Clemens, 349, 350

Other Music Titles Available from Pro/Am Music Resources, Inc.

BIOGRAPHIES & COMPOSER STUDIES

ALKAN, REISSUE *by Ronald Smith*. Vol. 1: The Enigma. Vol. 2: The Music.

BÉLA BARTÓK: An Analysis of His Music *by Erno Lendvai*.

BERNARD STEVENS AND HIS MUSIC: A Symposium *edited by Bertha Stevens*.

JANÁCEK: Leaves from His Life *by Leos Janácek. Edited & transl. by Vilem & Margaret Tausky*.

JOHN FOULDS AND HIS MUSIC: An Introduction *by Malcolm Mac-Donald*.   ← ?

LIPATTI *(Tanasescu & Bargauanu)*: see PIANO, below.

MASCAGNI: An Autobiography Compiled, Edited and Translated from Original Sources *by David Stivender*.

MICHAEL TIPPETT, O.M.: A Celebration *edited by Geraint Lewis. Fwd. by Peter Maxwell Davies*.

THE MUSIC OF MY TIME by Joan Peyser. (Series subtitle: *Something About the Music 1*. See also *Something About the Music 2*, below.)

THE MUSIC OF SYZMANOWSKI *by Jim Samson*.

THE OPRICHNIK: An Opera in Four Acts by Peter Il'ich Tchaikovsky. *Transl. & notes by Philip Taylor*.

PERCY GRAINGER: The Man Behind the Music *by Eileen Dorum*.

PERCY GRAINGER: The Pictorial Biography *by Robert Simon. Fwd. by Frederick Fennell*.

RAVEL ACCORDING TO RAVEL *(Perlemuter & Jourdan-Morhange)*: see PIANO, below.

RONALD STEVENSON: A Musical Biography *by Malcolm MacDonald*.

SCHUBERT'S MUSIC FOR PIANO FOUR-HANDS *(Weekly & Arganbright)*: see PIANO, below.

SOMETHING ABOUT THE MUSIC 1: see THE MUSIC OF MY TIME, above.

SOMETHING ABOUT THE MUSIC 2: Anthology of Critical Opinions *edited by Thomas P. Lewis*.

A SOURCE GUIDE TO THE MUSIC OF PERCY GRAINGER *edited by Thomas P. Lewis*.

Other Music Titles Available from Pro/Am Music Resources, Inc.

THE SYMPHONIES OF HAVERGAL BRIAN *by Malcolm MacDonald*. Vol. 2: Symphonies 13-29. Vol. 3: Symphonies 30-32, Survey, and Summing-Up.

VERDI AND WAGNER *by Erno Lendvai.*

VILLA-LOBOS: The Music *by Lisa M. Peppercorn.*

THE WORKS OF ALAN HOVHANESS: A Catalog, Opus 1 – Opus 360 *by Richard Howard.* With insert thrugh Opus 400.

XENAKIS *by Nouritza Matossian.*

GENERAL SUBJECTS

ACOUSTICS AND THE PERFORMANCE OF MUSIC *by Jürgen Meyer.*

AMERICAN MINIMAL MUSIC, REISSUE *by Wim Mertens. Transl. by J. Hautekiet.*

GOGOLIAN INTERLUDES: Gogol's Story "Christmas Eve" as the Subject of the Operas by Tchaikovsky and Rimsky-Korsakov *by Philip Taylor.*

HISTORY THROUGH THE OPERA GLASS: From the Rise of Caesar to the Fall of Napoleon *by George Jellinek.*

THE MUSICAL INSTRUMENT COLLECTOR, REVISED EDITION *by J. Robert Willcutt & Kenneth R. Ball.*

A MUSICIAN'S GUIDE TO COPYRIGHT AND PUBLISHING, ENL. EDITION *by Willis Wager.*

MUSICOLOGY IN PRACTICE: Collected Essays by Denis Stevens *edited by Thomas P. Lewis.* Vol. 1: 1948-1970.

MY VIOLA AND I, REISSUE *by Lionel Tertis.*

THE NUTLEY PAPERS: A Fresh Look at the Titans of Music (humor) *by James Billings.*

PEACE SONGS *compiled & edited by John Jordan.*

PERCUSSION INSTRUMENTS AND THEIR HISTORY, REV. EDITION *by James Blades.*

THE PRO/AM BOOK OF MUSIC AND MYTHOLOGY *compiled, edited & with commentaries by Thomas P. Lewis.* 2 vols.

THE PRO/AM GUIDE TO U. S. BOOKS ABOUT MUSIC: Annotated Guide to Current & Backlist Titles *edited by Thomas P. Lewis.* 2 vols.

Other Music Titles Available from Pro/Am Music Resources, Inc.

RAYMOND LEPPARD ON MUSIC: An Anthology of Critical and Personal Writings *edited by Thomas P. Lewis.*

GUITAR

THE AMP BOOK: A Guitarist's Inroductory Guide to Tube Amplifiers *by Donald Brosnac.*

ANIMAL MAGNETISM FOR MUSICIANS: Making a Bass Guitar and Pickup from Scratch *by Erno Zwaan.*

ANTHOLOGY OF FLAMENCO FALSETAS *collected by Ray Mitchell.*

ANTONIO DE TORRES: Guitar Maker—His Life and Work *by José Romanillos. Fwd. by Julian Bream.*

THE ART OF FLAMENCO *by D. E. Pohren.*

THE ART OF PRACTICING *by Alice Arzt.*

THE BURNS BOOK *by Paul Day.*

CLASSIC GUITAR CONSTRUCTION *by Irving Sloane.*

THE DEVELOPMENT OF THE MODERN GUITAR *by John Huber.*

DICCIONARIO ENCICLOPEDIO ILUSTRADO DEL FLAMENCO *by Jose Blas Vega & Manuel Rios Ruiz.* 2 vols.

THE FENDER GUITAR *by Ken Achard.*

THE FLAMENCOS OF CÁDIZ BAY *by Gerald Howson.*

THE GIBSON GUITAR *by Ian C. Bishop.* 2 vols.

THE GUITAR: From the Renaissance to the Present Day, REISSUE *by Harvey Turnbull.*

GUITAR HISTORY: Volume 1—Guitars Made by the Fender Company *by Donald Brosnac.*

GUITAR HISTORY: Volume 2—Gibson SGs *by John Bulli.*

GUITAR HISTORY: Volume 3—Gibson Catalogs of the Sixties *edited by Richard Hetrick.*

GUITAR HISTORY: Volume 4—The Vox Story *by David Petersen & Dick Denney.*

GUITAR HISTORY: Volume 5—The Guild Guitar *by E.G. Beesley.*

GUITAR HISTORY: Volume 6—The High-Performance Marshall Handbook *by John Boehnlein.*

Other Music Titles Available from Pro/Am Music Resources, Inc.

GUITAR REPAIR: A Manual of Repair for Guitars and Fretted Instruments *by Irving Sloane.*

GUITAR TRADER VINTAGE GUITAR BULLETIN. 6 vols.

THE HISTORY AND DEVELOPMENT OF THE AMERICAN GUITAR *by Ken Achard.*

AN INTRODUCTION TO SCIENTIFIC GUITAR DESIGN *by Donald Brosnac.*

LEFT HANDED GUITAR *by Nicholas Clarke.*

LIVES AND LEGENDS OF FLAMENCO, 2ND EDITION *by D. E. Pohren.*

MANUAL OF GUITAR TECHNOLOGY: The History and Technology of Plucked String Instruments *by Franz Jahnel. English vers. by Dr. J. C. Harvey.*

MAKING MUSIC SERIES: THE GURU'S GUITAR GUIDE *by Tony Bacon & Paul Day.* MAKING 4-TRACK MUSIC *by John Peel.* WHAT BASS, 2ND EDITION *by Tony Bacon & Laurence Canty.* WHAT DRUM, 2ND EDITION *by Geoff Nicholls & Andy Duncan.* WHAT GUITAR: The Making Music Guide to Buying Your Electric Six String, 3RD EDITION. WHAT'S MIDI, 2ND EDITION *by Andy Honeybone et al.*

THE NATURAL CLASSICAL GUITAR, REISSUE *by Lee F. Ryan.*

PACO DE LUCÍA AND FAMILY: The Master Plan *by D.E. Pohren.*

THE RIOPLATENSE GUITAR *by Rich Pinnell.* 2 vols.

THE SEGOVIA TECHNIQUE, REISSUE *by Vladimir Bobri.*

THE SOUND OF ROCK: A History of Marshall Valve Guitar Amplifiers *by Mike Doyle.*

THE SPANISH GUITAR/LA GUITARRA ESPANOL. English/Spanish Edition.

THE STEEL STRING GUITAR: Construction and Repair, UPDATED EDITION *by David Russell Young.*

STEEL STRING GUITAR CONSTRUCTION *by Irving Sloane.*

A WAY OF LIFE, REISSUE *by D. E. Pohren.*

WHAT IS FLAMENCO? *Editorial cinterco.*

THE WIND CRIED: An American's Discovery of the World of Flamenco *by Paul Hecht.*

Other Music Titles Available from Pro/Am Music Resources, Inc.

PERFORMANCE PRACTICE / "HOW-TO" INSTRUCTIONAL

THE BOTTOM LINE IS MONEY: A Comprehensive Guide to Songwriting and the Nashville Music Industry *by Jennifer Ember Pierce.*

GUIDE TO THE PRACTICAL STUDY OF HARMONY *by Peter Il'ich Tchaikovsky.*

HOW TO SELECT A BOW FOR VIOLIN FAMILY INSTRUMENTS *by Balthasar Planta.*

IMAGINATIONS: Tuneful Fun and Recital Pieces to Expand Early Grade Harp Skills *by Doris Davidson.*

THE JOY OF ORNAMENTATION: Being Giovanni Luca Conforto's *Treatise on Ornamentation* (Rome, 1593) *with a Preface by Sir Yehudi Menuhin and an Introduction by Denis Stevens.*

MAKING MUSICAL INSTRUMENTS *by Irving Sloane.*

THE MUSICIANS' THEORY BOOK: Reference to Fundamentals, Harmony, Counterpoint, Fugue and Form *by Asger Hamerik.*

ON BEYOND C *(Davidson)*: see PIANO, below.

THE STUDENT'S DICTIONARY OF MUSICAL TERMS.

TENSIONS IN THE PERFORMANCE OF MUSIC: A Symposium, REVISED & EXTENDED EDITION *edited by Carola Grindea. Fwd. by Yehudi Menuhin.*

THE VIOLIN: Precepts and Observations *by Sourene Arakelian.*

PIANO/HARPSICHORD

THE ANATOMY OF A NEW YORK DEBUT RECITAL *by Carol Montparker.*

AT THE PIANO WITH FAURÉ, REISSUE *by Marguerite Long.*

EUROPEAN PIANO ATLAS *by H. K. Herzog.*

FRENCH PIANISM: An Historical Perspective *by Charles Timbrell.*

GLOSSARY OF HARPSICHORD TERMS *by Susanne Costa.*

KENTNER: A Symposium *edited by Harold Taylor. Fwd. by Yehudi Menuhin.*

LIPATTI *by Dragos Tanasescu & Grigore Bargauanu.*

ON BEYOND C: Tuneful Fun in Many Keys to Expand Early Grade Piano Skills *by Doris Davidson.*

Other Music Titles Available from Pro/Am Music Resources, Inc.

THE PIANIST'S TALENT *by Harold Taylor. Fwd. by John Ogdon.*
THE PIANO AND HOW TO CARE FOR IT *by Otto Funke.*
THE PIANO HAMMER *by Walter Pfeifer.*
PIANO NOMENCLATURE, 2ND EDITION *by Nikolaus Schimmel & H. K. Herzog.*
RAVEL ACCORDING TO RAVEL *by Vlado Perlemuter & Hélène Jouran-Morhange.*
SCHUBERT'S MUSIC FOR PIANO FOUR-HANDS *by Dallas Weekly & Nancy Arganbright.*
THE STEINWAY SERVICE MANUAL *by Max Matthias.*
TECHNIQUE OF PIANO PLAYING, 5TH EDITION *by József gát.*
THE TUNING OF MY HARPSICHORD *by Herbert Anton Kellner.*